Democratic Narrative, History, and Memory

Democratic Narrative, History, and Memory

✻ ✻ ✻

EDITED BY

Carole A. Barbato

AND

Laura L. Davis

THE KENT STATE UNIVERSITY PRESS

KENT, OHIO

Library of Congress Catalog Card Number 2011047787

ISBN 978-1-60635-119-2

Manufactured in the United States of America

Library of Congress Cataloging-in-Publication Data

Democratic narrative, history, and memory / edited by Carole A. Barbato and Laura L. Davis.

p. cm. — (Symposium on democracy series)

Essays based on and revised from presentations at the 2009 Kent State University Symposium on Democracy.

Includes bibliographical references and index.

ISBN 978-1-60635-119-2 (pbk. : alk. paper) ∞

1. Kent State Shootings, Kent, Ohio, 1970—Congresses. 2. Collective memory—United States—Congresses. 3. Mass media—Social aspects—United States—Congresses. I. Barbato, Carole A. II. Davis, Laura L. III. Kent State University Symposium on Democracy.

LD4191.O72D46 2012

378.771'37—dc23

2011047787

16 15 14 13 12 5 4 3 2 1

Contents

Preface

CAROLE A. BARBATO AND LAURA L. DAVIS

On May 4, 1970, an international spotlight focused on Kent State University after a student protest against the Vietnam War and the presence of the Ohio National Guard on campus ended in tragedy. Twenty-eight guardsmen fired sixty-seven shots in thirteen seconds. They killed Kent State students Allison Krause, Jeffrey Miller, Sandra Scheuer, and William Schroeder and wounded nine other students, permanently paralyzing Dean Kahler.

The demonstration at Kent State marked a climax of the student activism and protest of the 1960s, a historical period encompassing the shootings at Kent State. The student protest movement was rooted in the civil rights movement of the late 1950s and early 1960s.[1] On college campuses, the generation gap—the divide between generations in lifestyle, culture, politics, and values—of the 1960s also was strongly felt. Those in positions of authority—parents, campus administrators, politicians, and law enforcement officials—squarely lined up on one side of the divide, with rising numbers of students on the other.

On May 4, the Ohio National Guard, called into town by Kent's mayor, literally lined up on campus on one side of the grassy central area known as the Commons. Students gathered five hundred feet away at the campus Victory Bell. Most students were observers; many felt aligned with the general counterculture movement; some were campus activists. Many students were consciously exercising their First Amendment rights of freedom of assembly and freedom of speech as they gathered for the May 4 rally.

In a statement read by press secretary Ron Ziegler, President Richard Nixon responded to the shootings by commenting, "This should remind us all once again that when dissent turns to violence it invites tragedy," an assertion of authoritarian values seen by many as lacking in sympathy.[2] For a large proportion of Americans, from members of Congress to the average citizen on both sides of the generation gap, the shootings constituted a watershed moment that changed their perspectives on the war in Vietnam. May 4, 1970, became the day the war came home in the American imagination, the day that American soldiers killed American children on U.S. soil.[3] For college students, the shootings at Kent State spurred the largest national student strike in U.S. history. "More than half the colleges and universities in the country (1350) were ultimately touched by protest demonstrations, involving nearly 60 percent of the student population—some 4,350,000 people in every kind of institution and in every state of the union."[4]

What Nixon failed to see, his staff recognized: the shootings at Kent State became one of the major symbolic events of the Vietnam War as well as the 1960s era, marking the beginning of the end of Nixon's presidency, as his chief of staff, H. R. Haldeman, noted.[5] "By January 1973, when Nixon announced the effective end of U.S. involvement," Vietnam War historian Mark Barringer writes, "he did so in response to a mandate unequaled in modern times."[6] During these years, the legal aftermath of the events of May 4, 1970, was well on its way to becoming, as Kent State legal scholar Thomas Hensley explains, "one of the longest, costliest, and most complex set of courtroom struggles in American history," setting civil rights precedent in the U.S. Supreme Court.[7]

In 2000, on the thirtieth anniversary of the event, Kent State University established an annual Symposium on Democracy. The symposium was founded as a living memorial to honor the memories of the four students who lost their lives in the May 4 shootings, with an enduring dedication to scholarship that seeks to prevent violence and to promote democratic values and civil discourse. This volume presents a collection of essays based on and revised from presentations at the 2009 symposium. Through a range of disciplinary lenses, these essays explore the complex relationships among experienced events, memory, and portrayal of those events in order to probe the deepest questions of human experience. While connections among the essays cross over from multiple directions, they have been gathered in three groupings that offer one set of possibilities for making meaning. Essays in the first group move from the particular history of May 4, 1970, to eternal concerns of peace and violence, silence and giving voice. Those in the second group address the part played by corporate—and noncorporate, if you will—media in shaping public memory and raising public consciousness. The essays in the final grouping examine acts of remembrance and reconciliation within local communities and the long history of discrimination existing within the national American community. Like the first two groups of essays, this group directly and indirectly proposes ways in which we can move toward social justice.

On the occasion of the tenth annual symposium, historian Jay Winter addressed the Kent State community as "the silence-breakers, who recognize, with Joseph

Brodsky, that 'the past won't fit into memory without something left over. It must have a future.'" Winter noted of the Kent State community that it is our "achievement to shape that future through framing of active knowledge in this place and at this time about the injustices that occurred here."[8]

For more than forty years, the Kent State community has answered the claim that other human beings have on us, so that we preserve the stories of those who have been lost—both to honor the lost and to reveal universal meanings.[9] We at Kent State are negotiating, in a literal sense, the space between memory and history, between social remembering and historical analysis—as Jerry M. Lewis, in his essay in this volume, applies the terminology of James Wertsch. For the 2009 symposium, scholars national and international were invited to join us in thinking through how to preserve Kent State's history for future generations, so as to respectfully acknowledge the past and to serve the future.[10] The scholarly examinations of the 2009 Symposium on Democracy informed the thinking, planning, and decision making for a May 4 Visitors Center. The two main features of this center are a guided walking tour of the seventeen-acre historic site and a permanent exhibit. The walking tour provides visitors the facts of the event, which had become draped in myth and misunderstanding.[11] Acknowledging the many voices and multiple perspectives regarding the events of May 4, the exhibit invites visitors to explore those facts within the social and historical context of the times, in order to better understand the events of that day and to reflect on their impact and meaning for today.

For many at Kent State, and for many in other communities that have experienced violence, the historical event is a lived event. And so acts of scholarship are sometimes acts of remembrance and commemoration at the same time. This volume emanates from a commemorative act, and at the same time it seeks to find historical meaning. That historical meaning not only holds relevance for a particular community but also speaks indelibly to the human community.

History begins with the actual, but any analysis will be a process of—as captured in the title of the 2009 symposium—"Re-membering: Framing, Embracing, Revising History." Many of the essays in this volume offer a treatment of the Kent State story. Others reflect on similar experiences in other communities, sometimes giving the measure of the scope of the Kent State event; on chronologies, short and long, within other communities; and on individual experience. As a collection (to make a turn on a phrase offered during the 2009 symposium), they make meaning of past history in order to serve the future.[12]

Notes

1. *The Report of the President's Commission on Campus Unrest* (Washington, D.C.: GPO, 1970), 21–22.
2. Quoted in A. J. Langguth, *Our Vietnam: The War, 1954–1975* (New York: Simon and Schuster, 2000), 570.
3. Vicki Goldberg, among others, has identified May 4, 1970, as the day the war came home: "The Vietnam War is tied up in a handful of corrosive pictures: Malcolm Browne's photograph of a Buddhist monk calmly immolating himself to protest his Government's policies, Eddie Adams's picture of the South Vietnamese chief of national police blowing out the brains of a Vietcong suspect on a Saigon street, Ron Haeberle's pictures of the My Lai massacre, Nick Ut's image of a little girl so badly burned by napalm she has ripped off all her clothes and is running straight toward us. In John Filo's photograph of a girl screaming about death on an Ohio campus, taken 25 years ago on May 4, the war came home." "Photography View: In a Rifle's Flash, a Lasting Icon of a Nation's Pain," *New York Times*, Apr. 30, 1995, <http://www.nytimes.com/1995/04/30/arts/photography-view-in-a-rifle-s-flash-a-lasting-icon-of-a-nation-s-pain.html?pagewanted=1>.
4. Kirkpatrick Sale, *SDS* (New York: Random House, 1973; New York: Vintage Books, 1974), 636. Also, a study determined that the May 4 shootings were the single factor causing the national student strike. *On Strike . . . Shut it Down: A Report on the First National Student Strike in U.S. History, May 1970* (Chicago, Ill.: Urban Research Corporation, 1970), 1.
5. H. R. Haldeman, with Joseph DiMona, *The Ends of Power* (New York: Time Books, 1978), 107.
6. Mark Barringer, "The Antiwar Movement in the United States," in *Encyclopedia of the Vietnam War: A Political, Social, and Military History*, ed. S. C. Tucker, 34–36, <http://www.english.illinois.edu/maps/vietnam/antiwar.html>.
7. Thomas R. Hensley, "The May 4th Trials," in *Kent State and May 4th: A Social Science Perspective*, 3rd ed., ed. Thomas R. Hensley and Jerry M. Lewis (Kent, Ohio: Kent State Univ. Press, 2010), 64. Parents and wounded students were blocked for years by the Eleventh Amendment, which prohibits citizens from bringing civil suit against governmental officials acting in their official capacities. The important concept of *sovereign immunity* was modified by the U.S. Supreme Court, which determined in a case brought by the parents of the slain students that it may be used as a legal defense, but not to block a trial (76–77).
8. Jay Winter, "Remembering Injustice and the Social Construction of Silence" (keynote address, 2009 Symposium on Democracy, Kent State University, Kent, Ohio, May 3, 2009).
9. Jay Winter, personal communication with the editors, Aug. 26, 2008.
10. In "Photographic Evidence of the Ukrainian Genocidal Famine, 1932–1933," scholar Roman Serbyn defined *collective memory* as "what people as a collection make of their past history in order to serve the future" (address, 2009 Symposium on Democracy, Kent State University, Kent, Ohio, May 1, 2009).
11. As an iconic event, the student protest and subsequent shooting of students at Kent State by members of the National Guard on May 4, 1970, is well known. However, the particulars of the four days in May that comprise the event are much less well known and are the subject of much disinformation. Because the events of May 4, 1970, are the

focus of, or relevant to, the discussion in many essays in this volume, the editors have provided a chronology of those events in an appendix, based on information from the key sources, most of which are no longer in print. The chronology is informed by the perspective of the forty years that have passed since that date, by the more than forty combined years of research and teaching on May 4 by the chronology's authors, and by the positioning of May 4, 1970, within the literature on the 1960s.

12. See note 10.

Part I

From History to Humanity

Introduction

Claire A. Culleton

"What three things can never be done?" American poet Muriel Rukeyser asks in *The Book of the Dead,* her epic that memorializes 476 West Virginia miners who died of silicosis building a tunnel for Union Carbide in the early 1930s. Rukeyser responds to her own question with chilling and exacting reprehension: "Forget. Keep silent. Stand alone."[1] For more than forty years, a generous community of students and faculty at Kent State University, local townspeople, and committed supporters from all over the world have worked to ensure that we do not forget the events of May 4, 1970; keep silent about the personal, cultural, and historic resonance of those events; or leave families, friends, and others affected by the May 4 tragedy standing alone.

The essays that follow grew out of an annual symposium founded on campus in 2000 to commemorate the painful events of May 4, 1970, and to encourage scholarship that seeks to prevent violence and injustice and to promote democratic values and civil discourse. The 2009 Symposium on Democracy focused on memory and remembering, on the recent status accorded to memory by historians, and on the subsequent "memory boom" inspired by such privileging. Philosopher Tzvetan Todorov remarked on the twentieth century's fin de siècle obsession with memory in his 1992 book *Les Abus de la memoire,* and he cautioned in a later work that "memory is a forgetting . . . a *partial* forgetting," an admonishment shared by French anthropologist Marc Augé, who suggests, "Memory is framed by forgetting in the same way as the contours of the shoreline are framed by the sea."[2] Jay Winter, keynote speaker at the 2009 Democracy Symposium and author of this volume's third essay, "Remembering Injustice and the Social Construction of Silence," remains dissatisfied by such binary either/or approaches to memory and forgetting, and he suggests that in order "to transcend the now saturated field of memory studies"—what he calls elsewhere "the efflorescence of interest in the subject of memory inside the academy and beyond it"—we acknowledge *silence,* liturgical, political, and essential silence. Doing so, he suggests, allows us to "transform silence about injustice into something active, purposeful, dynamic."[3] This is not to suggest that we do away with Rukeyser's imperative, only that we reconstruct it, as the essays in this section suggest.

Increasingly, and especially toward the end of the twentieth century, monuments and museums across the world have incorporated spaces that specifically invite purposeful silence and reflection. The United States Holocaust Memorial Museum (1993) in Washington, D.C., for example, has the Hall of Remembrance, a solemn, simple space designed for individual reflection. The museum itself, suggests architect James Ingo Freed, is "a resonator of memory."[4] Similarly, the Oklahoma City National Memorial (2000) features a reflecting pool that not only provides visual reflection but also summons purposeful silence. Here at Kent State, Bruno Ast's May 4 Memorial (1990), built in the natural setting of a campus hillside, instructs visitors to "Inquire, Learn, Reflect." Ironically, victims of injustice used to come up *against* silence. It stood in the way of reflection. Silence accompanied, attended, and always sided with institutional power, with hegemony. Now, however, silence is being invited to *enact* power and to transubstantiate injustice. The very dynamic of silence, then, once used to conspire against victims of injustice, has been invested with ameliorative and transformative power. Purposeful silence, in other words, can strengthen resolve rather than dismantle it, can lead to reparation instead of obstruction. No longer the last refuge of brute power, silence can be both sanctuarial and redemptory.

These sites for silence also offer us a space for memory, and therein lies the rub, for "whatever the specific content of the many contemporary debates about history and memory may be," Andreas Huyssen notes in *Present Pasts: Urban Palimpsests and the Politics of Memory,* "underlying them is a fundamental disturbance not just of the relationship between history as objective and scientific, and memory as subjective and personal, but of history itself and its promises."[5] The essays that comprise the first section of this spirited volume grapple with the changed and changing relationships between history and memory, silence and activism, memorializing and remembrance. "In virtually all acts of remembrance," Winter notes, "history and memory are braided together in the public domain, jointly informing our shifted and contested understandings of the past."[6] At Kent State, those shifted and contested understandings of the past commingle with the present every spring as commemorations and public observances of May 4 near. The annual Symposium on Democracy at Kent State University is one of those sites, one of those spaces, where panelists and conferees work to understand the topography of tragedy and to historicize and interpret not only May 4, 1970, and its international aftermath but critical and consequential events leading up to, contextualizing, and even auguring May 4.

The era preceding what the world knows as "Kent State," for example, was a decade marked by political strife, split by the generation gap, and divided by trenchant pro- or antiwar positions. It was an era of timeless and universal upheaval, an era synonymous with the Vietnam War, the peace movement, the civil rights movement, and bureaucratic intransigence; consciousness raising, counterculture rebellion, sexual liberation, and psychedelia; nonviolence, direct action, urban disorder, and widespread college and university campus activism. The 1960s inspired Panthers as well as Pranksters, sit-ins as well as standoffs, demonstrations to end the war and demonstrations to bring the war home. It produced the Chicago Eight as well as the Oakland Seven, and gave rise to demagogues as different as chalk and cheese. As the tumultuous decade drew to a close and the nation still reeled from the dynamic social, cultural, and political events of the 1960s, our small university in America's heartland was placed in an international spotlight after thirteen seconds of rifle fire by Ohio National Guardsmen left four students dead, one permanently paralyzed, and eight other students wounded during a student demonstration against the war. The episode at Kent State shocked the nation as it watched the film footage on the nightly news, and it became a defining moment for generations of Americans.

Tom Grace, whose essay opens this volume, was an undergraduate history major at Kent State and had attended several antiwar protests on campus before the May 4, 1970, demonstration. That day he took an Ohio National Guard bullet to the left foot. "I remember telling someone once that I enrolled in Kent State to study American history and, through no intention of my own, became a part of it," he says. "I guess if you're looking for irony, there it is."[7] Grace's essay, "Kent State and Historical Memory," examines the first five anniversaries of the campus shootings from a first-hand, local perspective, five years in what he calls "the long battle over the memory of the Kent State killings." The shootings of May 4 constituted a polemic event that quickly altered already changing relationships between parents and children, families and friends, local shopkeepers and customers, students, faculty, and administrators, and instantly traumatized a city of 25,000 people. Its aftermath bewildered an entire generation in Kent and its environs, and, in a flash, confounded a small and parochial police force as well as a large and multifaceted university administration. Grace knows this as well as anyone and focuses his essay on the persistent triangulation of three specific groups in the early historical aftermath of the shootings (1970–75). He analyzes the poles of extreme opinion that characterized each group with stakes in the memory war: those who wanted to keep attention squarely focused on the political significance of Kent State, those who wanted to neutralize its meaning, and those who insisted on blaming the young students and demonstrators for the violence. There are few places in America, Grace concludes, where twentieth-century public memory has been fought over more than Kent State. At risk, as always in such cases, "is the power of a commemorative site to keep the story alive as opposed to entombing it in the realm of the unspoken, of a past that is made to disappear yet once again."[8] In his essay, Grace invokes the

Kent State memory wars as a way into larger issues that direct his inquiry and makes broader gestures outward to place the contested terrain of Kent State within the context of the struggle for civil rights, student power, and the rejection of existing forms of political and cultural authority that characterized movements of the 1960s and 1970s.

Chris Powell's essay, "Kent State Comes to Canada: Internationalizing the Antiwar Movement," demonstrates the impact that the antiwar movement of the 1960s, subsequent campus unrest, and the May 4, 1970, tragedy had across North and South America, Europe, the Antipodes, and parts of Asia and Africa. As such, his essay is a remarkable record of chronologies that marks the international potency of youth and protest culture in the 1960s and 1970s and stands as a corrective to what he calls the case study "trend in recent years regarding the writing of the history of the antiwar movement." Industriously researched, Powell's essay traces over two decades an international component of the antiwar movement and links national and international opposition to the Vietnam War with civil rights and free speech movements mobilizing around the globe.

Jay Winter's essay on the social construction of silence focuses attention not on what has been said, argued, organized, or historicized about the Kent State shootings but on the larger subject of the performative nature of silence. "Silence is always part of the framing of public understandings of war and violence," he writes. His essay identifies several useful enactments of silence, from the liturgical to the strategic to the essentialist, and ends with a provocative, almost counterintuitive discussion of the advantages of silence.

The three essays in this opening section, then, interpellate Rukeyser's imperative that we never forget, keep silent, or stand alone. In fact, they enjoin us to do the opposite: transform standing alone into a contemplative gesture that leads to inquiry, learning, and reflection; appropriate silence into a purposeful political act; and—if Augé and Todorov are correct when they suggest that memory is framed by forgetting and that memory *is* a forgetting—anticipate forgetting the events at Kent State as we remember them, as well, no matter how heartbreaking that reality.

Notes

1. Muriel Rukeyser, *The Book of the Dead,* in *The Muriel Rukeyser Reader,* ed. Jan Heller Levi (New York: W. W. Norton and Co., 1995), 46.
2. Tzvetan Todorov, *Hope and Memory: Lessons from the Twentieth Century* (Princeton, N.J.: Princeton Univ. Press, 2003), 127; Marc Augé, *Les forms de l'oubli* (Paris: Payot and Rivages, 1998), 4.
3. Jay Winter, *Remembering War: The Great War Between Memory and History in the Twentieth Century* (New Haven, Conn.: Yale Univ. Press, 2006), 1.
4. James Ingo Freed, quoted in "Inside the Museum: The Architecture," United States Holocaust Memorial Museum, <www.ushmm.org/museum/a_and_a/>.
5. Andreas Huyssen, *Present Pasts: Urban Palimpsests and the Politics of Memory* (Stanford, Calif.: Stanford Univ. Press, 2003), 2.
6. Winter, *Remembering War,* 6.
7. Erin Kosnac and Melissa Hostetler, "Then I Was Shot. Tom Grace: Discovered the Irony," *The Burr,* special edition, May 4, 2000, <http://www.burr.kent.edu/archives/may4/shot/shot4.html>.
8. Huyssen, *Present Pasts,* 101.

Kent State and Historical Memory

Thomas M. Grace

As news spread in May 1970 of the fatal shootings at Kent State University (KSU), outraged students throughout the country went on strike to protest the violent suppression of peaceful dissent, while countless other people expressed the view that Kent's protesters only got what was coming to them. In many ways the simultaneous outrage and backlash framed the subsequent debate over the memory and meaning of Kent State: Were the students casualties of a deliberate act of injustice that must be remembered in order to be rectified? Were they unarmed combatants in a war to stop a war? Were the students themselves primarily responsible for what happened—the killings an object lesson in what happens when dissent turns into confrontation? Or was it all just a tragic mistake (like the war itself, as some believed), the wounds of which could be healed only through acts of public commemoration?

The initial phases in the long battle over the memory of the Kent State killings pitted those who labored to highlight the political significance of May 4 against those who preferred to first enshrine it as a day for mourning and reflection and later neutralize its meaning. Those who insisted on blaming the students also had a large stake in the memory war and sought to either deactivate the importance of the shootings or deny them political worth. Political antagonists who clashed at Kent State following May 4 included members of the antiwar movement at Kent and elsewhere, for whom May 4 became a symbol of the justice of their cause and the immorality of the American government; Kent State University authorities, who wanted to redirect and defuse the political significance of the shootings and, in 1977, ultimately to literally bury their memory; Governor James Rhodes and the Ohio National Guard, who sought not only to exonerate themselves but also to shift the blame to the students and to the plaintiffs in criminal and civil damages cases against the National Guard and officials considered responsible for the shootings.

While beyond these varying antagonists was a large, anonymous population engaged in or concerned with the events of May 4, the groups just named were most closely connected to the conflict at Kent State and figure most prominently in how the day is remembered in history and public memory.[1]

History says that the past is a cluttered place that rests on contested terrain. From the observance of the first anniversary of the killings in 1971 until 1975, the ongoing war in Southeast Asia and the campaign against it coincided with a battle over the memory of the shootings at Kent State. For five successive anniversaries and beyond, antiwar activists clashed with the KSU administration over whether May 4 would be a battle cry for justice or simply a day for remembrance and sorrow. As a result of the killings and the persistence of antiwar activism, some left-of-center wits soon dubbed the school "Kent Police State University" and regarded the shootings as a clarion call to further action.[2] This condemnation of KSU had sufficient staying power that in the 1980s, university officials eager to escape the heavy hand of the past were considering advice to drop "State" from the school's name.[3]

The association of the university with infamy persisted both despite and because of efforts by interested parties—notably the university administration, Governor James Rhodes, and the Ohio National Guard—to advance agendas very different from that of the antiwar left. Some of these parties sought to dominate interpretation of the day or erase its memory, either by building over the site of the shootings or by altering the university's name. Others sought to shed their association with the events of May 4, by demonizing and indicting Kent's antiwar cohort and, later, by covering the ground where the protesting students were shot. Such efforts failed, however; far from giving authorities control of the message or the meaning of May 4, they galvanized opposition. After reporting the death of the students, the local paper, whose publisher was the president of Kent State's board of trustees, issued a front-page editorial calling for "the sternest repression," while the Portage County grand jury that indicted antiwar students devoted paragraphs in its report to the vulgarities chanted by the protesters, but made no mention of the fatalities.[4]

That the killings later achieved such prominence in collective memory had much to do with the scope of the reaction by American students in the immediate wake of the fatal shootings. Numbers outline the magnitude: students staged demonstrations of some sort on better than half of all college campuses; more than five hundred universities closed for a period of time; and Kent State and fifty others were shut down for the remainder of the academic year. Historians know the statistics, while protesters—estimated at 4,350,000 people—can still call to mind their participation.[5] Reaction first to the United States' invasion of Cambodia and then to the Kent killings touched every corner of Ohio and the nation.

Most of this is well documented. What is less known is the role played by former Kent State students or those connected with its campus activists to spread the strike, which helped position the shootings in the public consciousness. Often they did so as individuals rather than as representatives of a particular organization. At Akron University, Bill Whitaker, once associated with Kent State's chapter of Students for a Democratic Society (SDS), was speaking at an antiwar rally when police approached the law student to tell him what had just transpired at Kent. Akron University shut down days later.[6] Seven thousand students marched at Ohio's Bowling Green State University—where Cleveland native Charlie Tabasko had organized an SDS chapter before becoming a regional SDS organizer, building chapters in Cleveland and at Kent.[7] Like most SDSers, Tabasko avoided the extremist edge and did his protesting in early May near Case Western Reserve University, where Danny Thompson and Tony Walsh—two of Kent's pioneer activists in the early and mid-sixties—also numbered among the estimated four thousand antiwar protesters who marched on Cleveland's Euclid Avenue the evening of May 4, 1970.[8] Hunter Havens likewise joined the throng protesting on Euclid Avenue, just as he had in January 1969, when he skipped high school to travel with the Cleveland and Kent SDS and participate in an anti-inaugural confrontation in Washington, D.C.[9] John McCann and Barbara Gregorich—another pair of veteran radicals who had organized Kent State's chapter of the Congress of Racial Equality (CORE) in 1964—also worked in Cleveland against the war.[10] The SDS collapsed in mid-1969, but following the Cambodian invasion and the Kent killings, a new wave of protest affected communities contiguous to colleges across much of the nation. In Cleveland, campus buildings at Case Western, John Carroll, Cleveland State, and Cuyahoga Community College suffered minor damage as protesters expressed their outrage.[11]

While the protests were not organized by students directly connected with Kent State, spontaneous demonstrations nevertheless spread throughout Ohio following the shootings. At Miami University of Ohio, authorities fearful of violent protest over the killings shut down classes.[12] In nearby Cincinnati, students occupied three campus buildings on May 4, continuing to hold them even after the campus closed on May 8.[13] The prolonged demonstrations persisted into late May 1970, when National Guardsmen were called to the only section of the state still largely untouched by protest: Ohio University in Athens. The oldest college in Ohio was the last major one to close, after a firebomb damaged another ROTC building and students broke windows in downtown Athens.[14] At Ohio State University, which experienced protest even before the announcement of the Cambodian invasion, students were wounded by shotgun fire.[15] Days before the protests that swept the state in the wake of the Kent shootings, Governor Rhodes had defended the forceful use of National Guard troops in Columbus, saying there had been "less trouble in Ohio as far as . . . building . . . fires than any other state."[16] Continuing to voice this hard line, Rhodes vowed on May 3 that he would "eradicate" the "dissident groups" and "drive them out of Kent."[17] By the end of May, his frequent deployment of National Guardsmen, which many came to see as inflammatory, had caused virtually all of Ohio's state universities to erupt in protest following the killings in Kent.

Those with Kent connections were involved in demonstrations across the country. Historian Lance Buhl, who had organized the first desegregation sit-in in the city of Kent in 1960 and was nearing the end of a decade of graduate work in May 1970, took time off from his studies to help plan a peaceful rally at Harvard, where he was enrolled, to protest the Kent killings.[18] Elsewhere in Boston, former Kent State students Roy Inglee (once a leader of the Kent Committee to End the War in Vietnam) and Bob Bresnahan organized protests before Bresnahan headed to Washington, D.C., to assist with the most hastily planned national antiwar demonstration ever held in the United States.[19]

With so many universities silenced by closure, 100,000 protesters responded to an emergency call by a reconstituted student movement, the New Mobilization Committee to End the War in Vietnam ("New Mobe"), to demonstrate in the nation's capital the weekend after Kent State. "After Kent," said one of the antiwar group's staff, "the response just catapulted."[20] One who threw herself into the planning was Judy Gollust, who had been part of every dissident group at Kent from CORE to SDS; Judy left a rally in New Haven, Connecticut, on behalf of indicted members of the Black Panther Party to help the New Mobe build the massive Washington, D.C., protest on May 9.[21] The size and ferocity of the protests produced genuine alarm; "Washington took on the character of a besieged city," recalled National Security Council adviser Henry Kissinger. "The Executive Branch was falling apart."[22] It cannot be known precisely how many KSU students went to the huge march, but activists like Jerry Persky, Rick Felber, and Mike Alewitz—all fired on at Kent State—were among hundreds who did. Having begun to shake off the fear that they and others felt after the shootings, they were ready to protest once more.[23] Alewitz, a Student Mobilization Committee leader, found his way to the speaker's rostrum at the Mall and told the huge and angry crowd what the National Guard attack had been like.[24] At the height of its greatest potential power, however, the antiwar movement lacked credible leadership: the SDS had collapsed nationwide almost a year before the fatal shootings; the national headquarters of the moderate Vietnam Moratorium Committee had dissolved in April 1970; and the organizers of the hastily arranged Washington protest were bitterly at odds, despite the swelling crowds of antiwar activists, including tens of thousands of newcomers.[25] Nevertheless, Kent students organized an impromptu outdoor session at the rally—"the only 'spread the strike' group discussion held during yesterday's antiwar demonstration," noted the *Washington Post* on May 10.[26] Thrust into the limelight in an unexpected role, students who witnessed the shootings realized the need not only to organize, but also to systematize the protest against the killing of their classmates.

One site for the new protests was Jackson, Mississippi, still a bastion of conservative, Old South thinking. Danny Thompson, a Kent State student, had been arrested there in June 1961 for his actions as a freedom rider seeking to desegregate interstate bus travel. Violent death as a price for civil rights activism was nothing new in the city in 1970; Medgar Evers's assassination in 1963 was only the best-known example. Despite the danger, however, students at the predominantly African American Jackson State College organized a demonstration for May 7 against the Cambodian invasion and the killings in Ohio.[27] Then at a rally on May 9, a *Daily Kent Stater* photographer, speaking to a hundred students, preached a message of interracial unity against "racism, [and] a senseless war."[28] The rally ended without incident, but only days later, just after midnight on May 15, city and state police unleashed a hail of gunfire at Jackson State students, wounding twelve and killing twenty-year-old Phillip Gibbs and high school student James Earl Green, eighteen.

When word of the Jackson State killings reached Chapel Hill, students tore through the University of North Carolina campus, breaking windows.[29] However, although reaction to the invasion of Cambodia and the shootings at Kent raged in every part of Ohio and in much of the nation, response to the Jackson killings was far more muted. Jackson State did not make the covers of *Time* and *Newsweek*. The selective nature of public outrage paralleled the near-confinement of protests to university campuses, although strikes did erupt as far away as the Pacific coast. Barbara Brock and Ron Wittmaack, who had participated in Kent's first pickets against the war in May 1964 and February 1965, were entering the Student Union at San Francisco State (SFS) when they heard news of the killings at their alma mater, Kent State. As they had done many times before, the two SFS graduate students joined demonstrations protesting the shootings at Kent.[30] On May 6, fearing still more protests over the events at Kent, California's governor, Ronald Reagan closed all campuses of the University of California system for four days.[31]

The initial wave of protests ended where many of the May 1970 protests started—in the Midwest. At Southern Illinois University (SIU), students first broke windows in the building where the Reserve Officers' Training Corps (ROTC) was housed. Later, students did $100,000 worth of damage to businesses in Carbondale, a level of destruction far exceeding that of Kent, Ohio. Speaking of the slain at Kent State, one SIU student, using the vernacular of the day, said: "Them cats don't want flowers. They want you to carry on the struggle where they left off. Don't just have a memorial service—have a struggle service."[32]

In the spring of 1970, concern about the U.S. invasion of Cambodia and its domestic consequences spread everywhere. Nixon administration officials worried not so much about the deaths on campus, but about the outbursts the killings had generated.[33] Nixon's own presidential commission later echoed the observation of an anonymous National Guard officer in reporting that, "The crisis on American campuses has no parallel in the history of the nation. This crisis has roots in American society as deep as any since the Civil War."[34] The president of Columbia University, a campus that had already known plenty of protest, called May 1970 "the most disastrous month . . . in the history of American higher education."[35] The scope of the protests helped establish the importance of the Kent State shootings as a decisive moment in the ten-year struggle against the Southeast Asian war. The massive, often rancorous student response to what many saw as unjustifiable killings preserved the May 4 shootings in modern American memory. Further, the view, widespread in both scholarly circles and in the popular imagination, that the killings silenced dissent at Kent State is mistaken. On the contrary, students at Kent State spent the next five years carrying on what the young activist at SIU called a *struggle service.*

What of those who had to contend institutionally with the shootings? Presiding over a student body that had more than doubled in size (to 21,000 students) between 1963 and 1969, Robert I. White, the president of Kent State University, had spent much of his tenure before May 1970 trying to run the school free from both student input and outside interference.[36] To do so, he had sought to navigate between an increasingly resistive student population and Governor Rhodes, who, together with other self-appointed guardians of public morality, was trying to exert unwanted political oversight.[37] As the decade wore on, White found it ever more difficult to circumvent outside intrusion.[38] In the spring of 1969, White deemed it necessary to call Portage County sheriffs to the campus to aid KSU police in making nearly eighty arrests over six weeks, and to ban the controversial SDS organization from the campus.[39] Thereafter, the law enforcement arms of the federal government, as well as the U.S. House of Representatives Committee on Internal Security, which investigated SDS after President White had banned the local chapter, took an increasing interest in campus affairs.[40]

The events of May 1–4, 1970, and Governor Rhodes's deployment of the National Guard ended any hope that Kent State's president, White, could operate the campus free from outside intervention. On the day of the killings, the Portage County prosecutor obtained a court injunction to shut down the university.[41] Students were ordered to vacate the campus, and authorities then combed all campus dorm rooms, ostensibly searching for weapons.[42] The school remained closed until graduation ceremonies on June 13 and the beginning of summer quarter on June 22.[43] In the glare of national attention, White's administration established several university commissions to determine the nature of the antagonisms that had made Kent State an instant symbol of death and dissent. While White's administration recognized that President Nixon's Cambodian gambit had triggered the disorderly protests, the university's Office of Alumni Relations (writing in the pages of *Kent* magazine) asserted that President Nixon and Governor Rhodes had properly branded outsiders as primarily responsible for "ignit[ing] the fire[s]" of Kent's protests.[44] Appropriating rhetoric from the president and governor, the magazine went on to explain what many of Kent's citizens believed, that the trouble could be attributed to "will-o-the-wisp characters who move from campus to campus, from confrontation to confrontation fomenting unrest and inciting to violence."[45] This targeting of imagined outsiders, more phantom than real, enabled President White to suggest that the disorders of May 1–4 stemmed from unwanted imports rather than Kent's homegrown protesters. In reality, the sequence was reversed: some Kent State students—realizing the magnitude of what they had seen on May 4 and acting on their anger—spoke as eyewitnesses at protests that sprang up elsewhere. Before the fatal shootings, virtually all of the protesters at Kent State either were or had been students there.[46]

As spring gave way to summer and summer to fall, the public hate engulfing Kent and Portage County diminished, giving way to uncertainty. Talk of killing hundreds of students, instead of merely four, mostly subsided or else found more discreet outlets, such as a petition organized by Doris Amick, chair of the Portage County Citizens for Law Enforcement, whose group gathered eight thousand signatures supporting the National Guard.[47] Meanwhile, however, university officials, worried that coverage by the five hundred journalists who descended on the town after the killings, and the resulting opprobrium, might undermine Kent State's enrollment, resorted to draconian measures.[48] Determined to preserve order, university and town officials mulled over how many new police hires would be necessary to enforce authority.[49] Promising to "move with assurance and resolve," President White conceded that the new measures would "seem like a police state to students."[50]

Paralleling local efforts, the Ohio General Assembly adopted House Bill 1219, legislation making campus "'disruption'" a new category of crime, and appointed Seabury Ford, Portage County's GOP chairman and an ally of Rhodes, the outgoing governor, a hearing officer charged with the law's enforcement.[51] Ford, who had once served in the same 107th Armored Cavalry Ohio National Guard unit that had supplied six of the eight guardsmen later indicted by the U.S. Justice Department, also acted as an assistant grand jury prosecutor in cases arising from the events of May 4. In that capacity, he ignored the culpability of those who had fired the fatal shots and instead indicted one KSU professor and twenty-four young people, mostly KSU students (the "Kent 25")—including two of those wounded—for their alleged roles in the May protests.[52] Namesake of an ancestor who had served as Ohio's last Whig governor, Ford declared in a newspaper interview that the guardsmen "should have shot all troublemakers."[53] Outrage over the remark cost him his job. Yet Ford made it clear that he represented popular, man-in-the-street opinion. Overlooking the fact that no disturbance had existed before the National Guard broke up the peaceful demonstration of May 4, Ford justified use of lethal means, insisting that the shootings "stopped the riot. . . . It just stopped it flat."[54]

Ford's remark represented one pole of opinion, little shared by KSU students or faculty, and KSU officials tried to set a different tone. In place of recrimination, administrators substituted collective mourning. Swift closure of the campus on May 4 denied the university community its public grief over the deaths. When classes resumed in fall 1970, administrators, faculty, and students assigned various meanings to the May 4 dead, whom many counted as casualties of the Southeast Asian war. Vietnam veteran Tim Butz, Ralph Abernathy of the Southern Christian Leadership Conference, Ira Sandperl of the California Institute for Non-Violence, the ubiquitous Phil Ochs, and student body president Craig Morgan (who would soon find himself among the Kent 25), addressed five thousand mourners in late September.[55] Overshadowing them all was Dean Kahler, a shooting victim who had been paralyzed. A forgiving Kahler told a capacity crowd that he was glad to be alive. Later, two thousand students held an unplanned candlelight vigil at the site of the killings, beginning a tradition that continues to this day on the anniversary of the fatal shootings.

Despite such promising beginnings, which seemed to offer signs of unity within the bereaved community, tensions were evident. As the war in Southeast Asia expanded not only into Cambodia but, in February 1971, into Laos, the KSU administration found little middle ground on which to operate. Ira Sandperl's presence at Kent State indirectly led to the 1971 creation of the Center for Peaceful Change (CPC), yet the center's various constituencies had very different ideas on whether and how to promote social transformation, while those on the antiwar left saw the CPC as a tool of cooptation.[56] The continuation of the war and demands for Kent State to end what the activist left saw as university complicity with it, the indictment of students by the county grand jury, and the persistence of racial tension between the administration and the leadership of the Black United Students (BUS) virtually guaranteed that unity within the bereaved community would prove elusive.[57] Anonymous bomb threats, whether symbolic or real, emptied classroom buildings now and again.[58] Rallies denouncing the war, a bomb attack on BUS headquarters, sporadic arrests of BUS leaders and peace activists, and the indictment of the Kent 25 kept social activism alive, despite efforts to undercut the protests by White's administration and Portage County officials. These irritants all took a continuing toll, as the campus newspaper chronicled through the 1970–71 academic year.[59]

Still, the administration appreciated that the first anniversary of the killings could not pass without a remembrance of some kind. In February 1971, a week after a protest against the invasion of Laos led to arrests for flag desecration, President White appointed Craig Morgan, the student body president, graduate student Steve Sharoff, and KSU's mild-mannered vice president, Richard Bredemeier, to head the president's May 4 Commemorative Committee (M4CC).[60] Burdened by ongoing campus tensions, including the arrest of BUS leaders for assault on the very day that White's appointments were announced, committee members could not avoid the troublesome present.[61] Blasting what its members called "repression" and decreeing that the time for whites to aid African Americans had reached a point of "now or never," BUS called for action.[62] Despite a heavy snowfall, two hundred students conducted a nighttime march on the president's home, demanding that charges against the students be dropped. A week later, President White announced his retirement, to take effect at the start of the fall 1971 quarter.

Divisiveness brought on by the long war hastened President White's departure, just as measures being taken against dissident students made consensus impossible. Promoting a view that "it happened to us all," the M4CC appealed for input from the larger student body.[63] Left-wing students would have none of it and rejected any notion of a community of suffering. Rather, the antiwar left claimed possession of the May 4 dead and wounded and organized in their name. Two former members of the SDS, Ken Hammond (one of the most prominent of the Kent 25 defendants) and Vietnam veteran Ken Johnson, led the formation of a May 4 Coalition as an alternative to the university-sponsored committee.[64] Having battled the university since the spring of 1968, leftist activists, including those heading the coalition, saw White's administration as being complicit in the war, if not in the campus killings.[65] Dissent developed even within the university-sponsored M4CC as some faculty members broke with it to support May 4 Coalition plans for a separate commemoration. Still another allied group, the May Day Coalition, worked at mobilizing students to attend a national protest in Washington, D.C., aimed at shutting down the capital the week of May 3 to dramatize opposition to the continuing war in Southeast Asia.[66]

The M4CC encountered additional obstacles when it announced plans to include poet Rod McKuen among the presenters at the commemoration, whose work activists and some critics found sentimentally vapid. Deciding the campus could do without McKuen's inspiration, a teaching fellow sarcastically asked in a letter to the student paper why the committee had not also invited Liberace and Norman Rockwell or had the remembrance "blessed by Rex Humbard."[67] Believing that the committee had earned such scorn, four of those wounded in 1970 contributed their own letter. In the first collective statement issued by May 4 wounded, they charged that the M4CC was "totally unrepresentative of the people . . . whom it [May 4] was designed to commemorate."[68] McKuen canceled his appearance, while additional members of the M4CC backed away from their support of the official commemoration.[69]

In the end, differences between the university and the antiwar left proved insurmountable. Amid credible rumors of National Guard deployment to the area and promises by the administration to bar nonstudents from the commemoration by forcing those attending to furnish proof of their student status, separate observances went on.[70] Drawing from the example of the spontaneous vigil held after the first memorial service the previous fall, Professor Jerry Lewis and sociology student Michelle Klein ignored administrative negativity and organized a candlelight march on the eve of the shootings.[71] On May 4, the Victory Bell, which had called students to the fateful rally, sounded in memory of those killed at Kent State and Jackson

State. Whether speaking at the official ceremony, as did Jesse Jackson, or at a May 4 Coalition event, as did Julian Bond, speakers were well received by the estimated ten thousand people who attended one or both observances; most knew or cared little about the sponsorship of the events.[72] Following the May 4 Coalition program, antiwar students occupied KSU's new ROTC building (which had replaced the one destroyed by fire) for some hours, but the only demonstrators arrested that day numbered among the hundreds of people from Kent State who had left campus to participate in a failed attempt to close down the nation's capital by filling its streets. One of these was Jim Russell, who had been wounded in the May 4 shootings.[73]

Three years later, in speaking of Nixon's resignation in August 1974, amidst the Watergate crisis, President Gerald Ford assured Americans that "our long national nightmare is over."[74] The new president's remarks not only offered the nation immediate comfort but also would have future utility when, in April 1975, the United States' withdrawal and the surrender of the South Vietnamese government to Communist forces finally ended the Vietnam War. Reactions to the war's end ranged from distress to relief and, in some cases, jubilation. At Kent State, on the occasion of the fifth commemoration of the May 4 killings, some students reacted with triumph to the war's end, reflecting the radicalization the war had engendered. Bitter after the federal government had, months earlier, dropped a conspiracy case against eight National Guardsmen and linking the campus killings to the war, crowds of Kent State students heralded what they saw as a victory for their cause. "When the actions of our government were condemned," noted one Ohio daily in its coverage of the commemoration, "the overwhelming young rally audience responded with enthusiasm rarely seen in this post-demonstration era."[75] Days earlier, Michelle Klein, the KSU graduate who had helped organize the 1971 candlelight march, offered another perspective on her obligation to the past. Referring to those, like herself, who had been students on May 4, she said: "There aren't many of us left (on campus) and we've become a cadre for people to point to."[76] Klein and others like her were visible links to a lethal past that they would not allow other Kent State students to forget.

Like President Ford, KSU officials wanted to believe that their own nightmarish half-decade had ended. They asserted that the end of the Vietnam War should likewise signal the end of public observances of the May 4 killings and their pluralistic acceptance of the commemorations.[77] Others disagreed, however. Current and former KSU students Alan Canfora, Dean Kahler, and Robby Stamps, all casualties of the National Guard, maintained that it was vital to remember the struggle, in which "the wounds of Kent State are felt still," as a national paper put it.[78] Together the three men, whose fates had been randomly joined together by gunfire and who had come to better appreciate the use of the past, established the May 4 Task Force to carry on the commemorations. In the years following, students who cycled in and out of the Task Force have kept alive the memory of that day for successive generations. By the fortieth anniversary of the Kent shootings, two constants remained: the candlelight vigil honoring the dead and an insistence on linking the vocal antiwar principles of the student protesters of May 1970 to the struggles of the present.

Of those factions interested in maintaining or downplaying the memory of the May 4 Kent State shootings, those with a direct stake included not only KSU activists and the university administration but also Ohio's governor and members of the Ohio National Guard, believed by many students to be collectively guilty of reckless homicide.[79] For the governor and the guardsmen, the repercussions of the May 4 killings and the memory of those events required a transfer of blame. The day following the shootings, Specialist 4 William Herschler rode back to the Wooster Armory with fellow guardsmen. Although he later denied making the remark, Herschler is reported to have said, "I just shot two teenagers," and his sergeant, Matthew McManus, told the FBI five days after the killings that Herschler "seemed to fire his weapon into the crowd . . . his whole clip of eight rounds in a semi automatic fashion."[80] Herschler returned to Wooster partly to vote in the May 5 primary, in which Governor Rhodes was a candidate for the Republican nomination for the U.S. Senate. His run for national office made Rhodes even more determined to control the political damage arising from the shootings at Kent State by National Guardsmen he had called out. At a May 5 news conference, two days after he had promised to "eradicate" those he said were "the worst type of people that we harbor in America," Rhodes called the events of May 4, "the most sorrowful day in my life," and then ordered John McElroy, his chief of staff, to draft a proclamation giving him retroactive authority to have dispatched the National Guard troops to Kent four days earlier.[81]

Narrowly losing the May 1970 primary, Rhodes bided his time, trying to say as little as possible publicly about Kent State.[82] As eight guardsmen faced federal trial, he nursed his ambitions to return to the Ohio governor's mansion. Speaking to what he may have believed was a closed campaign event in October 1974, candidate Rhodes told a group of GOP supporters in Wayne County—home base to some of the guardsmen facing trial—that all he did on May 4 "was perform my duty."[83] Weeks later, just as Rhodes achieved his campaign objective, the guardsmen attained their own goal when criminal charges against them were suddenly dismissed. Rhodes hailed the dismissal, proclaiming, "Once again justice has prevailed."[84] Eventually, Rhodes became the longest-serving chief executive in Ohio's history, winning two additional terms from 1975 to 1983. Throughout his years as governor, Rhodes avoided talking publicly about the killings, although his silence often spoke volumes, as when, during his third term as governor, Rhodes watched with seeming approval as Kent State officials constructed a gymnasium annex atop much of the ground where guardsmen had faced students seven years earlier. Ten months before his death at the age of ninety-one, Rhodes finally broke his silence, suggesting that his actions at Kent State, while ending unpleasantly, represented the will of the people. Conceding that the shootings at Kent State were "a terrible thing," he added a caveat: "But no one plans a train wreck, either. It just happened and life goes on."[85] The former governor's death generated considerable attention and comment, most of it predictable. Within days of his death in March 2001, one dispassionate newspaper columnist wrote of the former governor's failure to address the shootings: "James A. Rhodes took a secret to his grave. . . . [Kent State] is still an open wound."[86] It was a wound that only justice for and answers about May 4 could heal.

Initially, guardsmen involved in the shootings had been instructed by officers "not to talk about it [May 4] to the media or to anyone."[87] While National Guard commanders began circulating tales of rooftop marksmen, enlisted men, noncommissioned officers, and their company officers spoke for attribution only through their after-action reports.[88] Sgt. William James Case of Troop G, 107th Armored Cavalry, wrote in his report why he had fired in the air: "Only God can take lives and . . . I didn't get the order from him to aim at any human, no matter how hard they threw the rocks. I just couldn't shoot them."[89] Case was in the minority. James Pierce, another member of Troop G, called the students "animals," and wrote in his report, "After the firing I felt no remorse because it seemed to be the only way to defend myself."[90] Others spoke even more freely under the cover of anonymity. Another guardsman in Troop G complained about the stream of profanity they had endured and told a reporter, "It's about time we showed the bastards who's in charge."[91] Another from an unidentified unit put it more crudely, suggesting the mission involved sanitizing a foul place: "I felt like I'd just had an order to clean up a latrine."[92]

Company A, 145th Infantry, the other unit on the hill, hailed from rural Wayne County and served under a farmer. "Of the guardsmen interviewed," two reporters wrote, "none showed any remorse over the casualties inflicted." The reporters further observed of the fatal encounter that the guardsmen "accepted it, as one of them said, as something 'that had to happen sometime.'" Identified only as a dairy farmer, one guardsman raged about "hippies and longhairs . . . if they want to use force, they will receive force."[93] A more sympathetic account of the same unit appeared the following month, but even when the author of the article carefully questioned men who did not discharge their weapons, his findings were much the same as those who authored the earlier story. One guardsman fancifully imagined the students having taken their arms. Another, forgetting that guardsmen had also thrown rocks at students, recalled the death of the biblical Goliath from a stone. A third insisted on deconstructing the language of the fatal scene, telling the reporter, "I don't feel it was a killing. It was a shooting with death involved."[94]

A third unit engaged in the shootings that day, Company C, 145th Infantry, had only two members on the hill, although other guards in that detachment had been the first to aim their rifles at students on the Commons and although its commander,

Portage County detective Captain James Ronald Snyder, had been the first to strike a protester.[95] Snyder said flatly, "My men were not remorseful. . . . [N]o one has ever expressed to me any regrets for what happened."[96] Such sentiments caused one National Guard officer to describe the ferocity at Kent as being "like the Civil War."[97] One of the journalists observed, "The differences between those students and guardsmen . . . go beyond the tragedy at Kent," and averred, "They are divided by differences in outlook . . . in background and behavior."[98] The demonstration at Kent State presented guardsmen deployed there, some nursing cultural resentments, with a chance to fix what many saw as a lawless America. Asked years later whether he had modified his self-described "hard-core" views, guardsman and helicopter pilot Robert Gabriel remained steadfast: "I didn't feel sorry for the people that got killed. I really didn't."[99]

Since their initial, mostly anonymous statements to journalists in the wake of the shootings, the guardsmen who had been present—outside their usually careful court testimony—generally followed the lead of the governor and kept silent. Those who fired deadly weapons at Kent State have sought quite a different outcome to the memory wars than Kent State's students or even its faculty; the guardsmen have seemed rather more concerned with keeping May 4, and the roles they played in the fatalities, a closed book. More talk, they have reasoned, brings more attention, and more attention brings more tarnish. Some may continue to feel that the protests at Kent State, once equated with a latrine by an anonymous guardsman, are a part of the American past best ignored and forgotten. Reopening the discussion simply reopens the wound and the possibility of further blame being assigned to the guardsmen.

The Portage County grand jury proceedings of October 1970, which returned indictments of twenty-five people and their trials a year later, represented the first legal encounter for those with a stake in assigning blame for Kent State. After most charges against the Kent 25 were dismissed, parties retaining an interest in remembering or forgetting intersected again in court with the 1974 criminal cases against the National Guard and in a 1975 civil damages case filed on behalf of the plaintiffs' families against those responsible for the shootings. As the war in Southeast Asia raged on throughout the latter part of the Vietnamization phase of the conflict (during which the U.S. sought to replace American forces with South Vietnamese soldiers) so did efforts to win a federal probe of the conduct of the National Guard at Kent State. Other than activists in Kent's antiwar left, who feared being targeted by Nixon's Justice Department, most liberals and fair-minded middle-of-the-roaders wanted a federal investigation.[100] Spearheaded by several twenty-somethings, KSU students—with the support of the parents of the four slain undergraduates—gathered ten thousand signatures on petitions supporting a federal inquiry.[101]

This liberal pressure for an inquiry did not come at a good time in the oscillating political fortunes of Richard Nixon. The president had gone from winning reelection by a landslide in November 1972 to embroilment in the Watergate crisis just a year later. This political entanglement significantly affected the Justice Department, which had initially complied with Nixon's directive in November 1970, to avoid an investigation of the National Guard.[102] In August 1973, under the direction of Attorney General Elliott Richardson (who had succeeded two predecessors forced to resign under a cloud of scandal), the Justice Department revisited the issue and opened an investigation. At first, prospects for the investigation looked poor. Only months later, Richardson and his deputy themselves were fired by President Nixon after they refused to dismiss the Watergate special prosecutor. Moreover, Richardson's replacement was Senator William Saxbe of Ohio, a confidante of former Governor Rhodes and an inactive officer in the Ohio National Guard. However, after Saxbe told the Senate Judiciary Committee he would recuse himself from any dealings with the revived investigation of Kent State, a federal grand jury was impaneled. By December 1973, President Nixon had been so weakened politically that the grand jury investigation could finally go forward.[103]

Those seeking justice for or at least answers about the shootings at Kent State remained thwarted, however, by the vagaries of cultural populism in the 1970s. Justice Department attorneys returned indictments against eight Ohio National Guardsmen in March 1974, winning praise from a number of Ohio's Democratic representatives and families of Kent State students. "At last the blame has been . . . placed where it should be placed," said the mother of slain student Jeff Miller.[104] The indictments brought criticism from the state's Republicans, however, and from guardsmen's families. Saying perhaps more than he knew, the father of twenty-eight-year-old guardsman Lawrence Shafer compared the actions of his son and the other indicted men to those of a leading participant in a mass murder of civilians in Vietnam: "It was just like Lt. William Calley. They were only doing what they were told."[105]

Nixon's resignation in August 1974 in the wake of the Watergate crisis shook public confidence in government and certainly contributed to a series of huge midterm congressional losses for the Republican Party that year. Yet in Ohio that same year, James Rhodes managed to recapture the governorship following a constitutional hiatus. Two days after an exceedingly close vote, state election officials named Rhodes the unofficial winner on November 7, 1974.[106] The shell-shocked incumbent, John J. Gilligan, declared that he had been "destroyed by a media campaign . . . as if a rifle had shot me."[107] In late October, concurrent with the final election push in Ohio, the Justice Department commenced a bid to prove that the actual rifle fire by eight Ohio guardsmen had been "indiscriminate and unjustified."[108] In a remarkable twist of fate, on the very day Rhodes was declared the unofficial winner of the gubernatorial election, the Justice Department prosecution rested its case following ten days of testimony. Then, in an apparent coincidence, the presiding judge notified the prosecutor that he soon "might have something in writing."[109]

He did. At the start of the trial, the *New York Times* had speculated that "questions about what really happened on the [Kent State] campus are likely to linger even after . . . [the guardsmen's] fate is decided," yet few were prepared for the judge's written decision.[110] On November 8—the same day it was announced that former President Nixon's near-fatal illness would prevent him from testifying at a criminal trial for his onetime aides—Federal Judge John J. Battisti threw out the case against the guardsmen the *Times* had called "the alleged triggermen."[111]

Following the dismissal of the case and against the backdrop of army lieutenant William Calley being released after three years of home confinement following his conviction for murdering unarmed Vietnamese civilians, no less than half of the happy defendants—guardsmen Barry Morris, Matthew McManus, William Perkins, and James Pierce—autographed a trial exhibit photograph that showed them firing the fatal salvo at the students.[112] The Justice Department prosecutor later disclosed that he had "no problem with what the judge did."[113] Of course, many others had plenty of reasons to object to the decision, which did little to mend the deep fissure over the shootings. *Time* magazine asserted that the closed case left open "the restless search for justice" that seemed "likely to haunt the U.S. on through history."[114] The news that guardsmen were inscribing crime scene photos ensured that Kent State's wounds would fester rather than heal.

The magazine's coverage concluded dimly, "The parents and survivors can hope only for the token solace of damages in a series of civil suits now pending."[115] Book chapters and entire volumes have been devoted to this civil litigation, which involved two U.S. Supreme Court cases and one decision (*Scheuer v. Rhodes*), a lengthy fourteen-week tribunal in 1975, a successful federal appeals court decision handed down in the wake of a six-month campaign by activists at Kent to stop the construction of a gymnasium on the site of the shootings, and an out-of-court settlement in January 1979, just after the start of a second federal civil damages trial.[116] All told, the various judicial proceedings resulted in what KSU professor Thomas Hensley described as "one of the longest, costliest, and most complex set of courtroom struggles in American history."[117] The end of the litigation stipulated the signing of a statement by the sitting governor, two former generals, and twenty-five current and erstwhile members of the Ohio National Guard who remained as defendants. Guardsman Larry Mowrer, whose poor distance vision prevented him from seeing where he was firing, was the first to sign, indicted shooter James Pierce, the last.[118] Some called the written accounting an apology. Others, such as one of the signers, Adjutant General Sylvester Del Corso, loath to soothe Kent's lingering wound, maintained that it was nothing of the kind: "There is no apology," he said. "We expressed sorrow and regret just as you would express condolences to the family of someone who died."[119] Someone who died. Semantically, the phrase has a passive quality, considering the contextually active circumstances in which four people were fatally shot at distances ranging from 265 to 390 feet from their assailants.

Memorials marking sites of the dead were designated in 1999 after the May 4 Task Force pressed the university to do so. Speaking of the parking lot memorials and the Task Force, Mrs. Doris Krause, whose daughter Allison died more than 340 feet away from the National Guard position, insisted, "if . . . [they] hadn't applied pressure, nothing would have happened."[120] Yet the university has had half a dozen presidents since May 1970 and with the many administrative changes has come acceptance: "a much more positive view of its own history," as one knowledgeable alumnus put it in May 2007.[121] Over the years, on the anniversary of the killings, thousands of people, including not only the families of the dead and wounded but also university presidents, have stood vigil on the spots of the parking lot where the students were killed. Although most of the practice football field where the guardsmen maneuvered and once aimed at the students has given way to a now-underused gym annex, the sites where four young people were shot to death remain open, which is vital to recalling who they were and why they were killed.

Thus an otherwise unremarkable parking lot, surrounded and edged by a grassy apron and hillside, has become a place where memory merges with memorial and granite funereal forms. Yet memory is not history. As one specialist reminds us, "Memory is often owned, history interpreted."[122] At the same site where memory dwells, keepers of the past have weighed in. A descriptive marker erected in 2007 by the Ohio Historical Society is a reminder of the difference between what the same specialist, historian David Blight, calls "the authority of . . . evidence . . . [and] the . . . authority of . . . experience."[123] With regard to the former, historical practitioners insist on research and evidentiary standards when fashioning a reconstruction of the past; with regard to the latter, however, the participants and witnesses of the events of May 4 base their authority on their empirical memories. Despite the difference between history and memory, the two can and do intersect, however. America contains few instances more contested than the fight over the twentieth-century public memory of the shootings at Kent State. Iconic photographs, annual commemorations, memorials and markers, news stories, and continuing representations in popular culture serve to keep the memory alive, while historical judgments based on evidence and sensitive to context compete with resentments still voiced on talk radio and expressed through (often anonymous) Internet raging.

For those most aggrieved, fury may have subsided, but the divide remains. Justice has not been done. As one essayist put it so well, it may be that Kent State is, like Vietnam, "The War that Won't Die."[124] When one considers those most affected, the families of the four slain students, Steinbeck's 1945 novel, *Cannery Row,* comes to mind. "It's all fine to say that 'Time will heal everything,' . . . but when you are [involved], there is no passage of time, people do not forget and are in the middle of something that does not change."[125] For Jeff Miller's mother, there is always the photo, the ubiquitous Pulitzer Prize–winning photo. For her, that does not change.

Still, she had to find a way to become accustomed to the sight of her lifeless son and did so by imagining him asleep instead of dead. For the heartbroken mother, though, Jeff and his three classmates were not the only losses, for, as she once wrote, the "myth of a benign America where dissent is broadly tolerated was one [more] casualty of the shootings at Kent State."[126] By determining who would construe the significance of the shootings at Kent State, and, in so doing, achieving a small measure of justice, activists not only kept the memory of the killings from fading from public view but also helped define them as a watershed event in post–World War II American history.

Notes

1. This essay is based in part on a longer study, Thomas M. Grace, *Kent State: Death and Dissent During the Long Sixties, 1958–1973* (Amherst, Mass.: Univ. of Massachusetts Press, forthcoming).
2. "University to Get Tough, Kent City Officials Told," *Kent-Ravenna Record-Courier,* Sept. 17, 1970; photo of students wearing "Kent Police State University" T-shirts, *Daily Kent Stater,* Oct. 22, 1970.
3. "Beyond May 4 and Into the Future," *Cleveland Plain Dealer,* May 4, 2000.
4. "University Must Oust Hooligans," *Kent-Ravenna Record-Courier,* May 4, 1970; James A. Michener, *Kent State: What Happened and Why* (New York: Random House, 1971), 446–61; Justice Department memo, Nov. 4, 1970, courtesy of May 4 Center; "Grand Jury Report," in *The Killings at Kent State: How Murder Went Unpunished,* by I. F. Stone, 145–58 (New York: New York Review, 1970).
5. Kirkpatrick Sale, *SDS* (New York: Vintage Books, 1974), 636–38.
6. Bill Whitaker, interviews by author, Nov. 21, 1999, and Jan. 24, 2006; political ad attacking John Seiberling based on his association with Bill Whitaker, *Akron Beacon Journal,* Nov. 2, 1970.
7. Charlie Tabasko, interview by author, Sept. 8, 2002; "BGSU Students Demonstrate," *Cleveland Press,* May 1, 1970; "Here Are Colleges Facing Protests," *Cleveland Press,* May 7, 1970.
8. Danny Thompson, interview by author, June 23, 2001; Tony Walsh, interview by author, Feb. 19, 2000; "4,000 at CWRU Honor Dead at Kent," *Cleveland Press,* May 5, 1970.
9. Hunter Havens, conversation with author, May 4, 2000.
10. Barbara Gregorich, communication with author, Jan. 7, 2002. Gregorich supplied information about John McCann.
11. For Case and John Carroll, see "2 ROTC Fires Reported Here," *Cleveland Press,* May 7, 1970; for Cleveland State, see "Two Hurt, Five Arrested in CSU Violence," *Cleveland Press,* May 7, 1970; and for Cuyahoga Community College, see "Campuses Mourn KSU Victims, Marchers Smash Door at CCC," *Cleveland Press,* May 5, 1970.
12. "Three Ohio Universities Shut Down," *Cleveland Press,* May 7, 1970.
13. "Cincy Students Block Traffic; 145 Arrested," *Cleveland Press,* May 2, 1970; "Ohio College Students Protest," *Cleveland Press,* May 8, 1970.

14. "Millions Protest Against Cambodian Invasion," *Guardian* (New York), May 23, 1970; "Here Are Colleges Facing Protests," *Cleveland Press,* May 7, 1970
15. "Demonstrations at Ohio State," *Guardian* (New York), May 9, 1970; "Judge Called Soft in OSU Riot," *Cleveland Press,* May 1, 1970; "Guard Restores Order to OSU," *Cleveland Press,* May 6, 1970.
16. Joe Eszterhas and Michael D. Roberts, *Thirteen Seconds: Confrontation at Kent State* (New York: Dodd, Mead and Co., 1970), 14.
17. David Schmoll, Governor James Rhodes Press Conference, May 3, 1970, CD copy of tape provided by Bob Carpenter, 89.7 WKSU, May 4 Collection, Special Collections and Archives, Kent State University Libraries, Kent, Ohio.
18. Lance Buhl, interview by author, Apr. 18, 2000.
19. Roy Inglee, interview by author, Apr. 2, 2000; Judy Gollust, communication with author, Feb. 20, 2006.
20. "Antiwar Rally Puts New Life in Mobe Group," *Washington Post,* May 9, 1970.
21. Gollust, communication with author, Feb. 20, 2006.
22. Tom Wells, *The War Within: America's Battle Over Vietnam* (Berkeley, Calif.: Univ. of California Press, 1994), 430.
23. Jerry Persky, interview by author, Aug. 27, 2000; Rick Felber, conversation with author, Mar. 29, 2007, and letter to author, Apr. 28, 2007; Mike Alewitz, interview by author, Nov. 18, 2005.
24. Alewitz, interview, Nov. 18, 2005.
25. Wells, *War Within,* 409, 437–46.
26. "200 Students Plan 'Kent State in Exile' at Oberlin College," *Washington Post,* May 10, 1970.
27. Tim Spofford, *Lynch Street: The May 1970 Slayings at Jackson State College* (Kent, Ohio: Kent State Univ. Press, 1988), 18–32.
28. Ibid., 97–114.
29. "Millions Protest Against Cambodia," *Guardian* (New York), May 23, 1970.
30. Barbara Brock and Ron Wittmaack, joint interview by author, Feb. 19, 2000.
31. "Here Are Colleges Facing Protests," *Cleveland Press,* May 7, 1970.
32. Robbie Lieberman and David Cochran, "'It Seemed a Very Local Affair': The Student Movement at Southern Illinois University at Carbondale," in *The New Left Revisited,* ed. John McMillian and Paul Buhle (Philadelphia, Pa.: Temple Univ. Press, 2003), 11–27.
33. Wells, *War Within,* 430–37; H. R. Haldeman, *The Haldeman Diaries: Inside the Nixon White House* (New York: G. P. Putnam's Sons, 1994), 159–65.
34. Haynes Johnson, "The Tragedy at Kent: A Generation in Conflict," *Washington Post,* May 7, 1970; *Report of the President's Commission,* 1.
35. William Leuchtenburg, *A Troubled Feast: American Society Since 1945* (1979; Glenview, Ill.: Scott, Foresman and Co., 1983), 245.
36. On the tensions with Rhodes, see "Bowman Nixes Rhodes on 'Super Board,'" *Daily Kent Stater,* Jan. 24, 1963; "Presidents Refuse Regent Board OK," *Daily Kent Stater,* Feb. 7, 1963; Richard G. Zimmerman, "Rhodes's First Eight Years, 1963–1971," in *Ohio Politics,* ed. Alexander P. Lamis and Mary Anne Sharkey (Kent, Ohio: Kent State Univ. Press, 1994), 72–73. For examples of the pressure exerted on White from outside the university, see letters about the chartering of the Young Socialist Alliance in January 1965, in Robert

I. White Papers, box 14, file 41, Special Collections and Archives, Kent State University Libraries, Kent, Ohio.

37. "Though Not Sardines, We're Packed In Tight—Over 1,000 Turned Away," *Daily Kent Stater,* Sept. 25, 1964; Thomas R. Hensley, *The Kent State Incident: Impact of Judicial Process on Public Attitudes* (Westport, Conn.: Greenwood, 1981), 25.
38. Hearings Committee on Internal Security, Ninety-First Congress, First Session, June 24 and 25, 1969, *Investigation of Students for a Democratic Society,* Part 2, Kent State University (Washington, D.C.: GPO, 1969), 549.
39. Ibid., 488; "Arrest 6 for ROTC Disruption," *Daily Kent Stater,* May 27, 1969; William Armstrong and Barclay McMillen, "Kent State, May 4, 1970: Who Really Was Responsible for the Shootings?" 1999, May 4 Collection, box 131, file 14, Special Collections and Archives, Kent State University Libraries, Kent, Ohio.
40. "Former Chief Reveals Agents Were at KSU," *Daily Kent Stater,* May 14, 1971
41. Hensley, *Kent State Incident,* 68.
42. Eszterhas and Roberts, *Thirteen Seconds,* 286–87.
43. "Struggle to Recovery," *Kent* magazine 3, no. 6 (June 1970): 13, 18, 22. Published by Kent State University Office of Alumni Relations.
44. Ibid., 4.
45. Ibid.
46. For instance, all thirteen casualties on May 4, 1970, were KSU students.
47. Michener, *Kent State: What Happened,* 446–61; Scott L. Bills, "Introduction: The Past in the Present," *Kent State/May 4: Echoes Through a Decade,* ed. Scott L. Bills (1982; Kent, Ohio: Kent State Univ. Press, 1988), 18–22, 126; "Guard Supporter Happy with Judge's Decision," *Kent-Ravenna Record-Courier,* Nov. 8, 1974; Stuart Taylor et al., *Violence at Kent State: The Students' Perspective* (New York: College Notes and Text, 1971), 16–17.
48. "Kent State U. Enrollment Up," *Kent-Ravenna Record-Courier,* Sept. 26, 1970.
49. "Beef-up of Kent Police Force Due," *Kent-Ravenna Record-Courier,* Sept. 17, 1970.
50. "University to Get Tough, Kent City Officials Told," *Kent-Ravenna Record-Courier,* Sept. 17, 1970.
51. Jim Quilligan, "Perspective," *Daily Kent Stater,* Oct. 1, 1970, 3–4.
52. Ibid.; "Offenses Against Society," *Daily Kent Stater,* Oct. 1, 1970.
53. "Ford's Resignation Asked—By KSU Faculty Senate President Nurmi," *Kent-Ravenna Record-Courier,* Oct. 26, 1970; "Ford Off Track," *Kent-Ravenna Record-Courier,* Oct. 26, 1970; "Say Ford Ousted as Grand Jury Counsel," *Kent-Ravenna Record-Courier,* Oct. 28, 1970; Michener, *Kent State: What Happened,* 534–35.
54. "A Time to Remember May 4," *Kent-Ravenna Record-Courier,* Sept. 29, 1970.
55. Ibid.; "'Violence solves nothing,' Crippled KSU Student Says," *Kent-Ravenna Record-Courier,* Sept. 11, 1970; "The Fifth Victim of Kent State," *Life,* Oct. 16, 1970, 42–43.
56. "The Nonviolent Alternative: Research Strategy and Preliminary Findings," in *Collective Violence,* ed. James F. Short Jr. and Marvin E. Wolfgang (Piscataway, N.J.: Aldine Transaction, 2009), 355–69; "Two Extend 'Think Week' Nonviolence Theme," *Daily Kent Stater,* Nov. 10, 1970; Gloria Hepplewhite, "Baez, Sandperl . . . Preach Organized Love," *Daily Kent Stater,* Nov. 20, 1970; Ken Hammond, communication with author, June 23, 2009; Ken Johnson, communication with author, June 24, 2009; Joe Cullum, communication with author, June 23, 2009.

57. "Dr. White Rejects Yippie Demands," *Daily Kent Stater,* Oct. 29, 1970; "25 Indicted; Guardsmen Absolved," *Kent-Ravenna Record-Courier* Oct. 16, 1970; "White Cancels Black Homecoming," *Daily Kent Stater,* Oct. 14, 1970.
58. Most bomb threats were just that; see "Bomb Threats Increase," *Daily Kent Stater,* Nov. 10, 1970. One was real; see "Bomb Shatters Black Calm," *Daily Kent Stater,* Oct. 27, 1970.
59. "I. F. Stone Asks: 'No First Amendment Here?' 2,000 at Rally," *Daily Kent Stater,* Oct. 27, 1970. For the trial of BUS leaders arrested on Nov. 19, 1970, see "Blount, May Expect Decision Today," Jan. 19, 1971; "Two Face Hearings," Nov. 25, 1970; "Dragnet Total: 18, Arrests Continue," Oct. 27, 1970; "Injunction Halts Possible Protest," Oct. 15, 1970, all in the *Daily Kent Stater.* For the toll on Kent State's president, see "Dr. White's Mail Is 'Frightening,'" *Daily Kent Stater,* Nov. 5, 1970; "White: KSU Situation Volatile," *Kent-Ravenna Record-Courier,* Oct. 15, 1970.
60. "White Picks May 4 Committee," and "Police Nab Three 'for Flag Desecration,'" both in the *Daily Kent Stater,* Feb. 11, 1971.
61. "Blount/Perry Charged with Assaulting Student Senator," *Daily Kent Stater,* Feb. 11, 1971.
62. "200 Students March in Snow to White's House," *Daily Kent Stater,* Feb. 12, 1971; "Help Free BUS Two!" *Daily Kent Stater,* Feb. 19, 1971.
63. Kent State University public service advertisement, *Daily Kent Stater,* Mar. 5, 1971.
64. "Coalition Protests May 4 Plans," *Daily Kent Stater,* Apr. 2, 1971.
65. Kenneth J. Heineman, *Campus Wars: The Peace Movement at American Universities in the Vietnam Era* (New York: New York Univ. Press, 1993), 37–39, 179, 248, and passim. White also faced suits by the families of those killed and wounded on May 4, 1970. For this, see Joseph Kelner and James Munves, *The Kent State Coverup* (New York: Harper and Row, 1980), 15, 35, 62.
66. Bob Downing and Jim Nichols, "May 4 Subcommittee Seek Approval," *Daily Kent Stater,* Apr. 9, 1971; "Coalition Implementing Plans," *Daily Kent Stater,* Apr. 16, 1971.
67. "Brewster, McKuen Highlight May 4 Plans," *Daily Kent Stater,* Apr. 6, 1971; Elliot Podwell, letter to editor, *Daily Kent Stater,* Apr. 21, 1971.
68. "Four Wounded Last May Condemn Memorial Plans," letter to editor, *Daily Kent Stater,* Apr. 23, 1971; Joe Eszterhas, "Ohio Honors Its Dead," *Rolling Stone,* June 10, 1971, 14–18.
69. "Aligns with Coalition Forces/May 4 Subcommittee Seeks Approval," *Daily Kent Stater,* Apr. 9, 1971.
70. "'No National Guard in Area' Gilligan: May 1–4 for Campus People," Apr. 21, 1971; "Gilligan Wrong About Guard—Troops in Ravenna May 1–4 Preparation for Summer Camp," Apr. 22, 1971; "Makes Third Change—Gov. Cancels Guard," Apr. 23, 1971; "KSU Remembers Its Dead—7,000 Attend Memorial Service," May 5, 1971, all in the *Daily Kent Stater.*
71. "The Candlelight Vigil: 'A Way of Participating,'" in Bills, *Kent State/May 4,* 172–73.
72. "Coalition Rally Develops into Sit-in," *Daily Kent Stater,* May 5, 1971.
73. "Student Views Washington Mayday," *Daily Kent Stater,* May 12, 1971; "May Day Protesters—Who Were They?" *Akron Beacon Journal,* May 23, 1971
74. "Robert Hartmann, 91, Dies; Wrote Ford's Noted Talk," *New York Times,* Apr. 19, 2008.
75. "Days of Sorrow, Five Years Later," *Lake and Geauga County Telegraph,* May 5, 1975.
76. "Generation Ruined for Antiwar Beliefs," *Akron Beacon Journal* May 1, 1975.
77. "Introduction," in Bills, *Kent State/May 4,* 34.

78. Daniel St. Albin Greene, "When a World Collapsed—Kent State Wounded Tell Their Grim Story," *National Observer,* May 3, 1975.
79. "May 4 Shootings Seen as Murder by Students," *Daily Kent Stater,* Feb. 3, 1971; Taylor et al., *Violence at Kent State,* 16–17.
80. For Herschler, who insisted, "I never told Sgt. McManus that I fired my entire clip," see Manuscript Group 804, box 36, file 462, Kent State Collection, Manuscripts and Archives, Yale University Library. For the claim about him shooting, see FBI statement of Sgt. Matthew McManus, Ms. Group 804, box 36, file 473, Kent State Collection, Manuscripts and Archives, Yale University Library.
81. "'I'm relieved, pleased by jury verdict': White," *Kent-Ravenna Record-Courier,* Aug. 28, 1975. For the retroactive authority, see Kelner and Munves, *Kent State Coverup,* 159–68; "McElroy Called Shots, Rhodes Testifies," *Cleveland Plain Dealer,* Oct. 19, 1974.
82. Richard G. Zimmerman, *Plain Dealing: Ohio Politics and Journalism Viewed from the Press Gallery* (Kent, Ohio: Kent State Univ. Press, 2006), 10.
83. "Would Repeat KSU Callout, Rhodes Says," *Cleveland Plain Dealer,* Oct. 20, 1974.
84. "Judge Acquits 8 in KSU Shooting—Guardsmen Freed," *Kent-Ravenna Record-Courier,* Nov. 8, 1974.
85. "Kent State Photos Freeze Tragedy in Time," *Columbus Dispatch,* May 4, 2000.
86. David Giffels, "A Talkative Man Seals a Three-Decade Silence," *Akron Beacon Journal,* Mar. 5, 2001.
87. The quote is from guardsman James McGee, a member of Troop G, 107th Armored Cavalry, found in Ms. Group 804, box 36, file 472, Kent State Collection, Manuscripts and Archives, Yale University Library. Also see "Guards Heed Silence Order," *Wooster Daily Record,* May 8, 1970.
88. Justifications for the shooting, including alleged sniper fire, received mention in most coverage, but were given little credence in papers such as the *Washington Post.* See, for example, Richard Harwood and Haynes Johnson, "Guardsmen Kill 4 Students," *Washington Post,* May 5, 1970.
89. William James Case, who fired his weapon, but not at any of the students, was a member of Troop G. His report is in the Charles Thomas Papers, May 4 Collection, box 64, file 17, Special Collections and Archives, Kent State University Libraries, Kent, Ohio.
90. For Pierce, see Ms. Group 804, box 36, file 472, Kent State Collection, Manuscripts and Archives, Yale University Library.
91. Haynes Johnson, "The Tragedy at Kent: A Generation in Conflict," *Washington Post,* May 7, 1970.
92. "Kent State: Martyrdom That Shook the Country," *Time,* May 18, 1970, 13.
93. "Guardsmen Kill 4 Students," *Washington Post,* May 5, 1970.
94. William Barry Furlong, "The Guardsmen's View of the Tragedy at Kent State," *Sunday New York Times Magazine,* June 21, 1970.
95. For those in Company C who were among the guardsmen firing their weapons, see Peter Davies, *The Truth About Kent State: A Challenge to the American Conscience* (New York: Farrar, Straus, Giroux, 1973), 227–28.
96. Michener, *Kent State: What Happened,* 391.
97. Johnson, "The Tragedy at Kent," *Washington Post,* May 7, 1970.

98. Ibid.
99. "Enforcing the Law: 'What did they expect?'" in Bills, *Kent State/May 4,* 122.
100. Author's recollection of the controversy over the federal grand jury.
101. Davies, *Truth About Kent State,* 189–91
102. Ibid., 166–204; Richard Reeves, *President Nixon: Alone in the White House* (New York: Simon and Schuster, 2001), 213, 381.
103. For the chain of events, see Hensley, *Kent State Incident,* 108; William A. Gordon, *The Fourth of May: Killings and Coverups at Kent State* (Buffalo, N.Y.: Prometheus Books, 1990), 111–13. For the Ohioan's confirmation, the impaneling of the jury, and Nixon's low approval numbers, see "Saxbe by 75 to 10" and "KSU Grand Jury Starts Today," Dec. 18, 1973; "Gallup Polls 26% for Nixon, A Low," Feb. 4, 1974, all in the *Cleveland Plain Dealer.*
104. "Four Slain Kent Students Cleared Now, Parents Feel," *Cleveland Press,* Mar. 30, 1974; Hensley, *Kent State Incident,* 110.
105. "'Doing their job,' Says Guardsman's Father," *Cleveland Press,* Mar. 30, 1974; Hensley, *Kent State Incident,* 109.
106. "Rhodes Is Elected After He Concedes," *New York Times,* Nov. 7, 1974.
107. Hugh C. McDiarmid, "The Gilligan Interlude, 1971–1983," in Lamis and Sharkey, *Ohio Politics,* 99.
108. "After 4 Years Former Ohio Guardsmen Go on Trial," *New York Times,* Oct. 20, 1974.
109. "Guard Case Dismissal Possible," *Akron Beacon Journal,* Nov. 8, 1974.
110. "After 4 Years," *New York Times,* Oct. 20, 1974.
111. "Judge Acquits Guardsmen in Slayings at Kent State," *New York Times,* Nov. 9, 1974.
112. "Calley Parole Slated Nov. 19," *Kent-Ravenna Record-Courier,* Nov. 9, 1974. The image is in Gordon, *Fourth of May,* last of the photo galleys between 144–45.
113. "Guard's Prosecutor Admits He Never Expected to Win," *Akron Beacon Journal,* May 4, 1975.
114. "The Guardsmen Go Free," *Time,* Nov. 18, 1974.
115. Ibid.
116. Kelner and Munves, *Kent State Coverup,* 268–70.
117. Hensley, *Kent State Incident,* 84.
118. For the text of the statement, see ibid., 122–23.
119. "A Late Apology," *Time,* Jan. 15, 1979.
120. "Students from Then and Now Pass On Painful Lessons of Kent State," *New York Times,* Apr. 28, 2000.
121. "Thirty Years Ago, Trustees and Protesters Faced Off Over the Gym," *Daily Kent Stater,* Aug. 14, 2007.
122. David W. Blight, "Introduction: The Confluence of History and Memory," in his *Beyond the Battlefield: Race, Memory, and the American Civil War* (Amherst, Mass.: Univ. of Massachusetts Press, 2002), 2.
123. Ibid.
124. Carol Wilder, "The War That Won't Die," <http://www.carolwilder.net/index.html>.
125. John Steinbeck, *Cannery Row* (1945; New York: Penguin Books 1994), 136.
126. Elaine Holstein, "Anniversary: May 4, 1988," *Vietnam Generation* 2, no. 2 (1990): 46.

Kent State Comes to Canada

Internationalizing the Antiwar Movement

CHRISTOPHER POWELL

The Vietnam War and the movement that arose in opposition to it have been framed as American phenomena. American men donned uniforms and weapons and fought America's war in Southeast Asia, while back home an increasing number of Americans protested the war. That the Vietnamese played significant roles on both sides of the war is secondary to the narrative. That troops from Australia, New Zealand, the Philippines, South Korea, Taiwan, and Thailand fought alongside U.S. troops, though in significantly smaller numbers, is almost forgotten entirely.[1] So too are the international aspects of the antiwar movement. With the exception of a growing body of literature concerning the anti–Vietnam War movement in Australia, opposition to the war has been perceived as a purely national phenomenon, confined within the borders of the United States. In fact, however, the antiwar movement was international in scope, with demonstrations against the war taking place throughout Europe, Latin America, the Antipodes, and even parts of Asia and Africa. How the movement manifested in Canada in response to the May 1970 shootings at Kent State University stands as a case in point.

In the United States, the antiwar movement developed quietly during the early 1960s, and grew steadily over the latter half of the decade, following the introduction of U.S. combat troops in 1965. Development of the movement in Canada not only paralleled that in the United States from early on but was inextricably linked to protests in that country. In Canada, antiwar protest reached its climax—in terms of frequency of protests, confrontations with police forces, and regional representation, if not always in terms of numbers of participants—in the demonstrations that followed the U.S. invasion of Cambodia and the shootings at Kent State University. Antiwar activism in Canada in May 1970 demonstrates both the existence of a national antiwar movement there and its links to a much larger international movement that has largely been overlooked.

A vast body of literature exists concerning the antiwar movement in the United States, but only Fred Halstead's 1978 *Out Now* touches on the movement's international dimensions. Halstead's primary argument—the most forceful of the positions taken about the antiwar movement—asserts that along with the efforts of the Vietnamese themselves, it was protest at home that ended the war.[2] Halstead's work is unique in other ways as well. Unlike most of those writing about the antiwar movement, Halstead was not an academic but a participant-observer who was the first to offer a full-length account of the antiwar movement. He earned his credentials in the labor movement and as a leader within the Trotskyist Socialist Workers' Party (SWP), and his Marxist ideology undoubtedly informed his internationalist approach to the antiwar movement.[3]

According to Halstead, the Madison-based National Coordinating Committee to End the War in Vietnam and the Berkeley-based Vietnam Day Committee coordinated the first International Days of Protest to End the War in Vietnam in October 1965. In addition to protests in sixty cities across the United States involving 100,000 citizens, demonstrations took place in twelve European cities and in Canada, Australia, Mexico, and Chile.[4] The second International Days of Protest in March 1966 drew twice as many people: within the United States it involved fifty thousand in New York, seven thousand in San Francisco, and significant demonstrations in one hundred other cities, while internationally, protests took place in one-third of the world's countries and on every continent.[5] Thus, even before historians in North America began writing of the antiwar movement, Halstead had made clear that it was an international phenomenon. Despite Halstead's lack of scholarly credentials, *Out Now* is a recognized pillar of the literature concerning the antiwar movement.

All North American scholarly works dealing with the antiwar movement before and after the publication of *Out Now* are limited to how the movement manifested in the United States; moreover, they agree on its impact in shaping U.S. foreign policy, asserting that opposition to the war limited successive administrations in their ability to execute the war effort. Kirkpatrick Sale's 1973 *SDS,* a study of the new left organization Students for a Democratic Society, is one of the earliest of these works. Sale argues that the SDS—and by extension the antiwar movement—did much to shape public opinion against the war, and further, that the SDS revived an American left and transformed political possibilities.[6] Sale failed to recognize, though, that the new left in the United States was part of a much larger, internationally revived movement. Events in Paris, Prague, Mexico City, and Canada indicate that a changed and resurgent left was a worldwide phenomenon.[7] The SDS and its Canadian counterparts, first the Combined Universities Campaign for Nuclear Disarmament and then its successor organization, the Student Union for Peace Action (SUPA), went so far as to exchange representatives on each other's governing bodies.[8] In addition, it was not uncommon for members of the SDS to travel to Canada to conduct training sessions. One example involved Carl Oglesby, once a Kent State student. During the weekend of May 1, 1965, the future SDS president met with SUPA members in Toronto for discussions on Vietnam and the importance of nonviolence. Oglesby's suggestions to both groups included continuing to stage demonstrations around U.S. federal buildings and weapons manufacturers, picketing university classes whose departments received research grants from the U.S. State Department, organizing a second March on Washington, and calling a major nationwide student strike.[9]

A generation later, in 1990, Charles DeBenedetti and Charles Chatfield published *An American Ordeal: The Antiwar Movement of the Vietnam Era.* Still regarded as one of the most important works in the literature of the antiwar movement, *American Ordeal* presents a liberal analysis of antiwar dissent and asserts that while protest did not end the war, it kept the issue in the public eye long enough for both citizens and politicians to conclude that the war was a mistake and the United States should get out. However, the authors add that the "cultural power" of dissent "compromised its political effectiveness."[10] The public images of violence and disorder often unfairly associated with protesters did more to alienate the public than to mobilize it. Examination of contemporary public opinion indicated increasing resentment of protesters while at the same time increasing agreement with them. Tom Wells's 1994 study, *The War Within: America's Battle Over Vietnam,* is likewise representative of the national narrative on the antiwar movement. Wells sees antiwar action as more effective than DeBenedetti and Chatfield do, asserting that protest was instrumental in restricting, deescalating, and ending the war.[11] But despite his encyclopedic examination of the antiwar movement, his subtitle signifies his focus on events within the United States.

While recent scholarship on the history of the antiwar movement has tended to take a case study approach, rather than the grand narrative treatment preferred by earlier historians, it still has avoided an international perspective. Newer works have followed the path established by Sale in looking at specific antiwar groups within the United States. One such study, Mitchell Hall's 1990 *Because of Their Faith,* examines the group Clergy and Laity Concerned about Vietnam (CALCAV). Hall argues that CALCAV "helped influence public opinion against the war, limited government options in conducting the war, and defended the right of dissent."[12]

Amy Swerdlow likewise studied another prominent antiwar organization, Women Strike for Peace (WSP). However, Swerdlow's perspective deviates somewhat from the thrust of most studies of antiwar activism in that she is more concerned with the impact of the war on women than on women's contribution to ending the conflict. She argues that by engaging in antiwar activism, members of WSP underwent a process of radicalization that transformed them, as she puts it, "from feminine to feminist."[13]

In his 1999 work *The Turning,* Andrew Hunt selects for his case study the Vietnam Veterans Against the War (VVAW), in which he discusses the process of radicalization that many Vietnam veterans underwent on their return to the United States. Like members of WSP, VVAW members were radicalized, but through their direct participation in the war. According to Hunt, the VVAW actually transformed the antiwar movement and "contributed significantly to ending the war in Vietnam."[14]

In contradistinction to Hunt's study of those who fought in the war, Michael Foley's 2003 *Confronting the War Machine* is an examination of those who refused to fight. In relating the story of the Boston-area Resistance, Foley's concern is with reversing the perception of those who risked jail and alienation for refusing induction (and also refusing to go to Canada) as cowards and traitors and elevating them to the moral status of civil rights activists.[15] While tending to agree with the broad consensus that the antiwar movement helped end the war, Foley leans toward the position that the United States withdrew from Vietnam primarily because the government finally concluded that it could not win. However, this is not Foley's primary concern. He concludes by saying, "Whether or not the antiwar movement prolonged the war is not a particularly meaningful issue. A more important one is a moral one: to what extent is a citizen responsible to his country when the government is engaged in a violent war that he deems 'illegal,' 'immoral,' and 'obscene?'"[16]

Campus Wars, Kenneth Heineman's 1994 contribution to the discussion, is a somewhat enigmatic piece, being neither a general history of the movement nor a study of a specific antiwar organization. It is, rather, a case study approach to a constituency within the movement, specifically, students at four state universities: Kent, Michigan, Pennsylvania, and SUNY-Buffalo. Through his study of this constituency, Heineman argues that the antiwar movement was by no means the sole preserve of students at elite universities but also encompassed the sons and daughters of America's working class. Interestingly, Heineman is one of the very few scholars to reject completely the consensus that protest helped to end the war. He directly argues that the United States withdrew from the conflict because it could not win militarily.[17]

In her more recent study, the 2005 *¡Raza Si! ¡Guerra No! Chicano Protest and Patriotism During the Viet Nam War,* Lorena Oropoza, like Heineman, examines a constituency rather than a specific organization, in this case Mexican Americans and their opposition to the Vietnam War. Taking an approach similar to those of Swerdlow and Hunt, she argues that the war did more to change Mexican Americans than their antiwar activism did to affect the war. Noting that the Mexican American community was unique in being the only ethnic minority group in the United States to organize against the war as a constituency, Oropoza informs us that it did so by establishing the National Chicano Moratorium Committee, an offshoot of the fall

1969 national moratorium that drew hundreds of thousands of U.S. citizens into antiwar activism.[18] During 1970, the Chicano Moratorium staged more than a dozen demonstrations across the United States, culminating in a march, on August 29 in Los Angeles, in which between twenty thousand and thirty thousand Mexican Americans took part—the largest gathering of Chicanos ever. Despite the peaceful nature of the march, police ferociously attacked it, opening fire on unarmed protesters and killing three. Not surprisingly, the Chicano killings did not take on the iconic status accorded those at Kent State; Oropoza marks the brutal suppression of the Los Angeles march as the end of the Chicano antiwar movement.[19]

In sum, scholarly treatments of the antiwar movement from the 1970s to the present have moved from grand narrative on a national scale to more limited case studies of specific antiwar organizations and constituencies within the United States, exhibiting an increasingly narrow focus rather than moving to transcend the national boundaries of the United States. Addressing this oversight by considering the international connections of the antiwar movement is important because the war in Vietnam itself had global implications. While the United States and the Democratic Republic of Vietnam can be considered the primary belligerents, a full history of the Indochina conflict reveals that it involved numerous countries from most continents. Just as successive administrations required at least the silent complicity of U.S. citizens to continue waging war in Southeast Asia, so too did the war require a degree of international legitimacy—hence the importance of having Australian, New Zealander, Filipino, South Korean, Taiwanese, and Thai boots on the ground. The countries supplying these people played the role of a coalition of the willing, while the noncombatant support of other countries reinforced the legitimacy of U.S. intervention in Vietnam. For the antiwar movement to be effective, therefore, an international perspective was essential: it was vital to send a message to the governments of those countries to stop supporting the U.S. war effort. It is in this context that Canada's contribution to the antiwar movement must be understood. Canada was not only a military ally and major trading partner of the United States but a recognized middle power in international diplomacy in its own right: its support of U.S. intervention in Vietnam—sometimes quiet, sometimes not—therefore helped legitimize America's war effort. The early recognition of this reality by some Canadians led to the emergence of the antiwar movement north of the border.

The movement developed differently in Canada than in the United States. In the latter country, early antiwar activism (at least before the Gulf of Tonkin incident, which served as the pretext for introducing U.S. combat troops to Vietnam) emanated from radical student organizations.[20] In Canada, however, the pioneers of antiwar activism tended to emerge from the Communist Party in the guise of the Canadian Peace Congress.[21] Canada's governing Liberal Party, despite welcoming draft dodgers, generally supported the U.S. war effort for several reasons. First, Canada's administration agreed with the U.S. interpretation of the conflict in Southeast Asia as a case of Communist aggression against a sovereign nation—as opposed to a civil war or an unfinished revolution. In fact, in the early stages of the war, Canada's opposition Progressive Conservative Party (PC) advocated sending troops to assist its military ally in Vietnam, citing the examples of its Commonwealth partners Australia and New Zealand.[22] Second, Canada's political and diplomatic elite regarded Canadian access to U.S. policy makers as essential. According to scholar Douglas Ross, "Ottawa was not going to forsake its entrée to the corridors of power in Washington by publicly calling for unilateral US retreat from the Asian mainland. Credibility as a sympathetic ally of the United States had to be sustained. . . . The price for access to Washington decision-makers was substantial: a self-imposed prohibition on moral criticism of the US."[23] Third, Canada had a vested interest in supporting the United States' war aims in Vietnam. Throughout the war, Canadian corporations netted hundreds of millions of dollars in profits by providing military supplies to American armed forces.[24] It was this issue that Canadian antiwar activists latched onto. From early in the conflict, one slogan that distinguished the movement in Canada was "End Canadian Complicity."[25]

Around the time of the 1964 Gulf of Tonkin incident, Canadian Communists were joined in their antiwar efforts by groups similar in ideology to the U.S.-based Committee for a Sane Nuclear Policy. These included the Canadian Campaign for Nuclear Disarmament and its youth wing, the Young Canadian Campaign for Nuclear Disarmament; the Combined Universities Campaign for Nuclear Disarmament; and the youth wing of the New Democratic Party, the New Democratic Youth.[26] They were also joined by Voice of Women, the Canadian counterpart to the WSP.[27] Others were drawn in through their connections with the SDS. The first major antiwar demonstration of the era, organized by the SDS on April 17, 1965, in Washington, D.C., included participants from Montreal, Toronto, and British Columbia.[28] Beginning in the fall of 1965, Trotskyists, affiliated through the Fourth International (the international association of Communist parties that followed the line of Trotsky, as opposed to Stalin's Third International) with the Socialist Workers Party in the United States, began to exercise a growing influence on the antiwar movement in Canada.[29] Hence, from early in the war, participants in the movements in both countries worked together.

As the war in Southeast Asia ground on, the antiwar movement in Canada became increasingly integrated into the larger international movement, although admittedly protest was initially limited to Canada's three major cities, and numbers were small. During the first International Days of Protest, for example, demonstrations took place only in Montreal, Toronto, and Vancouver. In Montreal and Vancouver, protesters numbered 150 and 500 respectively.[30] In Toronto, three demonstrations occurred, with protesters at the largest numbering 800, of whom about half were members of the SUNY-Buffalo chapter of the SDS, who felt their voices would be heard more clearly if raised outside the United States.[31] The presence of these American students in Toronto demonstrates that not only were Canadians willing to travel to the United States to demonstrate—as for the April 17 march in Washington—but American activists who could would reciprocate.

Five months later, during the second International Days of Protest, the movement in Canada demonstrated a degree of growth and consolidation. In central Canada, rather than organizing protests in scattered cities, organizers concentrated on building a mass demonstration in the nation's capital, Ottawa. On March 26, 1966, between 2,000 and 3,500 people marched to the U.S. Embassy and on to Parliament Hill.[32] According to Ian Angus, one of its organizers, participation in international protests was quite intentional: "We viewed the antiwar movement as *international* [emphasis in original]. . . . [O]bviously we in Canada couldn't stop the war ourselves, but we could (and did) have an effect as [a] Canadian contingent of a world-wide effort. That's one reason why we often held demos here on the same days as they were being held in the US—to maximize the global impact of the protests."[33] On the west coast, between 3,000 and 4,000 students rallied at the University of British Columbia on March 25.[34] The following day, between 2 000 and 5,000 people protested at the Vancouver Court House.[35] Smaller protests, usually involving a few hundred participants, took place in Victoria, Edmonton, Regina, the northwestern Ontario twin cities of Fort William and Port Arthur (today known as Thunder Bay), and Toronto.[36] Significantly, the March 24–26 protests also marked the first stirrings of antiwar dissent in Maritime Canada when thirty people attended a meeting in Saint John, New Brunswick.[37] These demonstrations during the second International Days of Protest were Canada's largest antiwar protests up to that time. For the first time, all regions of Canada apart from the sparsely populated North fielded antiwar demonstrations, indicating not only that the movement was part of a larger international one, but that it had itself become truly national in scope.

The October 1967 Mobilization to End the War, best known for its march on the Pentagon, saw demonstrations take place across Canada.[38] The largest ones were in Vancouver, Toronto, and Montreal, with protesters in those cities numbering 1,000, 4,000, and 1,500 respectively.[39] Throughout 1968, taking their cue from American students protesting against Dow Chemical for its production of napalm, Canadians protested against the corporation across the country.[40] The 1969 Moratorium to End the War was the most successful grassroots antiwar protest of the era in the United States. Organizers actively encouraged international participation—and got it. In Paris, under the leadership of the Communist Party, 20,000 marched in solidarity; in Copenhagen, 10,000; and in London, 15,000. Several thousand marched in Berlin, Stuttgart, and Frankfurt, while even in Addis Ababa seventy-five American expatriates marched.[41] Like other national and international protest campaigns, the moratorium engendered significant protest efforts throughout Canada.[42] Hence, by

May 1970, Canada had achieved a long-established national antiwar movement that was well integrated with international peace efforts.

The events of late April and early May 1970 significantly mobilized antiwar efforts both in the United States and internationally. Following the U.S. invasion of Cambodia on April 29, activists in the United States called for a national student strike. By May 3, strike action had commenced on sixty campuses.[43] Then on May 4, at Kent State University, Ohio National Guard troops opened fire on protesters, killing four and wounding nine. The shootings acted to spread the strike. By mid-May, 536 campuses were shut down across the United States, and demonstrations were held on more than half of all U.S. campuses.[44] On May 9, one hundred thousand protesters converged on Washington, D.C., to protest the invasion of Cambodia and the shootings at Kent State.[45] Reaction to the invasion of Cambodia and the shootings at Kent State was not limited to the United States. In West Berlin, 10,000 marched; in London, 5,000. In Paris, between 50,000 and 200,000 people protested. Demonstrations also took place in Turin, Barcelona, Geneva, Copenhagen, Tel Aviv, Johannesburg, Tokyo, and throughout Australia.[46] In Canada, the antiwar movement responded to the invasion of Cambodia and the killings in Ohio with anger, energy, and diversity. Moreover, its response was national in scope, with demonstrations reaching from British Columbia to Newfoundland. Indeed, May 1970 represents the zenith of antiwar activism in Canada. While except in Toronto the protests were not as large as previous demonstrations, it must be kept in mind that most previous demonstrations had been months in the planning. Reaction to Cambodia and Kent State was immediate, with demonstrations in some cases being mounted within hours of the shootings in Ohio.

The most notable demonstration in this respect occurred in Montreal. The McGill University Student Society distinguished itself by organizing both a memorial service and a march within twenty-four hours of the shootings. The service was held the evening of May 5 at McGill. From there between 600 and 1,000 students marched in a candlelit procession to the U.S. Consulate, carrying four coffins symbolizing the four slain students.[47] Participation by American draft dodgers and especially deserters was significant, indicating that many draft-age Americans had not put the war behind them on arriving in Montreal.[48] Although generally peaceful, a few protesters threw rocks toward the end of the demonstration, breaking several consulate windows. Other students deposited their lit candles in nearby trashcans, inflaming their contents. When many refused to disperse, police used a moderate amount of force to break up the demonstration.[49]

The Montreal demonstration was significant for several reasons. Most noteworthy was its immediacy, which illustrated both the students' organizational abilities and the strength of feeling held by many Montrealers regarding the killings at Kent State. Second, the May 5 march marked the end of large-scale antiwar protest in that city. The antiwar movement had originally been supported by a strong component of Québécois nationalists, but that constituency was increasingly receding from the antiwar movement into its own cause; indeed, in a predominantly French-speaking city, the May 5 demonstration was an almost exclusively Anglophone event.[50] This withdrawal of Québécois nationalists from the antiwar movement, especially in Montreal, would soon be speeded by the crisis of October 1970, initiated by the kidnapping and murder of Québec Labour Minister Pierre Laporte by the Front de Liberation du Québec, and the attendant declaration of martial law.[51] With the exception of one last gasp—a mass march in April 1971—the march of May 5, 1970, would be Montreal's last mass antiwar protest.[52]

In Toronto, the Trotskyist-dominated Vietnam Mobilization Committee (VMC) played the leading role in protesting the events in Cambodia and at Kent State. Following the announcement of the U.S. invasion of Cambodia, the VMC immediately began making plans for a major demonstration on May 9, to coincide with the rally in Washington, D.C., and other international actions. Significantly, its leader, George Addison, was called to meetings in Washington, D.C., to help plan the action there, further illustrating the integration of the movements in the two countries. After the shootings in Ohio, the VMC stepped up action by holding rallies and vigils at the U.S. Consulate every day leading up to the Saturday march.[53] As in Montreal, the number of people mobilized in Toronto within twenty-four hours of the Kent State shootings was striking. On Tuesday night, approximately 500 people showed up at the U.S. Consulate. The demonstration remained relatively peaceful for the first hour, but police moved in when a group began yelling "pigs" at police and attempted to burn an American flag.[54] This group was likely the May 4 Movement (M4M), described by Myrna Kostash in her 1980 book *Long Way from Home* as an ad hoc coalition of new leftists, radicals, and student activists named for the day of the Ohio shootings, as well as for the day in 1919 when students and intellectuals in China mounted a mass protest out of which emerged the Chinese Communist Party.[55] Demonstrations at the consulate continued the following day. Picketing began at eleven o'clock that morning, with numbers eventually reaching 500.[56] Although the VMC posted marshals in front of the consulate to keep order, another group down the street, probably the M4M, began to cause a disturbance. Ultimately, eight individuals from the second group were arrested.[57]

Red, White, and Black, a newly formed antiwar group of American expatriates, organized a memorial for Friday, May 8.[58] It commenced at dawn at Queen's Park, the site of Ontario's Provincial Parliament, just south of the University of Toronto. Twelve clergy, including representatives from the Jewish, Anglican, Quaker, and Unitarian communities, addressed the seventy-five early risers.[59] The memorial service not only demonstrated that disapproval of the events in Cambodia and at Kent was not the sole domain of various stripes of radicals but also showed the contribution of Toronto's American expatriate community to the overall protest movement.

Toronto's largest antiwar event, scheduled for Saturday, May 9, was attended by between 5,000 and 15,000 demonstrators and became the largest Canadian antiwar demonstration of the Vietnam War.[60] The two main groups involved were the M4M and the VMC.[61] Although the VMC led a significantly larger portion of the demonstrators, including Communists, Trotskyists, and representatives from labor and churches, its members presciently separated themselves from the M4M participants, remaining peacefully across the street from the consulate. In contrast, M4M demonstrators attempted to block traffic. When police moved in, the crowd moved south on University Avenue and began a preplanned campaign of smashing the windows of local businesses. Seven thousand dollars' worth of damage was reported and ninety-one demonstrators were arrested.[62]

Protests in Ontario were not limited to Toronto. In Ottawa, 200 demonstrators marched from the U.S. Embassy to the National War Memorial, where they cheered as effigies of Prime Minister Trudeau and U.S. President Nixon were burned.[63] In St. Catharines, a small industrial city near Niagara Falls, about 125 people demonstrated on May 6. Another demonstration was scheduled for May 10 at the Peace Bridge connecting Fort Erie and Buffalo, but it is unclear if it took place as local papers gave it no coverage.[64] Two demonstrations took place in Hamilton on May 9.[65] These smaller demonstrations show how widespread the antiwar movement was, especially in Ontario; dissent was not limited to the major cities.

Outrage over events in Cambodia and at Kent State was also evident in Western Canada. Demonstrations took place in the provincial capitals of both Alberta and Saskatchewan.[66] In Vancouver, as in Toronto, protesters staged a series of demonstrations. The first occurred at the U.S. Consulate two days after the shootings in Ohio. It lasted about an hour and attracted 250 demonstrators.[67] Protests continued on Friday.[68] The largest demonstration in western Canada took place thirty miles from Vancouver that Saturday. Assembling at the International Peace Park at the Canada-U.S. border near Blaine, Washington, a group of Yippies calling itself the NLF—the Northern Lunatic Fringe—was joined by between 500 and 1,000 others. The march was a burlesque of Nixon's invasion of Cambodia. "In solidarity with the people of the Third World and with white youth we make this symbolic invasion of the United States," a spokesperson for the group stated. "Of course we won't go into the US more than 22 and 7/10 miles and will withdraw by June 30," he continued, echoing the president's promises on Cambodia.[69] On arriving in Blaine, the protesters were confronted with a mixed reception. Many local residents waved and gave the peace sign from windows, while others engaged in fistfights with their northern neighbors. Some protesters also took to violence, smashing windows and throwing rocks at cars.

Police reacted only when demonstrators began desecrating U.S. flags, when they clubbed and maced the crowd, maneuvering it back to the border. Along the way, stone-throwing demonstrators caused $50,000 worth of damage to a shipment of General Motors automobiles being shipped to Canada on the Great Northern Railway.[70] The level of violence and the number of arrests at Blaine, Vancouver, Toronto, and Montreal was new to the Canadian antiwar movement, indicating the profound anger that people felt over the invasion of Cambodia and the killings at Kent State. Douglas Ross, in his book *In the Interests of Peace: Canada and Vietnam, 1954–1973,* states that the demonstrations in Toronto and Blaine did much to discredit the antiwar movement in Canada. As evidence he offers a quote by a Progressive Conservative member of Parliament, who declared that the events in Blaine were caused by "a large group of hoodlums, queers, and just plain fools."[71] In fact, however, response to such demonstrations was more complex, and not all protests resulted in violence and arrests. The day after the events in Blaine, the International Peace Park was once again the scene of protest over the invasion of Cambodia. This time it was conducted by the British Columbia Conference of the United Church of Canada, the country's largest Protestant church, which had been meeting that week and had passed a resolution condemning the U.S. invasion of Cambodia.[72] The rally attracted some 500 churchgoers. Their only action was to lay flowers at the Peace Arch.[73] The Blaine demonstration signified the last mass anti–Vietnam War march in British Columbia.

Similar response to the development in the war and the Kent State shootings was noticeably lacking in Atlantic Canada, where antiwar demonstrations had been few and far between throughout the 1960s. The only city in which a protest was reported was St. John's, Newfoundland. On May 9, thirty U.S. expatriates, most of them faculty members of Memorial University of Newfoundland, protested at the U. S. Consulate there.[74] This demonstration was the only such protest in Canada that was composed exclusively of Americans. The faculty members, and those who joined them, spoke as citizens of the United States, indicating to their government that its actions both abroad and at home were unacceptable. Perhaps the professors' actions are explained by the way in which the shootings at Kent State changed the nature of protest. Until then, dissent had targeted the war itself and its many brutal manifestations in Southeast Asia. After the deaths of the four students in Ohio, focus shifted from Indochina to the United States: rather than concentrating on what the United States was doing to those people over there, activists drew attention to what the U.S. government was doing to its own people. As Kirkpatrick Sale put it, "The lesson was unmistakable, and not lost upon most students: the government would go to any lengths, including killing, to repress the forces working for significant change in America, and from now on death had to be considered part of the stakes of student protest."[75] In this respect, American faculty members, especially those acting from the safety of Newfoundland, felt they had an obligation to protest.

Reaction in Canada did not end with the protests occurring the weekend of May 9–10, 1970. The Trotskyist-led Student Mobilization Committee (SMC) in the United States called for demonstrations on Memorial Day, May 30, to commemorate new unjust fatalities in the United States and to stoke public anger over Cambodia and Kent State. Many such calls were published in *The Militant,* the newspaper of the Socialist Workers Party (SWP).[76] On May 9, police in Augusta, Georgia, had fatally shot six young African Americans who had been protesting that a young black man had been beaten to death in police custody earlier that week. On May 14, police killed two more young African Americans in Jackson, Mississippi, following demonstrations there.[77] Memorial Day demonstrations were decidedly smaller than the protests that had taken place in the immediate wake of the Kent State shootings. The largest was in New York City, attracting 10,000 people, compared to the 100,000 who had marched in Washington on May 9.[78] This is partly explained by the fact that the Memorial Day demonstrations were supported not by the larger antiwar movement in the United States but rather by the SMC, their primary sponsor, and its supporters in the Socialist Workers Party. In Canada by the end of 1968, the Trotskyist movement had become the undisputed leader of the antiwar movement. Its leadership of the Vietnam Action Committee (VAC) in Vancouver, the VMC in Toronto, and similar groups in other cities was pivotal in promoting the Memorial Day actions. Demonstrations took place in the twin cities of Kitchener-Waterloo as well as in Ottawa, Toronto, and Vancouver. While two of the stated aims of the demonstrations were by then standard slogans of the antiwar movement in Canada—"U.S. Out Now" and "End Canadian Complicity"—two more slogans were added to conform with the stated aims of the SMC in the United States: "Stop the Murder of U.S. Students" and "Free Speech, Freedom to Demonstrate."[79] Not surprisingly, Toronto hosted the largest Memorial Day march in Canada; under the leadership of the VMC, 800 demonstrators marched from Queen's Park to City Hall.[80] The featured speakers at some of these events again illustrated the links between the Canadian and American antiwar movements, and in particular the cross-border character of the Trotskyist-supported organizations organizing them. Among the speakers in Toronto, for example, was twenty-eight-year-old Mike York, one of four eyewitnesses to the Kent State shootings then touring the United States and Canada with SMC support. York gave his account of what he witnessed at Kent State on May 4.[81] The only Memorial Day weekend demonstration in Canada that took place outside Ontario was held in Vancouver on Sunday, May 31, sponsored by the VAC. The featured speaker there was Mike Alewitz, leader of the Kent State chapter of the SMC.[82] That the SMC would allocate two of its four eyewitness speakers to Canadian cities for the Memorial Day demonstrations indicates the importance it placed on generating support for the antiwar movement in Canada. As a Trotskyist-led organization, the SMC sought to build not just an American antiwar movement, but an international one. The May 31 demonstration in Vancouver brought to a close a month of protests in Canada that had been sparked by the U.S. invasion of Cambodia and the shootings at Kent State.

That month, May 1970, represented the zenith of antiwar activism in Canada. After the wave of protests in the immediate wake of the Cambodia and Kent State events, antiwar activism in both the United States and Canada experienced a dénouement. South of the border, antiwar forces rallied for one last protest campaign in April 1971, under the leadership of the newly established and Trotskyist-led National Peace Action Committee (NPAC).[83] This campaign was joined by thousands in Canada, picketing from coast to coast.[84] By the end of 1972, however, antiwar dissent as a mass movement had all but disappeared. This was partly a result of war weariness: people had been protesting the war in increasing numbers since combat troops had been introduced in March 1965, and they were tired. More significantly, however, it was because America's active role in the war was coming to an end. Draft calls had been decreasing throughout the early 1970s, and the number of American troops being withdrawn was increasing. The U.S. government might have ignored the activists' demand of "Out Now," but it was slowly withdrawing U.S. troops, and with their departure, one of the primary slogans of the antiwar movement lost its power. America *was* getting out. In January 1973, Henry Kissinger and Le Duc Tho signed the cease-fire agreement that led to the speedy withdrawal of the remaining U.S. combat forces from Vietnam. Although the United States continued to bankroll the Republic of Vietnam's war effort against North Vietnam, once American soldiers were no longer doing the fighting the antiwar movement in North America lost much of its raison d'etre. The movement had been growing since before the Gulf of Tonkin incident of 1964. As the war escalated in Southeast Asia, however, opposition in Canada and around the world became increasingly incorporated within a larger international movement. From the first major antiwar demonstration of April 1965 in Washington, D.C., activists from across Canada had joined their American cousins in marching against the war. Canadians continued marching, in growing numbers and from increasingly diverse regions, through the International Days of Protest of 1965 and 1966, the mobilization campaigns of 1967 and 1968, the Moratorium of 1969, following the 1970 invasion of Cambodia and the killings at Kent State, and into 1971. Every significant antiwar campaign that took place in the United States was mirrored by corresponding Canadian action.

The effectiveness of the antiwar movement in Canada likewise mirrored the impact of the movement in the United States. If one looks simply at the primary slogans of the Canadian movement—"U.S. Troops Out Now" and "End Canadian Complicity"—it did not achieve these goals. American troop withdrawals were gradual and occurred only after eight years of combat. And as for the sale of arms and military supplies to the United States for use in Vietnam, Canada continued to function as

America's arms bazaar until the fall of Saigon in April 1975. Like the U.S. antiwar movement, however, Canada's movement did keep the issue of the war in the public eye and provided citizens with a vehicle to express their increasing revulsion with the methods America employed to defeat its enemies.[85] In this respect, a push-pull dynamic was at work. While the antiwar movement actively recruited newcomers to its cause, U.S. aggression—particularly its bombing campaigns—pushed new members into its ranks. Canadian antiwar activists participated as both world citizens and citizens of their own country in opposing the U.S. war in Southeast Asia. Globally, they joined with Americans and citizens of many other nations in speaking directly to the government of the United States, denouncing its intervention in Indochina. While it probably had little direct influence on White House policies, Canadian participation in the antiwar movement added to an international effort to deny legitimacy to American military adventurism. In this, the Canadian movement enjoyed a considerable degree of success. At no time was this more apparent than in May 1970, following the brutal invasion of Cambodia and the gunning down of unarmed students at Kent State University. Canadian anger manifested itself immediately and on a national scale, an outrage shared by Australians, New Zealanders, French, Germans, Italians, Israelis, South Africans, and members of many other nations. It was also in this period that most of Canada's few incidents of violence occurred. Domestically, the movement in Canada challenged its own government. Canada initially had been vocal in its support of the U.S. war effort. Even if at times it voiced slight discomfort with American methods, it always was quick to reiterate its belief in the rightness of America's cause. The best example of this was the speech given by Prime Minister Lester B. Pearson at Temple University in April 1965, when he meekly suggested that bombing the DRV might not be the best way to win the war but at the same time stood firm in his support of the U.S. mission.[86] By 1968, largely as a result of growing public protest, Canada had begun to take a different approach. Although never going on record as opposing U.S. intervention is Southeast Asia, the Canadian government simply stayed silent on the issue rather than anger its mighty ally.[87] Thus Canada's antiwar movement at least succeeded in ending its government's role as America's cheerleader.

Notes

1. George C. Herring, *America's Longest War: The United States and Vietnam, 1950–1975*, 4th ed. (Boston, Mass: McGraw-Hill, 2002), 180–81.
2. Fred Halstead, *Out Now! A Participant's Account of the Movement in the U.S. Against the Vietnam War* (New York: Pathfinder Press, 1978), 843.
3. Ibid., 7–9.
4. Ibid., 81–112.

5. Ibid., 172–73.
6. Sale, *SDS,* 656–57.
7. For an in-depth discussion of this topic, see George Kastiaficas, *The Imagination of the New Left: A Global Analysis of 1968* (Boston, Mass.: South End Press, 1987).
8. National Council Report—March 20–21, "Vietnam," *SUPA Newsletter* 1, no. 1 (Apr. 1965): 1; Minutes, SUPA National Council Meeting, Mar. 20–21, 1965, Toronto, Combined Universities Campaign for Nuclear Disarmament, William Ready Library and Archives, McMaster University, Hamilton, Ontario, box 22, file 2; "National Council Meeting of Students for a Democratic Society," *SUPA Newsletter* 1, no. 2 (May 4, 1965): 3. SUPA members attending the SDS National Council meeting included Henry Travainen, Tony Hyde, Tom Hathaway, Liora Proctor, Arthur Pape, and Dimitri Rousopoulis.
9. Untitled, *SUPA Newsletter* 1, no. 2 (May 4, 1965): 4–5.
10. Charles DeBenedetti, with Charles Chatfield, *An American Ordeal: The Antiwar Movement of the Vietnam Era* (Syracuse, N.Y.: Syracuse Univ. Press, 1990), 1, 396.
11. Wells, *War Within,* 579.
12. Mitchell Hall, *Because of Their Faith: CALCAV and Religious Opposition to the Vietnam War* (New York: Columbia Univ. Press, 1990), x. While Hall does discuss CALCAV's financial support of American draft dodgers and deserters in Canada, the organization did not involve itself with antiwar activism in Canada.
13. Amy Swerdlow, *Women Strike for Peace: Traditional Motherhood and Radical Politics in the 1960s* (Chicago, Ill.: Univ. of Chicago Press, 1993), 1–4.
14. Andrew Hunt, *The Turning: A History of Vietnam Veterans Against the War* (New York: New York Univ. Press, 1999), 192, 201.
15. Michael Foley, *Confronting the War Machine: Draft Resistance During the Vietnam War* (Chapel Hill, N.C.: Univ. of North Carolina Press, 2003), 9.
16. Foley, *Confronting the War Machine,* 346.
17. Heineman, *Campus Wars,* 9, 2.
18. For a full account of the national moratorium, see Paul Hoffman, *Moratorium: An American Protest* (New York: Tower Publications, 1970).
19. Lorena Oropoza, *¡Raza Si! ¡Guerra No! Chicano Protest and Patriotism During the Viet Nam War Era* (Berkeley, Calif.: Univ. of California Press, 2005), 6, 9, 145–52, 160–63, 172.
20. Herring, *America's Longest War,* 142–47; Halstead, *Out Now,* 34–37.
21. Gary Moffat, *History of the Canadian Peace Movement Until 1969* (St. Catharines: Grape Vine Press, 1969), 80. For more on Communist Party connections with the Canadian Peace Congress, see Victor Huard, "The Canadian Peace Congress and the Challenge to Postwar Consensus, 1948–1953," *Peace and Change* 19 (Jan. 1994): 1, 25–50; Reg Whitaker and Gary Marcuse, *Cold War Canada: The Making of a National Insecurity State, 1945–1957* (Toronto: Univ. of Toronto Press, 1994), 366–67.
22. Douglas A. Ross, *In the Interests of Peace: Canada and Vietnam, 1954–1973* (Toronto: Univ. of Toronto Press, 1984), 256, 296.
23. Ross, *In the Interests of Peace,* 383–84.
24. For a full discussion of Canadian political and corporate involvement in the Vietnam War, see Victor Levant, *Quiet Complicity: Canadian Involvement in the Vietnam War* (Toronto: Between the Lines, 1986).

25. Ian Angus, interview by author, Nov. 6, 2006.
26. "Ottawa Report on Action in Ottawa, in Connection with the Viet Nam Incident," Combined Universities Campaign for Nuclear Disarmament, box 13, Vietnam, 1964–1965, William Ready Library and Archives, McMaster University, Hamilton, Ontario.
27. Kay Macpherson, with Christine Donald, *When in Doubt, Do Both: The Times of My Life* (Toronto: Univ. of Toronto Press, 1994), 98.
28. Sale, *SDS,* 185–86; "March on Washington," *SUPA Newsletter* 1, no. 2 (May 14, 1965): 3.
29. Angus, interview, Nov. 6, 2006.
30. Royal Canadian Mounted Police (RCMP) Report, National Coordination [*sic*] Committee to End the War in Vietnam—USA, Oct. 20, 1965; also (Vancouver) Committee to End the War in Vietnam Newsletter. Both documents found in Canadian Security Intelligence Service (CSIS), RG 146, Access to Information Application A-2006–00327, Vancouver Vietnam Day Committee disc 1, stack 4, LAC, Ottawa; "Student Anti-war Protest Grows," *Ukrainian Canadian,* Nov. 1, 1965, 1, 3, clipping in CSIS, RG 146, Access to Information Application A-2006–00427, Students for a Democratic Society, USA; "150 Gather in Dominion Square: Jagan Flays US Policies at Student Viet Nam Protest Day Demonstration," *Montreal Star* (Canadian Press), Oct. 16, 1965, 30; "The Great Student Viet Nam Protest," *Toronto Daily Star,* Oct. 18, 1965, 29.
31. "Great Student Viet Nam Protest," 29; Martin Knelman, "Beards and Sneakers in Protest Parade," *Globe and Mail,* Oct. 18, 1965, clipping in CSIS, RG 146, Access to Information Application A-2006–00427, stack 1, Students for a Democratic Society, U.S.A.; "Toronto Protest Draws 800," *Montreal Star,* Oct. 18, 1965, 29; "Students Plan Viet Protest Marches," *Toronto Daily Star,* Oct. 16, 1965, 2; Richard Reive, "Plan Peace March on US Consulate," *Varsity,* Oct. 15, 1965, 3; Judy Pocock, "U of T SUPA," *SUPA Newsletter* 1, no. 10 (Oct. 26, 1965), 14; "Peaceful Protest," *Varsity,* Oct. 18, 1965, 1.
32. "Marchers Show War Opposition," *Regina Leader-Post,* Mar. 28, 1966, 1, 8; "Thousands Rally Round Peace Flag," *Victoria Daily Colonist,* Mar. 27, 1966, 1, 3, clipping in Communist Party of Canada (CPC), box 49, file 01, LAC, Ottawa; "Canada a Growing Protest Movement," *Sanity,* Spring 1966, 7; "Protest Viet War: 2,000 March at Ottawa," *Montreal Star,* Mar. 28, 1966, 33; "Marchers Show War Opposition," *Regina Leader Post,* Mar. 28, 1966, 1, 8.
33. Angus, interview, Nov. 6, 2006.
34. Ray Burns, "UBC Leads West Coast Anti-war Movement," *Canada-Vietnam Newsletter,* June 1966, in CSIS, RG 146, Access to Information Application A-2006–00327, Vancouver Vietnam Day Committee, disc 1, stack 5; "Quality Publication Considered for Van VDC," *Vancouver Vietnam Day Committee Newsletter,* May 4, 1966, (clipping in same file as preceding article); Sandy Read, BC SUPA, "3,000 March at UBC," *SUPA Newsletter* 2, no. 6 (Apr. 19, 1966): 15.
35. RCMP Report, Mar. 30, 1966, National Coordination [*sic*] Committee to End the War in Vietnam, USA, Access to Information Application A2006–00312; "Babes-in-Arms Join City Peace Parade," *Vancouver Province,* Mar. 28, 1966, clipping in CPC, box 49, file 1.
36. "Rally to Rap Viet Nam War," *Victoria Colonist,* Mar. 10, 1966, 1, and "Babes-in-Arms," *Vancouver Province,* both clippings in CPC, box 49, file 1; "Protest Viet War," *Montreal Star;* "Marchers Show," *Regina Leader-Post;* form letter, William Spira, Secretary, Toronto

Committee to End the War in Vietnam, n.d., in Robert Kenny (hereafter, Kenny), box 54, file 1, Thomas Fisher Rare Book Room and Archives, University of Toronto; RCMP Report, March 30, 1966 in CSIS, RG 146, Access to Information Application A2006–00312, stack 7, National Coordination [*sic*] Committee to End the War in Vietnam, USA; "Canada a Growing Protest Movement, *Sanity;* "Cross-Canada Mobilization," *Workers' Vanguard;* "A Call to Action—Stop the War in Vietnam," Flyer, Saskatchewan Peace Council, Mar. 2, 1966, and RCMP Report, Apr. 18, 1966, National Coordination [*sic*] Committee to End the War in Vietnam, USA, both documents in CSIS, RG 146, Access to Information Application A2006–00312, stack 10; Russ Rothney, "Notes from the Lakehead," *SUPA Newsletter* 2, no. 6 (Apr. 19, 1966), 15; RCMP Memo, R. McKirnan, S/Insp, May 12, 1966, Winnipeg, CSIS, RG 146, Access to Information Application A2006–0312, stack 12, National Coordination [*sic*] Committee to End the War in Vietnam, USA.

37. "Speakers Express Views Against Vietnamese War," *Evening Times Globe,* Mar. 26, 1966; Barry Lord, "CEWV Formed in Saint John," *Canada-Vietnam Newsletter,* July 1966.
38. Halstead, *Out Now,* 340–99.
39. RCMP Report, "International Day of Protest—October 21, 1967, Province of Quebec," Oct. 25, 1967, CSIS, RG 146, Access to Information Application A2006–00309, Committee to End the War in Vietnam—Sir George Williams University, Montreal, Quebec, Part 01; RCMP Report, "International Day of Protest—October 21, 1967—British Columbia," CSIS, RG 146, Access to Information Application A2006–00425, Vietnam Action Committee, Vancouver.
40. Wells, *War Within,* 84, 193–94; *The Conference Table,* Feb. 1967, in CSIS, RG 146, Access to Information Application A2006–00309, Sarnia Citizens' Committee to End the War in Vietnam, Sarnia, ON, Part 02.
41. Hoffman, *Moratorium,* 173.
42. "It Was America's Biggest Protest: While a Sprinkling of Canadians Demonstrate Against Viet War," *Gateway,* Oct. 16, 1969, 1; Naomi Lyons and Leo Beinglas, "1200 for Peace Join Teach-in, *McGill Daily,* Oct. 16, 1969, 1, 5, 6; "McGill Joins It," *Gateway,* Oct. 15, 1969, 3; "Philosophers Back Vietnam Moratorium," *Georgian,* Oct. 15, 1969; Peter Whelan, "U.S. Consulate-General Picketed by 150," *Globe and Mail,* Oct. 16, 1969, 39.
43. *On Strike,* 1–2, 8, 15.
44. Sale, *SDS,* 635–41.
45. Halstead, *Out Now,* 644–45.
46. "Hundreds Injured in Anti-war Rioting Around the World," *Toronto Daily Star,* May 11, 1970, 4.
47. "Memorial Set for Tonight," *Montreal Star,* May 5, 1970, 2.
48. Renée Kasinsky, *Refugees from Militarism: Draft-Age Americans in Canada* (New Brunswick, N.J.: Transaction Books, 1976), 130; Larry Swartz, interview by author, June 21, 2002.
49. Mark Daly, "Memorial March Erupts in Violence," *Montreal Star,* May 5, 1970, 1, 2.
50. Steve Scheinberg, interview by author, Nov. 25, 2006.
51. Margaret Conrad and Alvin Finkel, *Canada: A National History,* 2nd ed. (Toronto: Pearson-Longman, 2007), 383–84.
52. Claude Demers, "Montreal Tells Trudeau to Pressure Nixon," *Young Worker* 2, no. 5 (May 1971): 4, CPC, box 59, LAC; photo and caption only, *Montreal Star,* Apr. 26, 1971, 3.

53. George Addison, interview by author, Oct. 22, 2006; "Protest Cambodia Invasion, Four Murders in Ohio" (poster), Kenny, box 54, file 1; "Stop Spadina Will Still Hold Demonstration," *Globe and Mail*, May 8, 1970, 5.
54. Lisa Hobbs, "Students Clash with Metro Police in Demonstration at U.S. Consulate," *Globe and Mail*, May 6, 1970, 1, 2; "Toronto Protesters Clash with Police," *Toronto Daily Star*, May 6, 1970, 3.
55. Myrna Kostash, *Long Way from Home: The Story of the Sixties Generation in Canada* (Toronto: James Lorimer and Co., 1980), 224.
56. Don Delaplante, "Metro Police Arrest Eight Demonstrators after Anti-war Clash Outside U.S. Consulate," *Globe and Mail*, May 7, 1970, 1, 2; "A Front Line View of War Protests—In Toronto and Cambodia: 75 in Toronto Picket Consulate," *Toronto Daily Star*, May 6, 1970, 3.
57. Delaplante, "Metro Police," 1, 2; "8 Held in Toronto Protest against Killings," *Toronto Daily Star*, May 7, 1970, 3.
58. "In Toronto . . . At the Red, White and Black You Can get Almost Anything You Want," *AMEX* 2, no. 3 (Apr./May 1970): 24.
59. Oliver Clausen, "Memorial Service at Queen's Park: Clergymen Assail U.S. Acts in Asia," *Globe and Mail*, May 9, 1970, 5; "U.S Consulate," *Toronto Daily Star*, May 8, 1970, 2.
60. There is some argument as to the number of demonstrators. Kostash asserts there were 15,000 present. See Kostash, *Long Way*, 224–25. *AMEX* reported between 5,000 and 10,000. See "Toronto," *AMEX* 2, no. 4 (June 1970), 18–20. Articles in the *Globe and Mail*, however, place the number at 5,000. See "Timetable of an Angry Confrontation," *Globe and Mail*, May 11, 1970, 15; Peter Churchill et al., "91 Arrested at Antiwar Rally: Protesters Fight, Shatter Windows During Downtown Toronto Chase," *Globe and Mail*, May 11, 1970, 1, 2; Michael Valpy, "They Brought in Horses for No Reason at All, Lawyer Charges," *Globe and Mail*, May 11, 1970, 5.
61. Kostash, *Long Way*, 224; Churchill et al., "91 Arrested at Antiwar Rally," 1, 2; "Protest Cambodia Invasion" (poster);"Stop Spadina," 5; "Timetable," 15; Churchill et al., "91 Arrested at Antiwar Rally," 1, 2.
62. Kostash, *Long Way*, 224–25; "Timetable," 15; Churchill et al., "91 Arrested at Antiwar Rally," 1, 2; DGB, "Peace City," *Harbinger*, 14; "91 Protesters Are Taken into Custody," *Globe and Mail*, May 11, 1970, 5; "Youth Jailed 60 Days for Knocking Officer Off Horse at Protest," *Globe and Mail*, May 12, 1970, 5; "Here is a List of People Arrested in Toronto Protest Saturday," *Toronto Daily Star*, May 11, 1970, 2; Greg Kealey, interview by author, Apr. 7, 2007; RCMP Report, "Protests and Demonstrations re: United States Action in Vietnam, Ontario," June 24, 1970, Report 2, CSIS, RG 146, Access to Information Application A2006–00315, stack 10, Vietnam Mobilization Committee to End the War in Vietnam, USA.
63. "Trudeau Burned in Effigy," *Toronto Daily Star*, May 11, 1970, 4; Churchill et al., "91 Arrested at Antiwar Rally," 1, 2.
64. "Vietnam Libre Banners Fly," *Hamilton Spectator*, May 7, 1970, 10.
65. "War Protesters Peaceful as Record Crowd Marches on City Hall, Post Office," *Hamilton Spectator*, May 11, 1970, 7; "Weekend of Demonstrations," *Daily Mercury*, May 11, 1970, 1.
66. Roberta Lexier, "Student Activism at the University of Saskatchewan, Regina Campus, 1963–1974" (master's thesis, University of Regina, 2003), 89–90; "Oppose U.S. Invasion, Motley Urges," *Edmonton Journal*, May 11, 1970, 29.
67. "250 Demonstrate Here," *Vancouver Express*, May 7, 1970, 3. See also photo on page 1.

68. "Near Riots Spur New Police Request," *Vancouver Express,* May 12, 1970, 3; "Vancouver Police Break Up Protest, *Saskatoon Start Phoenix,* May 9, 1970, 1.
69. "Blaine: Canadians Invade US in Mockery of Cambodia Attack; Gate of 'Peace Arch' Is Bolted Shut," *AMEX* 2, no. 4 (June 1970), 17.
70. "Blaine: Canadians Invade US," 17; "500 Protesters Bounced from U.S. After 'Invasion,'" *Toronto Daily Star,* May 11, 1970, 4; "Violence in the Name of Peace: Canadian Mob Invades Blaine," *Vancouver Express,* May 12, 1970, 1; Kostash, *Long Way,* 223–24.
71. Ross, *In the Interests of Peace,* 330.
72. "Peace Plea on Sunday," *Vancouver Express,* May 9, 1970, 11.
73. "Church Peace Rally Goes off Quietly," *Vancouver Express,* May 12, 1970, 2; "500 Protesters Bounced from U.S.," 4.
74. "Americans Petition U.S. Consul," *St. John's Telegram,* May 11, 1970, 1.
75. Sale, *SDS,* 641.
76. Many such articles were later published by the Socialist Worker's Party in *May 1970: Birth of the Antiwar University* (New York: Pathfinder Press, 1971). For an example, see Sid Finehirsh, "Extend the Strike, Organize, Build to May 30," originally published May 22, 1970, in *May 1970,* 30–33.
77. "Avenge the Augusta 7," *Daily Planet,* June 8, 1970, 8; Halstead, *Out Now,* 646. For a complete account of the shootings at Jackson State, see Spofford, *Lynch Street.*
78. Halstead, *Out Now,* 650.
79. "Vietnam Action Committee," (handbill), n.d.; "All Out to End the War, World Day of Protest, Sat, May 30 at Victory Square," (poster), both found in CPC, box 49, file 11.
80. "Shouts, Name-Calling, But No Violence at City Hall Rally," *Toronto Daily Star,* June 1, 1970, 4; "Toronto Anti-war Rally Orderly," *Kitchener Waterloo Record,* June 1, 1970, 1; "6,000 At Toronto's City Hall for Peaceful Anti-war Rally, *Guelph Daily Mercury,* June 1, 1970, 2. Headlines indicating 6,000 in attendance at this rally are misleading. Many of those present were those remaining from an anti-Soviet demonstration by Canadians of Eastern European descent that had preceded the antiwar demonstration.
81. "Shouts, Name-Calling," 4; "Toronto Anti-war Rally," *Kitchener Waterloo Record,* 1; "6,000 At Toronto's City Hall," 2.
82. "War, Grapes Bring Protesters Out," *Vancouver Province,* June 1, 1970, 21; Randy Furst and Dick Roberts, "Over 100,000 in Washington, May 9," in *May 1970: Birth of the Antiwar University* (New York: Pathfinder Press, 1971), 28–30.
83. Halstead, *Out Now,* 653–60, 680–712; DeBenedetti and Chatfield, *American Ordeal,* 304.
84. "Canadian Peace Marchers Were Generally Peaceful," *Vancouver Sun,* Apr. 26, 1971, 3.
85. Ross, *In the Interests of Peace,* 258.
86. Ibid., 14, 23, 324–25.
87. Ibid., 23.

Remembering Injustice and the Social Construction of Silence

Jay Winter

Silence is a place where no one says what everyone knows. In the face of injustice, silence of this kind conveys complicity. These remarks are addressed to you, the silence-breakers, who recognize, with Joseph Brodsky, that "the past won't fit into memory without something left over. It must have a future."[1] It is your achievement to shape that future through your framing of active knowledge in this place and at this time about the injustices that occurred here thirty-nine years ago.

In the brief time I have to speak to you today, perhaps it would be useful to reflect on silence: on how it happens, how it is enforced, how it ends. Some silences, I believe, are salutary; others are damaging. To distinguish between them requires reflection on memory and forgetting and on the curious omission of silence as a third kind of recollection, one in which events are both remembered and forgotten at the same time.

Consider these remarks by one of the most powerful commentators on memory, the French anthropologist Marc Augé: "Memory is framed by forgetting in the same way as the contours of the shoreline are framed by the sea."[2] There is some truth in these words, but there is something else in them, something left out, and that is silence.

Marc Augé's elegant formulation of the embrace of memory and forgetting draws upon a long tradition of philosophical and literary reflection. It is time, though, to go beyond it, in the effort to transcend the now-saturated field of memory studies dominated by scholarship that adopts this binary approach, for the topographical metaphor employed here is clearly incomplete. We need to see the landscape of the shoreline in all three dimensions. Doing so enables us to observe a vertical dimension to the creation and erosion of the shoreline, which is dynamic, unstable, and at times, intrusive. I speak of those deposits below the surface of the water, which emerge with the tides or with other environmental changes. In the framework of how we think about memory and forgetting, these hidden shapes cannot simply be ignored because they are concealed at some moments and revealed at others. They must be examined as part of the cartography of recollection and remembrance.

Silences: Liturgical, Political, Essentialist

We call these hidden deposits *silence*. The composer John Cage said all that needs to be said about the performative nature of silence. It exists in the world, and is defined by the world according to certain arbitrary but powerfully reinforced conventions. Those who first heard his composition *4′33″* in 1952 were stupefied by silence. What Cage did was to invite concertgoers to come together facing a pianist who sits at a piano and does not touch the keyboard for four minutes and thirty-three seconds precisely. What Cage showed them, much to their discomfort, was that silence is "the presence of ambient and unintentional noise rather than the complete absence of sound."[3] In these remarks, I want to draw attention to focused, directed, and purposeful silence, not conceived of as the absence of sound, but as the absence of conventional verbal exchanges.

In this landscape, silences are spaces either beyond words or conventionally delimited as left out of what we talk about. Topographically, they are there whether or not they come to the surface; and their reemergence into our line of sight can occasion a reiteration of the interdiction on talking about them or the end of the interdiction itself.

Critically, therefore, we cannot accept the commonplace view that silence is the space of forgetting and speech the realm of remembrance. Instead, I offer the following definition of silence. Silence, I hold, is a socially constructed space in which and about which subjects and words normally used in everyday life are not spoken. The circle around this space is described by groups of people who at one point in time deem it appropriate that there is a difference between the sayable and the unsayable, or the spoken and the unspoken, and that such a distinction can and should be maintained and observed over time. Such people codify and enforce norms that reinforce the injunction against breaking into the inner space of the circle of silence.

The reasons for this cultural practice are multiple, but in the context of war and violence, the primary, although not the only, impulses underlying the social construction of silence are three. In the first place, silence is always part of the framing of public understandings of war and violence, since these touch on the sacred, and on eternal themes of loss, mourning, sacrifice, and redemption. I term these uses of silence *liturgical silences*. They are clearly linked to fundamental moral problems, described in reflections on theodicy, or the conundrum as to why, if God is all good, evil exists in the world. Such liturgical silences are essential parts of mourning practices in many religious traditions, since not speaking enables those experiencing loss to engage with their grief in their own time and in their own ways.

Consider, for example, the paradox that the Kaddish, the Hebrew prayer for the dead, does not include the words *death, dying, grief,* or *bereavement,* all terms for conditions or states of mind associated with the seven days of mourning passed together by the families in mourning. The prayer is silent over the critical reality this practice marks. Mourning practices always touch on such matters, since they address the fragility of life and the limitations of our own understandings of our mortal existence.

The second impulse behind the social construction of silence addresses problems of social conflict more directly. Here silence is chosen in order to suspend or truncate open conflict over the meaning of or justification for violence, either domestic or transnational. The hope here is that the passage of time can lower the temperature of disputes about these events, or even heal the wounds they cause. I term these uses of silence *political* or *strategic silences.*

One example may suffice to illustrate the host of such usages. In 1975, Francisco Franco's forty-year dictatorship in Spain ended peacefully with his death. In short order, a socialist government came to power, and proceeded to refashion the country as a dynamic and stable member of the new European order. The price of that transition was the postponement or adjournment *sine die*—that is, permanently—of any formal and public inquiry into atrocities committed during and after the civil war of 1936–39. Spain's new democracy chose peace over justice, order over any open investigation of the abundant evidence on atrocities that—like the underwater sand bars to which I referred earlier—was present but invisible. Not seeing what everyone saw and not saying what everyone knew became a strategy accepted by everyone at the time to ensure the success of a peaceful transition to democratic rule.[4] Since such accords are matters of negotiation, they suffer from all the faults of political compromise. With time, their hold over the parties begins to loosen, a new generation comes to power, and, although silence is still ordained at the national level as wise and necessary, people start talking, looking, digging, writing, and, inevitably, accusing. And how could it be otherwise when the scale of accusations is monumental? Here we can see that silence, like memory and forgetting, has a life history, and, when new pressures or circumstances emerge, can be transformed into its opposite in very rapid order.

Some transformative moments are well known. Heidegger's silence about Nazi crimes, and his complicity in them, echoed similar lacunae in many German discursive fields after 1945. Paul Celan's poetry ruptured them. More recently, silence about war and violence ends when victims are invited to come forward and are given a forum ensuring that what they say will be heard. One such effort is South Africa's Truth and Reconciliation Commission, set up in 1995 in part to bear witness to crimes perpetrated under apartheid; numerous other truth commissions have been established for similar purposes.[5]

The third impulse behind strategies of silence arises from considerations of privilege. That is, who has the right to speak about the violent past? One nearly universal answer is to privilege one group of people who pass through an experience as thereby having the right to speak about it, as against others who were not there and thus cannot know and cannot judge that experience. Only those who were there, so this argument goes, can claim the authority of direct experience required to speak about these matters. This is what I term *essentialist silences.*

There are many examples of such distinctions. Soldiers frequently speak about their war experiences only to other soldiers. Efrat Ben-Ze'ev has studied an annual reunion of the members of a unit in the Israeli army of 1948; this event, and others like it, continue to this day.[6] In other cases, soldiers express a kind of sexist rejection of the very capacity of women to enter and understand this masculine realm. Still others take an essentialist line, in defining experience as internal and ineffable. When, forty years ago, I addressed a conference on the First World War at the Royal Military College, Sandhurst, one of the participants, Charles Carrington, who was a noted author and survivor of the Great War, urged me to choose another profession. The reason: "You will never know the war; only we who were there can know what it was like." This was said with avuncular kindness.

Other such strictures are more acerbic. Time and again, patriots ask how anyone can criticize soldiers and the choices they make under fire if they haven't been there. And when a conflict is still unfolding, what right do civilians have to criticize what the combatants do? Then there is the charge that moral issues are too easily framed by those who had the moral luck to avoid extreme or violent situations. And even among those who endured suffering, distinctions are made between those who knew the worst and those who luckily never reached such a point. Primo Levi, for example, said that even Holocaust survivors like him did not know the worst: that knowledge was restricted to those at the bottom of the world he had inhabited in Auschwitz—those who had already become the living dead.[7]

Another aspect of essentialist silence concerns those who have survived a war and kept secrets about their past. Condemnation is the easy way out for people who live comfortable lives. Shoshana Felman took this tack in considering the puzzle posed by the fact that her colleague, the great literary critic Paul de Man, had written anti-Semitic prose in a Belgian newspaper in 1940. This unsavory fact came to light only after de Man's death in 1982. How do we interpret his behavior? Felman not only sees his scrupulous scholarship as distinct from his earlier behavior but further suggests that his silence about his own past was a profound philosophical reflection on the terrible difficulty of all moral judgment, including judging those who as young men and women succumbed to the temptation of fascism.[8] While not sharing this conclusion, I feel Felman's argument does offer a telling riposte to what E. P. Thompson termed the "enormous condescension of posterity"—the tendency to look down on those stuck in predicaments we ourselves might not have resolved in any morally superior manner.[9]

The problem with this approach to silence is its characteristic essentialism. Few any longer subscribe to the romantic definition of experience as ingested, visceral, and objectively present in the lives and minds of only some individuals. According to this view, experience is theirs and theirs alone. In contradistinction, experience is much more fruitfully defined as a set of events whose character changes when there are changes in the subject position of the person or group that shared those events—changes through age, migration, illness, marriage, religious conversion, and so on.[10] Students of memory in the cognitive and neurosciences no longer view their subject as fixed, as in a computer's hard drive, but more as dynamic and unstable, as in a collage. The work of Elizabeth Loftus has deepened our understanding of implanted memories, ones suggested to individuals by outsiders and sometimes by clinicians in therapeutic relationships. The danger of such interventions is evident.[11] If memory changes radically over time, then we must abandon the notion that not only memory but the right to speak about memory is the property of only a chosen few who recall the experience of what Calvin termed *election.*[12] Relegating the rest of us to silence must be seen as a strategy of control, of cutting off debate, of ad hominem assertions of a kind unworthy of serious reflection.

Who does have the right to speak is a troubling question. War stories are never uncontested and they change over time as the people who frame them grow old, move on, and pass away. When the victims of violence have the sanction to speak out, as in a court of law or truth commission, then they become the authors not only of their stories, but also of their lives. Not speaking can entail accepting someone else's story about what happened to you, or it may be an assertion of dignity by those who, like rape victims, have passed through indignity. The central point is that the entitlement to speak about war and violence is in no sense universal. Some have the right; others do not. The difference between the two categories is a matter of social and cultural codes, which can and do change over time.

The Advantages of Silence

To those who work in this field, it is evident that the vast array of writing on memory and forgetting has reached an impasse, one imbedded in the time of its creation. I believe that introducing the category of socially constructed silence into the literature provides a way out of some of the difficulties in the current literature, where memory and forgetting are constructed as polar opposites.

The memory/forgetting divide is a matter of perennial philosophical reflection. Paul Ricoeur's magisterial survey of this literature goes back to Plato and Aristotle and the extent to which the *eikon* and the *topos,* the trace and the place, have been understood differently in the domain of memory and in the domain of history. But even his extraordinary survey is a tract for the times, reflecting many of the intellectual currents behind the current memory boom. His book, published in 2000, reflected decades of thought on this subject. "I am troubled," he wrote, "by the disturbing spectacle that gives an excess of memory here and an excess of oblivion there."[13] This comment echoed similar remarks by the French historian and publisher Pierre Nora on our surfeit of ersatz memory, in *lieux de mémoire,* and on a lack of imbedded, lived memory, in *milieu de mémoire.*[14] According to these and other French commentators, memory had become a commodity, an unavoidable sign of ethnic identity, a repository for romantic wishful thinking about the past, for which people paid substantial sums in theme parks, museums, and historic sites around the world.

The memory boom is the outcome of many different processes, some commercial, some technological, some political. I do not share the critical viewpoint of these French writers, since the growth in interest in commemorative projects arises as much from changing political circumstances as from market opportunities. There is a substantial literature on this subject, which I need not summarize here.[15]

In this discussion, it is evident that the Holocaust has been at the heart of the huge spiral of publications, lectures, exhibitions, museums, and Internet sites we have today. Initial oblivion, eventual entry into the realm of public memory: these two phases of public acknowledgment of the Holocaust have unfolded in sequence and have inflected many inquiries into other crimes and other abuses elsewhere in the world.[16]

It is impossible to miss the shadow of the Holocaust in the philosophical realm inhabited by Ricoeur. The third part of his study is on forgiveness, on the need to recognize the moral fallibility of all who judge the past, and therefore on the need to aim at a kind of redemptive approach to history and memory, the effort to construct what he terms *happy memory.* In English, the term appears absurd; in French it has more resonance, but it still has the scent of incense about it, the notion that to remember is to understand, and to understand is to forgive. There is too a psychoanalytic form of this position. To know is to heal is a premise of some forms of psychotherapy. We must bear in mind, however, that Freud said that his hope was to turn neurosis into normal unhappiness; no happy memories here.

Healing, acknowledgment, recognition, forgiveness: these were the hallmarks of the memory boom in the 1990s, the time when Nelson Mandela moved from prison to the presidency of South Africa and when Bishop Desmond Tutu drove forward the notion of a truth and reconciliation process for the victims and the perpetrators of the crimes of the former regime. In this environment, remembering is the key to repentance and forgiveness, while oblivion is complicity in crimes still hidden from sight. Suffice it to say that there are huge problems imbedded in this approach; why repentance should follow remembrance and, indeed, why healing should follow remembrance are questions with no easy answers. Many survivors of the Holocaust, as well as many people born long after the end of the Second World War, are uncomfortable with this fundamentally religious or spiritual approach to these matters. Primo Levi did not forgive those who told him that in Auschwitz, there was no *why;* neither did Paul Celan forget those who destroyed his family—indeed, his entire world. They remembered and they wrote, but healing was not their purpose or their fate. Victims insist on attention to other issues as well: compensation for truncated lives and for stolen property matter too. The difficulties with this nearly sanctified part of the memory boom are endless, and require us to seek another way. As long as we stay in this morally charged domain, we are unlikely to emerge with anything other than an updated version of Foxe's *Book of Martyrs.*

It is my contention that by privileging the category of silence and the socially sanctioning activity of silencing, we can get beyond this moralized and moralizing moment. The prime advantage of this approach is that we escape from the shadow of the Holocaust which, while unavoidable as a subject of moral significance, has tended to frame our subject in terms of the sanctification of speech and the denigration of silence about war, violence, and the victims of both. Speech, I claim, is morally neutral, and so is silence. Both can be deployed in morally defensible and morally deplorable ways.

Silence and War

If we see that the question of how to remember war and violence is one that both antedated the Holocaust and has persisted long after it, we also can escape from an exclusively Eurocentric approach to this matter. Since the Second World War, the institutions of war have fragmented. Whereas before 1945 our attention was fixed more on international conflict, now it is fixed more on transnational or internal conflict. We focus more than ever before on organized violence within states and between nonstate agents and territorial states. This is in part because the decades following the end of World War II were dominated by wars of national liberation, leaving in their wake fundamental social, ethnic, and political cleavages that, in turn, have bred armed conflicts of many different kinds. The genocide in Rwanda, and the ongoing massacres—some say genocide—in Darfur are two African examples of the terrible plight of people caught in these postcolonial ethnic conflicts. Crimes committed in Bosnia during the Yugoslav civil war, in Colombia, Lebanon, Sri

Lanka, Kashmir, Afghanistan, and Iraq have arisen from what may be termed the postnational and postcolonial setting of armed conflict.

Clearly, as war evolves, the stories we tell about it evolve in turn. Today, the collage of organized violence and the suffering it entails is much more complex, even dizzying in its shifting character. The tale of war can no longer be told primarily or exclusively within the unfolding saga of nationalism and the achievement of self-determination and national dignity.

When thinking about contemporary warfare, it is essential to take a step back from our current preoccupations. The Westphalian system of conflicts between states that we tend to take for granted as the natural order of things is nothing of the kind. It is not universal and not timeless. African warfare has developed its own character, outside a European system of states, while efforts by colonial powers to keep their hold on colonies struggling for independence usually took on the kind of fragmentary character we mistake as unprecedented. Nothing could be further from the case. Still, the catastrophe of the two world wars has left its imprint on what Samuel Hynes terms our "war in the head," our shared assumptions about what war is.[17]

It follows that while we adjust our attitudes toward war and war crimes, we may likewise need to adjust our notions of remembrance. The decentering of the experience of war and violence may make it less useful to apply the categories of memory and forgetting, which frequently assume that the story is determined by a top-down approach to political power configured in a national state. This is the landscape of George Orwell's *1984*, which was a dystopia set in London during the Second World War, and of Albert Camus's *The Plague*, set in Algiers in the same time period. Shifting our attention away from the hegemonic state or police apparatus to a broader social landscape may help reconfigure our understanding of subtler processes in the framing of debate through the construction of silence. This shift could also help us chart the life cycle of silence in such a way as to show how different memory agents use different means to puncture the balloon of silence and put words in its place.

Attention to silence and silencing also helps us turn the voice of our discussion from the passive to the active. Elsewhere I have called for greater rigor in the use of the terms *memory* and *forgetting*, such as to point to the person or group remembering or forgetting whenever possible.[18] Unfortunately, the terms *collective memory* and *national memory* have entered everyday speech, and thus have lost any concrete meaning they may once have had. If we turn our discussion toward silence and silencing, there is usually someone not speaking and frequently someone making sure that those who break the rules know the consequences of doing so. Those individuals the historian Carol Gluck has termed "memory activists" are also those who break silences and change the boundaries between what can and cannot be said. Social agency is the domain of the social construction of silence. On this point,

I side with Michel de Certeau, as against Michel Foucault, in asserting that not all cultural practices can be collapsed into discourse.[19] Silence is one such practice with a life history of its own.

Why Now?

One reason to adopt a different optic in the field of memory studies is that the social context in which we think about the subject is changing. From the time of Ernest Renan at the end of the nineteenth century to Benedict Anderson's seminal study of "imagined communities," the nation state and the mobilizing power of nationalism have provided the force and focus of several generations of scholarship on memory and remembrance.[20]

Since the 1960s, however, a different international environment has emerged. In some respects, what we term *globalization* is merely the reiteration of trends already in motion before the First World War, but the huge movements of capital, goods, and labor in the late twentieth century and since present us with a changing demographic landscape. To be sure, the nation state has not died, but its power has been eroded, in part by a surge in emigration from what we now term globally "the South"—Africa, South Asia, and Latin America—to "the North"—Europe and the United States. An unspecified but very large part of this population movement from developing to developed nations is illegal. That is, people are moving from developing to developed nations through normal visa channels if they can, but through illicit channels when they must.

This dramatic trend in population movement is a challenge to the integrity of the nation state. In many parts of the world, the state is less that institution with the authority to declare war than that institution with the power to determine who enters its territory. That power is now in question. The result is the presence among us of very large silent populations—silent because they are not supposed to be here. Such people occupy menial jobs in developed economies and constitute a huge reservoir of poorly paid labor. Speaking up would call attention to their illicit presence. They are silent, too, in that they have no political voice in the country to which they have come. On occasion, that can mean they have no rights at all and face hostility, harassment, arrest, and deportation. Stephen Frears's 2002 film *Dirty Pretty Things* opened a window onto this subterranean world, one that is hard to look at. Our silence about the presence of these people among us is something on which we should reflect.

If you travel to any major city, anywhere in the developed world, take an evening off, and dine in a local café, you are likely to be in the company of these newcomers, just off stage, washing dishes or cleaning up.[21] Most of the time, we too are silent about them, preferring to avoid a direct confrontation with the problem of undocumented immigrants, who consequently lead a shadow life, filled with dangers and uncertainties.

This changing demographic reality is bound to affect the way we look at the nation state and the historical questions we ask about our common cultural heritage. If memory and forgetting bracketed our understanding of nationhood and nationalism at the high water mark of what Charles Maier termed the age of territoriality, then it may be possible to see that now, in a transnational age, it makes sense not to dispense with memory and forgetting, but to develop a wider vocabulary to explore the sphere of signifying practices in the contemporary world.[22] I suggest that exploring the subject of silence and its social construction is one such analytical development.

Silence as a Cultural Practice

Now that I hope I have persuaded you of the value, indeed the necessity, of the study of silence, I want to turn to the ways in which the processes of silencing and respecting silences are socially conditioned. Let us consider several of them.

Speech: Free and Unfree

The courts help enforce silence in many different societies. In this domain, some rules apply, and some of these rules are coercive. Even in liberal societies, there are limits to free speech. No one has the right to shout "Fire!" frivolously in a crowded space; in some countries, a speaker who denies that the Holocaust happened can be prosecuted and imprisoned. There are other, well-known instances in which the law itself inscribes and enforces boundaries as to what can be said with impunity. Until May 2008, blasphemy was a crime in Britain. A charge of offending Muslim beliefs brought opprobrium (and calls for his death) onto the head of Salman Rushdie after the 1998 publication of his novel *Satanic Verses,* a work of satirical fiction that devout Muslims found highly offensive. His book was burned in Yorkshire, but, outside Britain, some religious authorities went further. The Ayatollah Khomeini issued a *fatwa* or judgment rooted in Islamic law, calling for Rushdie's death, forcing the author to go into hiding for a decade.

The normative enforcement of silence is a much more subtle and multifaceted domain. British libel laws were notoriously more advantageous to the defense than were American libel laws. This difference permitted the British publisher Robert Maxwell to cover up his crimes for decades before his death. The risks of prosecution for libel were simply too great for the whistleblowers or the newspapers who knew that he was a charlatan and a thief. The law is an important domain in the social construction of silence, one which, like all others, changes over time and place.

The confessional is a site of speech the content of which is privileged even in a court of law. The same is true for exchanges with a doctor, a lawyer, or a spouse. All inhabit a space in which what is said is—and must remain—no one else's business. At times, we accept the validity, even the necessity, of violating these rules, but only in extremis. Victims of rape or sexual abuse can anticipate a veil of silence draped over their suffering in everyday conversation, although in a court of law, they may have to speak about torture or injury that outside the courthouse is unspeakable. Even in this case, though, victims may remain silent, since the speech act may be performative—that is, the pain described is inflicted once again through testimony. All such statements mix revelation with silences, and who are we to say that the damaged person who refuses to speak even then is mistaken or culpable?

Poetic License

Are writers among the unseen legislators of rules about silence? Do they help us break it? In some respects, the answer to both questions is yes. However, the realm of silence with which writers deal is embedded in complex social practices of specifying and obeying codes of delicacy or tact. Consider this mundane instance of socially censored speech: even though there is no legal obstacle to discussing in public a painful divorce with one of the parties to it, many people would hesitate long before doing so. In contemporary Britain, polite conversation may avoid many subjects, aside from the weather, on the grounds that the primary purpose of social exchange is to avoid embarrassing anyone. Why embarrassment is a state to be avoided at all costs is a question we need not entertain here, though it raises clearly the variations existing between different societies' rules of decency and proper comportment.

Humor frequently describes and violates such rules of tact. We have already noted the Rushdie case, but there is a much longer tradition of vicious denunciation of injustices through black comedy. Humor, even the savage kind, provides a cover of indirection for statements that, if said in bland prose, could result in accusations of slander, libel, or treason. In his wickedly satirical *A Modest Proposal,* for example, Jonathan Swift suggested a novel solution for Ireland's economic woes—that the Irish sell their babies to the rich for food—even going into detail on how to prepare them as tasty dishes. Voltaire's *Candide* hid moral indignation in the folds of his modest tale. More recently, a completely different sensibility made anti-Semitism into the stuff of brilliant fiction. Louis-Ferdinand Céline's prose is filled with anti-Semitism of an unmistakable kind. "'The vertigo of words,'' style with "a sense of delirium," is how Céline described these diatribes, which did not prevent his masterpiece, *Voyage au bout de la nuit* (*Journey to the End of the Night*), from appearing in the classic Bibliothèque de la Pléiades series in 1952.[23]

What can be said in a joke is not at all what should be said in what is thought of as polite conversation. Consider the following joke about Alzheimer's disease. We should not fear this illness, the joke begins, because when you have it, every day you meet new and interesting people. Is this mockery of the mentally disabled, or of the suffering of their loved ones? Yes, on both counts. Is it a way of talking about a condition most people prefer to leave in the shadows? Yes again. And perhaps, too, mockery is a gentle form of the recognition of fallibility, like ethnic jokes one makes about one's own people, to puncture piousness or self-importance. Terms such as *tact, taste, good breeding, sensitivity,* and *manners* describe the comportment of those who do not say such things. And it is precisely this silence that gives satirists and comedians their challenge.

Sometimes, it is said, they go too far. But where is too far? There are no hard-and-fast rules. The comedic team of Monty Python ended their 1979 film *The Life of Brian,* a spoof on the New Testament, with a scene in which a chorus of men bound to crosses sing together, "Always look on the bright side of life." This ditty drove traditionalists in Britain up the proverbial wall, at least initially. Thereafter, Anglican clergymen urged their congregants to sing along. Travesty, or cross-dressing, is another Monty Python specialty. Here prejudices against homosexuality and the blurring of conventional sexual roles and postures are exposed by deliberately vulgar exaggeration, in which comedy speaks the unspoken social prejudices and self-deceptions of mainstream or polite society. In this case, though, it is unclear whether the mockery undermines or fortifies the prohibition on talking about certain subjects. Laughter can reduce tensions, but it rarely eliminates them.

Indeed, in some contexts, buffoonery can carry a message others fear to voice. There is a long tradition of granting license to liminal characters, like court jesters and fools, who can speak truth to power. Consider *King Lear,* in which the fool tells the king: "I had rather be any / kind o' thing than a fool, and yet I would not be / thee, nuncle: thou hast pared thy wit o' both sides / and left nothing i' th' middle."[24] A risky thing for a courtier to say? Yes, but not for a fool, who knows what everyone else knows, but has a socially sanctioned transgressive role. He tells Lear what he comes to learn—that once he lets go of the reins of power, his royal trappings amount to nothing. He is but an old man, dependent on his children to keep him alive. And yet no one in court would ever dare to say such a thing. Comedy speaks truth to power and lives to tell the tale another day. Social deviants may be permitted to defy the rules of polite society and call the great ones to book for their crimes and misdemeanors. Clowns can mimic; comics, mock; and the mentally ill can point out what others prefer to leave unsaid. It was no accident that the Soviet Secret Police used the drug Haldol to silence dissidents; it was the chemical straitjacket used to control psychotic people, and therefore very effective in silencing dissent.[25] Psychiatric patients in many countries are in this category of deviant speech: they could express fears others left unsaid.[26]

Silence can be shocking, and intentionally so. Harold Pinter's plays redefined theater as a space dominated by silences occasionally interrupted by words. The menace imbedded in the relations between the characters in his plays was heightened, at times excruciatingly so, by long periods of wordlessness. Again, humor cloaked some painful issues. In *The Homecoming,* a son comes to his father's house to introduce his new bride, who says nothing. The father takes his time, and then responds that he had asked his son never to bring his whores home. Outrageous, to be sure, but also a very probing jab at the London Jewish world that Pinter offended by his marriage to a non-Jewish woman, Vivien Merchant. Theatre has exposed hypocrisy, especially sexual hypocrisy, since George Bernard Shaw and Henrik Ibsen, but what Pinter added to the mix was the potent brew of silence, one that has endured. His Nobel Prize in Literature is in part a recognition of this achievement.

All the arts have the potential for speaking without words. In a performance of Verdi's opera *The Lombards and the First Crusade* in the Florence Opera in 2005, the scene in which the Crusaders take the city of Jerusalem was expressed in the form of total darkness and the background sounds of battle, punctuated by silent cameos of three or four members of the cast fixed in poses of prisoners under torture in Abu Ghraib prison in Iraq. The sight of a man on a box with a pointed cap on his head and electrodes attached to his arms needed no commentary. The image is now iconic; it tells its own story.

The same is true with respect to the photograph taken of Che Guevara's dead body in 1967, although here the image took on a life of its own. Instead of silently saying, "We got him. He is dead. One less revolutionary to worry about," the photograph of a handsome man laid out like Christ after the crucifixion, unintentionally but powerfully sacralized his death and turned his death mask into a revolutionary icon. Images speak in ways that are hard to control.

Amnesty

Amnesty comes from the Greek *amnēstia,* meaning "oblivion." It is a legal remedy providing a way in which societies wrestling with intractable political and social conflicts can draw an arbitrary line separating a *then* when legal and other grievances were pursued and a *now* when, in the interest of the collective, no further reckoning is permitted. Amnesty is not synonymous with forgetting. It tries to bypass the paralysis that can attend the settling of scores ad infinitum. After an amnesty, the words "I accuse" may still be uttered, but they have no legal force.

Drawing a legal line in the sand in this way requires a consensus that more justice is done by ceasing open conflict over the past than would be done by continuing to pursue one's enemies. Over time, that consensus may break down, leading to a renegotiation of the terms of amnesty. This happened in Argentina in 2005, when the country's Supreme Court struck down as unconstitutional the amnesty laws covering crimes committed by the government in the pursuit of its Dirty War in the late 1970s and 1980s. Today, a similar process of legislative nullification is under way in Chile.

The recent uncovering of mass graves in Spain shows the way in which amnesties may begin to unravel. Francisco Ferrándiz notes that "the public disclosure of caches of bones, products of the tragic legacies of war and violent conflict, elicits heartbreaking stories that had previously been suppressed or only whispered." Older people may have preferred to live with a past "thrown into oblivion," but their children and grandchildren may think otherwise.[27]

The stabilizing effect of amnesty itself is unstable over time. Indeed in November 2007, the Spanish parliament passed a Law of National Memory, opening up the whole subject of injustice and atrocities committed during the Civil War seventy years before. Sentences handed down by Franco's courts were declared illegitimate, and local and national authorities were instructed to help individuals to locate and exhume the bodies of Franco's victims still buried in mass graves. In addition, all statues and other symbols of the Franco regime were to be removed from public places. The Spanish prime minister drove this measure through, in part on principle and in part because his own grandfather had been executed during the Civil War. His silences—and indeed Spain's silences—were now transformed into both words and deeds.[28]

Amnesty Is Not Eternal

Amnesty of a different kind was practiced in South Africa's Truth and Reconciliation Commission. This commission was formed to achieve the purging of individual guilt through the public and complete admission of guilt by those who came forward. The Christian character of this form of truth telling as an alternative to judicial punishment made it attractive to some but not to others. Those who suffered injury still have to find healing; others have to find homes or other forms of material comfort to replace those they were deprived of. The performance of guilt may or may not yield the reconciliation of the victim and the perpetrator. What happens instead is that the victim gets to the microphone, seizes his or her own story, and therefore becomes a subject and not just an object in history. This is of great importance, but what the victim says may itself contain silences.

Cambodia, Kent State, and the Reconfiguration of Silence

To this point, I have tried to highlight the utility of reflecting on silence as a strategy of commemoration. At Kent State today, we mark events on which there have been nearly forty years of judicial silence. Many have cried out of wrong, and they have not been heard. Injustice is indigestible; it sticks in our throats and remains an obstacle, a puzzle, a condition. Perhaps the framing of this day by this symposium and those to come, and the framing of that day of forty years ago by the opening of the visitors center designed by the visionaries at the heart of this project, offer us an opportunity. The chance we have is not to transcend injustice, which is an impossibility, but to transform silence about injustice into something active, purposeful, dynamic. We must, as it is written in stone nearby, inquire, learn, and reflect on these matters. But I would like to add a fourth admonition. We need to respond to them. And silence—dignified, expansive, controlled, and directed—is a language we shape as a road to remembrance. "To be silent is still to speak," wrote the French philosopher Maurice Blanchot.[29] And to construct a space of meditation, for visitors to this place, is one way—in my view an appropriate way—to ensure these events and their meanings are never forgotten.

Notes

This essay was the keynote address at the tenth annual Symposium on Democracy at Kent State University, May 5, 2009. Kent State founded the symposium to honor the memories of the four students who lost their lives on May 4, 1970. On that day, members of the Ohio National Guard fired at demonstrators, wounding nine Kent State students, and killing Allison Krause, Jeffrey Miller, Sandra Scheuer, and William Schroeder.

1. As told by Joseph Brodsky to the author, Jan. 1, 1995.
2. Marc Augé, *Les formes de l'oubli* (Paris: Payot and Rivages, 1998), 4.
3. Branden W. Joseph, "John Cage and the Architecture of Silence," *October* 81 (Summer 1997): 80–104.
4. Mary Vincent, "Breaking the Silence? Memory and Oblivion since the Spanish Civil War," in Efrat Ben-Ze'ev, Ruth Ginio, and Jay Winter, *Shadows of War: A Social History of Silence in the Twentieth Century* (New York: Cambridge Univ. Press, 2010), 47–67.
5. Louise Bethlehem, "Now That All Is Said and Done: Reflections on the Truth and Reconciliation Commission in South Africa," in Ben-Ze'ev, Ginio, and Winter, *Shadows of War*, 153–70.
6. Efrat Ben-Ze'ev, "Imposed Silences and Self-censorship: *Palmach* Soldiers Remember 1948," in Ben-Ze'ev, Ginio, and Winter, *Shadows of War*, 181–96.
7. Primo Levi, *Survival in Auschwitz* (New York: Basic Books, 2002), 146.
8. Shoshana Felman, "Paul de Man's Silence," *Critical Inquiry* 15, no. 4 (Summer 1989): 704–44.
9. E. P. Thompson, *The Making of the English Working Class* (London: Victor Gollancz, 1963), 18.
10. Joan W. Scott, "The Evidence of Experience," *Critical Inquiry* 17, no. 4 (1991): 773–97.
11. Daniel Schacter, *The Seven Sins of Memory* (Cambridge, Mass.: Harvard Univ. Press, 1999), 20–23; Elizabeth Loftus, *Eyewitness Testimony* (Cambridge, Mass.: Harvard Univ. Press, 1979); Veronica Nourkova, Daniel M. Bernstein, and Elizabeth Loftus, "Biography

Becomes Autobiography: Distorting the Subjective Past," *American Journal of Psychology* 117, no. 1 (2004): 65–80.

12. Winter, *Remembering War,* chap. 1.
13. Paul Ricoeur, *La mémoire, l'histoire, l'oubli* (Paris: Seuil, 2000), xi.
14. Winter, *Remembering War,* 33.
15. Nancy Wood, *Vectors of Memory: Legacies of Trauma in Postwar Europe* (Oxford: Berg, 1999), is a good place to begin. See also Aleida Assmann, *Erinnerungsräume: Formen und Wandlungen des kulturellen Gedächtnisses* (Munich: C. H. Beck, 1999).
16. Andreas Huyssen, *Twilight Memories: Marking Time in a Culture of Amnesia* (New York: Routledge, 1995); Lawrence Langer, *Holocaust and the Literary Imagination* (New Haven, Conn.: Yale Univ. Press, 1975); James E. Young, *At Memory's Edge: After-images of the Holocaust in Contemporary Art and Architecture* (New Haven, Conn.: Yale Univ. Press, 2000).
17. Samuel Hynes, *The Soldiers' Tale* (New York: Penguin, 2000).
18. Jay Winter and Emmanuel Sivan, "Setting the Framework," in *War and Remembrance in the Twentieth Century,* ed. Jay Winter and Emmanuel Sivan, 6–39 (Cambridge, UK: Cambridge Univ. Press, 1999).
19. For a fuller discussion, see Winter, *Remembering War,* chap. 1.
20. Ernest Renan, *Qu'est-ce qu'une nation?* ed. Philippe Forest (Paris: Pierre Bordas et fils éditeur, 1991); Benedict Anderson, *Imagined Communities* (London: Verso, 1983).
21. See Kiran Desai, *The Inheritance of Loss* (New York: Atlantic Monthly Press, 2005).
22. Charles Maier, "Consigning the Twentieth Century to History: Alternative Narratives for the Modern Era," *American Historical Review* 105, no. 3 (2000): 807–31.
23. Jay Winter, "Céline and the Cultivation of Hatred," in *Enlightenment, Passion, Modernity: Historical Essays in European Thought and Culture,* ed. Mark S. Micale and Robert L. Dietle (Stanford, Calif.: Stanford Univ. Press, 2000), 238.
24. William Shakespeare, *King Lear,* ed. Alfred Harbage (Baltimore, Md.: Penguin Books, 1973), 1.4.176–78.
25. Paul Calloway, *Soviet and Western Psychiatry* (London: Moor Press, 1992).
26. Svenja Goltermann, "On Silence, Madness, and Lassitude: Negotiating the Past in Post-war West Germany," in Ben-Ze'ev, Ginio, and Winter, *Shadows of War,* 91–112.
27. Francisco Ferrándiz, "The Return of Civil War Ghosts: The Ethnography of Exhumations in Contemporary Spain," *Anthropology Today* 22, no. 3 (2006): 7–12.
28. "Spain Confronts Past under Franco," *Spiegel Online International,* November 2007, <http://www.spiegel.de/international/europe/0,1518,514796,00.html>.
29. Maurice Blanchot, *The Writing of the Disaster,* trans. Ann Smock (Lincoln: Univ. of Nebraska Press, 1995), 11.

Part II

Corporate Media Culture and Public Memory

Introduction

Paul Haridakis

Columnist Walter Lippmann once claimed that the media are our windows to the world—particularly the world beyond our direct experience.[1] In the years since, media scholars have devoted considerable attention to ascertaining the media's influence on our opinions, perceptions, and behavior. They have disagreed, however, over the extent of the media's power in that process. Some claim that the media set the public agenda. As Cohen put it, the press "may not be successful in telling people what to think, but it is stunningly successful much of the time in telling its readers what to think *about*."[2] Others attribute even more power to the media, suggesting that not only do they tell audience members what to think about, but the way they frame stories also guides interpretation of the images and events portrayed.[3] Still others assert that the media are not particularly influential, and that audience members' individual differences mediate and generally limit the extent of media effects.[4] Although scholars disagree over whether the media shape perceived reality or simply reinforce preexisting attitudes and opinion, they generally agree that the media do tell stories and shape how they are presented.

The following four chapters, making up part two of this book, all undertake such inquiry and reflection on the media's presentation of significant U.S. cultural events. Although their authors don't draw specific conclusions about how media portrayals shaped understanding of events portrayed, they do remind us of the importance of examining the potential short-term and long-term effects of the media's portrayals of those events. Collectively, the authors ask us to consider how those portrayals may have shaped perceptions at the time, and how ongoing coverage of these past events may reshape or reinforce memories of them.

Together, the chapters focus on portrayals of war, protest, and other specific cultural events from the 1940s to the 1970s generally, and the May 4, 1970, tragedy at

Kent State University specifically. Their analyses of the media portrayals remind us that these were tumultuous times in the United States. It is important to reflect on the media images they review because dependence on the media is more intense during times of societal conflict.[5] Further, the more we rely on the media to help us interpret events covered, the greater the potential that this coverage can shape our perceptions of reality. In different ways—sometimes explicitly and sometimes implicitly—all of the chapters in this section consider the role of the media in shaping our perceptions.

The chapters provide readers with a context for learning about or remembering the events portrayed and an opportunity to reflect on them and elaborate on them—and to consider the possibility that our views and experiences are inextricably intertwined with such media portrayals. For most of us, in other words, our memories are mediated memories. Both for readers who did and for those who did not directly experience the events covered, these authors suggest that one cannot discount the influence of media portrayals that have become part of our recollections of these events. Their essays, then, help us to consider that the amalgamation of media images we have in our memories have become a part of our perceived reality of the events they portray. In hindsight, we need to consider the times the events occurred, the media's role in shaping our perceptions and memories of those times, the accuracy of the media portrayals, and the consequent accuracy of our memories.

Edward Morgan's essay, "Lost History/Lost Democracy: Media Culture and the 1960s," reviews what he refers to as the media culture of the 1960s. Rather than focusing on a particular media organization or medium, he suggests that in the headlights of the early twenty-first century, the 1960s are reflected in rather dichotomous media images today. At times, the 1960s are framed by corporate and political actors in terms of nostalgia. Often, however, the 1960s are framed by the media in a way that allows current corporate and political interests advancing a political shift to the right to blame the nation's present ills on the cultural events of that earlier decade. He refers to this latter media frame as a backlash to the 1960s that "trivializes the kind of empowering democratic awakening" of the era.

Although Morgan seems particularly concerned with the latter, each of these very different frames marginalizes 1960s culture. Whether the media are cast as playing a central role in the 1960s or as agents of social control returning us to "the hegemony of consumer-driven capitalism," Morgan emphasizes that the memory we have of the 1960s is itself a media product, produced strategically by powerful interests in the United States. His conclusions are supported by research suggesting not only that the media do play a role in setting the public agenda, but also that the media's own agendas are set by powerful social forces, including political leaders and the newsworthiness of events they cover.[6]

While Morgan raises the possibility that the 2008 election of Barack Obama may telegraph a shift in the political pendulum back to the left, his analysis simultaneously asks readers to consider that even this counter-backlash manipulates 1960s images and raises critical concerns about the honesty and integrity of the media's historical picture of that era and those developing that picture.

Devan Bissonette takes a different approach in his analysis of media images in his essay, "Visualizing the Limits of Democracy in the Silence of the Cold War: The Photography of *Life* Magazine and the Unraveling of the American Century." Rather than dealing with media culture generally, Bissonette focuses on a single media organization, *Life* magazine. Focusing on *Life*'s photographic images from the 1950s into the 1970s, he considers how editorial decisions were reflected in *Life*'s portrayal of critical historical events of the era. Bissonette highlights a trajectory of the magazine over those three decades from seeing itself as a purveyor of the "American Century" to viewing itself as a questioner of such an idealized vision of America. Bissonette suggests *Life* used its pages to raise those questions and present "alternative ideologies."

Given the shock of events during the period being examined—events such as the violence and conflict surrounding the civil rights movement, demonstrations over the Vietnam War, and other social protests—*Life*'s staff, according to Bissonette, came to question "the nation's morality and intellectual prowess." He suggests that *Life* magazine's critical photographic portrayals of government actors emerged only when the editors felt those actions fell outside societal norms (e.g., the use of intimidation and the denial of citizens' lawful rights). At the same time, he suggests that the magazine was equally critical of those challenging authority when their actions likewise fell outside acceptable societal norms (such as their use of violence), arguing that the magazine's social justice frame led it to cast a negative eye on those questioning American authority in a violent rather than a nonviolent manner.

The message with which Bissonette leaves the reader is that *Life*'s progression through the decades, like that of many of its readers, was a journey of social conscience that led it to become a supporter of social justice. He concludes by asserting that "*Life,* through its photographs, came to capture the failures of American democracy. . . . If the price of consensus was silence and violence, *Life* was ready to encourage a new style of unity that was explicitly open to those who respectfully questioned democracy's shortcomings and sought solutions to reinvigorate the national promise."

Like Bissonette, Janet Leach and Mitch McKenney focus their attention on a single media organization, the *Akron Beacon Journal.* In their essay, "'Of Loss and Learning': How Anniversary Coverage Affects Understanding of May 4, 1970," they focus specifically on a single issue of that newspaper, the thirtieth commemoration of the May 4, 1970, shootings at Kent State University. Like Morgan, they offer an analysis of a contemporary media portrayal of a historical event. Unlike both Morgan and Bissonette, however, Leach and McKenney do not suggest a subjective media agenda or a predetermined media orientation or reinterpretation of history.

According to their analysis, the newspaper's editorial and journalistic decisions were directed toward objectivity and reflected a conscious decision not to take a position on what happened at Kent State in May 1970. The editors instead wanted to educate readers and put the Kent State events into context. They explain the editorial process and decision making that went into a conscious attempt at objectivity, as in the assignment of journalists who were either born after 1970 or were too young to have firsthand knowledge of the events portrayed. But they also assert that the reporters "knew it would be a risk if their work contradicted the existing paradigm surrounding the shootings."

Whereas Bissonette discusses the editorial decisions and philosophy of a media organization over decades, Leach and McKenney focus on the editorial processes pertaining to a single issue. This is not to suggest that the latter study is less important than the former. As they assert, a single issue's "anniversary coverage serves as a lens through which to examine the past" and helps readers "reevaluate their impressions and understanding of important historic events." Interestingly, like Bissonnette's assertion that the staff of *Life* magazine was influenced by its coverage of historic events, Leach and McKenney note that the anniversary coverage of Kent State also changed the *Beacon Journal*'s reporters "personally and professionally."

Daniel Miller and Suzanne Clark's chapter, "Wars on Trial in Three Landmark Documentary Films: *Night and Fog, Hearts and Minds,* and *Taxi to the Dark Side*," returns us from an analysis of objective reporting to assessment of conscious media attempts at taking a position. They assess three documentary films that cover three different wars: *Night and Fog* (1955), covering World War II; *Hearts and Minds* (1975), covering the Vietnam War; and *Taxi to the Dark Side* (2007), covering the war in Afghanistan. Assessing the images presented in those films, they explain how three different filmmakers cast a critical eye on wartime events—specifically human rights abuses—that occurred during those wars. The films reviewed documented war atrocities, but also are a stark reminder that such abuses still occur. The social commentary in the films analyzed by Miller and Clark didn't challenge the government's authority to wage war or the potential necessity of war. Rather, it specifically challenged wartime actions that exceeded the bounds of moral acceptability, such as the circumvention of human rights by means of abuse, torture, and more extreme crimes against humanity.

While Bissonette suggests *Life* magazine came to critically evaluate government injustice during the tumult of the 1950s through the 1970s, Miller and Clark discuss how filmmakers questioned not just authority but also the inaction of ordinary citizens, who were perhaps complacent during the perpetration of abuses by those in authority. Miller and Clark show us how the media can be more than mere purveyors of social justice, as referenced by Bissonette, by reflecting social conscience. That is, the media can lead us to question not merely our nation's actions but also our own action (or inaction) as members of a nation.

In this context, it is interesting for the reader to look at these essays in cross-section, examining their analyses of media treatments at the point of intersection when the media either take a position or do not take a position in their portrayals of groups engaged in societal conflict—specifically powerful societal interests and those who challenge them.[7] That point of intersection is most pronounced during contentious times—and the times examined in these essays were tumultuous.

Although the authors of the chapters in part two leave their readers to ponder the extent of the long-term impact of the media portrayals discussed, they do remind them that, as Morgan says, "the wider public typically encounters both protest and the target of protest through the visual and interpretive filters of the media." Our memories of events are largely mediated ones. This is particularly true for events for which we have no direct personal experience—and that accounts for most of history.

In recollecting past events, the authors of these essays leave us with a more implicit, but no less important consideration: although we see events as framed by the media, we also interpret them through our own social and psychological filters. Therefore, although media portrayals can be lauded or criticized, the long-term effects of the events they portray may be attributable as much to the audience as to the media.

Perhaps we give the media too much credit for change or stability. Our failure to engage in civic life may be attributable to our own malaise rather than to the media's encouragement of such passivity. If we think of the 1960s with nostalgia rather than remembering the social upheaval, perhaps it is because that is the recollection we choose rather than the recollection forced on us by the media. If we acquiesce to such developments as free speech zones,[8] a lack of universal health care for all citizens or of social support for those who are less fortunate, military control of media coverage, electronic surveillance, USA PATRIOT Act searches of library patron reading materials, and the reemergence of corporate monopolization and of the deregulation that encourages it, perhaps it is because we choose not to see the blemishes of our society that Bissonette references. Perhaps we refuse to accept any blame for those blemishes, as the films reviewed by Miller and Clark emphasize. Perhaps we simply want to blame past decades for them, as Morgan stresses.

If we do not accept blame for societal flaws or call for beneficial social change, it may be because we neither are nor wish to be any more socially conscious than we were when fear drove us to acquiesce to the internment of Japanese Americans during World War II, the activities of the House Un-American Activities Committee in the 1950s, and the failure of our justice system to push for convictions of those responsible for the murder of innocent students at Kent State University in 1970.

In short, the essays in this section suggest that while we may have lived through tumultuous times, they did not create tumultuous change. That possibility does not diminish the scholarly debate that these essays spur, however. We always need to be aware of the influence media have on us, especially on our views of important political and cultural events. We can learn from revisiting media images such as those examined in these essays. As we learn, reflect, and remember, perhaps we will find ways to use the media to help remedy the social ills that exist today, rather than blaming the media for them. Then we may not come to marginalize the fight for civil liberties as the same old 1960s complaints, or regard protests against war as anti-American, or demean ideals such as peace and love as naïve and silly notions of youth angst.

If we are to continue to learn from past mistakes, we need to recognize that improving society requires assessing what we did right and what we did wrong. It requires us to correct misinterpretations—whether media induced or otherwise. Learning, reflecting, remembering, and, at times, revising history are an important exercise in the attempt to make ourselves and our society better. That is the goal of these chapters. Indeed, it is the goal of this book and of the symposium that spawned it.

Notes

1. Walter Lippmann, *Public Opinion* (New York: Macmillan, 1922).
2. Bernard C. Cohen, *The Press and Foreign Policy* (Princeton, N.J.: Princeton Univ. Press, 1963), 13.
3. David Tewksbury and Dietram A. Scheufele, "News Framing Theory and Research," in *Media Effects: Advances in Theory and Research,* ed. Jennings Bryant and Mary Beth Oliver, 17–33 (New York: Routledge, 2009).
4. Joseph T. Klapper, *The Effects of Mass Communication* (New York: Free Press, 1960).
5. Wilson Lowrey, "Media Dependency During a Large-Scale Social Disruption: The Case of September 11," *Mass Communication and Society* 7 (2004): 339–57.
6. Maxwell McCombs and Amy Reynolds, "How News Shapes Our Civic Agenda," in Bryant and Oliver, *Media Effects,* 1–16.
7. See, for example, Michael P. Boyle et al., "Newspapers and Protest: An Examination of Protest Coverage from 1960 to 1999," *Journalism and Mass Communication Quarterly* 82 (2005): 638–53; and Frank E. Dardis, "Marginalization Devices in U.S. Press Coverage of Iraq War Protest: A Content Analysis," *Mass Communication and Society* 9 (2006): 117–35.
8. Paul Haridakis and Amber Ferris, "The Use of 'Speech Zones' to Control Public Discourse in Twenty-First-Century America," in *The Impact of 9/11 and the New Legal Landscape: The Day that Changed Everything?* ed. Mathew J. Morgan, 39–56 (New York: Palgrave Macmillan, 2009).

Visualizing the Limits of Democracy in the Silence of the Cold War

The Photography of *Life* Magazine and the Unraveling of the American Century

Devan Bissonette

On the eve of World War II, Henry Luce, the editor-in-chief of *Life* magazine, published an article laying out his dream for "the American Century."[1] He believed that if American democracy became a model for others, all the world's peoples could be lifted "from the level of the beast to . . . a little lower than the angels."[2] Americans embraced his ideological call-to-arms, steeped in Western traditions, capitalist works, and Christian goals, a call that permeated *Life*'s pages in the months after Pearl Harbor, making it the most popular magazine in the United States by the war's end.[3] With Luce's eager approval, *Life* transformed itself into the showroom for the wonders of the American Century in the postwar world. Yet in seeing and showing the nation's triumphs and tragedies as it climbed toward its manifest destiny, *Life* visualized practices of exclusion and intimidation. Evidence of factional conflict proved that some Americans were being denied their lawful, democratic rights, tearing *Life*'s image of a contented American people. As it became clear that the price of the American Century was silence and violence, *Life* reconsidered the benefits of a public blindly unified behind what looked like the hollow promise of the postwar world and began to stand with responsible dissent, recognizing that the establishment was, at times, denying instead of defending democratic virtues.

The end of the Second World War ushered in what historian Lizabeth Cohen calls the "Consumers' Republic."[4] The public, less than a decade removed from the Great Depression, was inundated by messages preaching the importance of indulging one's personal wants in the marketplace for both personal enjoyment and the good of the national economy. This emphasis on consumerism was an ideal foundation from which to sell Luce's American Century. Sales pitches for state-of-the-art goods and services, ready-made for the busy lives of its middle-class readers, surrounded *Life*'s articles.[5] It was a trumpeting of mass culture on a scale no magazine had been able to do before. This idealized vision, however, came with a hefty price. In making America appear the wealthy, moral, and capitalist melting pot advertisers desired, *Life* glossed over a multitude of troubles hidden beneath the veneer of tranquil affluence. This blind spot was facilitated by the birth of a truly popular and inclusive mass culture, based on the ethic of mass production and consumption. Moreover, the climate created by the cold war allowed mainstream media outlets to demand consensus—or silence—from the citizenry, all in the name of national security.[6] If *Life*'s readers looked closely, they might have noticed that the promise of prosperity lining the magazine's pages was visibly limited by race and framed by explicit gender and class roles.

Life's ability (with a readership encompassing about one-quarter of the population) to blanket the nation with stories reflective of an imagined consensus was essential in visualizing a nation united in common purpose.[7] However, this same ability guaranteed that if social unrest became sufficiently widespread to require regular reporting, the constructedness of *Life*'s vision would be exposed as wishful thinking, or, worse, willful misrepresentation. This was precisely what happened in the later 1950s. Demographic shifts, brought about by the burgeoning of new industries, the rise of the civil rights movement, and the postwar baby boom, allowed alternative ideologies to gain an audience, particularly among America's youth. Since these changes held too much potential for dramatic copy to be ignored, *Life* magazine and other media that had cultivated national unity began, through their weekly reporting, to expose social injustices.[8] *Life*'s efforts to explain away America's problems, however, only kept them in the public's mind.

From their lofty perches in New York City, *Life*'s editors, although not necessarily its subordinate writers, refused to acknowledge the very real shortcomings of cold war America, a willful omission that made it hard to sustain the magazine's vision of America's democracy as the ideal model of government for all the world's people to follow. This helps explain the widespread shock that emerged in the magazine's pages after the forced integration of Little Rock High School in Arkansas and the launch of the Soviet Sputnik satellite in the fall of 1957.[9] Like *Life*'s staff, many Americans were suddenly questioning the nation's morality and intellectual prowess. This included Henry Luce. These concerns pushed him to change *Life*'s tone toward America's age of affluence, laying the groundwork for the death of the American Century. After reminding staff to emphasize Soviet weaknesses and the morality of the *Brown v. Board of Education* decision that made school integration a reality, Luce asked if editors might consider, and here Luce included himself, why they had been too reticent to discuss "what's wrong with . . . Americans." Maybe, he thought, their collective silence had precipitated the sudden crisis of the American spirit.[10]

Though *Life* had traditionally minimized the frequency of racial confrontations across the South, by the start of the 1960s the threat these posed to domestic peace had caught the magazine's attention. With ample evidence in the news that black Americans were being denied their lawful rights, *Life* focused coverage on the morality of those who fought for equal rights.[11] The Rev. Martin Luther King Jr. was one African American leader who frequently found himself in *Life*'s spotlight. As King was being led to an Atlanta jail on dubious charges during the first week of November 1960, *Life* did more than portray him as a sympathetic victim; as a reward for King's refusal to act out despite his unjust arrest, *Life* framed him as a martyr. Its lead photo drove home this theme of self-sacrifice, presenting King with his head bowed low and a melancholy look in his eyes as he willingly, if grudgingly, accepted his punishment for the greater good. King was treated as a man not all that dissimilar from Christ on his way to the Crucifixion. As it so often did in praise of great men, *Life* ended its piece with a shot of King's family, reminding its audience that the minister was, like the magazine's middle-class readers, a family man.[12]

Life's tolerance for those who, like King, were victimized by democracy's failed promises proved absent when their own behavior, in its view, provoked violence.[13] When, in 1961, efforts to desegregate interstate buses and segregated bus stations across the South through integrated Freedom Rides erupted into hostility, the magazine accused the riders of "deliberately and knowingly asking for trouble." Pictorially, readers encountered a far more troubling message about the means necessary to ensure that equal rights were a reality for all Americans. In one image, National Guardsmen stand at the ready in the aisle of the busload of Freedom Riders, making it appear that minority rights would only come at the point of a soldier's bayonet.

Paul Schuzter, Untitled (1961), from "Asking for Trouble and Getting It," *Life*, June 2, 1961, 46–47. Photograph copyright Time, Inc.

The look on the face of one seated protester left viewers wondering if these troops were really interested in the undertaking.[14]

When the University of Mississippi erupted into violence over the admission of African American student James Meredith in October 1962, *Life*'s article created the impression that Confederate soldiers and Yankee marshals had turned the campus into a Civil War battlefield. Its worst venom was unleashed against the bigoted Mississippians whose raucous behavior, it concluded, had brought shame on "their state and their nation."[15] The following May, the citizens of Birmingham, Alabama, drew equal ire from *Life* for forcing the nation to glimpse just how far some white Americans were willing to go to reinforce the racial status quo. As its story opened, firemen lunged at defenseless black protesters with a "battering ram" of water. The dramatic, two-page image did what other media refused, making the moral high ground obvious from the outset. *Life* proudly explained that its pictures were "frightening because of the brutal methods being used by white policemen in Birmingham . . . [and] because the Negro strategy of 'nonviolent direct action' invites that very brutality—and welcomes it as a way to promote the Negroes' cause, which, under the law, is right."[16] The magazine used its narrative powers to evoke sympathy in the hearts and minds of its readers with the protesters—but not with their tactics. As never before, police became the villains in a *Life* story. Even an image, later in the article, of a black minister imploring protesters to disperse showed a police officer lurking in the background, suggesting that the reverend's words were spoken under duress.[17] If the forces of law and order were aligning against those who asked only to have their lawful rights protected, what did this say about the underlying democratic ideals at the core of the American Century?

Life's search for the moral citizenry necessary to usher in the American Century was dealt another blow in the summer of 1964, when the shooting of a black youth, James Powell, by a white police officer in Harlem, New York, set off several days of rioting there. The incident became a model for large-scale urban racial violence throughout the 1960s and the most disturbing example to that point that access to the benefits of the consumer's republic was limited by the color of one's skin.[18] "What [set] the New York riots apart," said *Life* on July 31, was "the blind desperation of the rioters. They have gone—or as they feel, been driven—beyond reason." An image later in the piece of nightstick-wielding policemen menacing African Americans gave some credence to the sentiment expressed by Harlem's residents that they were driven to retaliate. The image of an African American girl crying over her classmate Powell's death added a rather troubling postscript to the article about the smoldering community. The caption noted her angry cry to police moments after the shooting: "Come on, shoot another nigger!"[19] Readers were left all but certain that confrontations like this would grow commonplace, and, at least in its pictures, *Life*'s coverage gave ample evidence that the black community was justified in feeling pushed "beyond reason."[20]

A March 1965 civil rights protest in Selma, Alabama, provided another sign that equality had distinct limits. A police blockade set up to stop a planned march turned into a violent attack when officers set on the peaceable group in a frenzy. *Life*'s photographers made the cruelty of the police impossible to miss.[21] With a groundswell of fresh sympathizers materializing in the aftermath and Martin Luther King Jr. in town to help lead a second march, all eyes were focused on the South. Despite an agreement with officials designed to ensure peace, officers again forced marchers to turn back. Understanding that the retreat weakened King's credibility in the civil rights movement and therefore support for nonviolence, *Life* leapt to his defense later in the issue.[22] With a policeman pictured in the foreground of one image from the second march, his billy club at the ready, there was ample reason to think marchers were certain to be beaten by police had King not backed down.[23] *Life*'s already serious concerns over the nation's ability to repair the gaping wounds to its democratic façade were growing more visible by the week. No matter what the magazine said, the American Century was looking more and more like a dangerous mix of racial and class warfare.

Only months later, the Watts riot in California proved that *Life*'s passion for social justice had begun to interfere with its narrative of national consensus, as it had begun to appear that unity required systemic inequality. *Life* pictured turmoil on the cover of its August 27, 1965, issue, but portrayed a black citizen of Watts as a victim, not a perpetrator, discarding the chance to treat the incident simply as a race riot. Color photographs of National Guardsmen, bayonets fixed and ready for action, drew an eerie parallel between events at Watts, past civil rights disturbances, and Vietnam. While *Life* did not speak directly of class conflict, including violence aimed at black businesses, it did admit that the residents of Watts "were manhandled by cops all through the riots."[24] The magazine was showing an uncharacteristic uncertainty in its depiction of the combustible mix of racial and class animosities bubbling in cities across America, for the very people expected to keep the peace were pictured encouraging disorder.[25]

In July 1967, Newark, New Jersey, became the next flashpoint for the deteriorating state of racial equality in America. There, simmering tensions between white and black citizens exploded after a white policeman arrested a black taxi driver. Cries of brutality quickly escalated into violence. Readers could be excused if they thought they were looking at a typical week's coverage of Vietnam, for, as with *Life*'s coverage of the Watts riots, the imagery was similar save for the black faces. "The Newark riot really started in Watts," claimed *Life* columnist Shana Alexander. It "was the turning point, a moment as significant in the long agony of American Negro history as John Brown's raid on Harpers Ferry."[26] *Life* uneasily described the vicious tactics used by police against looters, graphically depicting how innocent victims (like a young boy shot by a police officer, who then casually walked by his bleeding victim) were the real tragedy of Newark. As it had done after the Watts riot, the magazine cautiously pointed to one of the perpetrators, admitting that the "trigger-happiness of the police . . . did not enhance the reputation" of local authorities, a behavior made all the more perplexing since "so few police and Guardsmen were hit by [the] snipers" who supposedly set them off.[27] *Life* dared not say it plainly, but, as the black community told reporters, rumors of snipers seemed designed to encourage looting—and reprisals—to continue unabated.[28] It was easy for readers to conclude, from the language and photographs in *Life*'s article—including the photographs of the bleeding child and indifferent police officer—that an imminent threat to their safety was not the primary motivation for the police's trigger-happy actions.

The oversimplified desire of Luce and his editors to cast liberty and democracy, under the guise of the American Century, as inalienable American rights to be waved in the face of the Soviet Union, was failing, but not simply because of racial strife. Evidence of how the student movement would challenge the magazine's passion for the American Century surfaced in May 1960, after a protest against a House Un-American Activities Committee (HUAC) hearing in San Francisco.[29] In *Life*'s view, youthful activists senselessly "rushed police" who then "broke out hoses. When 400 cops tried to drag them away a riot ensued—tooth and nail *vs.* nightstick."[30] The accompanying photograph offered a far different story. In it, water cannons battered defenseless students with high-powered streams. There was no sign of rioting—from the protesters at least.[31] How could students involved in this and similar protests not distrust the media, let alone the government who turned its hoses on them when they dared exercise their constitutional right to free speech?

The young's distaste for America's moral and political hypocrisy soon spilled into street protest, prompting *Life* to give their "seasonal rite of rioting" a new visual emphasis.[32] As a National Guardsman with bayonet fixed stood among a smiling group of kids, *Life*'s flippant attitude toward the latter's behavior evaporated. The young were now recognized as a very real threat to order, even if they had a point. Just how much *Life*'s attitude toward this generation was fluctuating became clear in its coverage of events in Berkeley, California, in December 1964. "Panty Raids? No! Tough Campus Revolt," it concluded, had infected Berkeley, where students were "carrying on in a way that ma[de] panty raids look decorous."[33] The young had launched something more than a challenge to the establishment; they had forced a confrontation with its failures. It was the last thing a consensus-minded magazine wanted to report. Later in the article, *Life* rightly found a far-reaching meaning behind the passion of the Free Speech Movement (FSM) for protest, speaking of "a new breed of student leader" emerging from the tumult, noting that such leaders were eager to adapt the tools of civil disobedience they had learned in the South to venues across the country.[34] Despite such coverage, *Life*'s editors so far saw the FSM as only a minimal tremor in the status quo, regarding deteriorating race relations as a far more immediate threat to President Lyndon Johnson's Great Society than the students' critique of liberalism. That was about to change.

Hoping to draw fresh readers to the magazine as a mixture of declining advertisements and rising print costs added to *Life*'s troubles in the 1960s, its editors printed increasingly spectacular pictures of confrontations between ostensibly legitimate authority figures and civilians.[35] Its increasingly moderate tone toward the social crises of the decade was largely attributable to the death of Henry Luce early in 1967.[36] Hedley Donovan, Luce's successor, was now able to make good on his pledge to employees that the magazines of Time, Inc., would strive to abandon their frequent conservative bent. For readers who had gorged themselves on the magazine's celebration of all that made the nation great, *Life* seemed to be losing sight of "what *Life* almost alone could celebrate," in the words of former managing editor Ed Thompson, namely, "the satisfactions of normal living." Its passion for the American Century was also growing cold as Donovan saw to it that democracy, prized as it remained by his magazines, was no longer off-limits for criticism.[37] Increasingly, the dark side of American society filled *Life*'s pages. Nevertheless, it stubbornly clung to the belief that brighter days lay ahead. That, too, was about to change.

Thanks to Donovan's prodding and the course of the news, *Life* in 1968 rethought the hypocrisy behind its textual narrative of American exceptionalism and its visual storyline of exclusion and intimidation. The process began on May 10, when, in its study of a student takeover at Columbia University, *Life* gave members of the student generation a rare chance to present their side of the story in a mainstream magazine. Its familiar antidisruption narrative was lost amidst the words of six Columbia students.[38] Any hope that a responsive political system would quell these institutional troubles was dashed when the Democratic National Convention erupted into violence. Photos of defenseless protesters beaten and bloodied by Chicago's finest exposed a democracy *Life* had once exulted as a beacon of hope for oppressed peoples around the world as one whose morality and passion for democracy was limited by race, class, gender, and age.[39] The young, it gloomily concluded months later, "and the future, are saddled with the same fallible human instincts and impulses" of their elders, "which they demonstrate daily by the very cunning and violence of their assaults on the established, if lamentable, order of things."[40] It was hardly proof that the enlightened, moral republic at the heart of the American Century had ever existed.

No matter what degree of sympathy *Life* had with youths who protested the nation's ills, it was tempered by fear that their cries could invite anarchy; as the violence spread to Cornell's campus in late April 1969, it announced the event with the grim headline, "The Guns Come to Cornell." Images of well-armed and defiant-looking black men spoke to the fear of black power latent in the crisis that was growing nationally. The unspoken linkage between militancy and blackness revealed by its imagery troubled the magazine greatly. While attacking the presence of weapons, *Life* noted both that they were unloaded and that, as the offending students claimed, their white counterparts already had guns on campus.[41] By giving the students' side of the story, *Life* pointed to the underlying social problems behind the crisis. It did something similar in its coverage of the University of California, Berkeley, on May 30, where students, tired of waiting for university officials to act on their request to turn an empty, weed-invested lot into a park, started the transformation themselves. Civic responsibility once again brought out the National Guard and resulted in needless violence. *Life*'s imagery of a campus brimming with guardsmen made it hard to dispute those who considered the establishment part of the problem.[42]

Racial strife, though fading from *Life*'s pages (and Richard Nixon's agenda) at the start of the new decade, received one last airing out from African American photographer Gordon Parks. As one of the few newsworkers trusted by the black community, Parks captured images no other mainstream reporter could: images of police confrontations from the perspective of the Black Panthers.[43] It was further evidence that many problems in America were skin deep. "To understand these kids," Parks explained, "you have to understand racism as a black man knows it. Their enemy *is* the police. And if you are part of that silent majority that wants the police to wipe them out, then you are the enemy too."[44] The white-dominated media, Parks could well have added, was one of those adversaries. Some hope for the future came from an unlikely source, Black Panther Bobby Seale. We fight for "the same [opportunities] the white man fights for," he told Parks. "A decent education for our children, good jobs, good housing. . . . In fact we want just about the same things Martin Luther King wanted."[45] The story was another example of how *Life*'s enthusiasm for American culture had become tempered by a critical eye, even while the magazine retained its long-held commitment to consensus and domestic peace, albeit one modified from its earlier idealistic view to be more expressly moral and democratic.

Donovan, whose discomfort with the direction Richard Nixon's administration was taking on social issues had grown palpable by the start of the 1970s, had begun using *Life*'s pages to question the president's behavior toward his critics. This task was facilitated by the elevation of Ralph Graves to *Life*'s managing editorship, replacing the conservative and patriotic George Hunt. The new team's most powerful salvo occurred after Nixon's decision to escalate the Vietnam War into Cambodia in the spring of 1970 had provoked a new wave of campus protests in response. At Kent State University in Ohio, the magazine's worst fears came true when members of the Ohio National Guard killed four students during an antiwar protest. On its May 15 cover, in stark yellow lettering superimposed on the black-and-white photograph of a wounded student, his peers rendering aid, *Life* addressed the issue with the headline

"Tragedy at Kent." The magazine began by blaming Nixon for making the decision to invade Cambodia in isolation and against advice and for refusing to mend the nation's wounds.[46] However, it also sought to communicate a more fundamental concern to its readers about human life. Lest its images give the wrong impression, *Life* used dramatic language to paint a picture of "embattled Guardsmen [who] . . . tried to bluff the students into submission by aiming their rifles at them." The result, "before it ended, in senseless and brutal murder at point-blank range," was that "Kent State had become a symbol of the fearful hazards latent in dissent, and in the policies that cause it."[47] The act was not mere tragedy, *Life* said, but senseless murder. The photographic timeline of life and death that etched the memory of Kent State into the minds of readers was climaxed by a quote from Arthur Krause, whose daughter Allison had died that day. *Life* turned Krause's bitter questions into a headline—"'Is this dissent a crime? Is it a reason for killing?'"—making it appear that by borrowing Krause's words, *Life* was speaking as a surrogate parent to the nation. The photograph of a dead student below the headline was a silent but clear *no.*[48] These kids were innocent victims, it declared, and deserved far better than death at the hands of their government. In attacking its government and defending student protesters, *Life* went against the sympathies of many of its middle-American readers. It had no patience for Nixon's consensus, which, it appeared, required turning the other way when the government committed murder. While unity remained its goal, *Life* now sought to define it in its own new democratic language.

In subsequent months, *Life* latched its hopes for renewing America's democratic spirit to a series of calls to repair the national spirit and the passion, though not necessarily the specific ideology, behind the American Century. According to the June 19 issue of *Life,* the class of 1970 had one "last chance to sound the alarm one more time, to try to tell their parents, their teachers and their country just how bad things looked to them."[49] It was time, the magazine said, that they listened. A mock graveyard later in the article, a graveyard full of tombstones marking a generation's lost souls, spoke visually of the cost of ignoring their pleas once again. While *Life*'s editors accorded responsible dissenters ample respect, they were distracted by extremists and their penchant for dramatic copy, as when antiwar protests again came to Washington, D.C., in May 1970. Arresting demonstrators before they had a chance to protest was hardly a sign of enlightened democracy, yet *Life* shrugged at the internments: even though the arrests "showed more respect for practicality than for constitutional rights . . . they worked."[50] One *Life* reporter asked the D.C. police chief, Jerry Wilson, if he felt the mass arrests were unconstitutional. "That's a judgment I'll leave to the American people," he replied. Opposite his troubling words, *Life* placed a shot of officers walking past a cross left by antiwar protesters. It was a familiar type of image indicative of finality. Had dissent died on the cross thanks to armed policemen and an administration that preferred expediency to law?[51] Just as

Life had once derided Southerners who ignored federal law, it could not ignore the disregard for basic constitutional rights coming from the establishment.

Life's growing urgency to cure the malaise of the national spirit was not simply a product of its desire to fix the nation's problems. Thanks to a $17 million budget shortfall projected for 1973, management decided *Life*'s span must come to an end. That did not stop staff in the magazine's final issue from leaving its readers with hope that the wounds of recent years might yet heal and allow the nation to reunite under a banner of peace and understanding. At the issue's end, Ralph Graves spoke of the importance of *Life*'s nearly four-decade mission to see the world: "As a magazine, we tried to talk to you across all barriers and special interests. We didn't want to reach you as skiers, or teen-agers, or car-owners, or TV-watchers, or single women, or suburbanites, or inhabitants of New York City, or blacks, or whites. Instead, we wanted to talk to you as people, who share the common experience of humanity. I still believe that such talk is important to our country. I am sorry with all my heart that *Life* can no longer make that contribution."[52] In an odd commentary on the magazine, if not on the public's desire to forget a past whose call for unity currently seemed so out of place, the company's stock price rose six points after *Life*'s demise was made public.[53]

"A little of America belongs to every man and woman everywhere who has had faith in democracy and hope in a world of peace and justice," Henry Luce said as he concluded his call for the American Century. Each, he continued, must put their faith in leaders who embrace these ideals "to decide exactly where and when and how the American people shall take their stand at Armageddon."[54] As *Life* examined protest after protest that attacked the government's failure to guarantee democratic rights regardless of race and age, its absolute certainty in right and wrong eroded. Its photographs, which trivialized critics of American government for years, began to represent dissenters as legitimately oppressed instead of mere rabble-rousers. Long before most media admitted the limits of American citizenship, *Life*'s images revealed practices of exclusion and intimidation that proved Americans were being denied their lawful rights at home. Once the cornerstone of the postwar consensus and the American Century, *Life,* through its photographs, came to capture the failures of American democracy. Two narratives emerged from the chaos, one verbal and one visual. Not until 1968 did their realignment begin. If the price of consensus was silence and violence, *Life* was ready to encourage a new style of unity that was explicitly open to those who respectfully questioned democracy's shortcomings and sought solutions to reinvigorate the national promise. Once the champion of all things American, *Life,* by the start of the 1970s, had become far less hesitant to recognize that the establishment was, at times, the villain. Even in the face of death, however, *Life* never abandoned Henry Luce's faith in Americans, if they would only look at themselves in the mirror, blemishes and all, to right the wrongs of the past and to work toward making the democratic values the nation, if not the American Century, was founded on a reality for all citizens. Until then, Armageddon would have to wait.

Notes

1. In 1936, Henry Luce and several top employees prepared to launch *Life,* America's first national photojournalism magazine. Its prospectus mixed Luce's belief in the triumph of the American spirit, Christian morality, and mankind's ability to progress with the public's desire for entertainment, escape, and hope Robert T. Elson, *Time Inc.: The Intimate History of a Publishing Enterprise, 1923–1941,* vol. 1, ed. Duncan Norton-Taylor (New York: Atheneum, 1968), 277–79; Otha B. Spencer, "Twenty Years of *Life:* A Study of Time, Inc.'s Picture Magazine and Its Contributions to Photojournalism" (Ph.D. dissertation, University of Missouri, 1958), 189.
2. Henry R. Luce, *The Ideas of Henry Luce,* ed. John Jessup (New York: Atheneum, 1969), 104.
3. Thanks to the dramatic and emotional photography *Life* printed during World War II, the magazine's skyrocketing audience made it among the most powerful opinion-makers in the country. *Life* had found a visual language capable of expressing humanity's successes and failures by emphasizing and personalizing the emotions of the moment. James L. Baughman, *Henry R. Luce and the Rise of the American News Media* (Boston, Mass.: Twayne Publishers, 1987), 118; Elson, *Time Inc.* vol. 1, 384, 404–6, 461–67, 480–81; W. A. Swanberg, *Luce and His Empire* (New York: Charles Scribner's Sons, 1972), 175; Ralph G. Martin, *Henry and Clare: An Intimate Portrait of the Luces* (New York: G. P. Putnam's Sons, 1991), 202; notes on George Frazier's *It's About* Time, box 17, folder, "Luce: Book Research (2)," W. A. Swanberg Papers, Rare Books and Manuscript Library, Columbia University, New York, N.Y. See also Wendy Kozol, Life*'s America: Family and Nation in Postwar Photojournalism* (Philadelphia, Pa.: Temple Univ. Press, 1994).
4. Lizabeth Cohen, *A Consumers' Republic: The Politics of Mass Consumption in Postwar America* (New York: Vintage Books, 2003), 121, 195.
5. James L. Baughman, "Who Read *Life?* The Circulation of America's Favorite Magazine," in *Looking at* Life *Magazine,* ed. Erika Doss (Washington, D.C.: Smithsonian Institution Press, 2001), 46; Theodore Peterson, *Magazines in the Twentieth Century* (Urbana: Univ. of Illinois Press, 1964), 36, 41, 99–101; David E. Carter, "The Changing Face of *Life*'s Advertisements, 1950–66," *Journalism Quarterly* 46, no. 1 (1969): 90–91; Andrew Heiskell with Ralph Graves, *Outsider, Insider: An Unlikely Success Story* (New York: Marian-Darien Press, 1998), 58.
6. David Halberstam, *The Fifties* (New York: Villard Books, 1993), 132–34; David Abrahamson, *Magazine-Made America: The Cultural Transformation of the Postwar Periodical* (Cresskill, N.J.: Hampton Press, 1996), 38; and Kozol, Life*'s America,* 79.
7. "The Five Billionth Copy of *Life,*" *Life,* July 21, 1958, 92–93; "*Life* in the '60s," *Time,* May 19, 1959, 55.
8. Alan Nadel, *Containment Culture: American Narratives, Postmodernism, and the Atomic Age* (Durham, N.C.: Duke Univ. Press, 1995), 4; Cohen, *A Consumer's Republic,* 73; Abrahamson, *Magazine-Made America,* 39.

9. While most writers accepted the slanting of the news as part of the cost of working for the company, some more liberal writers learned subtle ways of putting in their own opinions despite the best efforts of their editors. Swanberg, *Luce and His Empire,* 188.
10. Robert T. Elson, *The World of Time Inc: The Intimate History of a Publishing Enterprise, 1941–1960,* vol. 2, ed. Duncan Norton-Taylor (New York: Atheneum, 1973), 409–10; Halberstam, *The Fifties,* 528; "Soviet Satellite Sends U.S. into a Tizzy," *Life,* Oct. 14, 1957, 34–37; Martin, *Henry and Clare,* 334.
11. Fred Powledge, *Free at Last? The Civil Rights Movement and the People Who Made It* (New York: HarperPerennial, 1991), 245; Maurice Isserman and Michael Kazin, *America Divided: The Civil War of the 1960s* (New York: Oxford Univ. Press, 2000), 61
12. "Martyr of the Sit-Ins," *Life,* Nov. 7, 1960, 123–34.
13. Powledge, *Free at Last?* 257–64; Harvard Sitkoff, *The Struggle for Black Equality,* rev. ed. (New York: Hill and Wang, 1993), 93–96; Mary L. Dudziak, *Cold War Civil Rights: Race and the Image of American Democracy* (Princeton, N.J.: Princeton Univ. Press, 2000), 159.
14. "Asking for Trouble and Getting It: The Ride for Rights," *Life,* June 2, 1961, 46–55.
15. "Let Old Glory Wave Alone over Ole Miss" (editorial), and Story of the Week "On the Mississippi Campus, the Bitter Siege of Violence," "Battlefield: Where the Law Won," and "Now, the Lonely Decision for Right or for Wrong," by Lillian Smith, all in *Life,* Oct. 12, 1962, 6, 32–44.
16. "They Fight a Fire That Won't Go Out," *Life,* May 17, 1963, 26–36.
17. Reporter Hugh Sidey credited the "visual impact" of the story with changing the country's attitude toward civil rights. Powledge, *Free at Last?* 513–14; John Kaplan, "The *Life* Magazine Civil Rights Photography of Charles Moore, 1958–1965," *Journalism History* 24, no. 4 (Winter 1999): 134.
18. Powledge, *Free at Last?* 591–92.
19. "Harlem's 'Long Hot Summer' Begins," *Life,* July 31, 1964, 14–23.
20. Richard Lentz, *Symbols, the News Magazines, and Martin Luther King* (Baton Rouge: Louisiana State Univ. Press, 1990), 130.
21. "Selma: Beatings Start the Savage Season," *Life,* Mar. 19, 1965, 30–37.
22. Isserman and Kazin, *America Divided,* 140–141; Sitkoff, *The Struggle for Black Equality,* 176–79; Lentz, *Symbols,* 151–53.
23. "Selma: Beatings Start the Savage Season," *Life,* Mar. 19, 1965, 30–37.
24. "Out of a Cauldron of Hate," *Life,* Aug. 27, 1965, 20–34.
25. Mark Hamilton Lytle, *America's Uncivil Wars: The Sixties Era from Elvis to the Fall of Richard Nixon* (New York: Oxford Univ. Press, 2006), 189–90; Isserman and Kazin, *America Divided,* 145; John Loengard, *Life Photographers: What They Saw* (New York: Little, Brown, and Co., 1998), 402–3.
26. Shana Alexander, "The Feminine Eye," *Life,* July 28, 1967, 14B.
27. Russell Sackett, "Revolt in the Newark Ghetto," *Life,* July 28, 1967, 16–28A.
28. Lytle, *America's Uncivil Wars,* 232.
29. Jo Freeman, *At Berkeley in the Sixties: The Education of an Activist, 1961–1965* (Indianapolis: Indiana Univ. Press, 2004), 40–41.
30. "Hose vs. Young Rioters," *Life,* May 23, 1960, 52–53.
31. "Letters to the Editor," *Life,* June 13, 1960, 17; Lytle, *America's Uncivil Wars,* 83.

32. "Teen-agers' Seasonal Rite of Rioting," *Life,* Sept. 18, 1964, 50.
33. "Panty Raids? No! Tough Campus Revolt," *Life,* Dec. 18, 1964, 46A–46B.
34. Lytle, *America's Uncivil Wars,* 169–73; Freeman, *At Berkeley in the Sixties,* 209–13.
35. For more on this escalation of imagery, see Devan Bissonette, "Between Silence and Self-Interest: *Time, Life,* and the Unsilent Generation's Coming-of-Age," *Journalism History* 35, no. 2 (Summer 2009): 62–71.
36. Curtis Prendergast with Geoffery Colvin, *The World of Time Inc: The Intimate History of a Changing Enterprise, 1961–1980,* ed. Robar Lubar (New York: Atheneum, 1986), 276; Maitland Edey with Constance Sullivan, *Great Photographic Essays from* Life (Boston, Mass.: New York Graphic Society, 1978), 17; Hedley Donovan, *Right Places, Right Times: Forty Years in Journalism, Not Counting My Paper Route* (New York: Henry Holt and Co., 1989), 267.
37. Edward K. Thompson, *A Love Affair with* Life *and* Smithsonian (Columbia: Univ. of Missouri Press, 1995), 256.
38. "Table of Contents," and "Mutiny at a Great University," both in *Life,* May 10, 1968, 3, 36–49; Todd Gitlin, *The Sixties: Years of Hope, Days of Rage* (New York: Bantam Books, 1987), 307–8.
39. "The Host and the Honored Guest at the . . . 1968 Democratic Convulsion," *Life,* Sept. 6, 1968, 18–32A.
40. Paul O'Neil, "Mired and Unfettered," *Life,* Jan. 10, 1969, 65–72.
41. Richard Reeves, *President Nixon: Alone in the White House* (New York: Simon and Schuster, 2001), 73–74, 78; "The Guns Come to Cornell," *Life,* May 2, 1969, 20–27; Lytle, *America's Uncivil Wars,* 343–44.
42. "Homecoming Day for the National Guard at Berkeley," *Life,* May 30, 1969, 42–43.
43. Gordon Parks, *Voices in the Mirror: An Autobiography* (New York: Doubleday, 1990), 284.
44. Parks called Cleaver "the most uncompromising individual I had ever met." Gordon Parks, "Black Panthers: The Hard Edge of Confrontation," *Life,* Feb. 6, 1970, 23–25.
45. Ibid., 24–25.
46. Cover, "Table of Contents," and "Nixon in a Crisis of Leadership," all in *Life,* May 15, 1970, 3, 28–29.
47. "Kent State: Four Deaths at Noon," *Life,* May 15, 1970, 30–37.
48. Ibid., 34–35.
49. "'70 Stages Its Last Confrontation," *Life,* June 19, 1970, 20–29.
50. "Table of Contents," Hugh Sidey, "The Presidency," and "The Day Washington Did Not Shut Down," all in *Life,* May 14, 1971, 3, 4, 30–39.
51. Reeves, *President Nixon,* 318–20.
52. Ralph Graves, "With Pride and Affection," *Life,* Dec. 29, 1972, 96.
53. Loudon Wainwright, *The Great American Magazine: An Inside History of* Life (New York: Alfred A. Knopf, 1986), 419; Donovan, *Right Places, Right Times,* 286.
54. Luce, *The Ideas of Henry Luce,* 104.

Lost History/Lost Democracy

Media Culture and the 1960s

EDWARD P. MORGAN

> The democratic ideal . . . is that the people are capable of and ought to be making their own history, that the making of history ought to be integrated with everyday life. . . . The reason that democracy persists as an ideal at all is that people at times have transcended their everyday lives in order to make history.
> —Richard Flacks

> [Advertising] makes all history mythical. . . . A people or class which is cut off from its own past is far less free to choose and to act as a people or class than one that has been able to situate itself in history.
> —John Berger

Speculation about the United States getting over the sixties is an almost reflexive media preoccupation that goes back to the end of the 1960s decade itself.[1] In 2008, Barack Obama's campaign for the presidency provided the mass media with yet another irresistible opportunity to revisit the 1960s era and ask once again whether the nation was ready to move beyond battles the media now widely attributed to the baby boom generation. As a presidential candidate, Obama himself was driven to declare, as early as September 14, 2007, "I come from a new generation of Americans. I don't want to fight the battles of the 1960s."[2] From that day until a year later, however, a search of Lexis-Nexis's major U.S. and world publications revealed 1,103 articles containing references to both Obama and the 1960s.

Typically what the mass media have *meant* by the term "the sixties" is an era marked by an unusually rebellious generation. Thus it should not be surprising that since about 1999, the sixties have been associated with, as Andrew Sullivan put it, the "debilitating, self-perpetuating family quarrel of the Baby Boom generation that has so long engulfed us."[3] Public memory of the 1960s era in the United States is largely a product of media accounts like Sullivan's.

Over the years, the media culture's public memory has been shaped by two forces. One has been a conscious, lavishly funded campaign to scapegoat the era for many of America's social ills in order to move the nation's political agenda to the right. The other is driven by the more nonpartisan forces of commercial media, typically playing off dramatic images, events, and personalities to generate interest among market audiences. Like much of consumer culture, these sixties evocations play off feelings of nostalgia, often in bifurcated form—that is, nostalgia for one's youth in the 1960s vs. nostalgia for the good old days before the sixties ruined everything.[4] In more recent years, advertisers and producers of pop culture have played on reaction against such nostalgia among younger audiences tired of the incessant media preoccupation with baby boomers.

Mass media discourse about the 1960s has thereby domesticated a politically volatile era in the service of a political spectacle that trivializes the kind of empowering democratic awakening that occurred some forty to fifty-five years ago. The period beginning with early civil rights activism around 1954 and continuing until the end of the war in Vietnam was one of awakened democratic assertiveness that grew out of contradictions of post–World War II America.[5] This assertiveness posed profound challenges to the United States' political economy and thus produced a backlash from both the political Right and the corporate Center that ushered in the long era of rightist-dominated neoliberalism. I suggest that the same two forces that have shaped public memory of the 1960s—ideological backlash and consumer-driven media—also played a significant role during the 1960s, influencing that era's trajectory in ways that helped to restore the hegemony of consumer-driven capitalism while eroding the democratic culture.

Two structural characteristics of mass media, reflecting broader structures of power and ideology, have played a crucial role in this transformation of the American political culture. First, reflecting a variety of institutional and market forces, the mass media produce an ideologically boundaried discourse that reinforces the polity's foundational institutions, ideology, and mythology.[6] Within the boundaries of this "legitimate" discourse, debate over the meaning of events typically occurs between Democrats and Republicans, liberals and conservatives, doves and hawks. As Daniel Hallin put it in his study of Vietnam War coverage, "Beyond the Sphere of Legitimate Controversy lies the Sphere of Deviance, the realm of those political actors and views which journalists and the political mainstream of the society reject as *unworthy of being heard* [emphasis added]."[7] In the excluded "sphere of deviance," one can find the views and arguments of those who challenge or critique the nation's prevailing myths, ideology, or institutions. Excluded from mainstream discourse, these views have found expression in the arenas of protest and alternative media.

Second, especially with the rise of television in the 1950s and 1960s, commercial imperatives have increasingly pushed mass media toward news-as-entertainment—the highlighting of dramatic news, powerful imagery, and compelling personalities—and away from coverage of complex issues and in-depth analysis and explanation.[8] The evocative power of television news drama could be seen in the NBC interview with congressman (and former SNCC activist) John Lewis at the moment Barack Obama was declared the newly elected president at 11:00 P.M. on November 4, 2008. Reflecting poignantly on "the struggle, the suffering, the pain and everything we tried to do to create a more perfect union," Lewis evoked a panoply of 1960s memories: Martin Luther King Jr., President Kennedy, Robert Kennedy, the "unmovable lines" of civil rights marchers in Selma, and the three civil rights workers killed in Mississippi. He concluded, "I feel very blessed to live to see this day."[9] Indeed, television's election night coverage resonated with the historic symbolism of Obama's election. Viewers could watch the exuberant multiracial crowd celebrating and shedding tears of joy in Chicago's Grant Park, where forty years earlier Chicago's police had waded into an antiwar protest with billy clubs flailing.

The democratic assertiveness of the 1960s era was grounded in protest, as one emerging group after another, from the early civil rights movement of the 1950s to the women's, gay rights, and ecology movements of the late 1960s, attempted to inject their grievances and demands into a national political agenda that had previously largely ignored them. Political scientist Michael Lipsky has argued that, for direct action protest to be effective, the "psychological distance" between the public and the protest must be shorter than the distance between the public and the protest target.[10] As suggested in the figure below, the wider public typically encounters both the protest and the target of the protest through the visual and interpretive filters of the media.

Fig. 1. Media and 1960s protest

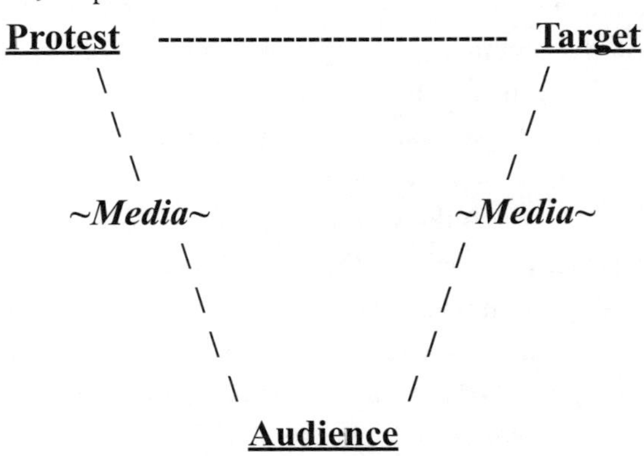

During the 1960s, the mass media helped to invite and spread protest activity, but they did so in terms that reflected their broader structural characteristics. Thus the media helped to shape, marginalize, and ultimately contain the era's protest movements.

In general, mass media coverage of 1960s protests revealed four prevailing characteristics: (1) it portrayed protest as a deviation from the preferred normal political process; (2) since it presented the protest as the news, rather than the argument the protest was intended to highlight, protests were considered significant primarily in terms of their potential impact on legitimate political actors; (3) it framed protests within the most immediate causal and temporal parameters, as if, as Todd Gitlin observed, they were "crime stories" about deviance;[11] and (4) it emphasized violence or the threat of violence in its stories about protests.

At least for several years of activism, for example, most national news reports on the civil rights struggle in the South framed their stories in specific, local terms rather than as instances of broader issues of nationally guaranteed rights. Thus, reports on the 1960 lunch counter sit-ins zeroed in on competing local claims over access to lunch counter seats. *Newsweek*'s first article, representative of the media treatment, portrayed the sit-ins as a struggle for "squatter's rights."[12] Moreover, from the outset, coverage of civil rights activism in the South was obsessed with the threat of racial violence stemming from the nonviolent protests, often failing to specify who might start the violence. Yet, when individual participants died in such clashes, the national media paid scant attention to the deaths of blacks while lavishing a great deal of scrutiny on the deaths of whites—a double standard that infuriated many black activists. Not only did the flagrant death of black Mississippian Herbert Lee—shot and killed in public view by a white state representative (later acquitted) during the voter registration drives of 1961–64—receive scant notice in the *New York Times,* but the *Times*'s account drew on the state representative's story without including a rejoinder from Robert Moses, one of the leaders of the voter registration drive, who worked closely with Lee and was featured elsewhere in the article.[13] In contrast, when two white activists from New York and one local black activist disappeared in Mississippi during the Freedom Summer drive of 1964 (later to be found dead), the national media were all over the story. They not only provided readers with in-depth narratives about the northern students, but also shadowed the massive FBI-backed manhunt ordered by the administration of Lyndon Johnson to find the activists and their killers.

The national media also clearly signaled their preference for normal political processes in which established elites and political authorities could work things out free from the pressures protest produced. In reporting on the Nashville and Knoxville sit-ins, *Newsweek* juxtaposed James Lawson, a trainer in nonviolent activism whom it identified as the "Negro agitator behind Nashville's sit-down disorders," with the men of "caliber" who were "taking the lead" in seeking "to be good neighbors."[14] In the pivotal protests in Birmingham and Selma, the news magazines likewise expressed "distaste for the confrontation that they believed was forced by [Martin Luther] King [Jr.]."[15] As Taylor Branch put it, the media "stressed non-partisan calm as the essential pre-condition for racial progress—much like the clergymen who criticized King in Birmingham."[16] News coverage in Selma revealed the mass media's fixation with a kind of impartial balance that nonetheless subtly indicated the media's preferences. Martin Luther King Jr. was presented as an overly impatient counterpoint to Sheriff Jim Clark and his "squirrel-shooting posse," and both were compared unfavorably to the moderate city public safety director, Wilson Baker, who was "desperately trying to keep the peace in the strife-stricken town."[17]

Media interpretation shifted sharply, however, when the nonviolent protesters in both Birmingham and Selma were openly and viciously attacked by the authorities, rather than by random white toughs. Both cases revealed the potency of media imagery in conveying a variety of subjective meanings to different audiences, including meanings that transcended the boundaries of so-called legitimate media discourse. Photographs from the Birmingham and Selma attacks were prominently displayed in many of the nation's (and world's) newspapers. In Richard Lentz's account, "Birmingham's enduring images were stark and simple. Arrayed on one side were the forces of good—the black men and women marching by the hundreds for the freedom that was their long-denied birthright as Americans. . . . Their encounters in the streets of Birmingham produced powerful images of brutality . . . of white men loosing fierce police dogs and training murderously efficient fire hoses on men, women, and, especially, children, who wanted no more than the rights of any American citizen. Shock waves surged through America, indeed the world."[18] As Birmingham businessman David Vann later commented about the Birmingham campaign, "It was a masterpiece [in] the use of the media to explain a cause to the general public."[19] These depictions provoked a groundswell of response that led President Kennedy and President Johnson respectively to introduce landmark civil rights legislation.

Similarly, visual images of the sit-ins, which contrasted with the narrowly interpretive texts of sit-in reports, spoke powerfully to young people in the North, attracting them to the cause. As Robert Moses put it, "The sit-ins, when they broke out, just grabbed me. The pictures of the Southern students. What I became aware of looking at them was *they looked how I felt* [emphasis added]. And I responded immediately to that."[20] Stokely Carmichael (Kwame Ture) likewise recalled that while he had found the sit-ins "politically inconsequential" when *reading* about them as a student in New York, his reaction was completely different "the first time I *saw* [emphasis added] on TV young Africans calmly sitting at a counter while racist abuse, blows, and the contents of ketchup bottles, full ashtrays, and coffee cups were dumped on their heads. That made a believer of me. Instantly."[21]

Many of the objectives of the Southern civil rights movement fit within the liberal framework of constitutional rights. Thus it became possible, after years of struggle and at significant cost to the Southern activists, for media images from the South to convey meanings that clearly violated nationally acceptable norms. Media coverage of 1960s movements shifted significantly during 1964–65, when activists began to target *national* policies and institutions, as opposed to brutal and dehumanizing regional deviations from constitutionally legitimized national norms. These years were marked by urban community organizing, the introduction of Lyndon Johnson's War on Poverty and the ensuing struggles in locales around the nation, the first of the decade's major "riots" in northern cities (Rochester and Harlem in 1964 and Los Angeles's Watts district in 1965), the participation of large numbers of white students in Mississippi Freedom Summer, the emergence of the Free Speech Movement at the University of California, Berkeley (and related activism on other campuses), a major escalation of the war in Vietnam in 1965, and early manifestations of counterculture in bohemian communities in New York and San Francisco.

Media coverage of these emergent movements followed the same structural imperatives as before—the *meaning* of these and later protest movements lay outside the boundaries of legitimate discourse, except as reinterpreted by credible liberals and doves, while media cameras were obsessively drawn to the movements' more extreme expressions of personal flamboyance or militancy. From the beginning, the riots provided some of the era's most stunning and disturbing visuals—city blocks as fiery infernos, National Guardsmen firing their weapons at rooftops or tenement windows, looters gleefully smashing store windows and carrying off prized goods, and dead black bodies on city sidewalks—yet media texts rarely probed for the underlying reasons for the upheavals, often singling out characteristics of the inner-city poor for blame. The black power movement and the later radical feminist movement were largely expressions of a democratic imperative of empowerment, but the media reinterpreted them as, respectively, black and female supremacy and typically equated them with the more virulent strains of white racism and male sexism; moreover, the media nearly always represented them by their most dramatic and vehement visual expressions. As for the antiwar movement, Melvin Small summed up years of national press and TV coverage by observing, "Time and time again, those who reported major antiwar demonstrations concentrated on violent and radical—albeit colorful—behavior on the fringes of the [antiwar] activity, undercounted the crowds, and ignored political arguments the protesters' leadership presented. In addition, because of a misapplication of the 'fairness doctrine,' especially on television, journalists bent over backwards to present the views and activities of counterdemonstrators and administration spokespersons in order to balance those of the doves."[22]

The mid-1960s were also the years in which the mass media discovered its dominant frame for understanding the spread of protest to national targets, namely that they reflected the preoccupations of a new generation. While mass media, and the market generally, have long been hyperconcerned about the fads and fashions of youth, the sheer numbers of postwar baby boomers, along with distinctive behaviors that emerged in the 1950s and 1960s, allowed the media to resort to a generational explanation for most of the phenomena emerging in the second half of the 1960s. The mass media consistently emphasized the youthful or student nature of protests, even when the protests were organized and significantly populated by older Americans. Perhaps more than any other 1960s phenomenon, the counterculture drew media cameras like moths to light. The newsmagazines in particular featured colorful spreads of the most bizarrely attired and provocatively behaving hippie youth in San Francisco's Haight-Ashbury district, and mass media, including popular music, hyped the 1967 Summer of Love, drawing a new wave of teenage runaways into the Haight and spawning the deterioration of that community. The media also dwelt on aberrant drug use by the young—aberrant because the drugs being used did not help the young adapt to the pressures of modern life, but instead helped them escape those pressures and rendered them less able (or inclined) to perform in the rat race. By seizing upon the excessive behaviors of some youth—which they often attributed to permissive parents or lenient officials—movement detractors shifted the cause of the protesting behaviors away from the very things the protesters were targeting, however effectively or ineffectively the latter did this.

The same two forces, commercial and ideological, that have reframed the meaning of the 1960s era in the years since created a dynamic during that decade that, along with the continued escalation of the war in Vietnam and government repression, helped produce the trajectory of the later 1960s. As protests grew, media discourse was full of debate between established liberals and conservatives over issues of poverty, higher education, the war, race, and gender. Yet both sides in this debate embraced and reinforced the legitimacy of American institutions. In the case of the war, for example, both hawks and doves in the media viewed U.S. intervention in Vietnam as legitimate and defensive in its origins and intent. However, the arguments and meanings that protest movements themselves expressed—that, for example, the war was an act of immoral American aggression against a nation that posed no threat to the United States—were excluded from mass media news accounts, except for truncated slogans or sound bites.

Within this frame, the arguments of protesters were treated as if they were illegitimate, if not incomprehensible. On those occasions when the mass media did grant some attention to outsiders' arguments, either they were editorially dismissive of the arguments, or establishment liberals within the media recast them into terms compatible with consensual norms. Thus, in response to the antiwar protests of fall 1965, James Reston of the *New York Times* sounded a common theme in a column titled "The Stupidity of Intelligence." Noting that it was "not easy, but let us assume" the protesters were "sincerely for an honorable peace," Reston dismissed the naïve youths for "inadvertently working against all the things they want. . . . [T]hey are not creating peace but postponing it."[23] On the other end of the 1965 media spectrum, the *National Review* headlined its report on the same protests, "The Day the Vietcong Attacked the United States."[24]

Perhaps nothing demonstrated more clearly the boundaries of mass media discourse than the media response to a 1967 speech by Nobel Peace Prize–winner Martin Luther King Jr., in which he publicly denounced the war and "the greatest purveyor of violence in the world today—my own government."[25] The national press swiftly condemned King's speech. Dismissing much of King's address as "sheer inventions of unsupported fantasy," the *Washington Post* declared that many who listened to King "with respect will never again accord him the same confidence."[26] The *New York Times* scolded King for doing a "disservice" to his "cause of Negro equality" and accused him of "whitewashing Hanoi," ignoring King's own caution that he was not suggesting that North Vietnam and the National Liberation Front were "paragons of virtue."[27] *Life* magazine called King's speech a "demagogic slander that sounded like a script for Radio Hanoi."[28]

At the same time, the commercial and journalistic imperatives of the media pushed them to attend to what they considered the more newsworthy aspects of protest activities—typically those that were visual: their more extreme postures, unusual appearances, symbolic actions, dramatic conflicts, and, most compellingly, acts of violence. Not surprisingly, then, the mid-1960s were the years when the media spectacle began to take center stage, the years when, as John Sanbonmatsu has argued, "expressivism became the dominant 'spirit' of the movement."[29] Along with the escalating war and government repression, this combination of textual exclusion and visual inclusion introduced a telling dynamic into the protest movements of the later 1960s era—one that provided the forces of backlash and commercial exploitation with ample material.

In the first place, mass media always spoke what William Gamson and Gadi Wolfsfeld have labeled *mainstreamese,* thereby alienating and radicalizing young people, since the boundaried language of "the system" could never accommodate the language of the movement. In the second place, the delegitimation of their perspectives and arguments about protest issues cast the young as outsiders and led to their withdrawal into enclaves that revolved around their particular outsider identity, to the growth of underground media that spoke their language—from Los Angeles's *Free Press* to Cambridge's *Old Mole,* hundreds of local underground papers cropped up in the mid-to-late 1960s—and ultimately to the increasing age-isolation of the young. Finally, the media's simultaneous exclusion of protesters' arguments and inclusion of their more volatile behaviors fostered an emphasis on symbolic action and increasing militancy as ways of being heard by political authorities and the wider culture. The display of Viet Cong flags, the performative militancy of the Black Panther Party, the trashing of symbols of gender oppression, the cultural theatrics of the Yippies—all were examples of the expressive politics of the later 1960s era.

While the new militancy did exert significant pressure on federal government officials, most notably with respect to its leaders' plans for the war in Vietnam, this media dynamic produced two outcomes of lasting significance. First, it produced a kind of "affective empowerment," as Lawrence Grossberg has put it, that began to supplant democratic engagement with the wider culture and, in a number of cases, gradually became a substitute for *real* instrumental movement empowerment.[30] Perhaps the most flamboyant practitioners of media theatrics were Abbie Hoffman, Jerry Rubin, and the Yippies. With an instinctive feel for media visuals and the subjective pulse of the alienated young audience they hoped to politicize, Rubin and Hoffman were, in effect, advertising men for the movement. As Hoffman put it, "We tear through the streets. Kids love it. They understand it on an internal level. We are living TV ads, movies. Yippie!"[31]

Second, the media-movement dynamic produced a media spectacle of agitated and alienated youth who became the focal point for two kinds of system response. As commercial media zeroed in on the appearances of 1960s youth, Madison Avenue began to use hip language to exploit the expanding youth market—in effect flattering the rebelliousness of the younger generation while enticing them into behavioral patterns that drew them further from the kinds of engagement that might build a broader movement for more fundamental societal transformation. In other words, the "living TV ads" Abbie Hoffman spoke of were ultimately directed away from oppositional activity and toward the system-reinforcing behavior of consumption. As Thomas Frank has argued, corporate America came to embrace the culture of rebellion and individuality; as younger age cohorts came into social consciousness, this commercial response co-opted the oppositional meaning of the counterculture and ushered in the culture of hip consumerism.[32]

Provocative media visuals also provided the forces of political backlash with images that were highly functional for their efforts to appeal to American audiences who felt alienated from, if not threatened by, what they were seeing. Beginning with Barry Goldwater's 1964 presidential campaign, through Ronald Reagan's 1966 gubernatorial campaign in California, and culminating with the 1968 presidential campaigns of George Wallace and Richard Nixon, political conservatives cast dramatic media images as lawless inner-city rioters and obscene dancers and blamed such scenes on nonviolent civil rights activism, liberal government handouts, and permissive parents. Thus, images offensive to conservative groups were linked to the Right's real political targets: liberal domestic policy, government regulation of the economy, and so-called liberal media. By linking these targets to what it regarded as an East Coast elite, the Right succeeded in creating a message with a populist spin that appealed not only to traditional Republican constituencies like small business and small-town Americans, but to formerly Democratic populations like the white South and the white working class.

During the 1970s, as the capitalist economy became significantly less profitable and productive, corporate America joined in this backlash against the 1960s. A 1975 report from the corporatist Trilateral Commission, for example, viewed the 1960s era as one of an "excess of democracy," in which new political voices—racial minorities, women, and the young—entered the political arena in force. According to the commission, the political and economic demands of these new political actors produced a "welfare shift" away from the postwar reliance on military Keynesianism, and their increasingly turbulent participation generated greater mistrust in government.[33] The environmental and consumer protection movements were also perceived as generating additional constraints on the private sector.

While their agendas were not identical, the political Right and the corporate Center converged in attacking what they labeled big government liberalism, advocating a return to what they called a free-market economy and urging more aggressive military interventionism in the aftermath of the Vietnam War. This convergence of interests and ideological themes, however, obscured a fundamental contradiction between an increasingly unregulated and unconstrained market economy on the one hand and the values of tradition, family, and local community often embraced by conservatives on the other. The presidential candidacy of Ronald Reagan proved to be the ideal vehicle to appeal to both constituencies while simultaneously obscuring their contradictions. Reagan's persona and rhetoric—his instinctive reference to simplified virtues of past and present, his praise of individual and national strengths as the basis for a new optimism, and his bombastic rhetorical attacks on communism—tapped into public nostalgia for an idealized past and echoed mythical themes traditionally found in grade school textbooks and popular culture. On the eve of his election, Reagan elaborated on his vision of the past: "Not so long ago, we emerged from a world war. Turning homeward at last, we built a grand prosperity and hopes, from our own success and plenty, to help others less fortunate. Our peace was a tense and bitter one, but in those days, the center seemed to hold. Then came the hard years—riots, assassinations, domestic strife over the Vietnam war. . . . For the first time in our memory, many Americans are asking, 'Does history still have a place for America, for her people, for her great ideals?'"[34]

With significant help from newly organized or revitalized foundations and think tanks, Reagan's election ushered in a neoliberal "regime" that has dominated U.S. political discourse from 1981 down to the present,[35] a period in which the 1960s era has been effectively reconstructed by political ideologues and commercial media alike. While neoliberal policies helped to generate a new gilded age in American society, Hollywood's 1983 film *The Big Chill* provided American audiences with a classic Reagan-era sixties story in which affluent ex-sixties rebels use the occasion of a classmate's suicide ("the only one of us to stay true to the sixties") to engage in a nostalgic and narcissistic reunion while clearly embracing their lives as yuppies.[36] With a musical score and themes that played to baby boom nostalgia, the popular film's theme of sixties sellouts conformed to the media's general take on the sixties as a phenomenon of youthful rebelliousness and self-indulgence. It also contrasted sharply with *The Return of the Secaucus Seven,* an earlier, smaller-market film directed by John Sayles, which presented a more accurate and authentic portrait of young 1960s radicals' efforts to retain their political values while dealing with the challenges of life in their early thirties.

Simultaneously, news media retrospectives played up reunions of various sixties gatherings and anniversaries of media-saturated events like 1960s assassinations, the 1963 March on Washington, the Watts riot, the 1967 Summer of Love, the Tet Offensive, the 1968 Democratic National Convention, and the Woodstock Festival. On the twentieth anniversary of the Summer of Love, *Newsweek* published an article titled "The Graying of Aquarius." Featuring a few quaint remnants from the past who still "cling to the values—and they're still called hippies" and observing that "not all hippies have made a successful adjustment to the 1980s," the magazine's portrait of the past was little other than a compilation of media imagery. The hippies the magazine managed to locate were "survivors of that once vast band of romantics who imagined that the mighty river of American civilization could somehow be turned from its course by sex, drugs, and rock and roll." "Someday," *Newsweek* concluded, "no one will believe there was a time when young men and women tried to stop a war with music and bring down a president with flowers; or that they could have sex with dozens of strangers and run the risk of nothing more serious than body lice."[37]

In the midst of 1987 references like these, *Washington Post* columnist Jonathan Yardley bemoaned what he took to be the fact that "the Sixties are back." His column voiced classic Reagan-era rhetoric about the 1960s era: "The Sixties had almost nothing to do with genuine ideological commitment or sense of purpose. . . . The Sixties were adolescent rebellion masquerading as a political movement. . . . The plain truth is that the Sixties were a period of unfettered self-indulgence on the part of the privileged children of America's middle class, and that the decade's legacy is, with the rarest of exceptions, lamentable."[38] However, Yardley took pains to distinguish his sixties from what the media had generally decreed were the *good sixties*—namely the Southern civil rights movement. His method was, to say the least, creative: "Apologists for the time like to claim, for example, that the civil rights movement was part of the Sixties, when in fact it had begun long before then." Yardley singled out Tom Hayden and Mario Savio as two sixties leaders who "had nothing to do with" the era's civil rights legislation, even though in both cases their activism in the Southern movement was, as for many, a crucial formative step leading to their later leadership roles. As it happened, Yardley's bad sixties "actually began around 1965,"[39] the same time that 1960s-era movements were beginning to target national institutions and policies and the media began to frame their coverage of protest in terms of a youthful generation.

Another emergent theme in the Reagan era that seemed to contradict the claim that sixties youth had no genuine ideological commitment was the charge that sixties radicals were somehow seizing control of the nation's colleges and universities. The primary basis of this assertion was the emergence of multicultural perspectives within liberal arts curricula. As feminists, racial minorities, and the occasional leftist academic sought to broaden the range of the traditional curriculum—sometimes, indeed, denouncing protectors of the canon—they were typically accused of propagandizing their students or seeking to delete the great works of Western culture. These rightist claims in the culture wars resembled attacks made during the 1960s by Southern white supremacists who claimed that black power meant black supremacy and by males who accused the women's movement of seeking to dominate men.

In 1994, in an attempt to build support for his Contract with America, Republican House Speaker Newt Gingrich attacked the centrist administration of Democrat Bill Clinton for attempting to carry out a Great Society "counterculture, McGovernick" legacy of the sixties.[40] Several years later, echoing a general media pattern, the *Wall Street Journal* labeled Clinton as the "leading edge of the baby boomers," citing his alleged "evolution" to the right, and "his fondness for fast food, his chronic difficulty getting organized, even his penchant for late night work."[41] The Right was equating its sixties targets with an aging boomer generation. The same year that Gingrich made his charge, the blockbuster film *Forrest Gump* told the beguiling story of the innocent Gump's life played out against a backdrop of events that confirmed virtually all of the Right's charges about the past. First, Tom Hanks's Gump was placed by computer creativity into black and white documentary footage from the good sixties of the Southern civil rights movement and an idealistic Kennedy administration. Soon, however, the film's actors played out the prevailing dark themes of the bad sixties: a Vietnam war in which invisible Vietnamese wreaked destruction on Gump's platoon; a New Left leader who not only excoriated returning soldiers and chanted seemingly mindless slogans but beat his girlfriend, Jenny; a threatening-looking, Black Panther–like gathering of black militants; and Gump's own best friend, Jenny, getting drawn into self-destructive drug use and sexual behavior that ultimately resulted in her death from AIDS.

Over these same years, television shows moved from *All in the Family*'s entertaining theme of generational conflict between 1960s-era stereotypes to an inverted version of the same conflict in *Family Ties*—a clash between Alex P. Keaton's brash younger-generation embrace of Reaganism and the weakly liberal nostalgia of his parents—in effect appealing to both sides of the media discourse. Adapting to market imperatives, popular movies recreated a variety of sixties stories in ways intended to appeal to mass 1980s-era audiences. A host of powerful Vietnam war soldiers' stories—from *The Deer Hunter* and *Coming Home* in 1978 to *Platoon, Hamburger Hill,* and *Full Metal Jacket* in the mid-1980s, to *We Were Soldiers* in 2002—depoliticized the war, with only a handful providing the merest metaphorical hints of the war's controversy (perhaps most notably the dichotomous characters being Sgt. Barnes and Sgt. Elias in *Platoon*). *Mississippi Burning* recreated the story of the deaths of three civil rights activists during Freedom Summer, but did so in a way that transformed black Mississippians into prayerful supplicants thankful for the FBI officials (playing a fictionally heroic role) investigating the crimes. Even films that sought to correct media misinformation—notably Spike Lee's *Malcolm X* and Mario Van Peebles's *Panther*—placed their historical characters in contexts that either domesticated the fears they generated (*Malcolm X*) or downplayed their political ideology and distorted the government role in their demise (*Panther*). As entertainment, these films essentially left audiences with little to do other than cheer (or jeer) and perhaps emulate, in some superficial manner, their compelling characters.

By 1997, conservative columnist George Will was acknowledging that the "national political discourse" was "driven by conservatives," but he noted that conservatives remained "aggrieved because politics seems peripheral to, and largely impotent against, cultural forces and institutions" permeated by what they consider "sixties sensibilities."[42] In 1999, one of the organizers of the conservative Moral Majority, Paul Weyrich, expressed despair over the degree to which American culture had "decayed into something approaching barbarism" in the years since Reagan's initial election. According to the self-styled "godfather" of the conservative movement, "politics has failed . . . because of the collapse of the culture . . . a collapse so great that it simply overwhelms politics." Americans, Weyrich lamented, "have adopted, in large measure, the MTV culture."[43]

From Jonathan Yardley's 1987 column to Weyrich's 1999 lament, right-wing attacks on sixties sensibilities repeatedly targeted what are in reality market-driven responses to forces initially unleashed during the 1960s era. The five-hundred-pound gorilla in the room that cannot be mentioned in this political discourse is capitalism and its incessant need for mass consumption, of particular importance in restoring capitalism's profitability and growth in both the post–World War II and post-1960s eras. An economy that drives marketers to anticipate the next fad while bombarding American youth with hip advertising at ever-earlier ages is the very market that began to play to alienated youth in the 1960s; it is, if anything, *typified* by Weyrich's MTV culture. Ironically, Weyrich's 1999 essay suggested a path for conservatives that mirrored the course taken by countercultural dropouts in the 1960s—that conservatives "separate [them]selves from the institutions that have been captured [*sic*] by the ideology of Political Correctness, or by other enemies of [their] traditional culture."[44]

Thus what passes for political discourse within market-dominated neoliberalism is really the devolution of society into fragmented enclaves of like-minded individuals whose beliefs about others unlike themselves continue to rigidify into self- and isolation-sustaining mythologies. That, it would seem, is the real sixties sensibility for which capitalism's mass media are significantly responsible.

For nearly thirty years in this cultural milieu, the Right's electoral resurgence has been facilitated by a politics of distraction employing references to the symbolic and imagistic politics of the sixties—welfare-freeloaders, anti-American peaceniks, spoiled youth, men- and family-hating feminists, tree-hugging hippies—all of whom have been part of a populist construction linked to liberal government and liberal media. This highly symbolic strategy succeeded in shaping political discourse for twenty-eight years, until the material politics of economics and war became so significantly salient that a voting majority elected the first African American president. From all appearances, there is little evidence that a regime shift involving a new coalition of interest groups has occurred with the Obama administration. Like Bill Clinton's election, Obama's seems to be an example of what Stephen Skowronek called the "politics of [temporary] pre-emption."[45] With the assistance of enormous corporate funding of election campaigns and the continuation of rightist attacks, neoliberalism remains the dominant paradigm. John Kennedy was accused by his contemporaries of giving "unwitting charge" to social movement activism, particularly among the young. Suggestions that Obama has done the same seem to have died on the vine.

Yet, as Paul Hawken observed in 2007, the world is alive with a "blessed unrest" of grassroots struggles for social justice and environmental sustainability.[46] In 2011, the Arab spring, the protests in the United States against state budget cutbacks and attacks on public employee unions, and mass actions in Greece, Italy, and Spain, among others, all suggest that neoliberalism may yet spawn its own demise and the revitalization of democracy.

Notes

1. Throughout these pages, I use *1960s* to mean the actual years or era of that time and *sixties* to mean ways the era is commonly referred to in the mass media.
2. *Times* (London), Sept. 15, 2007, 53.
3. Andrew Sullivan, "Goodbye to All That," *Atlantic,* Dec. 2007, 42. Rick Perlstein's critique of Sullivan's *Atlantic* article referred to the sixties as a "trauma" characterized by "two sets of contending Americans, each believing they were fighting for the future of civilization, but whose left- and right-wing visions of redemption were opposite and irreconcilable," "Getting Past the 60s? It's Not Going to Happen," *Washington Post,* Feb. 3, 2008. The framing of the 1960s as a battle between left and right was popularized by Maurice Isserman and Michael Kazin's *America Divided: The Civil War of the 1960s* (New York: Oxford Univ. Press, 2000).

4. For greater elaboration of these findings and the argument presented in this essay, see Edward P. Morgan, *What Really Happened to the 1960s: How Mass Media Culture Failed American Democracy* (Lawrence: Univ. Press of Kansas, 2010).
5. See Edward P. Morgan, *The Sixties Experience: Hard Lessons about Modern America* (Philadelphia, Pa.: Temple Univ. Press, 1991).
6. See, for example, Edward Herman and Noam Chomsky, *Manufacturing Consent: The Political Economy of Mass Media,* 2nd ed. (New York: Pantheon, 2002); Douglas Kellner, *Television and the Crisis of Democracy* (Boulder, Colo.: Westview Press, 1990); Daniel C. Hallin, *The "Uncensored War": The Media and Vietnam* (Berkeley: Univ. of California Press, 1989).
7. Hallin, *"Uncensored War,"* 117.
8. See W. Lance Bennett, *News: The Politics of Illusion,* 7th ed. (New York: Longman, 2006).
9. John Lewis, interview by Brian Williams, "Decision 2008: Election Night, 11:00 P.M." NBC, Nov. 4, 2008, <http://www.lexisnexis.com/lnacui2api/delivery/PreviewFrameDisplay.do?jobHandle=2826%3A304585627&fromCart=false&dnldFilePath=%2Fl-n%2Fshared%2Fprod%2Fdiscus%2Fqds%2Frepository%2Fdocs%2F7%2F62%2F2826%3A304585627%2-Fformatted_doc&fileSize=5000>.
10. Michael Lipsky, "Protest as a Political Resource," *American Political Science Review* 62 (December 1968): 1144–58.
11. Todd Gitlin, *The Whole World Is Watching: Mass Media in the Making and Unmaking of the New Left* (Berkeley: Univ. of California Press, 1980), 53.
12. "Squatter's Rights," *Newsweek,* Feb. 22, 1960, 27–28.
13. Claude Sitton, "Negro Vote Drive in Mississippi Is Set Back as Violence Erupts," *New York Times,* Oct. 24, 1961.
14. "A Pattern for Peace?" *Newsweek,* Mar. 21, 1960, 50–51.
15. Lentz, *Symbols,* 78.
16. Taylor Branch, *Pillar of Fire: America in the King Years, 1963–65* (New York: Simon and Schuster, 1998), 49.
17. Lentz, *Symbols,* 146. The reference to Clark's "posse" appeared in "Shades of Bull Connor," *Newsweek,* Feb. 1, 1965, 21, whereas *Time* observed that "A new Selma city administration, with the cooperation of many businessmen, is trying hard to clear the town's dark racist reputation by steering a more moderate course." "The Aim: Registration," *Time,* January 29, 1965, 21.
18. Lentz, *Symbols,* 75–76.
19. Quoted in Juan Williams, *Eyes on the Prize: America's Civil Rights Years, 1954–1965* (New York: Penguin Books, 1988), 191.
20. Michael Chandler, *Freedom on My Mind* (documentary film), directed by Connie Field and Marilyn Mulford (San Francisco: California Newsreel, 1994); DVD, 1995.
21. Stokely Carmichael with Ekwueme Michael Thelwell, *Ready for Revolution: The Life and Struggles of Stokely Carmichael (Kwame Ture)* (New York: Scribner, 2003), 139.
22. Melvin Small, *Covering Dissent: The Media and the Anti-Vietnam War Movement* (New Brunswick, N.J.: Rutgers Univ. Press, 1994), 2.
23. James Reston, "Washington: The Stupidity of Intelligence," *New York Times,* Oct. 17, 1965, Section E.

24. Timothy J. Wheeler, "The Day the Vietcong Attacked the United States," *National Review,* Dec. 14, 1965, 1157–59.
25. Martin Luther King Jr., "Declaration of Independence from the War in Vietnam," address delivered at the Riverside Church, New York, Apr. 4, 1967.
26. *Washington Post,* Apr. 6, 1967.
27. "Dr. King's Error," *New York Times,* Apr. 7, 1967; King, "Declaration of Independence."
28. *Life,* Apr. 21, 1967, 4, quoted in David Garrow, *Bearing the Cross: Martin Luther King, Jr., and the Southern Christian Leadership Conference* (New York: Vintage, 1988), 554.
29. John Sanbonmatsu, *The Postmodern Prince: Critical Theory, Left Strategy, and the Making of a New Political Subject* (New York: Monthly Review Press, 2004), 35.
30. See Lawrence Grossberg, "Rockin' in Conservative Times," in Grossberg, *Dancing in Spite of Myself* (Durham, N.C.: Duke Univ. Press, 1997), 257.
31. Quoted from Abbie Hoffman's *Revolution for the Hell of It,* in Gitlin, *The Sixties,* 326. Gitlin also observed that both Hoffman and Jerry Rubin "received job offers from three advertising agencies" after Chicago. Gitlin, *The Sixties.*
32. See Thomas Frank, *The Conquest of Cool: Business Culture, Counterculture, and the Rise of Hip Consumerism* (Chicago, Ill.: Univ. of Chicago Press, 1997).
33. Michel Crozier, Samuel P. Huntington, and Joji Watanuki, *The Crisis of Democracy: Report on the Governability of Democracies to the Trilateral Commission* (New York: New York Univ. Press, 1975), 70, 113.
34. Quoted in Daniel Marcus, *Happy Days and Wonder Years: The Fifties and the Sixties in Contemporary Cultural Politics* (New Brunswick, N.J.: Rutgers Univ. Press, 2004), 61.
35. Stephen Skowronek has written of political "regimes" that reflect configurations and coalitions of interests that dominate American politics over a span of time. Thus the New Deal regime spanned the years from 1932 until 1980, when Ronald Reagan was elected. I have drawn on common references to neoliberalism to suggest that the "regime" that came to power with Ronald Reagan's election might be termed a "neoliberal regime." See Stephen Skowronek, "The Changing Political Structures of Presidential Leadership," in *Debating Democracy: A Reader in American Politics,* 6th ed., ed. Bruce Miroff, Raymond Seidelman, and Todd Swanson, 295–308 (Boston, Mass.: Houghton Mifflin, 2009).
36. *The Big Chill,* directed by Lawrence Kasdan (Beverly Hills, Calif.: Carson Productions, 1983).
37. Jerry Adler et al., "The Graying of Aquarius," *Newsweek,* Mar. 30, 1987, 56, 58.
38. Jonathan Yardley, "Echoes of an Empty Decade: The 60s Are Back," syndicated *Washington Post* column published in the *Bethlehem Globe-Times,* Bethlehem, Pa., July 24, 1987.
39. Ibid.
40. See Dale Russakoff, "Gingrich Lobs a Few More Bombs," *Washington Post,* Nov. 10, 1994.
41. Gerald Seib, "To Understand President Clinton's Policies, You First Need to Understand the Generation He Comes From," *Wall Street Journal,* Jan. 20, 1997.
42. George Will, foreword to *Reassessing the Sixties: Debating the Political and Cultural Legacy,* ed. Stephen Macedo (New York: Norton, 1997), 3.
43. Paul Weyrich, "A Moral Minority," quoted in Roger Kimball, *The Long March: How the Cultural Revolution of the 1960s Changed America* (San Francisco, Calif.: Encounter Books, 2000), 276.

44. Ibid., 277.
45. Skowronek, "The Changing Political Structures of Presidential Leadership," 301–2.
46. Paul Hawken, *Blessed Unrest: How the Largest Movement in the World Came into Being and Why No One Saw It Coming* (New York: Viking, 2007).

"Of Loss and Learning"

How Anniversary Coverage Affects Understanding of May 4, 1970

Janet Leach and Mitch McKenney

If, as journalists say, news reports are the first draft of history, the *Akron Beacon Journal*'s initial reports of the shooting of students by the Ohio National Guard at Kent State University on May 4, 1970, represent the first of many drafts of history. The stories are straightforward, the headlines striking in their declarations:

"4 Dead, 11 Wounded as Guard Fires into Rioters at KSU"
"KSU Shock, Reaction Roll Across Nation, No One Is Sure Just How It Happened"
"'Not In Danger,' Guardsman Says"
"All Must Help Restore Order"[1]

The stories accompanying these headlines made up the *Akron Beacon Journal*'s Pulitzer Prize–winning entry for coverage of the shootings at Kent State in 1970. Murray Powers, then a Kent State University journalism professor and formerly the *Beacon Journal*'s managing editor, wrote in his four-paragraph letter nominating the newspaper for a Pulitzer in journalism, "What distinguishes the *Beacon Journal*'s work is that the nature of its disclosures, all under the pressure of a deadline, contributed to a common understanding of what happened May 4." In describing the *Beacon Journal*'s early efforts and its award-winning work, Powers goes on to say that "the stories reflect the shared belief of the reporters and their editors that Kent State deserved more than routine reporting. With the national mood quickly fragmenting, and the tendency to explain the shootings with slogans, accusations and epithets becoming dominant, the *Beacon Journal* staff responded to the mandate for thorough, accurate reporting that would reveal the truth about Kent State."[2]

A second Pulitzer nomination for the *Beacon Journal* that year was submitted for a ten-page special report, published on May 24, 1970, in which a team of journalists from the journal's parent company, Knight Newspapers, wove together stories and images from the shootings.[3] Unlike the winning Pulitzer entry, in which stories were reported and written in the first hours and days after the shootings, the May 24 report used vignettes, with just three or four sentences per passage, bringing in voices and context that hadn't been available earlier, when the story was still unfolding.

The newspaper's coverage then and in the years that followed set down what was known at the time: the myriad eyewitness accounts and official reports, understanding from personal perspectives, and continuing debates about how and why the shootings happened. Because of the special local significance of the Kent State shootings and lingering controversy over them, the *Beacon Journal* closely covered them and regularly revisited them, especially each May. In 2000, when the *Beacon Journal* was planning its annual coverage of May 4, its editors were in the position of many journalists who grapple with how to remember key dates in local and national history—Pearl Harbor, the D-Day invasion, September 11; they all try to offer coverage that can be useful, even when little may have changed between anniversaries. For the *Beacon Journal*'s editors, the thirtieth anniversary of the shootings was not a standard milestone, instead representing a substantial passage of time that they felt deserved a significant effort.[4]

Newspapers produce anniversary stories as tributes to or acknowledgments of extraordinary occurrences. Anniversary coverage serves as a lens through which to examine the past. For those readers who were not present at the time, it grants awareness of the event, helping them feel what it was like; for those who were present, anniversary coverage transports them back to the key date they lived through. By finding new, engaging ways to approach an anniversary, journalists can advance a story, giving readers tools to reevaluate their impressions and understanding of important historic events.

One aspect of preparing such coverage is appreciating how the audience may receive it. The *Beacon Journal*'s audience for stories about the May 4 events at Kent State comprises hundreds or perhaps thousands of people, including victims and their families; current and former KSU students, faculty, and staff; active and retired National Guardsmen; members of local law enforcement; public officials; residents of the city of Kent, Portage County, and surrounding areas; and medical and legal representatives. Many of these people still live in northeastern Ohio or in the Kent-Akron-Cleveland area. If they are old enough, they have knowledge of the original events and, no matter their age, they have personal opinions that may have changed over time. Being aware of those personal reactions is important for reporters seeking context for a decades-old story and shaping anniversary coverage.

Without sustained efforts to recall key events in a community's or nation's history, the stories of those events will change, inevitably and even dramatically, as memories fade and participants pass on. Examining the relationship between collective memory and the news, Kurt Lang and Gladys Engel Lang observe, "What is conveyed to the public via the news media can never replicate the event as experienced by the participants actually present at the scene of the action." Such reporting shapes public opinion, however, and provides a "mediation of events" that changes and redefines experience.[5] Future generations, they note, must depend on that mediation: "Looking at a critical event as it is happening by 'firehouse research' differs from a study of the same event by way of a retrospective 'look back' upon it. . . . The outside attention it gets converts the event into news and endows it with new meanings, and the various accounts will progressively overshadow any first-hand experience. The retrospective 'looking back' on events has to contend with the ever-changing consciousness of a shared historical past."[6] In this case, the *Beacon Journal*'s Pulitzer Prize–winning coverage was that "firehouse research," while the thirtieth anniversary coverage represents the "looking back" that becomes collective memory.

Jill Edy calls this type of anniversary coverage "commemorations."[7] Such commemorations require a commitment from the media to secure in their place known details. Details also may transform through the addition of new perspectives and the passage of time, during which both memories and participants might change. Details new to the story may affect understanding.

As the thirtieth anniversary of the Kent State shootings approached, the *Beacon Journal* sought to commemorate and put into context the events of May 4, 1970. For its coverage in 2000, dozens of *Beacon Journal* staffers prepared and produced "Of Loss and Learning," a sixteen-page report examining the original events of that day, exploring significant findings, reviewing government documents, and talking to people involved with or connected to those events. The special section included a long narrative story titled "May 4 Answers Lost in the Chaos"; then-and-now photographs; a two-page graphic illustration showing what happened where; and several personal essays, including the reflections of two *Beacon Journal* staff members—an artist who had been a National Guardsman on duty in Kent, though not on campus, at the time of the shootings and a staff photographer who had been a journalism student on campus and in Taylor Hall, near the shootings. Another essay related the frenzy of covering an ongoing, overwhelming event. Still another story, accompanied by a wide photograph, covered the controversial May 4 Memorial completed in 1990. One article explained the university's May 4 Oral History Project, while a detailed timeline traced events from five days before to twenty years after the shootings. The section also included both historic and new photographs, in black and white and in color, representing events from 1970 and later. Stories about political activism appeared next to photos of the burned-out ROTC building and the enduring image of Mary Ann Vecchio kneeling over the body of slain student Jeffrey Miller. The extensive compilation was, and is, memorable for the details it revealed, the history it recalled, and the strong opinions it reported.

On the cover of the *Beacon Journal* report were evocative photographs of the clothes worn by Allison Krause, Jeffrey Miller, Sandra Scheuer, and William Schroeder on the day they died—photos from government archives never previously published. The black-and-white images depicted the victims' clothes on hangers, as if in a clothing store display, with their shoes neatly perched to one side. For days, editors debated whether to publish the photos at all, invoking journalism ethics questions of taste, privacy, sensitivity, and exploitation. "What I really remember thinking was how personal this is, that you could not get past the fact that four people died, that it wasn't just a historical footnote anymore, that they were real people, with the clothing, and the shoes," said Susan Kirkman Zake, who was the *Beacon Journal*'s director of photography in 2000.[8] The choice to publish the newly unearthed photos—and to elevate them to the main cover art—signaled both to their own staff and to readers the importance the *Beacon Journal* editors attached to advancing the May 4 story and its continuing narrative.

Readers' reactions to the *Beacon Journal*'s special thirtieth anniversary section were mixed. Some readers wrote letters to the editor criticizing the decision to show the dead students' clothes from that fateful day. Others applauded the report for its descriptive summary. Still others commended the writing, and, in fact, "Of Loss and Learning" won several regional, statewide, and national journalism awards.

Just as newspaper anniversary coverage provides the touchstone or tribute necessary to validate important events, it also attempts to update such events, granting readers the opportunity to uncover and understand what was not known earlier. The test for the *Beacon Journal* in 2000 was to find something new and interesting in an historic event—a test that has long been challenging for news organizations.

In 2000, some of the people involved in the *Beacon Journal*'s original 1970 reportage still worked in the newsroom, and it would have been difficult to find a veteran staffer without strong memories of May 4, 1970. Editors selected lead reporters for "Of Loss and Learning" who did not have their own clear memories of the events—David Giffels, Chuck Klosterman, and Michael Weinreb. Giffels had been a child in 1970, while the other two had not yet been born. The editors chose these three to ensure that they would get all of their material from talking to others, rather than starting with their own recollections, as they put the events of May 4, 1970, into context for the new anniversary report.

The reporters sought to "get the truth from everybody," as Weinreb put it.[9] They hoped to break new ground, perhaps providing some answers to lingering questions about motivation for the shootings. Had students offered the National Guard direct provocation for shooting? Had the guardsmen been ordered to shoot? While the reporters knew "from the very beginning that we were dealing with something that had been done to death," Giffels said, they were optimistic.[10] As they worked, however, it became clear to the reporters that there would be no new answers to report because they were interviewing many of the same people about a familiar topic. "It was pretty obvious to us that we weren't going to find a smoking gun even though that's part of what we tried to do. . . . That was part of the lead of the story, that this is not what you want to hear," Giffels said. Still, the story still mattered to the three reporters, to the *Beacon Journal,* and to its audience—readers seeking the legitimacy, or mediation, of such tribute journalism. These included the witnesses to or participants in the actual events, others who had followed the story from its inception and as it unfolded over the years, and new readers looking for the historical implications of this local occurrence. The story mattered to them all, but for different reasons. Phone calls and letters to the newspaper after its publication of the special section indicated readers' intense interest in and emotional reaction to the topic, but there was no consensus about the story, its local significance, or its historical status.

The story certainly mattered to the staff writers of the *Beacon Journal.* Giffels saw the goal of the reporting as adding context to and getting to the meaning of a story that had been told; he believed that the accretions of time had given the story a façade, and he worried that people wouldn't be able to look at the events of May 4, 1970, in a new way, because the exterior was too hard to penetrate. Klosterman also sought to penetrate that façade, but while he asserted that journalists have an obligation to note anniversaries, he added that anniversary stories are problematic because of the risk of losing accuracy with each passing year.[11] Acknowledging the passage of time was likewise important to Weinreb, who noted that the media must sort out the views reported at the time from the views put forward in subsequent years. Weinreb also said he could have predicted the calls that came in from readers complaining, "Why are you writing about those crazy hippies again?" Beyond that, however, he found it was difficult to know whether the coverage "contributed something to the narrative" or otherwise had an impact. He compared such responses to reader reaction to stories revisiting the case of serial killer and Akron-area native Jeffrey Dahmer. "People are saying, well why are you bringing this up again?"

While acknowledging that "Of Loss and Learning" yielded no startling new revelations, Giffels, Klosterman, and Weinreb did assert that the report provided the events of May 4, 1970, with new perspective and context, and perhaps even granted readers some measure of understanding or a mechanism for resolving their own feelings about the shootings. The reporters also said the assignment changed them personally and professionally. Giffels, for example, was interested in taking a long look at the Kent shootings in part because the event was so personal to the community and to his colleagues in the newsroom, many of whom had won the Pulitzer Prize for their work on the original story. He wanted to look at May 4, he explained, "not just as history but as culture." In three decades, much had changed on the Kent State campus, in Ohio, and nationally, yet still he believed there was reason to explore different points of view, even for an emotionally charged subject that had already been deeply examined.

The *Beacon Journal*'s coverage of the shootings on previous anniversaries had focused largely on what were then the most recent developments: on the court cases of 1974 and 1975, for example, on the commemoration of 1980, or on the controversial memorial created in 1990. As time passed, readers were more likely to find a where-are-they-now story, to delve into the unresolved controversies, or to hear a voice that previously had been silent. With those angles already covered, and no breaking news, the reporters in 2000 signaled in their introduction that this section would tell a different kind of story:

> This is not what you want to hear.
>
> If you expect to read this story and understand what happened on May 4, 1970, you will be disappointed.
>
> If you look here for an answer, you will not find one. The answer to Kent State was lost 30 years ago in the sting of tear gas and the noise of rifles. For all the trying, it has never been found. Not in the thousands of pages of government documents; not in the nearly 20 books published on the topic; not in courtrooms or classrooms or candlelight vigils; not in the minds of people who have devoted a generation to its pursuit.
>
> The answer, in fact, has become a question. And that question is more important than anything else: Does this still matter?[12]

Noting the impact on the region, Giffels said the point of the section was to remember the terrible events of May 4, 1970, "in a reverential way and not a controversial way."

If accounts of historical events are subject to revision with fading memory and advances in technology, or if reporters recognize that a story can't get at the truth, what are the implications for truth that Murray Powers predicted would be found on the newspaper's pages? When anniversary stories revisit something that happened years ago, should news consumers believe what they read and see? The three principal authors of the *Beacon Journal*'s thirtieth anniversary section all said they were concerned that their accounting be accurate—not that they were cavalier about details in their other work, but that they wanted to be exactingly precise in their reporting of details and crafting of sentences to ensure their work had no errors that could cloud their credibility. Journalists seek the truth in day-to-day reporting.[13] This is a long-held and basic tenet of the profession, and, for the most part, it is attainable, as long as sources are truthful.

This was evident even in the early reporting of the Kent State tragedy. In the weeks after the shootings in 1970, John S. Knight—who built a newspaper publishing empire from Akron with the legendary motto "Get the truth and print it"—argued in correspondence with the FBI's then-director, J. Edgar Hoover, about the paper's interest in the truth about the shootings. After a story said the FBI "has concluded" the shootings were "not necessary and in order," Hoover complained. "The results of our inquiries into the Kent State matter," he wrote to Knight, "were furnished to the Department of Justice without recommendation or conclusion."[14] While acknowledging that *concluded* was a poor word choice, Knight noted, "There is no occasion to lecture the editor. We are quite as dedicated to the quest for truth as the FBI."[15] To Knight, presenting truth—not just assembling facts, but explaining things without ambiguity, to inform the reader's understanding—was not only possible, but the newspaper's main directive.

That directive carried through to 2000 when editors recognized that there were different versions of what happened, yet still sought understanding. Moreover, they added another journalistic goal: to provide insight. People who live through significant events sometimes demand that newspapers offer some commemoration of the events they remember and of which they were a part. According to Frederic C. Bartlett's classic study, *Remembering,* this may be because memory cannot proceed without some kind of social framework.[16] People want to make sense of their shared experiences and their place in history and depend on newspapers and other media to validate their memories of key events. For instance, editors regularly get complaints if there is no story on December 7 recalling the 1941 attack on Pearl Harbor. For newspapers that were intricately tied to significant events, readers' expectations for anniversary coverage can be even higher. This was especially true of the *Beacon Journal* and its coverage of May 4, according to the newspaper's director of photography, Susan Zake, who was connected with several May 4 anniversary stories over the years. Zake said the *Beacon Journal,* having established its authority in 1970, needed to "own" that story, maintaining its authority by providing exclusive, exhaustive, and unparalleled coverage of the 1970 Kent State shootings year after year. This sense of owning the story explains why the paper devoted extensive resources to the thirtieth anniversary, such as finding and interviewing retired Kent State police officer Harold Rice. Rice, who had been a campus police officer on May 4, 1970, had never before spoken publicly about his actions and observations. That kind of proprietary commitment shaped and continues to shape the newspaper's coverage of the shootings and readers' responses to that continuing coverage. It provides Bartlett's "social framework."

Newspapers use this framework to lead the conversation in communities. Sometimes that conversation revolves around significant past events. Carolyn Kitch explained how this is accomplished (in magazines) when "anniversary issues . . . reuse their own content as historical 'evidence' of the American past and their own roles in it."[17] Newspaper anniversary coverage also contributes to historical accuracy.

The journalistic media, according to Kitch, "function to create a collective national memory and situate themselves as public historians."[18] In these ways, newspaper anniversary or commemorative coverage serves a significant, sometimes controversial, function. That is clearly the case with "Of Loss and Learning," the *Beacon Journal*'s thirtieth anniversary special section, which provided awareness and insight into the Kent State shootings—a step toward understanding. The awareness came from new interviews, never-before-seen photographs, and detailed descriptions from essayists, which proved that this was a story still worth telling, while the insight came from the historical hindsight of thirty years. There is insight in what is not said, too, as the three reporters demonstrated when they wrote:

> Our messages would go out.
> "Would you talk about Kent State?"
> They do not get returned.
> One man, Larry Shafer, is polite but very firm: "I do not want to talk about it anymore." Another responds in sarcastic sing-song before hanging up abruptly: "Life is good. I want to stay upbeat. Bye-bye."
> They are former members of the Ohio National Guard, men called into the middle of something they were never given a chance to understand and whose aftermath has been—for them in very particular ways—as murky and stinging as tear gas.[19]

The refusal of some witnesses to discuss the shootings suggests they were weary of retelling their stories or couldn't foresee any good coming from revisiting the subject. Such silence is part of the insight: that these participants apparently felt no compulsion to unburden themselves publicly, even after thirty years, could signal to the reader that this emotionally charged story was and still is unresolved.

Just as the three young reporters worried about their coverage being wrong or incomplete, they knew it would be risky if their work contradicted existing paradigms surrounding the shootings. Readers seeing facts they did not recall might question the overall accuracy of the report rather than use the occasion to reexamine their own conclusions. At the same time, Klosterman observed, the reporters knew if they did a superficial job and simply repeated the contents of earlier stories, they could be "objectively galvanizing the preexisting perception of that event." All three reporters acknowledged the challenge posed by a readership that had been hearing about the shootings for thirty years. As Giffels noted, just as the region's culture had been static since the 1960s, as postindustrial Akron shrank, so too, the perceptions of May 4 "were set, and have been set" with a point of view: "I think within a couple of days of the event, people who were sort of mature, sentient people on

May 4, 1970, had their opinion about it that pretty much hasn't changed. And then people who gained an opinion about it since then have had their opinion almost completely influenced by those prevailing opinions."

Giffels added that he sees the effect of forming one's opinion as a sort of imprint. The initial reaction of anyone who was in northeastern Ohio in 1970 probably has not changed. Two common paradigms, Giffels summarized, would be those who dismissed the protesters ("These hippies are wrong and are trying to ruin our country") and those who believed the authorities overreacted ("The man is keeping us down"). For some, the imprint was immediate and fiercely resistant to challenges, and while others might consider different points of view, changing one's opinion is akin to changing religions. Unless reporters are patient and their work persuasive, their coverage will not change readers' perceptions because, as Giffels put it, "we need some things to be pillars of our worldview."

Klosterman noted likewise that the "collective assumed narrative" regarding the Kent shootings had been set decades before the three reporters set about asking questions in 2000. Some of the people they interviewed believed the reporters already had their story written and were looking for quotes: "They would look back at other stories written and figure, 'Oh, he wants me to say x to fill in the blank in his story.'" Giffels added that he began encountering that regional familiarity with the events of May 4 long before the thirtieth anniversary project. If the issue came up on an unrelated story, everyone had an opinion about the students or the guardsmen or Vietnam or social unrest and "people would just become . . . deadened to any new willingness to understand it."

As with any major story, over the years the May 4 coverage moved from the immediate and day-to-day developments to a more contemplative and thoughtful retrospective: journalism pivoting into history. As anniversaries arrive, media organizations reexamine the details—including their own coverage—and retell the story from perhaps a new vantage point, but with no less commitment to truth. For those involved with the *Beacon Journal*'s thirtieth anniversary coverage of the 1970 Kent shootings, the idea of truth was important but somewhat intangible. The writers and editors described wanting the story to have news—something the reader didn't know before—but, failing that, they wanted it to bring clarity—the kind that comes with distance. "I think it's an emotional clarity more than anything," Zake said. "I think it allows us to say that even if these kids were protesting, they didn't deserve to die. . . . I think it [anniversary coverage] allows us to separate things emotionally and make more just evaluations of what happened then, what was right and wrong about it."

These issues have consequences for what Edy calls "the meaning that a community makes of its past."[20] The consequences can be significant. As Michael Shudson observes, "It is worth noting how difficult it seems today to know how to think about the past, not just a particular past whose recollection promises to stir conflict, shame, or embarrassment, but 'pastness' in general. People are wary of the past, recognizing that it is often used as an ideological weapon and knowing that any account is vulnerable to challenge and revision."[21] Still, journalism and media organizations have a responsibility to document what happens and a commitment to retell the past for new, younger audiences. Without the information, analyses, and perspective that journalists provide, important social context can be lost. Thus, the *Beacon Journal*'s special thirtieth anniversary section attempted to provide context and succeeded in providing new perspective. Even without new or breaking news, the journalistic effort communicated meaning, informed opinion, and generated debate.

Weinreb said the reporters' efforts to unearth something new to say about Kent State "made us realize it had become a symbol as much as anything else." Klosterman wondered if journalists responsible for future coverage will worry less about retelling every detail and deal instead with moving toward the meaning: "Maybe our story was, in a weird way, the beginning of seeing the event only as metaphor. We talked about all the history, but it was only to get to the point of what could this mean to somebody trying to think about the world, and not just what happened that afternoon. And that's probably the direction these stories will be from this point on." Over the years, Klosterman continued, the truth of any story—on student unrest, or Vietnam, or the intersection of citizens and governments—becomes metaphor, because of all the "telling." But on the thirtieth anniversary of the killing of four college students, the *Beacon Journal* stood up and said this was real, more than a metaphor.

As generations pass and media transform, who or what will drive how we as a society remember significant events? Blogs, social media, and other user-generated content give equal weight to citizen journalists and media professionals. Messages and, by extension, memory, can be appropriated, falsified, or even surrendered to opinion and fabrication. Former longtime New York columnist Pete Hamill recently worried about the loss of the daily newspaper library, with its bound volumes and organized clippings: "They tell you all the detail that historians don't. How much was a pair of shoes? What did a guy pay to go to the ballpark in 1934 during the Depression? How many people were there?"[22] Beyond losing an authoritative contemporary source, you also lose that journalistic commitment to be complete.

With the *Beacon Journal*'s thirtieth anniversary effort and now-archived publication, details of the May 4 shootings exist in a print collection offering not only some measure of historical accuracy but also insight and reflection. It was complete, up to that point, even if it wasn't definitive. Kitch noted the importance of such journalistic efforts when she described their "understanding of the past as a way of—and their anniversary as an occasion for—imagining and assessing the future."[23]

Weinreb voiced a like concern when he explained that it is a key responsibility of the media to put events in a frame for the next generation and that a problem with online media today is that it moves too fast for any kind of retrospective. Klosterman questioned whether watching events such as September 11 unfold live on television helps people understand them more or remember them better. Unless people have direct experience of an event, they must rely on the media message. A hundred years from now, Klosterman predicts, a broadcast special about the shootings will have a dose of the requisite facts, as well as all the things that make it interesting, such as the music and culture.

The pervasiveness of news reports through a multiplicity of media may over time induce changes in public perception of both the events and their media coverage. Klosterman fears, for example, that the rising incidence, since the late 1990s, of violence in schools and other public places, such as Columbine High School and Virginia Tech, may be desensitizing students to campus violence, or at least making young people less surprised that students were shot and killed at Kent State. While Klosterman and his fellow journalists did not raise this idea in their thirtieth anniversary section on the events at Kent because they hadn't explored it fully, he noted that when he asked some students on campus "how crazy it would seem that people were shot out here, they were generally underwhelmed." The idea wasn't as jarring in 2000 as it had been in 1970, he said, because today's students have grown up with the idea that bursts of violence happen.

Klosterman also noted that as technologies advance, the potential grows for more visual re-creations of historic events—at least for those who take the time to report and research them. Weinreb noted the work he now does on such topics as the 1986 death of basketball player Len Bias: "I think there's an audience for that kind of stuff. The question is will there be resources for that stuff?" However, he believes news organizations "are making a mistake" if they don't spend time reexamining history, because—beyond fulfilling their responsibility—he is convinced there is an audience for such stories, even if that audience is online. "We don't know the form the feature is going to be," Weinreb commented, "but I guess I'm optimistic there's going to be some kind of form. People still buy books about historical events. I've got a book on my shelf right now about the history of the Dust Bowl, which is something I normally wouldn't have been interested in but the book won a Pulitzer Prize. Those sorts of things interest people."

Committing such anniversary coverage to print provides a more lasting record than radio or television broadcasts or here-today, gone-tomorrow Web links. A permanent form that can be searched and researched better serves both readers and history, we submit, than ethereal media. Still, none of the reporters who worked on the special section marking the thirtieth anniversary of the Kent shootings expected to find the *Beacon Journal* or any other news organization expending similar resources on coverage of its fortieth anniversary, primarily because of the changes in the economics of producing news that have taken place in the intervening decade. Three reporters working exclusively on one story for two months cost the equivalent of half a reporter's annual salary. Considering the photographers, artists, and editors required to produce such a section, the staff cost alone for similar coverage of Kent's fortieth anniversary could have reached into six figures. Nevertheless, Ann Mezger, who was the *Beacon Journal*'s section editor in 2000 and also the architect of many of the newspaper's historical anniversary sections, said in 2009 that whatever form it takes, such coverage connects history to current events, not only serving as tribute but updating the record for those who were around for the event recalled and bringing awareness of it to those who weren't.[24] Weinreb said he hopes editors keep finding ways to pursue such reporting, "because that's the only way we're going to remember this stuff, or get people to remember this stuff."

In the event, the *Beacon Journal*'s fortieth anniversary coverage of the Kent shootings was thorough, although many features were available only at the newspaper's website. The newspaper's editor, Bruce Winges, said that in light of the *Beacon Journal*'s unique past coverage of the event, a record offered by no other new media, planners at the paper recognized the value of maintaining that coverage and set a goal for the 2010 retrospective of talking to people from every side of the issue to provide "a living history." The print paper featured front-page coverage for four days, starting with "Lives Interrupted," stories from nine people who were at Kent State on May 4, 1970. Web exclusives included historical coverage, a chronology, and an eight-minute video. Winges said that while limited resources had required the paper to plan ahead, it was committed to ongoing coverage of the Kent shootings. "It's part of our community. There are still feelings here. . . . It's amazing that after forty years this can still be so divisive," Winges said.[25]

Revisiting important events is a journalistic responsibility that can help people understand the past, honor it, and remember their place in it. It also uses history to introduce the past to those lacking personal memories of it, sealing the newspaper's foundational role in culture and memory. Such coverage serves a role in maintaining a community's and a nation's touchstones, while providing interest and insight along the way. Kitch described it succinctly: "Anniversary journalism is thus an illustration of the role of journalism in collective memory and the role of collective memory in journalism. It provides a lens through which we may consider how, with the passage of time, journalists gain the cultural authority to tell the 'true story of America.'"[26]

Despite its value, however, many journalists are concerned that communities will be seeing less of such anniversary coverage. As news consumption changes, editors, struggling to meet increasing demands with decreasing resources, are being forced to be more selective, to weigh how many hours and meetings and pages an anniversary story is worth. For much less money, an anniversary date could be noted, of course, and remembrance events covered as they happen. Such cursory coverage, however, would deprive readers of the opportunity to read the work of journalists still committed to revisiting such stories in a meaningful way, journalists who see such opportunities for tribute, awareness, and insight not only as a responsibility, but as a good story.

Notes

Janet Leach was editor and vice president of the *Akron Beacon Journal,* and Mitch McKenney was its deputy metro editor in May 2000, when "Of Loss and Learning" was published.

1. The newspaper headlines appeared in the *Akron Beacon Journal* in 1970 on the following days: May 4 ("4 Dead 11 Wounded as Guard Fires into Rioters at KSU"); May 5 ("KSU Shock, Reaction Roll Across Nation" and "'Not in Danger,' Guardsman Says"); and May 10 ("All Must Help Restore Order"). The May 4 headline, written as news was breaking the first day, says that eleven people were wounded. In fact, a total of thirteen Kent State students were shot, of whom four were killed and nine wounded.
2. Murray Powers, Pulitzer Prize nomination letter, Jan. 24, 1971. Pulitzer Collection. Columbia University Libraries, Columbia University, New York.
3. "Tragedy in Our Midst—A Special Report," *Akron Beacon Journal,* May 24, 1970.
4. Janet Leach, personal recollection, 2009, based on her experience as editor of the anniversary issue of 2000.
5. Kurt Lang and Gladys Engel Lang, "Collective Memory and the News," *Communication* 11 (1989): 123.
6. Ibid., 124.
7. Jill Edy, "Journalistic Uses of Collective Memory," *Journal of Communication* 49, no. 2 (Spring 1999): 74.
8. Susan Kirkman Zake, interview by authors, Apr. 17, 2009; Leach, personal recollection. As editor of the paper at the time the anniversary section was published, Leach gave the final approval to use the photos of the dead victims' clothing. She remembers long and heated debate about the appropriateness of publishing the photos on the cover of the special section. While asserting then and continuing to assert that the photos would wrest readers' attention, she also acknowledged that, as one reader complained, they could be considered "disgusting."
9. Michael Weinreb, interview by authors, Mar. 24, 2009.
10. David Giffels, interview by authors, Mar. 12, 2009.
11. Chuck Klosterman, interview by authors, Mar. 23, 2009.
12. David Giffels, Chuck Klosterman, and Michael Weinreb, "Of Loss and Learning," *Akron Beacon Journal,* Apr. 30, 2000.
13. Society of Professional Journalists, "SPS Code of Ethics," 1996–2011, <http://www.spj.org/ethicscode.asp>.
14. Charles Whited, *Knight: A Publisher in the Tumultuous Century* (New York: E. P. Dutton, 1988), 277.
15. Ibid.
16. Frederic C. Bartlett, *Remembering: A Study in Experimental and Social Psychology* (Cambridge, UK: Cambridge Univ. Press, 1932), cited in Barbie Zelizer, "Reading the Past

Against the Grain: The Shape of Memory Stories," *Critical Studies in Mass Communication* 12, no. 2 (June 1995): 215.

17. Carolyn Kitch, "Anniversary Journalism, Collective Memory, and the Cultural Authority to Tell the Story of the American Past," *Journal of Popular Culture* 36, no. 1 (2002): 49.
18. Ibid., 45.
19. Giffels, Klosterman, and Weinreb, "Of Loss and Learning."
20. Edy, "Journalistic Uses of Collective Memory," 73.
21. Michael Schudson, *Watergate in American Memory: How We Remember, Forget, and Reconstruct the Past* (New York: Basic Books, 1992), 52.
22. Mark Bialczak, "Pete Hamill Talks about Newspapers, Fiction, and Life with Keyboard and Pen," *Syracuse Post-Standard*, Dec. 6, 2009, <http://blog.syracuse.com/entertainment/2009/12/pete_hamill_talks_about_newspa.html>.
23. Kitch, "Anniversary Journalism," 59.
24. Ann Sheldon Mezger, interview by Mitch McKenney, Feb. 25, 2009.
25. Bruce Winges, interview by Janet Leach, June 3, 2010
26. Kitch, "Anniversary Journalism," 62.

Wars on Trial in Three Landmark Documentary Films

Night and Fog, Hearts and Minds, and *Taxi to the Dark Side*

Daniel L. Miller and Suzanne Clark

> We have all tried very hard to escape what we have learned.
>
> —Randy Floyd, American pilot during the Vietnam War, *Hearts and Minds*

In the years since World War II, events have left the living with terrible, traumatic memories and moral questions they can remember only with pain, but cannot and must not forget. Do images give us a way to remember the conditions of war, and reflect ethically upon them? It has seemed to many, as Susan Sontag observes, that the power of photography might instead make us wary.[1] Does the emotional shock of pictures depicting the violence of war in fact shortcut the ability of the viewer to reason, producing a kind of voyeurism, while the repetition of iconic images flattens critical, ethical thought?

Some documentary films resolve this dilemma. Michael Rabiger states that documentary film at its best is like a court case.[2] Such films approach the truths of terrible memories through a process like that named by Jay Winter not memory but "remembrance," by including conflicting views through witnesses, images, and film technique.[3] Thus memory is not stopped but rather put on trial—weighed through the diachronic processes of historical perspectives. In *The Great War and Modern Memory,* Paul Fussell shows how the trench warfare of World War I changed writers' fundamental ways of thinking about the *other:* it created a polarized "mode of gross dichotomy" or "the modern versus habit" of irreconcilable opposition.[4] Having experienced the concentration camps of World War II, philosopher Emmanuel Levinas argues that ethics cannot exist in a timeless, either/or relationship to a truth about the other, but, rather, takes place only in diachronic, historical time, in the acts of responsibility called forth by difference—by the face of the other, which is not self and is more than self.[5] The films this essay will discuss include *Night and Fog,* a 1955 documentary about Nazi concentration camps, directed by Alain Resnais and written by Jean Cayrol; *Hearts and Minds,* a 1975 documentary about the Vietnam War, directed by Peter Davis; and *Taxi to the Dark Side,* a 2007 documentary about the torture policies practiced by the United States as part of the war on terrorism in Iraq and Afghanistan since 2001, written and directed by Alex Gibney. These films enact and question the traumatic human stories that are associated with war and the dehumanizing of the other, who in fact might be not the military enemy but rather the victim of patriotic mythologies. As the films show, these histories of violence may be deforming not only to the victims and the perpetrators, but also to those who think themselves not responsible.

Night and Fog (Nuit et brouillard) is a thirty-one-minute French documentary film that portrays the facts of historical evil in the Nazi concentration camps of World War II.[6] It was commissioned, produced, and distributed in 1955, under the auspices of the historian Henri Michel, the French Committee of the History of World War II (Comité d'Histoire de Deuxième Guerre) and the Archives of the Memory (Réseau du Souvenir), an association devoted to the memory of those deported to the camps. *Night and Fog* immediately came under scrutiny and censorship for two things: its depiction of French police officers during World War II guarding a contingent of deportees being herded toward trains to the camps and its use of horrific archival images, particularly during the last ten minutes of the film. Director Alain Resnais agreed to disguise the police emblems on the uniforms of the French officials but was allowed to retain the images used in the film's final ten minutes.

The film was inspired by *Poems of Night and Fog (Poèmes de la nuit et du brouillard),* the poetic memoirs of French author, resistance fighter, and concentration camp survivor Jean Cayrol, who wrote the script for the narration of the film. Cayrol was a victim of the Nazi regime's effort to make those who opposed it disappear by sending them to their deaths in the camps, as if into the night and fog. The policy, announced in 1941, was called NN, *Nacht und Nebel* (*Night and Fog*). While the film does not tell the stories of individuals, in its entirety it may be seen as a form of testimony. Because Cayrol is writing of a history he knew firsthand, even the expository dryness with which he relates facts becomes a public witness to the embodied horrors of the Nazi camps, the scope of which would fully emerge only later, through the testimonies about the Holocaust.[7]

The most innovative and provocative formal and aesthetic choices in the film arise both from the use of archival photos, which give face to the unthinkable, and from decisions to shoot footage of the deserted but intact camps of Majdanek and Auschwitz in color, and then to edit that together with the mostly black-and-white archival still and moving images, using analytical and idea-associative comparison montage, as well as the more dramatic collision montage in which idea A collides with idea B to provoke a new meaning, C. The color film of the cinematic present from the beginning gives us an unbelievable pastoral view of the setting of these crimes: "An ordinary village for vacationers, with a marketplace and a steeple . . . can lead all too easily to a concentration camp," the narrator points out. The camp always had this aspect, a "semblance of a real village," with the commandant and his family trying to lead an ordinary life, as a photograph of the couple at home at the camp attests.

The commandant of Auschwitz, his wife, and his dog at home next to the camp. Image captured by the author from the film *Night and Fog*, directed by Alain Resnais and Jean Cayrol.

The logic and thoroughness of the narrator's catalogue is undermined by what the images show: rows of naked people, a razored head, an arm with tattoos, a uniform with patches, stars, "N N" on the back of a shirt, red triangles, green triangles. The terrible economy of death is similarly catalogued in the pictures of things collected by the Nazis from the prisoners: glasses, women's hair (used to make cloth), bones (for fertilizer), skin (used like parchment for drawing illustrations). Eyes look out at us from the archival footage to express not vision but "continuous fear," as the film says. Here is the face of the other, whose experience we can hardly imagine even as we see.

The final six-minute sequence of the film begins with images of uniformed Nazi men and women prisoners shortly after liberation of the camps being led to form work details under the administration of the Allied troops. This is followed by iconic images of survivors looking out past barbed wire at the events, and then by particularly disturbing images focusing on the dead bodies of victims.

These images are in fact projected for shots of unusual length, in wide, medium, close-up, and extreme close-up views, and focused in many cases on the most physical of evidence: on the human bodies, the human face. The first image screened is that of Nazi female military personnel marching on the diagonal from left to right toward the camera. There is a cut to a nearly identical scene of Nazi male military personnel marching in the same direction. Each face can be seen for a few seconds as it grows in size moving toward the camera. There is then a collision cut, on the same action and direction of movement, of Nazi male prisoners of the Allies carrying dead bodies on their backs along a deep, wide trench, into which the bodies are to be deposited. The beautiful face of a dead woman comes into close view. The body is then fully exposed as the man carrying this woman on his back moves away from the camera behind a line of others and past the Allied guards toward the dumping ground. The marchers this time are moving not on military parade but in a macabre procession in which they labor to carry the abject bodies of the human beings whose deaths they have caused.

When Auschwitz is liberated by Soviet troops, a woman's body is carried on the back of a German soldier to a mass grave. Image captured by the author from the film *Night and Fog,* directed by Alain Resnais and Jean Cayrol.

The next cut is to a shot of two Germans throwing a body into a pile of bodies in the mass grave. The camera tilts down with the body, following it to its resting place against the multitudes already there. Next is a cut to a line of Germans now moving left to right toward the camera carrying human skulls. Then there is an eye line match cut (implying the same perspective) to three successive shots of Jewish prisoners gathered against barbed wire looking at something, which appears to be this act of gathering the bodies and the bones. With the first shot of the falling body, Cayrol's narration begins again, in concert with the visual images: "The inmates look on without understanding. Are they being freed? Will everyday life know them again?" This iconic portrait of their disbelief reflects how totally they had seemed to disappear in the night and fog of the camps.

Now the film cuts to black-and-white archival footage of a Kapo—a prisoner who supervised other prisoners—testifying before a tribunal. He is one who may have been forced to carry the bodies of his victims earlier. "I am not responsible," says the Kapo. Cut to a German officer testifying at a tribunal: "I am not responsible," says the officer. Cut to a close-up of another German face at the tribunal: "I am not responsible." In an idea-associative collision montage cut, the viewer then sees an image of a camp survivor. The narrator's voice asks, "Then who is responsible?" And the viewer is forced to look at a series of three images of human bodies in mass graves. Thus the film's editing emphasizes the astonishing disconnection between the actuality of millions of deaths and the efficient, dissociated apparatus that caused them.

It is at this point that the primary aesthetic stylistic strategy is employed, as the film cuts from the lingering image of the naked bodies to a color image of the wetland swamp waters now (in 1955) filling the depressions in the earth caused by the trenches of the mass graves. From this point through the last shot and sound, the film shows only contemporary (to 1955) color images of the now-abandoned camps, including the landscape: wide shots of the buildings, so seemingly detached from the events that transpired in them (not different from the images on a postcard, Cayrol had said earlier in the film), and the odd detail and detritus of the abandoned camps. The narrative ends with Cayrol saying these final words: "As I speak to you now, the icy water of the ponds and ruins fills the hollows of the mass graves, a frigid and muddy water as murky as our memory. We pretend it all happened only once, at a given time and place." Cut from the last image of the ruins of one crematorium with its peaked roof housing this narration emblematic of the broken-down house of mankind in which took place the worst of human acts—but precisely, very precisely, not the most isolated, unique, or singular of human acts. Then cut to black.

Resnais invented for this film some of the methods for questioning memory that would characterize the future New Wave, the avant-garde movement that marked a historical turn in French cinema. These were not just stylistic choices, but rather were designed to involve the audience in a diachronic experience of trauma that would serve to contradict the apparent normalcy of historical accounts. The collision cuts disrupt the audience's commonsense expectations and make the film more difficult to view in an ordinary state of distraction, where the question of who is responsible might seem easy to answer.

The Allies specifically ordered the process in which the Nazi military and German camp workers are engaged during the final archival sequences, to subject the perpetrators to the realities of the horrors they had either carried out themselves or else supported through their actions. These affecting images can be used to explore and illuminate the layers of mythologies employed by propagandists across history, which rose to martial crescendos during the intrawar Nazi ascendance to indoctrinate compliant publics with the ideologies of Aryan humanness and Jewish otherness. First, there is the myth that these Nazis, now forced to shoulder the dead bodies and thereby confront the harsh, undeniable realities of their false consciousness and assumptions, were invincible, and more human than those perceived as the other, demonstrated as pure delusion at this moment. Second, the very idea that these Jews, now deprived of all life and left only as physical human vessels, could have ever contained the deep levels of otherness with which the Reich's cultural and ideological apparatuses had invested them is visually shown to be false. Even in their deaths, these objects of the Nazi machine have neither disappeared into the night nor become inhuman objects that do not disturb us, as the sight of their vulnerable bodies demonstrates.

The final words of *Night and Fog* warn the viewer that the living have turned a blind eye to what surrounds them and a deaf ear to humanity's never-ending cries. The film was a landmark for a variety of reasons—not least of which are its unpopular theses. Cayrol's text assigned responsibility for the horror of the camps to the racism of the ordinary people who accepted them. The indictment of administrators and direct perpetrators, carried out institutionally in the justice tribunals such as Nuremburg and culturally in the fiction and nonfiction film and television representations of the postwar era, was expanded to include the public(s).

A similar warning issues from Peter Davis's 1974 documentary film *Hearts and Minds,* about the American war in Vietnam.[8] *Hearts and Minds* premiered at Cannes in 1974 and won the Academy Award in 1975 for the Best Feature Documentary, but, like *Night and Fog,* it encountered resistance. The former national security advisor, Walt Rostow, interviewed in the film, accused it of being misleading, claimed he did not get a chance to review his interview, and sought a restraining order. Columbia Pictures refused to distribute the film, which was finally released by Warner Brothers in 1975.

According to Peter Davis, the inquiry in *Hearts and Minds* centers on three questions: "Why did we go to Vietnam, what did we do there, and what did the doing do to us?" Importantly, he adds, "I didn't expect to answer those questions. I expected to address those questions both in shooting and later in editing."[9] *Hearts and Minds* rigorously films its witnesses speaking for themselves in the spirit of cinema verité, without script or rehearsal. In 1972 and 1973, the Vietnamese people testify to the cameras of Dick Pearce and the microphones of Tom Cohen at a time when their lives were still threatened for speaking out.[10] Their voices, individually and in concert, are not only powerful in this film but also unique in films about the Vietnam War. The testimonies of American combatants Randy Floyd, Bobby Muller, William Marshall, and George Coker (a former prisoner of war) are also significant and powerful in the film, for they were witnesses to the conduct of the war, to the effects of the war on the Vietnamese people, and to its effects on American veterans.

Hearts and Minds opens with a shot of a Vietnamese ox-drawn cart in a typical village in Vietnam. The camera pulls away from the cart to reveal the village and then cuts to images of laughing children in a field and of women in the field conducting their everyday lives. There is no sign of war. Finally, a soldier crosses into the frame—it is the intrusion of the war into the lives of Vietnamese people—and the film begins. This opening shot demonstrates how testimony will be framed by a democratically recorded context of sounds and images, in ways that lend the dignity of honesty to the speakers and to their stories. Two examples demonstrate. In the first, political prisoner and torture victim Nguyen Thi Sau is interviewed. She has been released but is crippled and blind from the torture. In addition to the interview, direct-cinema-style shots record her walking through her neighborhood, on narrow pathways framed by the buildings. Children and neighbors walk by in the background and occasionally turn to look on. The camera cuts to emblematic shots of the revealing detritus of an assault on a just-bombed-out village, its homes destroyed. The camera and microphones do not flinch when Vietnamese people walk into the frame, glare at the cameras, and announce angrily, "First they bomb and then they film," implicating the filmmakers themselves in the exploitation of the Vietnamese people. These scenes are edited into the film to document the accusation of these witnesses that the filmmakers themselves bear a responsibility, in particular for a voyeuristic depiction of war and suffering.

Hearts and Minds benefited from technological advances in filmmaking, including the invention of new small cameras and mobile sync sound, pioneered in the 1960s, that made it possible to film direct cinema, with the microphone synchronized to the image. By using this technology to record his evidence, Peter Davis brought to the film a cinema verité staging of the courtroom and trial, demonstrating the idea advanced by Rabiger that a documentary film carries out an inquiry into the truth by incorporating the testimony of participants and letting the audience judge the veracity of this evidence. Among primary witnesses, the oppositions are pronounced. Throughout the film, for example, the unrepentant all-American pilot George Coker is set in opposition to the repentant and obviously damaged American pilot Randy Floyd. Coker is filmed giving—honestly and forthrightly, it seems—celebratory speeches that reflect the earlier nationalistic atmosphere of the cold war; during seven years as a prisoner of war, he had had no contact with the growing American unease about the war. In contrast, Floyd, like other pilots in the film, tells a story of transformation through his experiences in Vietnam that is contrasted to his earlier dedication to the war, and the film ends with Floyd's emotional admissions of thoughtless damage to Vietnamese civilians.

Another scene of dramatic opposition shows the white, upper-middle-class, patriotic Emerson family (descended from Ralph Waldo Emerson) in their home in Massachusetts. Their beloved son Bing had graduated from Harvard and become a journalist before enlisting and serving as a helicopter pilot in the war. He died during a rescue mission. As David Emerson, his wife beside him, describes his views about the America that he believes in and his love for his son, he also declares his belief in the rightness of Bing's sacrifice, an endorsement for the struggle in Vietnam. Davis describes this interview as the most difficult one to film because of the pain he and his crew witnessed and recorded. The unstaged cinema verité filming keeps the sound of Emerson's voice while framing and reframing the moving camera, from David's agonized face, visibly torn about the truth, to the face of his wife, blank or traversed by a flash of pain, and then panning down to an extreme close-up of her hand gently caressing the model airplane her son had built as a young boy.

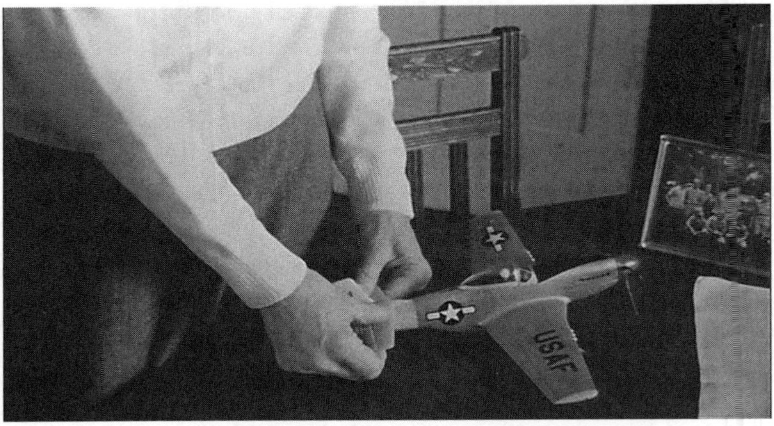

The hands of a mother, Mrs. Emerson, touching her son's model airplane as her husband speaks of the son's death in Vietnam. Image captured by the author from the film *Hearts and Minds,* directed by Peter Davis.

Such dramatic oppositions spark intense intellectual tension by providing varying views and sets of evidence. The primary aesthetic of editing in this film is *montage* of three primary types: (1) analytical montage, designed simply to edit shots together that analyze the evidentiary details of the event; (2) the classic idea associative montage, designed to juxtapose two shots or ideas that do not merely contribute to the sum of the whole meaning but create an entirely new meaning; and (3) idea associative collision montage, in which the new meaning relies on the dialectical collision of the shots/ideas juxtaposed. War is about collision, and not simply military collision but—at the heart of this film's meanings—intellectual, ethical, and moral collision on the deepest level of human conviction.

As in *Night and Fog,* archival footage provides compelling images in this film, including black-and-white newsreel footage that traces the long, seldom-disclosed history of the war and displays evidence of U.S. and U.S.-surrogate South Vietnamese forces instituting widespread programs of civilian destruction, assassination, torture, and governmental secrecy. In contrast, however, Davis incorporates images from American dramatic and instructional film media that promoted an ultra-patriotic, anti-Communist view of Vietnam's war and its conduct—the ground in which a general public acquiescence could be cultivated. Even more powerfully, the film employs idea collision montage to juxtapose irreconcilable images and stories. Davis uses color archival newsreel and file footage depicting not only images of war but also, as counterpoint, images of parades and other celebratory cultural events. In addition, Davis includes new color cinema footage of such mundane events as football games to portray a daily life that is distanced from the war.

The final seven-minute sequence of *Hearts and Minds* incorporates the types of presentation of images, sounds, ideas, and collision montage discussed above; it thus represents a link between *Night and Fog*, which preceded and influenced it, and the third film to be discussed, *Taxi to the Dark Side*. In collision editing style, Davis juxtaposes a scene of Richard Nixon speaking to released prisoners of war, praising the brave men who carried out the Christmas bombings of 1972, with archival footage of the bombing itself—footage that had alienated the world from U.S. policy when it was first broadcast. He follows this with a series of collision montage juxtapositions that contrast the pain of the Vietnamese with the views of the American military. Vu Duc Vinh, filmed in his North Vietnamese village with his destroyed home behind him, cries out, "My eight-year-old daughter was killed and my three-year-old son. Nixon! Murderer of civilians. . . . She was feeding the pigs. . . . She was so sweet. . . . No targets here, only rice fields and houses." The sound of a boy moaning and sobbing comes in over the farmer. There is a visual cut to a funeral in South Vietnam. Bamboo drums click loudly. A young boy sobs at a picture of his brother, the victim, a member of the military fighting on our side.

At this point the film displays its most controversial piece of editing: a collision cut to General Westmoreland, poised and calm in an interview by a sylvan South Carolina lake. "Well," he says, "the Oriental doesn't put the same high price on human life as does the Westerner."[11] The film then cuts to napalm bombs falling on a village, and, under this footage and sound of the bombs, viewers first hear the voice of former naval pilot Randy Floyd and then see his image. "During the missions," he says, " . . . the results of this game, this . . . exercise of my technical expertise, never really dawned on me." The film next cuts to the same village being bombed, but this time viewers see footage of burned children running, including Phan Thi Kim Phuc, the little girl captured in the iconic Pulitzer Prize–winning photo of the same event by Vietnamese photojournalist Nick Ut.

Mother with napalmed baby on a road in Vietnam after an American strike. Image captured by the author from the film *Hearts and Minds*, directed by Peter Davis.

The film cuts back to Floyd. "When I was there," he says, "I didn't drop napalm, but I dropped other things that were just as bad—CBUs . . . with something like six hundred pellets in each ball that would blow out as soon as it hit the ground—that would shred people to pieces." When Davis, off screen, then asks him, "Do you think we are learning anything from all this?" it is Floyd in the cinema verité interview, not a narrator, whose emotional reflections provide the final words of the film: "I think Americans have tried, we have all tried very hard, to escape what we have learned in Vietnam. People fighting for their own freedoms are not going to be stopped by just changing your tactics. Americans have worked extremely hard not to see the criminality that their officials and their policy makers have exhibited." The camera pans up and looks out over a seemingly endless line of graves, stretching into the distance of a barren brown earth landscape. The film then fades to black.

Peter Davis brings the audience back to the film and the questions he has posed in it in a dramatic direct-cinema parade sequence, powerfully shot. Intended to celebrate the peace treaty, the withdrawal of U.S. troops, and conclusion of the fighting, the parade is filmed from every viewpoint, from its interior and from the perspective of those observing it. The long sequence creates a series of collisions in the film. It does this first by contrasting the stark realities of the pain of the war and the victims piling up in South Vietnam with the bombastic, martial music and marching of Americans ten thousand miles removed from the violence. Floyd, as one of the perpetrators of the violence, has expressed a regret that is at odds with the parade. The images of the pain suffered by the Vietnamese children make the scenes of celebration ironic, while the collision montage interrupts any easy interpretation by the viewer. The signature theme is not celebration, but rather collision of ideas and attitudes within the culture and society itself. One of the very few scenes of protesters in the film comes into view, and, as the audience watches, fascinated, the parade ominously breaks down into hateful rhetoric, confrontation, and violent assault by a martial patriotism against those nonviolently opposing the war. This film resonates with *Night and Fog,* especially in its warning regarding the ongoing willingness of publics to turn away from knowledge and deny complicity. Both call on viewers to look at the past with a critical, questioning eye, to hold its darkest, most shadowy, hidden, and unsavory moments to the light, and to see the faces of those whose lives were not valued. Like *Night and Fog, Hearts and Minds* makes strong demands on an audience and questions the excess of patriotic fervor. In this, it links prophetically to the history told in *Taxi to the Dark Side.*

Released in 2007, *Taxi to the Dark Side,* like *Hearts and Minds,* won the Academy Award for a feature-length documentary film.[12] Director Alex Gibney was urged to take on the inquiry into the dark side of U.S. prisoner treatment under the Bush administration by his father, Frank B. Gibney (to whom the film is dedicated). An interrogator for the U.S. Navy during World War II, Frank told his son that stories charging U.S. forces with using torture in interrogations of prisoners of war suggested widespread violations by the United States of the ethics of war conventions. Alex Gibney found the story of Dilawar, an Afghani farmer, in a 2005 *New York Times* story by Tim Golden about Dilawar's death at Bagram prison in Afghanistan.[13] This film is resonant with the moral questions raised by the two previous films about the responsibility for the torture and death of those seen as the enemy, the other.

Like *Hearts and Minds, Taxi to the Dark Side* features revealing interviews with soldiers involved directly in the conduct of war crimes, participants in Dilawar's ordeal, and witnesses of events at Bagram.[14] The interviews focus primarily on the young American men who participated in terrible acts and, in some cases, were found guilty of the crimes. For Alex Gibney, it becomes especially important to understand that Dilawar's death is part of a larger crime, in which these guilty persecutors are also victims. The only prisoner interviewed in the film is Moazzam Begg, who describes his ordeal and the cavalier response of the U.S. soldiers holding him: "I was kidnapped, abducted, tossed in prison, tortured, threatened with further torture, without charge, without trial. Even many soldiers have said to me afterwards, 'Well, hell, if you weren't a terrorist when you came in here I am sure you will be by the time you leave just because of the way you've been treated.'" The film makes a nonverbal link between Begg and the soldiers. On camera, looking directly at the interviewer and the audience, Begg is lit as if he is a witness in a courtroom, in exactly the same way and with the same backdrop as the soldiers who testified, soldiers Begg witnessed at Bagram where he heard Dilawar crying for his mother. Thus Gibney's evidence puts the torture policy itself on trial and suggests visually as well as verbally that the treatment of prisoners made soldiers into victims as well as perpetrators. Unlike the wide-ranging interviews incorporated into *Hearts and Minds, Taxi* does not feature the testimony of other citizens of Afghanistan or Iraq as its key witnesses in interviews, but it does employ strategies to give them a face and a voice that are also powerful. It represents them first and foremost by focusing on Dilawar's story. Dilawar, aged twenty-two, was an Afghani son, brother, husband, father, and farmer-turned-taxi-driver. A poor man from a small community, he was detained, tortured, and murdered by young Americans at Bagram prison in December 2002. Afghani middlemen had turned him in, as happened to so many. Even his persecutors believed he was innocent.[15]

Dilawar's story is the heartbreaking central mystery of the film. Affecting images of Dilawar and his family at his home bookend the main body of the film. The official notice from the U.S. military announcing to his family that Dilawar had died at Bagram prison has on it the (brave) coroner's assessment. *New York Times* reporter Carlotta Gall made the shocking discovery when she visited the family and translated for the first time the official paper they showed her, written in English: the cause of death was marked as "Homicide." Who killed the vulnerable and innocent Afghani taxi driver, Dilawar?

The quest for an answer leads the film to a second narrative level, as the evidence begins to implicate members of a wider circle of responsibility. Gibney includes testimony from a host of interviewees about this larger context, from FBI Special Agent Jack Cloonan to Senator Carl Levin to psychologist and scholar Alfred McCoy.[16] These interviews are supplemented by archival footage of statements and testimonies from the popular media. The administration of George W. Bush is represented by footage of Vice President Richard Cheney; Secretary of Defense Donald Rumsfeld, who drafted new anything-goes rules for prisoner Sheik Mohammed al-Qahtani and others; Attorney General Alberto Gonzalez; John Yoo of the Office of Legal Counsel at the Department of Justice and author of what is known as the "torture memo"; and President Bush himself, who questioned whether the Geneva rules applied in the war on terror. The torture memo was classified in 2003 so that the public did not see what it alleged: the U.S. president has every right to impose torture policies because in acting for the military he is not bound by criminal law: treaties and the War Crimes Act apply only to uniformed enemy soldiers, and federal statutes against torture do not apply on military bases. Even more strikingly, Gibney shows the official, mostly redacted forms, memos, and transcripts that instituted the policies; childlike drawings of prisoners; images recorded by the military of hundreds of prisoners in the ubiquitous hoods, goggles, and earmuffs; the so-called party photos of prisoner torture and humiliation at Abu Ghraib prison in Iraq; and drawings and images of similar (in some cases identical) tortures, such as water boarding, collected from conflicts ranging from the Inquisition, to World War II, to the Vietnam War and Cambodia.

The use of recreated scenes or of digitally constructed or enhanced multimedia graphic images would not have been regarded as appropriate for the direct-cinema aesthetic of *Hearts and Minds,* but were in fact employed appropriately in *Taxi to the Dark Side.* In a New York studio, Gibney recorded scenes of actors as stark hooded figures hanging from wire on handcuffs through bars to use intermittently as stock images. In the most dramatic re-creation, Gibney used the written transcripts of video recordings to enact the torture sessions of Mohammed al-Qahtani at Guantánamo Bay. The video recordings were not made available to the filmmakers. Instead, actors portray the scenes of military personnel torturing al-Qahtani in a mixed multimedia representation, shot in close-up and extreme close-up, and in slow motion, against an antiseptic, stark, digitally produced white screen background. When the figures, represented in an abstract, pop-cultural style, put on party hats and sing to the National Anthem and the American flag, the irony resonates.

The final scenes of *Taxi to the Dark Side* begin twelve minutes from the end of the film with the pardon of everyone in command positions and the prosecution of all those who are not. They show how the Geneva Convention was circumvented. Pfc. Willie Brand, Sgt. Anthony Morden, Pfc. Damien Corsetti, and Specialist Glendale

Walls describe the conduct and consequences of their trials. All but Corsetti were convicted, and all were personally devastated. Then the film cuts to an outraged Alberto Mora, then general counsel to the U.S. Navy, who had sought unsuccessfully to end the use of torture at Guantánamo Bay, and who says in his interview, directly and unequivocally, "We fight not only to protect lives; we fight to protect our principles," a statement that articulates the perspective of Gibney's film.

Dilawar appears on screen for the final time, in a photograph showing him sitting by the pile of stones he had carried from the mountains to his family farm for building. There is a cut to a film of Dilawar's mourning brother, Shapoor, who asks, "What should I say to the Americans? My brother was innocent—he was barely more than a child—and they killed him." There is a cut out to a wider shot of Dilawar's daughter and father. Thus the images and sounds of Dilawar's home that opened the film and are revisited during it—images and sounds that testify to everyday life, dignity, and humanity rather than war—reappear at its end. Like the scenes opening *Hearts and Minds*, scenes of village life in Vietnam quite consciously removed, at first, from the war, these images from Dilawar's life in *Taxi to the Dark Side* accomplish the same effect. They demonstrate that people in their own country have humanity, lives, and families with children. They collide with the familiar images of power and the irrational excess of revenge. The film fades to black on the taxi in the fields of Afghanistan and fades up from black to a taxi in Washington, D.C.

A re-created mock-up of the shackling used on Dilawar at Bagram. Image captured by the author from the film *Taxi to the Dark Side*, directed by Alex Gibney.

In *Taxi to the Dark Side*, unlike *Night and Fog* or *Hearts and Minds*, the director himself speaks the words of the invested and self-revealing filmmaker. After Shapoor's last word, Gibney speaks: "There's a lot of other people out there that are going to run

Dilawar's daughter with his father. Image captured by the author from the film *Taxi to the Dark Side,* directed by Alex Gibney.

into this system unless it's fixed, and you only need one to remind yourself what it's capable of." His film does not chiefly indict the young men who carried out the torture; like the pilots and foot soldiers in Vietnam, they are depicted as scapegoats. Who should have been on trial? The recreated scenes and the reenactment of al-Qahtani's torture are not pictures of the real event, but the events of the sessions were not the true crimes. They are, rather, evidence—supported in the film by documents—of a real ethical event that continues, that exists in the ongoing history of torture, and that exceeds the literal moment of the murder. In the commentary, Gibney says that the shock of reading the transcripts came not just from what the torture sessions were doing to al-Qahtani but from what they were doing to those who were designing, conducting, and executing those sessions.

One of the cultural and social elements contained in *Hearts and Minds* and glaringly absent from *Taxi to the Dark Side* is the protest movement. Although Peter Davis made a conscious and appropriate decision in his film not to focus on protest—indeed, it is almost invisible—he did include sequences of soldiers who became leaders of protest, and a sequence of powerful images of antiwar protest in Washington, D.C., where hundreds of thousands of Americans from every walk of life gathered to protest the death in Vietnam and the corrupt policies of the U.S. government. And the final sequence in *Hearts and Minds,* the last image and thus the last word in the film, is punctuated by ugly public citizen violence against dissent. Like Peter Davis in *Hearts and Minds,* Gibney uses the credit sequence to add a coda to *Taxi to the Dark Side.* Gibney, sadly, had a more difficult task, with few images of widespread protest to draw on (although very large protests had occurred). The way that *Taxi to the Dark Side* shows protest is through the acts of representative individuals: first, by highlighting those courageous few souls in the administration who protested; second, by protesting himself through the production and distribution of his brilliant film; and, finally and most tellingly, by showing his father to his audience. Frank Gibney, in the film's last word and postscript, protests the conduct of America with the dignity of a distinguished human being who not only had fought for America throughout his life but who had specifically served as a military interrogator. Alex Gibney's father, then fatally ill, had asked to testify to the moral outrage represented by interrogations that violate the Geneva Convention.

How do the viewers of *Taxi to the Dark Side* now hear the warnings of Jean Cayrol in *Night and Fog,* that the crimes against humanity conducted in the death camps and acquiesced to by the citizens of many countries were not isolated but were repeated through history and must be seen, heard, remembered, and guarded against constantly and vigilantly? How could it be that the warnings given voice by Lt. Randy Floyd—that the United States as a nation was complicit in Vietnam in the same behaviors perpetrated by our enemies in World War II—were not heeded? How could it happen that crimes against the other were committed not as individual and atypical cases of torture but through the application of a torture policy?

As *Night and Fog* did in 1955 and *Hearts and Minds* did in 1974, *Taxi to the Dark Side* in 2007 used the considerable powers of the documentary film to raise questions about human ethics and violence within the context of a moral history. These documentaries do not flinch from displaying the terrible images that have, in iconic photographs, become touchstones for our historical memory. However, through the shock of the contrasts and contradictions revealed by collision montage, these three films put truth on trial and turn history from a series of *conclusions*—vulnerable to the "versus habit" that Fussell documents—to a process of *questioning.* This escape from polarized antipathy makes ethical responsibility possible, perhaps to protest the horrors that have depended on the acquiescence of citizens who think themselves not responsible.

Notes

1. Susan Sontag's *On Photography* (New York: Farrar, Straus, and Giroux, 1977) raised questions about the influence of images: she argued that audiences tend to view photographic evidence as if it represents reality, an unwarranted claim. Sontag later revised these in her analysis of war photography, seeing the images as part of the rhetoric of war, and the most terrible of them as the most demanding of our critical thought; see Sontag, *Regarding the Pain of Others* (New York: Farrar, Straus, and Giroux, 2003), 42.
2. "Like a prosecutor or an attorney for the defense," says Michael Rabiger, "the documentary director must decide how best to present the evidence and under what conditions." Regarding the audience, he writes: "The final version of a film can be likened to the final stage of a trial when the main issues are summed up for the jury. The jury must decide whom do they believe, whom do they like, whom do they disbelieve? With whom do they empathize, and whose version of events squares most with their own experience of life?" Michael Rabiger, *Directing the Documentary,* 4th ed. (Burlington, Mass.: Focal Press, 2004), 62–63.

3. Winter, *Remembering War.* See especially the introduction and the section titled "The Age of the Witness" in chapter 1, 27 ff. Winter argues that historical memory today is "fractured," and the very meaning of *memory* itself has become multiple and contested. He proposes that the quest of this generation for memory, or memory boom, in the wake of the Holocaust is about a process of remembering—*remembrance*. "Collective remembrance," he says, "is a matter of activity" and it privileges new voices, the agency first and foremost of survivors, of posttraumatic searchings—the witnesses, Winter, *Remembering War,* 28.
4. Paul Fussell, *The Great War and Modern Memory,* 25th anniversary ed. (New York: Oxford Univ. Press, 2000), 76, 79.
5. See discussions throughout Emmanuel Levinas's works on ethics and philosophy: for example, in the selections of *Basic Philosophical Writings,* ed. Adrian Peperzak, Simon Critchley, and Robert Bernasconi (Bloomington: Indiana Univ. Press, 1996) and in the essay collection *Entre Nous: Thinking of the Other,* European Perspectives, trans. Michael B. Smith and Barbara Itarshav (New York: Columbia Univ. Press, 1998).
6. *Night and Fog [Nuit et brouillard]* (documentary film), dir. Alain Resnais, narration written by Jean Cayrol, trans. Alexander Alan (Neuilly-sur-Seine, France: Argos Films, 1955); DVD, Criterion Collection, 2003. This edition of the film restores the original version, before censorship.
7. Partly for technical reasons, the film—although pioneering in its treatment of the Holocaust—preceded the era of focusing on the testimony of victims in historical remembrance, which Jay Winter saw as beginning in 1969 with Marcel Ophüls's *The Sorrow and the Pity* (*Remembering War,* 28). Nonetheless, the film in its entirety is a form of testimony.
8. *Hearts and Minds* (documentary film), dir. Peter Davis (BBS Productions, 1974); DVD, Criterion Collection, 2002.
9. Peter Davis, "Commentary," *Hearts and Minds.*
10. Vietnamese interviewed include, among others, Mui Duc Giang (coffin builder), Father Chan Tin (Catholic priest), Diem Chau (editor, *Trinh Bay* magazine), Gen. Nguyen Khanh (president of South Vietnam, 1964–65), Nguyen Van Tai (farmer and bombing victim), Vo Thi Hue and Vo Thi Tu (seventy-year-old sisters and bombing victims), and Nguyen Thi Sau andNgo Ba Thanh (political prisoners and torture victims).
11. Davis, "Commentary," *Hearts and Minds.* Davis goes on to describe the filming of Westmoreland's comment: when he said for the first time that Orientals value life less that Westerners, Davis was surprised and asked him to repeat that segment. A second take ran out of film, and five minutes later, during the third take, the general repeated the cliché once again.
12. *Taxi to the Dark Side* (documentary film), dir. Alex Gibney (THINKFilm, 2007); DVD.
13. Tim Golden et al., "In U.S. Report, Brutal Details of 2 Afghan Inmates' Deaths," *New York Times,* May 20, 2005, <http://www.nytimes.com/2005/05/20/international/asia/20abuse.html?pagewanted=1&_r=2>.
14. There are interviews of those indicted and found guilty and of others who were at Bagram, including Sgt. Thomas Curtis, Military Police, Bagram (not indicted); and Pfc. Damien Corsetti, Military Intelligence, Bagram (indicted, found innocent). Like Randy Floyd in *Hearts and Minds,* Spc. Tony Lagouranis, interrogator, Military Intel-

ligence, Iraq—transformed by his participation—provides a featured interview about his firsthand experience with the practices of interrogation. He was not at Bagram and was not indicted. Others involved were not interviewed: Eric Lahammer, Military Intelligence, Bagram and Abu Ghraib, who worked on Dilawar; Spc. Brian Cammack, who was tried and convicted for abuse; and Capt. Christopher Beiring, the only officer ever indicted, who was found innocent because of the lack of clear orders.

15. According to statistics given by Alex Gibney in his commentary to *Taxi to the Dark Side*, only 3 percent of those who were arrested for terrorist activity were, in fact, ever found guilty. The number of innocents like Dilawar put in prison must be staggering.

16. There are interviews of many military and intelligence personnel in positions of experience and power, including Special Agent Cloonan, FBI, who visited Guantánamo and denied the effectiveness of such interrogation; Col. Lawrence Wilkerson, U.S. Army, assistant to Colin Powell; Gibney's own father; reporters Tim Golden, Ruhallah Khapalwak, Carlotta Gall, and David Rohde, who originally researched, investigated, wrote, and broke the central stories documented; Scott Horton, chair of the NYC Bar Association's Committee on International Law, who advised judge advocate general attorneys outraged about the fog of ambiguity put out by the highest levels of the Pentagon; Clive Stafford Smith, lawyer for Guantánamo detainees (including Moazzam Begg), who said "Habeas Corpus is the essence of the law"; John Galligan, attorney for Willie Brand; sociologists, psychologists, and scholars such as Alfred W. McCoy, who has studied and written about the specific policies of this war as well as the broader historical contexts and antecedents of these policies (McCoy had been writing books about the drug wars since 1976); Carl Levin, one of the senators opposed to the policies; the courageous and outraged Alberto Mora, general counsel to the Navy, 2001–6; and other powerful political and military figures. For a full list of those who appear in the film, see IMDb.com, Internet Movie Database, Inc., 1990–2011, <http://www.imdb.com/title/tt0854678/fullcredits#cast>.

Part III

Memory, History, and Justice

Introduction

Kenneth J. Bindas

One of the key questions raised by the 2009 Kent State University Symposium on Democracy concerned the nature of memory and how individuals and society choose to remember or, in some cases, not remember events of the collective past. The conference's focus on remembering suggested that there is some disconnect not only in what we choose to recall, but in how memory is tied to the larger community. The shootings at Kent State University on May 4, 1970, of course, constitute one such contested memory in an era of contested events and are part of the larger collective memory concerning the transformation of the United States after World War II.

The study of memory is a tangled web of science, law, and humanities, where scientists look at the process through the lens of cognition, lawyers through validation, and students of the humanities through experience.[1] In recent years, this focus on memory has not only allowed the powerful and dominant culture to speak, but also granted the disenfranchised, abused, ignored, exploited, and forgotten the space to detail their experiences, in the hope that by giving legitimacy to these remembrances, some clarity or meaning regarding the larger social or political context might emerge. We, as readers or listeners, will better learn about our collective past through the addition of these new voices. Scholars, lawyers, and documentarians have played a central role in this process, seeking to draw inaudible or once silent voices to the discourse. Telling, collecting, and retelling these stories thus become a dialogue of intention—what the historical actor using her or his memory wants to detail and the information that the expert wants to focus on in order to *re*tell a story. Each approach the interview with specific intentions and, through a process of give-and-take, meet at the intersection of collective memory. But, as Cormac McCarthy's main character relates in *The Road,* "each memory recalled must do some violence to its origins . . . so be sparing. What you alter in the remembering has yet a reality, known or not."[2] Each memory exists both inside and outside its origins and is made valid by the social context of its creation and dissemination. So while memory is neither history nor truth, it does inform and give life to the larger story of humanity, providing insight into the continuing dialogue that is at the root of both memory and history.

Many events that have transpired since 1945, like those of May 4, 1970, at Kent, continue to be discussed and debated—as this volume suggests. In the weeks leading up to the 2009 symposium, for example, thirty-nine years after the events of that day, local newspapers carried several letters to the editor reflecting the long-standing division between those who want to leave the past alone and those who want more truth. Only a few days before the symposium, when confrontations between police and over-partying Kent State University students escalated, *YouTube* depicted some students yelling, "Remember May 4!" and singing the iconic "Four Dead in Ohio." To this cohort, any police action is a replay of the abuse of power that was evident in May 1970, regardless of their understanding of the context. The larger issue regarding memory and its place in the historical narrative, then, is how the past resonates with those not present or invested in the story. How do we as a society deal with the events of the past, and how do they become a part of the collective memory? This volume seeks to open and broaden this dialogue by referencing several landmark events that have taken place since 1945 and thereby placing them into the larger context of memory, its personal and social meaning, and the larger historical process.[3]

The authors in this section document the broadening of this dialogue, some focusing on the Kent State event and some on events from other periods and places, to discuss the meaning of memory in its personal and social contexts. All of the essays concern the difficult concept of assigning, accepting, and even deflecting responsibility. The essays also underscore the tensions between the memory and law, experience and the historical record, power and silence. While they discuss different events, they all illuminate the difficulty of trying to come to some closure regarding the events of May 4 and suggest that more memory work on that event remains to be done.

Cathy J. Collins examines the process of collective remembering and forgetting regarding the 1957 school integration crisis in Little Rock, Arkansas. Her analysis explores what, how, and why Little Rock chose to remember and what steps were taken to reconcile historical with social memory. She suggests that for Little Rock, the situation comes closer to *dis*-remembering, as the events since the creation of a commemoration committee in the mid-1990s fall more in line with Iona Irwin-Zarecka and Judith Miller's model of neutralizing memory by blaming the victim, becoming the victim, placing blame outside the community, and suggesting that Little Rock's race relations were not as bad as those of other places. She traces the rise and development of the commemoration committee preparing for the fortieth anniversary of the crisis in 1997 and the fiftieth in 2007, in order to document the tension between those wanting to use the events to promote racial healing (claiming everything is fine now) and those wanting to portray the events with historical accuracy. Some white residents were reluctant to participate in the historical approach, arguing that the situation was not that bad in Little Rock, that in a way the victims brought it on themselves, and that outside agents (the government and the media) turned a small event into a national crisis. Collins points out how this group simply refused—then and afterward—to confront the reality of the daily indignities suffered by the nine young black students and so contested the collective memory designed by the commemoration group. She concludes by arguing that the Little Rock crisis and the nine children who led the integration of Central High School remain largely invisible and serve as an example of how collective and social memory can be manipulated and reconstructed to either validate or marginalize the participants.[4]

In her essay, Renee Romano compares the events at Kent on May 4, 1970, with those which took place in Greensboro, North Carolina, on November 3, 1979. She does not suggest that the events were the same (the students at Kent were shot by the National Guard in the context of a series of antiwar demonstrations and activities, while at Greensboro Klansmen and American Nazis fired into a crowd of labor and civil rights activists taking part in a march organized by the Communist Workers Party), but she does assert that the two events "left a raw wound in both communities for decades." The festering of such wounds arises from the contested nature of history and memory, as both sides sought to have their stories validated within the community, and, failing that, through the legal system. Although neither the community nor the law provided a satisfactory way to reconcile the grief and hard feelings generated by the events, Romano posits that in Greensboro, the failure of the legal and social processes did eventually prompt community activists, labor leaders, university members, local politicians, and an ecumenical group to unite in creating the Greensboro Truth and Reconciliation Committee in 2004, to try to get the community to grow beyond the events of 1979. The committee's final report, issued in 2006, helped "establish a more honest narrative" related to the contested events and could serve as a model for Kent State University and its local community to move beyond May 1970 and begin to build for the future.[5]

Jerry M. Lewis, who was a witness to the shootings at Kent State on May 4, 1970, suggests the difficulty such a reconciliation process might encounter in Kent, positioning the personal memories of those who were at Kent on that day against those without vested interest in the narrative—a process that remains contested. Using anthropologist James Wertsch's model for collective remembering as his guide, Lewis places the annual remembrance activities associated with May 4 outside the historical collective memory process and within that of social or personal remembering. He traces the rise and development of three major social remembering events—the Candlelight March, the Candlelight Vigil, and the May 4 Commemoration—and one physical entity of remembrance—the May 4 Memorial—to suggest that the contest over social remembering has led to a dysfunctional relationship locally between memory and memorial. At the heart of Lewis's essay is a defense of the Kent State community's position within the social remembering stage, even while he suggests that the time has arrived for a process of historical analysis. Lewis contends, however, that historical analysis need not supplant social remembering, instead suggesting that the social memory process is an appropriate honoring of those killed and wounded and continues to serve as a historical reminder to the larger society.[6]

The three essays in this section are linked in their pathos and the desire they exhibit for open and forthright discussion. They are also joined with the rest of the essays in this volume in their willingness to continue the dialogue on the human process that allows us to remember and to share our collective memory so that, first and foremost, we do not forget, and furthermore, that we come to understand and accept our place within that collective memory.

Notes

1. For pertinent discussions of memory and history, see Maurice Halbwachs, *On Collective Memory,* ed. and trans. Lewis A. Coser (Chicago, Ill.: Univ. of Chicago Press, 1992); James W. Pennebaker, Dario Paez, and Bernard Rimé, eds., *Collective Memory of Political Events: Social Psychological Perspectives* (New York: Sage, 2006), especially Dario Paez, Nekane Basabe and Jose Luis Gonzalez, "Social Processes and Collective Memory: A Cross-Cultural Approach to Remembering Political Events," 147–74; Jaclyn Jeffrey and Glenace Edwall, eds., *Memory and History: Essays on Recalling and Interpreting Experience* (Lanham, Md.: Univ. Press of America, 1994), especially Paul Thompson, "Believe It or Not: Rethinking the Historical Interpretation of Memory," 1–16; and Paul Thompson, *The Voice of the Past: Oral History,* 2nd ed. (New York: Oxford Univ. Press, 1988).
2. Cormac McCarthy, *The Road* (New York: Knopf, 2006), 111.
3. The process of contextualizing such events is discussed in Jeffery C. Alexander, "Toward a Theory of Cultural Trauma," in *Cultural Trauma and Collective Identity,* ed. Jeffrey C. Alexander et al. (Berkeley: Univ. of California Press, 2004), 85–108.
4. For related discussions of how collective and social memory can be manipulated and deconstructed, see Kathryn L. Nasstrom, "Beginnings and Endings: Life Stories and the Periodization of the Civil Rights Movement," *Journal of American History* 86, no. 2 (September 1999): 700–711; Leigh Raiford and Renee C. Romano, "Introduction: The Struggle over Memory," in *The Civil Rights Movement in American Memory,* ed. Renee C. Romano and Leigh Raiford (Athens: Univ. of Georgia Press, 2006), xvi–xx; Edward P. Morgan, "The Good, the Bad, and the Forgotten: Media Culture and Public Memory of the Civil Rights Movement," in Romano and Raiford, *The Civil Rights Movement in American Memory,* 137–66; Scott A. Sandage, "A Marble House Divided: The Lincoln Memorial, the Civil Rights Movement, and the Politics of Memory, 1939–1963," in *Time Longer than Rope: A Century of African American Activism, 1850–1950,* ed. Charles M. Payne and Adam Green

(New York: New York Univ. Press, 2003), 492–535; and Roy F. Baumeister and Stephen Hastings, "Distortions of Collective Memory: How Groups Flatter and Deceive Themselves," in Pennebaker, Paez, and Rimé, *Collective Memory of Political Events,* 277–94.

5. *The American Historical Review* dedicated an entire forum to truth and reconciliation in history. *American Historical Review* 114, no. 4 (October 2009); see especially in that issue James T. Campbell, "Settling Accounts? An Americanist Perspective on Historical Reconciliation," 963–77. See also J. G. Stein, "Image, Identity, and Conflict Resolution," in *Peace, Conflict and Violence: Peace Psychology for the 21st Century,* ed. Daniel J. Christie, Richard V. Wagner, and Deborah DuNann Winter (Englewood Cliffs N.J.: Prentice-Hall, 2001), 189–208; William Chafe et al., eds., *Remembering Jim Crow: African Americans Tell about Life in the Segregated South* (New York: New Press, 2001); Jennifer Rittenhouse, *Growing Up Jim Crow: How Black and White Children Learned Race* (Chapel Hill: Univ. of North Carolina Press, 2006); Renee C. Romano, "Narrative of Redemption: The Birmingham Church Bombing Trials and the Construction of Civil Rights Memory," in Romano and Raiford, *The Civil Rights Movement in American Memory,* 96–134; and Larry J. Griffin, "'Generations and Collective Memory' Revisited: Race, Region, and the Memory of Civil Rights," *American Sociological Review* 69, no. 4 (August 2004): 544–57.

6. Analyses of the struggle between social memory and history related to Lewis's discussion include James Wertsch, *Voices of Collective Remembering* (Cambridge, UK: Cambridge Univ. Press, 2002), 15–66; Diane Barthel, *Historic Preservation: Collective Memory and Historical Identity* (New Brunswick, N.J.: Rutgers Univ. Press, 1996); Michael Frisch, "American History and the Structures of Collective Memory: A Modest Exercise in Empirical Iconography," *Journal of American History* 75, no. 4 (March 1989): 1130–55; Tom Grace, "Kent State: The Struggle for Memory and Meaning," *The Sixties: A Journal of History, Politics and Culture* 2, no. 2 (December 2009): 245–49; and Bernard Rimé and Véronique Christophe, "How Individual Emotional Episodes Feed Collective Memory," in Pennebaker, Paez, and Rimé, *Collective Memory of Political Events,* 131–46.

The Role of Forgetting in Remembering
The Desegregation of Central High School in Little Rock, Arkansas

Cathy J. Collins

I graduated from Central High School in Little Rock, Arkansas, twenty-five years after Ernest Green. I did not know this until nearly fifteen years later, when I became part of the official memory-making process by serving on the Planning Committee of the Central High Museum Visitor Center and the Advisory Committee to the Little Rock Central High Anniversary Commission. Indeed, my 1983 yearbook states, on a full-page picture of Central High School, "What amazed Mr. [Harry] Reasoner [of CBS News] and the other reporters was the fact that today's students at Central 'know very little or nothing at all' about the 1957 crisis."[1] Despite the fact that there was an ever-present monument to the desegregation crisis of Central High School—Central High School itself—Little Rock spent much effort in actively not remembering the events that had transpired. It was as if forgetting equaled having moved beyond the racial strife of the past.

Iona Irwin-Zarecka and Judith Miller, whose work examined the Holocaust, provide a framework for understanding Little Rock's memory-making process concerning that event as historical amnesia and purposeful forgetting. Irwin-Zarecka establishes four criteria for neutralizing memory: blaming the victim, seeing oneself as the victim, distancing the problem, and universalizing the problem.[2] Miller explains that memory is culturally suppressed through denial, shifting of blame, rationalization, and relativization.[3] After reviewing the historical and memory-making context in Little Rock, I will integrate Irwin-Zarecka's and Miller's approaches to examine the Little Rock collective memory process in terms of universalizing the problem, relativization, denial, rationalization, blaming the victim, seeing oneself as the victim, and distancing the problem.

The events surrounding the desegregation of Central High School contain the elements of a good novel—political intrigue, clandestine meetings, violence, sex (at least the imagining of it), twists and turns. Little Rock had the reputation of being a progressive city regarding matters of race.[4] Indeed, five days after the historic 1954 *Brown v. Board of Education of Topeka* decision, the Little Rock School Board affirmed that it would uphold the ruling.[5] However, the plans that Superintendent Virgil Blossom envisioned for the process of desegregating the schools shifted several times as reaction from parents and the *Brown II* decision injected different boundaries and requirements for fulfilling the law. By the time the Blossom Plan was enacted, only one high school was slated for minimal desegregation: Central High School.[6] The prolonged maelstrom of legal activity and resistance on all sides that followed was unexpected and contributed to the community trauma that erupted.

The more organized resistance to desegregation mobilized among the fundamentalist clergy and in the Capitol Citizens' Council and the Mothers' League, a group of white segregationist mothers whose children attended Central High School.[7] The Arkansas Council on Human Relations worked to establish an environment open to desegregation, including training students slated to desegregate the schools to react nonviolently to such resistance.[8] The selection of black students to desegregate Central High School began in the spring of 1957. More than 117 students initially signed up, of whom approximately 75 were selected, based on their academic and disciplinary records, to meet with Superintendent Blossom. By the time those students understood the limits of the plan—such as being banned from extracurricular activities, including band and sports—and the extent of the growing vocal resistance, only nine students—Melba Pattillo Beals, Elizabeth Eckford, Ernest Green, Gloria Ray Karlmark, Carolotta Walls LaNier, Terrence Roberts, Jefferson Thomas, Minnijean Brown Trickey, and Thelma Mothershed Wair—remained committed to desegregating Central High School.[9]

The Labor Day weekend before the schools were to open, a petition by a member of the Mother's League to block the desegregation of Central High School was granted by the state, then denied by a federal court. At 10:15 on the evening before school was to open, Governor Faubus announced that the Arkansas National Guard was already present at Central High School. The first day of school started without the nine black students. At least five hundred people had gathered to protest the desegregation of the school.[10] Plans for the nine black students to attend school the next day continued to shift well into the night. Elizabeth Eckford, one of the nine black students, did not have a phone and did not receive word of the final arrangements. She arrived alone the next day to face an angry mob. The guards were not her protectors as she had imagined they would be; she met the hate and anger of the mob alone. The other eight black students were likewise turned away by the National Guard.[11]

Two and a half weeks would pass before the students—known as the Little Rock Nine—would return to Central. During this time, the crowds at Central did not dissipate; nor did the legal activity.[12] On Monday, September 23, the city police replaced the National Guard. The police safely got the nine black students into the school building only to have to quickly enact a frantic plan to get them out.[13] They did not attend school the next day. Finally, the mayor of Little Rock requested assistance from the White House. In response, President Eisenhower authorized the secretary of defense to send in troops and federalized the ten thousand members of the Arkansas National Guard, who would now be under federal jurisdiction. That evening, one thousand paratroopers from the 101st Airborne arrived in Little Rock.[14]

Just after midnight, Superintendent Blossom coordinated with Daisy Bates, president of the Arkansas NAACP (National Association for the Advancement of Colored People), who served as the central point of contact for the Little Rock Nine, to have the students meet at her house in the morning. Accompanied by the principals of the black junior highs, she went to the parents' homes to inform them about the plan, as they were no longer answering their phones.[15] The next morning, with military precision, Central High School was integrated. Two hours later the school was evacuated for a bomb threat.[16] The 101st Airborne remained in Little Rock for a month; the federalized Arkansas National Guard remained for the entire school year.[17] As for the school itself, it remained in a constant state of tension. Amid bomb threats, calls by parents and anonymous hecklers, curious absences, and daily reports of incidents involving the Little Rock Nine, legal maneuvering became part of the school landscape.[18] In December, Minnijean Brown, one of the Little Rock Nine, was expelled from school for dumping chili on a student's head.[19] After the expulsion, Sammie Dean Parker, one of the student segregationist leaders, was suspended for a few days after passing out cards saying, "One Down Eight to Go!"[20] The lame-duck city government, unresponsive business community, and a noncommitted clergy provided little community support. Despite segregationist attempts throughout the year to impede the desegregation process, Ernest Green graduated from Central High School on May 27, 1958.[21]

While the school year had ended, the legal fight for desegregation had only just begun. A lawsuit to delay the desegregation process, *Aaron v. Cooper,* went all the way to the Supreme Court; its decision, handed down on September 15, 1958, directed the Little Rock School Board to resume its desegregation plan. In response, Governor Faubus closed all of Little Rock's high schools, although he did allow the football season to be played out, remarking that to cancel it would be "inhuman."[22] In the fall of 1958, a group of concerned white women formed the Women's Emergency Committee to Open Our Schools (WEC) and waged a campaign to open the schools. In October, Little Rockians voted to keep the schools closed rather than integrate (19,470 voted to keep schools closed; 7651 voted to integrate them). Schools remained closed for the entire 1958–59 school year.[23]

The second uproar within the white community came in the spring of 1959, when the business community got involved through the STOP (Stop this Outrageous Purge) campaign after segregationist school board members began to purge teachers and administrators who had been even slightly supportive of the desegregation of the schools. After a fierce and quick campaign, the voters recalled the segregationist school board members.[24] The schools finally reopened in August 1959. Fire hoses and police officers quelled a segregationist rally on that opening day.[25] It was not until 1973 that all grades of the Little Rock schools were desegregated. The Little Rock School District remained under court jurisdiction until April 2, 2009, when it was officially released from federal court involvement.[26]

In the Little Rock collective memory process, people had little opportunity to universalize its desegregation school experience. Instead, it was other communities and people that used the desegregation of Central High School as the benchmark with which to gauge their own desegregation process. When discussing my research into the memory-making process in Little Rock, a faculty member remarked that when his hometown of Seattle was desegregating, "they knew they were not Little Rock."[27] Little Rock craved its image in the outside world to be something other than this marker, yet little was done, individually and collectively, until the mid-1990s to actively reshape that image, other than trying to ignore and hoping to forget that the desegregation crisis had happened at all. Little Rock's official process of remembering the desegregation crisis ignited after a local white restaurant owner, Mark Abernathy, heard a speech claiming that in 1957 Atlanta and Little Rock were approximately the same size. Believing that it was time for Little Rock to reconcile with its past, he opened conversations with African American leaders and, after receiving an article from *Newsweek* on Black Heritage Tourism from Hillary Clinton, he formed a small planning committee.[28] Simultaneously, another small group emerged after Max Brantley, the white editor of the *Arkansas Times,* vacationed in Atlanta and wrote an article about it. After Brantley's article appeared, two white business leaders, Rett Tucker and Skip Rutherford, contacted him. All three men had children in the public schools and believed in the value of an integrated society.[29] Nonetheless, their altruistic motives were matched by their desire to restore Little Rock's image and take advantage of an economic opportunity. The two groups joined forces and created Central High Museum, Inc.

The memory-recovery process moved quickly. The new organization obtained a planning grant from the Arkansas Humanities Council and sought the aid of Johanna Miller Lewis, an assistant professor at the University of Arkansas at Little Rock; Lewis, together with her students, helped steer the group through the process of hiring architects and museum exhibit designers by the fall of 1996. That same fall, Mayor Jim Dailey appointed a Fortieth Anniversary Commission to oversee the official commemoration activities. In the fall of 1997, two years after the creation of Central High Museum, Inc., a visitor center was built and a major event undertaken to commemorate the fortieth anniversary of the integration of Central High. The ceremonies included a speech by President Bill Clinton and the presence of all of the Little Rock Nine. Commemoration activities continued after the fortieth anniversary: these included the creation of a Central High Commemorative Garden, the honoring of the Women's Emergency Committee, transference of the Museum Visitor Center to the jurisdiction of the National Park Service, the minting of a special commemorative coin, and the dedication of lifelike statues of the Little Rock Nine on the capitol grounds. The fiftieth anniversary prompted still more activities, including another reunion of the Little Rock Nine at Central High School and a speech by former President Clinton.

Constructing the official collective memory about the events surrounding the desegregation of Central High School required the negotiation of the official transcript of the themes, words, and images that would be displayed. Planning committee minutes for the Central High Visitor Center detailed discussions of a range of topics, including themes, historical concepts, timelines, word choices, artifacts, photographs, overall design, signage, outdoor lighting, and even the placement of windows. Consensus was often difficult to achieve as conversations happened at multiple levels simultaneously. These multifaceted discussions were often perceived as being contentious; a more accurate description, however, might be that they conveyed the differing goals that people wanted to achieve. Some wanted the history portrayed accurately; others wanted to use the historical events as a way to promote racial healing; many driving the process wanted to repair Little Rock's image; and some just wanted to reach a decision.

Virgil, one of the African American members of the Central High Museum Board, recalled the discussion of whether the confederate flag should be displayed: "It was thought by some that that flag should go up in our Visitor Center because it was a symbol of that time. We had had one board member, who was an African-American board member, say, 'If that flag goes up in that Visitor Center, I will tear it down.' . . . We had tremendous discussion about it. . . . The point was made the Jewish people wouldn't stand for a swastika being displayed prominently because that's too emotional, and we shouldn't, as African-Americans and as a community, have a confederate flag in that museum. The flag didn't go up."[30]

Rett Tucker, the white chair of the museum board and a co-chair of the Central High Anniversary Commission, explained that "the exhibit [for the Central High Museum Visitors Center] is the work of twenty-five people—what each word, each sentence said."[31]

The Little Rock Central High Celebration Commission, appointed by Little Rock's mayor, grappled with a similar clash of goals and perspectives. Beginning in the fall of 1996, the group toiled over its purpose and what activities it should sponsor. The commission agreed on two things: its name, and the large-scale plans (described earlier), proposed by Skip Rutherford, for a fortieth anniversary reunion of the Little Rock Nine on the grounds of Central High School together with a speech by President Clinton. By the end of February 1997, the commission had changed its name to the Little Rock Central High Anniversary Commission, bowing to objections that the word *celebration* would be perceived as an attempt to gloss over the unpleasant history of the desegregation crisis and the city's current racial climate. As for the anniversary reunion, plans for it moved forward, although hindered by a struggle between the white power structure and the leaders of the black community. Calls for greater inclusion and more voices led to the formation of an advisory committee and an expansion of the planned activities. The commission also conducted public forums. Ann Marshall, a white member of the Anniversary Commission, discussed one of those forums: "It [the planning process] was so factionalized. There were three main views coming out of it, and they just were not going to mesh. . . . So I volunteered to bring this group together over at Central and use a consensus-building model. . . . It just took 3 hours on a Saturday morning. I never prayed so hard about anything in my life."[32] Ironically, Rett Tucker remembered the Anniversary Commission getting under way around June, after all the conflict had dissipated.

Pervasive denial rendered the collective memory of the desegregation of Central High School incomplete. An important aspect of this denial was the belief that things were not that bad for the Little Rock Nine during the crisis. The narrative of many of the white students proclaimed this belief.[33] "We didn't even know. . . . I don't remember a bad incident except for the couple I told you about [books being thrown down, putting someone into a locker, the chili incident] that went on during the year," stated one white student who had graduated with Ernest Green.[34] Even Elizabeth Eckford's father participated in the denial, asserting that all that went on in the school was just some pushing and shoving.[35] At a principals' meeting in North Carolina, Jess Matthews, Central High's principal, described the school year in this way: "Most teachers and students have gone about their regular school program without the knowledge of any incidents. . . . No child has been physically injured, no persons in town have been killed or seriously hurt, and no teacher has resigned his or her position. There has been no mob violence on the campus or within the school."[36] Such denials left unexplored the hidden pain and disguised terror experienced by the Little Rock Nine and other members of the community who dared to support them during this time.

The historical accounts and commemoration activities tended to focus only on the terror relating to the mob scenes outside the school before the black students' successful entrance. However, my own interviews with the Little Rock Nine and the memoirs by Melba Pattillo Beals and Daisy Bates (*Warriors Don't Cry* and *The Long Shadow of Little Rock*, respectively) leave no doubt about the daily indignities suffered by the nine students. It is true that no one was killed or suffered serious physical harm, but once within the school doors, the Little Rock Nine endured a barrage of incessant physical, verbal, and psychological abuse, creating a climate of terror.[37] Terrence Roberts, one of the Little Rock Nine, later offered a glimpse into that terror:

> I didn't have any idea of how crazy things were going to become . . . I thought there would be some opposition because not everybody is going to be happy about this, but these people will show up, give voice to that opposition and go home, satisfied that they said their piece. Never did I realize that people would be into this thing with such furor and they weren't about to go home. In fact, the message was "unless you leave, we're not going anywhere." On a few occasions at the very beginning, I think we were in more danger than ever. I didn't realize it, but that day we had to be taken out very quickly by the police because the mob was surging in. That was pretty scary; when I look back . . . fear was so much a companion. I had never been that afraid in my life. I didn't know a human being could be that afraid.[38]

Roberts went on to explain, "It was tense most of the time. . . . There were a group of them who were so upset that we were there. . . . They were constantly doing things to make life miserable. So we had to constantly be on the alert for attacks."[39] Ernest Green, another of the Little Rock Nine, described it as "putting on your armor, turn[ing] your face into your game face and get[ting] ready to go to war. I mean it was that way every day."[40]

Compounding this fear was the lack of official reaction both to the presence of the black students at the school and to the abuse they were enduring. "There were teachers . . . that were helpful," recalled Ernest Green, but, he added, "There were others who were indifferent, and there were some who were beyond indifferent."[41] Elizabeth Eckford likewise vividly remembered this studied indifference: "I saw people all the time turning their backs and not even seeming to acknowledge having heard what they had to hear, seeing what they had to see. Some of them I know were saying, 'Well, you deserve what you're getting,' but it was not even acknowledging our humanity that was so horrible."[42] That the names of the Little Rock Nine are absent from the Commemorative Garden, while the key funders and designers are present, reinforces this aspect of not seeing their humanity.

White students refusing to join in the abuse found themselves suffering it in turn. Robin Woods Loucks, a white student, recalled the consequences of sharing a math book with Terrence Roberts:

> When he came into Algebra II, during the first day the blacks came to school, he didn't have a book. . . . The teacher said turn to page whatever. She even asked if someone would share a book. Nobody moved. Nobody moved . . .

none of the boys got up to share their book with him. It made me so angry, I suddenly jumped up and moved my desk over to his and we shared a book. And I tell you the silence was [dropped to a whisper] so heavy you could cut it with a knife.[43]

For that act Robin was followed home that day, stones and spit were hurled at her. Throughout the year, as she remained vocal in her support for the black students, she received hate calls and mail.

Community denial of the extent of suffering caused by the crisis is also evident in the length of time it took to commemorate the desegregation of Central High School and then in the initial attempt to couch that commemoration as a celebration. More curious, though, is the lack of negative memories about the planning process for the fortieth anniversary or about the juxtaposition of that anniversary with current racial incidents in Little Rock. Fatal police shootings of two African American males, one in December 1996 and one in January 1997, had prompted an intense examination of police-community relations. At the time of the fortieth anniversary activities in fall 1997, the city's Racial and Cultural Diversity Commission was being reorganized and thus was out of commission. And when the two classes from Central High School arrived for the dedication of the Commemorative Garden, one class was composed primarily of black students and the other primarily of white ones. The incident signaled that the end of de jure segregation in Little Rock did not erase the de facto segregation still filling the cultural landscape. The commemorative activities did little or nothing to link these realities of the politics of race to the events being commemorated.

Rationalization often supports denial. The argument that because no one was killed at Central High the black students there must not have experienced real terror is an example of such rationalization. Likewise, the belief (or at least, assertion) among Central High's white students that the incidents that they engaged in with the Little Rock Nine were just "innocent fun"—the types of pranks normally engaged in by students—signals their denial that their actions delivered a clear, direct statement of who was in power and control, and what role and place they expected the black students to occupy, rather than the message of indirect acceptance associated with normal teasing.[44]

Rationalization is also evident in the belief that minimal compliance did not grow out of the same roots that the white massive resistance to integration did. Numan V. Bartley used the term "massive resistance" to refer to the Southern white segregationists who used "interposition, propaganda, political insurgence and coerced conformity as its essential elements" to reject or suppress ideological change in the tradition of white supremacy.[45] John A. Kirk explained that the minimal compliance—doing only the bare minimum of what was required to satisfy desegregation law—placated those not wanting school desegregation by allowing token desegregation to serve as implementation of the law.[46] In the end, minimal compliance became a way for some whites, particularly the wealthier ones, to resist the means, but not the ends, of the staunch segregationist resistance.

The silence of Little Rock's business community and clergy, Superintendent Blossom's refusal to get widespread support for his desegregation plan, and the failure of key professional people—the chief of police, Federal District Judge John E. Miller, Governor Faubus, and federal government officials—to use the power of their positions to support the desegregation process all served to corroborate the efforts of the massive resisters. While such inaction probably was not intended to signal such support to the massive resistors, its consequence was a quiet resistance poised to quash any widespread effort toward desegregation under the guise of law and order. In the video shown as part of the exhibit at the Central High Museum Visitor Center, Elizabeth Eckford described a similar scenario inside the school. She surmises that the organized group of about fifty-five students committed to harassing her and the other black students must have had the tacit cooperation of many other students, as well as teachers and administrators, to so successfully terrorize the Little Rock Nine. By taking refuge in silence and invisibility, white individuals and businesses were able to rationalize that they were not actually responsible for the events happening inside and outside Central High School while sending a subtle message that they still supported a segregated way of life. Their silence was used as a way to rationalize their noninvolvement in the more heinous activities.

In the commemorative process, rationalization occurred in the use of symbolic gestures as a way of indicating that the harder issues had been addressed. The opening of the doors of Central High School by the U.S. president, Arkansas's governor, and Little Rock's mayor, on both the fortieth and fiftieth anniversaries of Little Rock's desegregation, was consciously staged to demonstrate how far the community had come. This may have been an effective ceremonial symbol, but, regrettably it exaggerated the city's progress over the past decades in overcoming the racism that, in 1957, so long kept the doors of Central High closed to those nine black students. The doors may now have been opened for the Little Rock Nine, at least acknowledging their tremendous sacrifices and those of their parents, yet our collective memory still does not go inside the doors with them to understand the terror and pain they endured.

While the Little Rock Nine are often held up as heroes in Little Rock's commemoration activities and while their lifelike statues on the lawn of the Arkansas State Capitol permanently symbolize that role, the nine students, sometimes Daisy Bates, and even the African American community, are just as frequently blamed, directly and indirectly, for the events that transpired. Many in the white community believe that more time to desegregate would have prevented the outbreak of hate and resistance; therefore, they argue, the fact that the Little Rock Nine were unwilling to wait makes them responsible for the ugly scenes around Central High. Many of the legal ploys used during that period demonstrated this desire for time. The reality is that there never would have been enough time to adequately prepare for the social change being ushered in. As Les Back and Vron Ware remind us, "Recognizing the extent to which white supremacism was a belief system that provided a rhythm to the very ear of the culture required an acknowledgment that any radical, concerted attempt to rid the country of racism would inevitably bring instability and anxieties in its wake."[47] The capacity to ask for more time reinforces the inequality that existed and the white privilege that kept it in place.

More insidious, though, are the accusations by the white students attending Central High School during the crisis that the Little Rock Nine ruined their senior year or cheated them out of it.[48] While it is understandable to be disappointed about having aspects of one's high school experience spoiled, the emotional place it still holds for many of these students, more than fifty years later, is noteworthy. Terrence Roberts described an incident that occurred on the first day of the training he was doing for the Little Rock School District during the 2001–2 school year. A white teacher stood up and declared, "You ruined my senior year."[49] Several Central High Museum board members recall being contacted by white students requesting that this perspective of how they were affected be reflected in the Museum Visitor Center.[50] Such requests recall a similar assumption of unrecognized privilege contained in a note sent to Ernest Green asking him to forgo attending his own graduation exercises, explaining, "It will be a time that I and hundreds of others do not wish to have marred. For the sake of your classmates and good common sense, please give your utmost consideration to this. I hope that you will let your unselfishness and good judgment dominate your decision."[51] Such attitudes and sentiments often serve as the bridge allowing Central High's white students to see themselves as the victims of the desegregation crisis: their school year was ruined, their Southern way of life destroyed.[52] The facts do not support such assertions, however. The military accounts of the year reveal that very few regular school activities were altered that year. Even the dance and football game scheduled three days after the 101st Airborne escorted the Little Rock Nine into the school were not canceled.[53] Much of this sense of victimization by white students may stem from reaction to the lost year of 1958–59, when, by the vote of its own residents, Little Rock's schools remained closed to prevent further desegregation.

Another aspect of the crisis cited as evidence that the whites were its real victims was the arrival of the 101st Airborne and the federalization of the National Guard; some white students and members of the white community remain convinced that the sending in of these troops transformed Little Rock into an occupied state. The presence of the military was the only theme common to all of my interviewees' descriptions of the desegregation crisis at Central High School. In contrast, very few talked about what it was like for the Little Rock Nine. Interestingly, the 1958 Central High yearbook reinforces this sense of the whites becoming victims of a military occupation from outside. All of the pictures of the events depicting the desegregation contain military personnel and equipment, and not one of them contains an image of the nine black students desegregating the school. In a less direct way, whites also regard Little Rock's beleaguered economy and sullied image as grounds to feel victimized. In the end, the Little Rock Nine served as the scapegoats for the white community's own actions of resistance, which escalated the ugliness of what transpired. This blaming and victimization process enacts white privilege and disavows the need for social change.

The other way that the collective white community avoids culpability is by shifting the blame, and the primary target of this blame is the governor. Many assign Governor Faubus sole responsibility for the decisions producing the desegregation crisis. There is no denying his role: he called out the Arkansas National Guard to deny entrance to the Nine; he finagled the Mother's League to file a lawsuit; he reneged on his agreement with the president; he signed anti-integration laws; and he closed Little Rock's high schools. Nevertheless, assigning sole responsibility to Faubus leaves unrecognized the myriad contributory actions of other individuals and groups, particularly those of the Capital Citizens' Council and the Mothers' League, which supported Faubus's decisions or failed to provide alternative courses of action. In his book about Nazi Germany, *In Hitler's Shadow,* Richard J. Evans makes a similar comparison to how Hitler became the sole demon of the Holocaust.[54] The amount of focus and ink given to Faubus, his life, and his role continues to divert attention and blame from the ways in which the collective white community supported a racialized, segregated way of life.[55]

Examining how interpretative significance is assigned within the events of the desegregation of Central High School illuminates another way the central issue of race often becomes invisible. The tendency to place the desegregation of Central High School into such contexts as constitutional issues (states' rights versus federal rights), class, gender issues, and miscegenation—sex—leaves race out of the equation.[56] It is not that these interpretative perspectives do not have merit or cannot inform our understanding and analysis of the desegregation of Central High School; it is that they often obscure the core issue that sparked the events in the first place—race. While these perspectives do not completely deny the role of race, they give it a back seat to other issues, regarding it merely as the catalyst for the events of the crisis. Some argue, for example, that the silence of Little Rock's upper class citizens allowed the city's more vocal working class residents, who were more directly affected, to be the spokespeople for the city. Would the same mob have shown up to protest the building of Hall High School, where the wealthier population of Little Rock sent their children? Or would nine wealthy white students or extremely poor white students have received the same hostile and violent treatment meted out to the Little Rock Nine? Class was a pawn in the politics of race. It is the absence of the context and relationship to race that makes the distancing of it so dangerous. By disassociating race from the main cause of the desegregation crisis, the difficulty of our racialized history never has to be addressed.

Exacerbating the distancing of the problem of race is the relativization of race—masking, hiding, or diminishing the deeper issues of racism while creating a façade of racial inclusion. While African Americans were part of the commemoration activities, their involvement followed a pattern: a black was accorded a place on the program only if he or she was one of the Little Rock Nine or had an official role (as a board member, for example). Even blacks having such official roles were assigned formal duties, such as giving the prayer or invocation or serving as master of ceremonies. At the dedication of the Commemorative Garden, the members of the Little Rock Nine were seated farthest from the podium and were the only ones seated in the sun. In contrast, a significant amount of time during the ceremony was spent honoring white people who had contributed to the commemoration. A similar spectacle of whites congratulating themselves for their self-imposed leadership occurred at the reception held just before the showing of the documentary film *Turning Points of History—The Little Rock Nine.* A year later, the Central High Museum Board held a fund-raiser to honor the original board members. Only five years had passed since the fortieth anniversary commemoration efforts. It seemed a bit out of place to honor white people for taking forty years to pay tribute to the nine brave students who desegregated Central High School.

The commemoration process also displayed a yearning to set at a distance the failures of the white community by overemphasizing the role of the Women's Emergency Committee (WEC) and the STOP campaign. The Women's Emergency Committee has been honored twice since the Fortieth Anniversary Commission. While its members' actions were laudable, they took such action only when they were forced to face the circumstances when the schools were closed, good teachers and administrators were being purged, and the economy was faltering. They were silent until their nonaction directly affected them and their own children. Their actions resulted more from self-interest than altruism. Although it is important to recognize the contributions of white members of the community, it is just as important to not let those actions overshadow the totality of the white involvement, or lack thereof, or have these actions be misinterpreted within the social norms of the present.

The desire to understand the perspectives of the white students involved in the crisis has resulted in a similar skewed picture of the desegregation crisis. While the white students' perspective is critical to a better understanding, the problem is that now there is more information about the white perspective than the black. This focus diminishes the issue of race and recognition of what the Little Rock Nine experienced inside the school and in their communities. In the development of the exhibit for the Central High Museum Visitor Center, few African American voices were brought into the actual exhibit. Yet a panel titled *View from Inside the School* was added to the exhibit after the class president and student body president for the 1957–58 school year threatened to organize a protest if it was not included. They wanted to protect the image of the white students by ensuring that others understood that most of the white students did not take part in harassing the black students but instead did nothing. The panel remained despite many, including many whites wanting it removed. The small panel speaks volumes to the enactment of power and privilege of the dominant group to construct the official collective memory.

Collective memory (i.e., collective forgetting) reflects and shapes human society. It relies on a historical context and provides insight into the societal structures that shape the current, and sometimes future, memory of the past. We reconstruct the past in accordance with our interpretation of the present. When faced with traumatizing historical events, the process of this remembering sometimes becomes a path to forgetting as well. Even as Little Rock has put a tremendous amount of effort into the memory-making process, much of it has supported the process of forgetting the cultural norms of segregation and racial hierarchy that permeated the original crisis. What we forget constitutes as much a part of collective memory as what we visibly or consciously remember. Commemorative and interpretative efforts can seek to dismiss, neutralize, and deflect the historical experience. What we need to distinguish about forgetting is that it speaks as much to what we cannot express about ourselves, our community, and our social interactions as it does about a specific historical event. While there was no outward malice or overt racism in the commemoration process, it did display a lack of understanding of how deeply imbedded the community's racial hierarchy was and still is. Even though Little Rock has made some progress in race relations and in dismantling the legalized portion of segregation, its efforts to commemorate the desegregation crisis amply demonstrate that the community still has not fully recognized the cultural patterns of race permeating the many facets of society and how they control our collective memory. In some ways, these gains preclude our capacity to fully engage the historical context of the desegregation of Central High School. We know better today the wrongness of much that occurred during the crisis, and yet we have not made enough progress to fully acknowledge that we did, and do, assign superiority and inferiority based on race. Perhaps someday our capacity to remember will be greater than our need to forget, for we will have fully reckoned with the cultural patterns of racial social hierarchy that supported the system of segregation, a system whose threatened demise touched off the events surrounding the desegregation of Central High School.

Notes

1. *The 1983 Pix*, 38 (yearbook), Central High School (Little Rock, Ark.: 1983), 20.
2. Iona Irwin-Zarecka, *Neutralizing Memory: The Jew in Contemporary Poland* (New Brunswick, N.J.: Transaction Publishers, 1990).
3. Judith Miller, *One by One by One: Facing the Holocaust* (New York: Simon and Schuster, 1990).
4. Arkansas Council for Human Relations, *Race Relations in Little Rock Before 1957*, MC 426, box 20, folder 197, Special Collections at University of Arkansas, Fayetteville, Ark.
5. Harry S. Ashmore, *Hearts and Minds: The Anatomy of Racism from Roosevelt to Reagan* (New York: McGraw-Hill, 1982), 251.
6. Numan V. Bartley, *The Rise of Massive Resistance: Race and Politics in the South During the 1950's* (1969; Baton Rouge: Louisiana State Univ. Press, 1997), 253.
7. See Graeme Cope, "A Thorn in the Side? The Mother's League of Central High School and the Little Rock Desegregation Crisis of 1957," *Arkansas Historical Quarterly* 57 (Summer 1998): 160–90; E. Q. Campbell and Thomas Pettigrew, *Christians in Racial Crisis: A Study of Little Rock's Ministry* (Washington, D.C.: Public Affairs Press, 1959); and Neil R. McMillen, "White Citizen's Council and Resistance to School Desegregation in Arkansas," *Arkansas Historical Quarterly* 30, no. 2 (Spring 1971): 95–122.
8. J. F. Henderson, *Some Observations on the Little Rock Story*, October 24, 1957, Pamphlet 01507, Special Collections, University of Arkansas Libraries, Little Rock, Ark.
9. Roy Reed, *Faubus: The Life and Times of an American Prodigal* (Fayetteville: Univ. of Arkansas Press, 1997), 205–9.
10. Daisy Bates, *The Long Shadow of Little Rock: A Memoir by Daisy Bates* (Fayetteville: Univ. of Arkansas Press, 1986), 61–68; Melba Pattillo Beals, *Warriors Don't Cry: A Searing Memoir of the Battle to Integrate Little Rock's Central High* (New York: Washington Square Press, 1994), 40–45.
11. Elizabeth Eckford, "Little Rock, 1957: The First Day," *Southern Exposure* 7 (1979): 38–39, Pamphlet 03812, Special Collections, University of Arkansas Libraries, Little Rock, Ark.
12. For additional information on legal activity, see Orso Cobb, *Orso Cobb of Arkansas: Memoirs of Historical Significance* (Little Rock, Ark.: Rose Publishing Co., 1989); Tony A. Freyer, *The Little Rock Crisis: A Constitutional Interpretation* (Westport, Conn.: Greenwood Press, 1984); Elizabeth Huckaby, *Crisis at Central High: Little Rock 1957–58* (Baton Rouge: Louisiana State Univ. Press, 1980); Reed, *Faubus.*
13. Beals, *Warriors Don't Cry*, 115.
14. Bates, *The Long Shadow of Little Rock*, 99–100.
15. Ibid., 100–103.
16. "I Saw it Happen in Little Rock," *U.S. News and World Report*, Oct. 4, 1957, 37–41, Pamphlet 04207, Special Collections, University of Arkansas Libraries, Little Rock, Ark.
17. Robert W. Coakley, *Operation Arkansas* (OCMH Monograph 158M) (Washington, D.C.: Histories Division, Office of the Chief of Military History, Department of the Army, 1967).
18. Huckaby, *Crisis at Central High.* For additional information on legal maneuvering, see Cobb, *Orso Cobb of Arkansas;* Freyer, *The Little Rock Crisis;* Huckaby, *Crisis at Central High;* and Reed, *Faubus.*

19. Minnijean Brown Trickey, interviews by author, Feb. 12 and Mar. 17, 2003.
20. Huckaby Papers, MC 428, box 2, file folder 16, Special Collections, University of Arkansas Libraries, Fayetteville, Ark.
21. Huckaby, *Crisis at Central High,* 210–17.
22. Freyer, *The Little Rock Crisis,* 154; Virgil T. Blossom, *It Has Happened Here* (New York: Harper, 1959), 185; Sara A. Murphy, *Breaking the Silence: Little Rock's Women's Emergency Committee to Open Our Schools, 1958–1963* (Fayetteville: Univ. of Arkansas Press, 1997), 101–2.
23. Murphy, *Breaking the Silence,* 90.
24. Ibid., chap. 8.
25. Will Counts, *Life Is More Than a Moment: The Desegregation of Little Rock's Central High* (Bloomington: Indiana Univ. Press, 1999), 26–29.
26. Cynthia Howell, "LR Schools Declared Desegregated," *Arkansas Democrat-Gazette,* April 3, 2009.
27. James Spickard, telephone conversation with author, fall 2001.
28. Mark Abernathy, interview by author, Feb. 13, 2003.
29. Max Brantley, interview by author, Feb. 13, 2003; Skip Rutherford, interview by author, Feb. 18, 2003; Rett Tucker, interview by author, Feb. 7, 2003.
30. Virgil (full name withheld by mutual agreement), interview by author, Feb. 9, 2003.
31. Tucker, interview by author.
32. Ann Marshall, interview by author, Feb. 18, 2003.
33. Two examples are R. Green (full name withheld by mutual agreement), interview by author, Feb. 12, 2003; and Beth Roy, *Bitters in the Honey: Tales of Hope and Disappointment across Divides of Race and Time* (Fayetteville, Ark: Univ. of Arkansas Press, 1999).
34. R. Green, interview by author, Feb. 12, 2003.
35. Elizabeth Eckford, interview by author, Dec. 5, 2002.
36. Quoted in Huckaby, *Crisis at Central High,* 191.
37. For additional information, see Cathy Collins, "Forgetting and Remembering the Desegregation of Central High School in Little Rock, Arkansas: Race, Community Struggle, and Collective Memory" (Ph.D. diss., Fielding Graduate University, 2004), *Dissertation Abstracts International,* AAT 3140183, DAI-A 65/07 (Jan. 2005): 2779.
38. Terrence Roberts, interview by author, Jan. 6, 2003.
39. Ibid.
40. "35 Years Later: Black and White Student Reunions," *Oprah Winfrey Show,* Jan. 15, 1996, transcript, Chicago, Ill.: Burrelle's Information Services.
41. Ibid.
42. Elizabeth Eckford, interview by author, Dec. 11, 2002.
43. Robin Loucks, interview by author, Mar. 17, 2003.
44. R. Green, interview by author; Roy, *Bitters in the Honey,* 271–300.
45. Bartley, *The Rise of Massive Resistance,* 237.
46. John A. Kirk, *Redefining the Color Line: Black Activism in Little Rock, Arkansas, 1940–1970* (Gainesville: Univ. Press of Florida, 2002), 93.
47. Vron Ware and Les Back, *Out of Whiteness: Color, Politics, and Culture* (Chicago, Ill.: Univ. of Chicago Press, 2002), 22.

48. R. Green, interview by author; Roy, *Bitters in the Honey,* 143–70.
49. Roberts, interview by author.
50. Annie Abrams, interview by author, Feb. 17, 2003; Ethel Ambrose, interview by author, Nov. 13, 2002; Tucker, interview by author; Virgil, interview by author.
51. Huckaby, *Crisis at Central High,* 203.
52. Ambrose, interview by author; Elizabeth Jacoway, interview by author, Mar. 18, 2003; Johanna Miller Lewis, interview by author, Feb. 10, 2003; Leon Modeste, interview by author, Feb. 12, 2003; Roberts, interview by author; Trickey, interviews by author.
53. Coakley, *Operation Arkansas,* 82.
54. Richard J. Evans, *In Hitler's Shadow: West German Historians and the Attempt to Escape from the Nazi Past* (New York: Pantheon Books, 1989).
55. For information on Governor Faubus, see Tony Badger, "The Forerunner of Our Opposition: Arkansas and the Southern Manifesto of 1956," *Arkansas Historical Quarterly* 56, no. 3 (1997): 353–60; Numan V. Bartley, "Looking Back at Little Rock," *Arkansas Historical Quarterly* 25, no. 3 (1966): 101–16; Bartley, *The Rise of Massive Resistance;* Tony A. Freyer, "Politics and Law in the Little Rock Crisis, 1954–1957," *Arkansas Historical Quarterly* 40, no. 3 (1981): 195–219; Freyer, *The Little Rock Crisis;* Tony A. Freyer, "The Little Rock Crisis Reconsidered," *Arkansas Historical Quarterly* 56, no. 3 (1997): 361–70; Tony A. Freyer, "The Past as Future: The Little Rock Crisis and the Constitution," in *Understanding the Little Rock Crisis: An Exercise in Remembrance and Reconciliation,* ed. Elizabeth Jacoway and C. Fred Williams (Fayetteville: Univ. of Arkansas Press, 1999), 141–51; Reed, *Faubus;* Roy Reed, "The Contest for the Soul of Orval Faubus," in Jacoway and Williams, *Understanding the Little Rock Crisis,* 98–105; David Wallace, "Orval Faubus: The Central Figure at Little Rock Central High School," *Arkansas Historical Quarterly* 39, no. 4 (1980): 314–29.
56. For information on constitutional and states' rights, see Bartley, "Looking Back at Little Rock"; Bartley, *The Rise of Massive Resistance;* Freyer, "Politics and Law in the Little Rock Crisis"; Freyer, *The Little Rock Crisis;* Freyer, "The Little Rock Crisis Reconsidered"; Freyer, "The Past as Future"; K. L. Hall, "The Constitutional Lessons of the Little Rock Crisis," in Jacoway and Williams, *Understanding the Little Rock Crisis,* 123–40; and Laura Miller, interview by author, Nov. 6, 2002. For information on class issues, see Pete Daniel, *Lost Revolutions: The South in the 1950s* (Chapel Hill: Univ. of North Carolina Press, 2000); P. C. Godfrey, "'Sweet little girls'? Miscegenation, Desegregation and the Defense of Whiteness at Little Rock's Central High, 1957–1959" (Ph.D. diss., State University of New York at Binghamton, 2001), *Dissertation Abstracts International,* 62 (07), 2585A, UMI No. 3019499, 2001); Roy, *Bitters in the Honey;* C. Fred Williams, "Class: The Central Issue in the 1957 Little Rock School Crisis," *Arkansas Historical Quarterly* 56, no. 3 (1997): 341–44. For information on gender issues, see Vivian L. Brewer, *The Embattled Ladies of Little Rock: The Struggle to Save Public Education at Central High* (Fort Bragg Calif.: Lost Coast Press, 1999); Lorraine Gates, "Power from the Pedestal: The Women's Emergency Committee and the Little Rock School Crisis," *Arkansas Historical Quarterly* 55, no. 1 (1996): 26–57; Godfrey, "'Sweet little girls'?"; *Women's Emergency Committee to Open Our Schools* (documentary film), produced and directed by Sandra Hubbard (Little Rock, Ark.: Morning Star Studio, 1998); Elizabeth Jacoway, "Down from the Pedestal: Gender and Regional Culture in a Ladylike Assault on the Southern Way of Life," *Arkansas Historical Quarterly*

56, no.3 (1997): 345–52; Roy, *Bitters in the Honey.* For information on miscegenation, see Godfrey, "'Sweet little girls'?"; Jacoway, interview by author; Roy, *Bitters in the Honey.*

Confronting the Legacies of Violence

Lessons from Kent State and Greensboro, North Carolina

Renee Romano

> There comes a time in the life of every community when it must look humbly and seriously into its past in order to provide the best possible foundation for moving into a future based on healing and hope.
>
> —Mandate, Greensboro Truth and Reconciliation Commission

Shots ring out as a group of heavily armed men opens fire on unarmed, peaceful protesters gathered for a demonstration. Several fall, mortally wounded; more are injured, some very seriously. Afterward, those in positions of authority and many in the larger community blame the protesters: it was their fault for making trouble; they were outside agitators seeking to foment revolution; they were Communists and deserved to die. Demonstrators and their supporters blame the killings on governing authorities, who, they charge, either ordered the killings or helped create an environment that encouraged and fostered violence and the excessive use of force. And, despite the existence of reams of evidence about the shootings, victims prove unable to secure justice through the legal system.

This scenario, in its basic outline, has a pattern that many survivors might recognize as their own, including those in the Kent State community. There, on May 4, 1970, members of the National Guard opened fire on students protesting the Vietnam War, killing four and wounding another nine. Yet while the description might resonate for many at Kent State, it specifically describes shootings that took place in Greensboro, North Carolina, on November 3, 1979, when a group of labor and civil rights activists calling themselves the Communist Workers Party (CWP) led a march to protest the Ku Klux Klan. When the protesters gathered at a black housing project in Greensboro to begin their march, a nine-car caravan of Klansmen and members of the American Nazi Party arrived on the scene. As four different television news crews shot video, Klansmen and neo-Nazis took guns from their cars and opened fire on the crowd, which included many children from the project among the demonstrators. Four of the CWP leaders were killed, and another ten people were injured.[1]

The 1970 shootings at Kent State are sometimes viewed as a singular event in American history. Philip Caputo, the famed writer who was a young reporter at the time of the Kent State shootings, describes the massacre as a "unique event . . . the first and only time American troops fired upon and killed American students."[2] Searching for a parallel, Caputo could find only the Boston Massacre of 1775, where British troops shot and killed American colonists. But those seeking parallels do not need to look as far back as the colonial era, nor need they ignore events that have taken place since the Kent State shootings. In Greensboro, as at Kent State, unarmed protesters faced a short but intense period of horrific violence initiated by a well-armed group.[3] Despite the one-sided nature of the violence, the media in Kent and in Greensboro held the protesters responsible for what happened. And perhaps most significantly, although the violence in each place only lasted seconds, it left a raw wound in both communities that has festered for decades. While many years have elapsed since these stark moments of violence, they remain present in the memory of many who were there and of others who heard about them at the time or since.

In both Kent and Greensboro, the ruptures that originally led to violence have continued in the form of debates and differences about what actually happened on those fateful days. History, these two episodes make clear, can become contested terrain in the face of politicized violence. At both sites, even some of the most basic facts of what happened have been debated for years. But when history itself becomes a field of contest, when there is no consensus about what happened or why, it can be difficult, if not impossible, to put a violent past to rest. The episodes at Kent State and in Greensboro have remained raw because the shootings have remained the subject of continued controversy, unanswered questions, and charges of conspiracy and cover-ups. Moreover, steps taken in both communities to try to rectify the violence demonstrate the limitations of common mechanisms of social repair—specifically the legal system—to bring divided communities back together or to settle disagreements in the historical record. For both the Kent State and Greensboro communities, the criminal justice system proved an inadequate mechanism for holding accountable those responsible for violence, for fostering community reconciliation and healing, or for establishing the historical record.

Yet the case of Greensboro provides not only a powerful parallel to Kent, but also an instructive comparison. For in Greensboro, the community has taken steps to grapple with its contested history by turning to a model popular outside the United

States, a truth and reconciliation commission. Greensboro's experience suggests that before communities can hope to find meaningful ways to move on from historic violence, they must first find mechanisms to establish some basic truths about the event. Assessing divergent historical accounts is a first step toward resolving long-standing social divisions.

In the introduction to a 1982 anthology on the shootings at Kent State, Scott Bills noted that at Kent State, "as with other sudden, violent historical events, the past lives uneasily in the present."[4] In Kent, as well as in Greensboro, the past continues to live in the present. But why? Why have these violent episodes remained so powerfully salient for more than three decades? These two events offer some clues about the kinds of violence that can prove difficult to resolve or move beyond. First, at both Kent State and Greensboro, a well-armed force used excessive violence to quell a nonviolent political protest. These shootings were not random acts of violence. In Kent, Ohio National Guard troops ordered to the campus to suppress antiwar protests opened fire two days later as students participated in a rally on the campus Commons. In Greensboro, Klansmen targeted the Communist Workers Party activists because the group advocated trade unionism, worker's rights, and interracial cooperation. These two incidents resulted from and reflected deep political divides.[5]

In both episodes, moreover, the violence was compounded by the fact that it was so popular. In both cases, many people felt the shootings were justified and that the protesters had gotten what they deserved. In a Gallup poll from May 1970, 58 percent of those polled believed that the demonstrators at Kent State bore the primary responsibility for the students' deaths. Only 11 percent held the National Guard responsible.[6] Indeed, some in the community openly questioned why the Guard didn't shoot more students. An FBI memo from the time insisted, "The students invited [the shooting] and got what they deserved."[7] The antipathy to the protesters was so widespread that it did not seem to matter that two of the four students killed at Kent had not been involved in the demonstrations at the time of the shooting.[8] Likewise, in Greensboro, the unpopularity of the Communist Workers Party made it easy for the larger community to blame the demonstrators and to excuse the Klan's violence. Influenced by the media, many people in Greensboro came to blame the CWP for instigating the violence with their anti-Klan rhetoric and for fomenting communism and social revolution.[9] Even the presence of many children at the housing project where the Klan opened fire did not shift sympathy to the demonstrators. No one who was there, it seems, could be truly innocent.

But it is not just the political nature of the excessive force, or its popularity, that has led the past to live uneasily in the present in Kent and in Greensboro. The two communities share another key characteristic: in both, the truth of what happened has been hotly debated and contested since the shootings took place. Signe Waller, a CWP member whose husband was killed on November 3, has called Greensboro a "city with two tales."[10] The same could be said of Kent, since in each city, two very different histories of what happened and who was responsible for the violence have developed.

In Greensboro, the media, political authorities, and many in the larger community have put forth a history of the events that insists that the shooting had nothing to do with Greensboro or its race or class relations. This interpretation depicts both the Klan and the Communists as radical outsider groups who chose, for whatever reason, to have their showdown in Greensboro.[11] In this version of the incident, the city and the police bear no responsibility for what happened, even though the CWP had left a map of the march route with the police and the police knew the Klan and Nazis were planning to confront the march and were bringing firearms. Yet city officials did not blame police for not being at the scene at the time of the shooting. The chief of police's official report on the incident found that the police planning and preparation were "adequate and proper," that the assigned personnel level was "sufficient," and that the police performed their duties "in a professional and reasonable manner."[12] Moreover, the local media, as well as the official reports, pinned much of the blame for the November 3 shootings on the demonstrators, even though Klan and Nazi members carried out nearly all of the shooting and all of the killed or wounded were CWP members or sympathizers. The local media quickly labeled the event a "shootout," insisting that the CWP had sought a confrontation and that both sides had been equally responsible for the gunfire.[13] This rhetorical shift—from *massacre* to *shootout*—came to dominate the general view of the event in Greensboro. A 1980 official report by the Greensboro Human Relations Commission maintained that the CWP "took on the Ku Klux Klan and the Nazis in a shootout at Morningside Homes, that left five people dead."[14]

For survivors of November 3, the truth of this event is completely different. To them, the shooting *was* a massacre, one that reflected long-standing, corrupt racist and class politics in Greensboro. The police, they insisted, knew what was going to happen at the march and deliberately decided not to protect the Communists or the poor blacks who lived in the housing project where the march began. Indeed, some CWP survivors claim that the local, state, and federal governments used the Klan to silence the Communists and to forestall their interracial organizing. In this view, the killings were nothing less than state-sponsored political assassinations, the work of "an organized death squad that rained death and terror on a poor, minority neighborhood." Many of the survivors began a crusade after the shooting to prove that the police and city officials were complicit in the violence of November 3 and that the episode was part of a long-standing pattern in Greensboro of repression of racial and class activism.[15]

Kent, like Greensboro, is a city with two tales. In Kent, the story that the guardsmen and their supporters tell portrays the student demonstrators as radicals and suggests that they may have been associated with terrorist groups such as the Weathermen. In this view, the students are seen as dangerous: guardsmen claim that they felt threatened by students who were throwing rocks and by what they thought was a sniper, and that they fired in self-defense. In this version of events, the shootings took place because of confusion and fear; they were not planned or organized and certainly were not part of any larger conspiracy.[16]

For victims of the May 4 shootings at Kent State and for many others who were there, though, there is no question that the shootings were unjustified and premeditated. Victims and their supporters insist that the guardsmen never faced any danger from the students; the students who were shot were too far away to have been threatening to the Guard, and some were shot in the back. All available data, including photos, confirm that a line of more than seventy guardsmen turned in unison and that twenty-eight opened fire, providing clear evidence of planning. Many believe that a superior officer ordered the guardsmen to fire, although the identity of that officer remains unknown. Victims and supporters also continue to raise questions about the burning of the Kent State ROTC building, which took place two days before the shootings, theorizing that it was the work of a government agent or undercover program seeking to stir up trouble or to justify harsh measures to control the student demonstrators.[17]

The divergent histories in Greensboro and in Kent have developed and survived despite a plethora of evidence about the shootings; in both cases, photographs and audio recordings of the shootings exist and have been exhaustively analyzed. There are videos of the shootings in Greensboro and an eight-millimeter film of the shootings at Kent State. Dubious claims about both events, circulated and popularized by the media, have survived despite contradictory evidence. In both Kent and Greensboro, the shooters' explanations that they were acting in self-defense gained widespread currency despite the lack of evidence that the shooters were in any real danger when they opened fire. These divergent accounts of the same historical events demonstrate the importance of what some scholars of historical memory refer to as *frames of remembrance.* How individuals or groups remember and understand an event can be influenced more by their political beliefs, social position, or preconceived notions of what happened than by facts or evidence. A general public predisposed to view public demonstrations as potentially dangerous threats to the status quo may easily accept a media account that paints nonviolent demonstrators as radicals or potential terrorists. As memory theorist Iwona Irwin-Zarecka points out, when individuals develop their sense of the past, their own experience, political views, and emotional needs become the key frame of reference for constructing a sense of history. Although the historical record is not a free-for-all that can be remade completely in contradiction to available evidence, studies of historical memory make clear that there is a great deal of space for individuals and groups to construct particular versions of the past that meet their contemporary political and cultural needs.[18]

These versions of history, moreover, can have important political consequences. As Michael Kammen suggests in his influential work *Mystic Chords of Memory*, the truth of the past is less important than the constructed memory of the past—often influenced by political figures and the media—that people carry with them. "What people believe to be true about their past is usually more important in determining their behavior and responses than truth itself," Kammen observes.[19] The vital importance of understandings of the past in shaping political behavior and cultural identity has ensured that the victims in these shootings have developed a strong alternative memory that seeks to keep alive their version of events. Activists both in Greensboro and at Kent State have engaged in various forms of "memory work," as they have sought to influence the collective understandings of what happened in each episode. This memory work has included writing books and giving interviews, planning commemorative ceremonies, proposing or building monuments to the shooting victims, researching charges of conspiracy, and holding meetings or symposia about the events.[20] In these ways, victims and their allies have sought to keep their version of the past alive and to challenge dominant framings that discount their reality of the events.

This ongoing contestation over the history and meaning of the two shootings makes both Kent and Greensboro classic examples of pasts that will not "lie down quietly," in the words of Desmond Tutu, the South African archbishop.[21] While Tutu's words referred specifically to his country's history of apartheid, a more general pattern holds true: violent incidents that are historically and politically contested, or where one group's reality of events is discounted and ignored, cannot be easily put in the past. As one newspaper noted ten years after the shooting, the Kent State incident refused to "stay quiet in its grave."[22] These pasts remain, in the words of religious scholar Solomon Schimmel, "wounds not healed by time."[23] The events in Kent and in Greensboro have proven particularly resistant to closure. The social and communal rifts engendered by the shootings in these two communities have not, and will not, go away on their own.

What mechanisms exist for grappling with or trying to resolve the kind of violence that took place at Kent State and in Greensboro? Can pasts that will not lie down quietly and that result in opposing versions of history be reconciled? Kent State and Greensboro make one thing clear: the courtroom is not an ideal space for grappling with a contested past. The criminal justice system provides perhaps the most popular and widely accepted form of justice seeking in the United States. Many victims of violence and their supporters immediately turn to the law and the legal process as a way to punish perpetrators and to hold instigators of violence responsible for their actions. If legal justice is thwarted at the time of the crime, victims or their families may spend decades struggling to bring alleged murderers before a jury.[24] Yet this most traditional method of trying to fix blame and ensure accountability is particularly limited in cases of violence leading to contested historical records. Even the briefest accounting of efforts by victims of Kent and Greensboro to find justice through the courts offers a sad illustration of the failings of the legal system to handle episodes of this kind of politicized violence. As victims in both cities discovered, the legal system "inevitably reflects and also is influenced by the prevailing social and political contexts."[25] At both Kent State and in Greensboro, victims and the families of those killed sought justice through both state and federal courts, but they found instead that the legal system was biased against them and refused to hear their claims fully or fairly.

The legal travails after the Kent State shootings demonstrate the difficulties of turning to the courts to achieve justice or affix blame when the gunmen are representatives of the state. Neither the state of Ohio nor the federal government wanted to indict or blame the Ohio National Guard for the shootings. President Nixon even sought to prevent the Department of Justice from investigating. When the state of Ohio convened a grand jury in October 1970, it indicted twenty-five of the protesters rather than any guardsmen. Continued pressure finally resulted in a federal criminal trial in 1974 for eight of the guardsmen who fired their guns, but a judge dismissed the case on the grounds of lack of evidence.[26] When the guardsmen faced charges in a federal civil trial the following year, the defense team successfully put the student protesters on trial instead. Defense attorneys called students terrorists and sought to associate students at Kent State with radical groups like the Weathermen. As one of the plaintiffs recalled, "They [the guards] weren't put on trial. We were."[27] In the end, the jury held that none of the guardsmen was legally responsible for the shootings, and it ordered the parents of the dead and of the nine survivors to pay court costs. The federal courts, in other words, accepted the guardsmen's position that they acted in self-defense.[28]

In Greensboro, unlike in Kent, the state of North Carolina quickly moved to arrest many of the Klansmen and Nazis who had been involved in the shooting, and six were put on trial for first-degree murder in 1980. From the start, however, the victims felt that the trial was rigged against them. During jury selection, the prosecutors asked potential jurors whether they "could be fair in this case even though the victims were communists who stood for everything we *hate* in America?"[29] One man who would serve on the jury answered that he thought it was less of a crime to kill a communist. The jury foreman, moreover, was a Cuban activist opposed to Castro and to communism. Perhaps not surprisingly, CWP members and relatives of those killed and injured felt the trial was inherently biased against them, and they decided not to testify, fearing their politics would only come under further attack if they took the stand.[30] The activists of the Communist Workers Party also felt that the existing evidence—which included many other witnesses and videotapes of the shooting—would speak for itself. But the jury ultimately acquitted the six Klan and Nazi defendants of all charges, on the grounds that they acted in self-defense. As one juror told the media after the trial, "From the very beginning, it was the Communists who did the attacking. It was the Communists who started beating the cars with sticks."[31] A second federal trial in 1984 ended in the same result, even though CWP members cooperated with the process and testified before the jury.

These trials did not reconcile the historical record or affix blame or accountability. Instead, they further delegitimized the victims' sense of the reality of what happened in Kent and in Greensboro. As one North Carolina editorial noted in the wake of the acquittals in the federal Greensboro trial, the verdict seemed to contradict reality: "The implicit message that the system has set forth—that no one was *really* murdered, that no one's rights were *really* violated—stands in shocking contradiction to the bloody events recorded on the video tape that day. Until reality and the verdicts are reconciled, justice has not been done."[32]

The trials that took place in Kent and Greensboro are extreme examples of the problems that can arise in the justice system, but even at its best, the legal system offers only limited potential for resolving the kinds of contestations of history that developed in the aftermath of these two shooting incidents. While legal trials can send a powerful message that no individual is above the law and that societal harms can be redressed through existing legal norms, the very nature of the legal process itself makes a trial a limited tool for addressing contested histories or charges of complicity and conspiracy.[33] A criminal prosecution must focus narrowly on whether the evidence proves the guilt of a particular individual. Trials thus allow for only a very narrow engagement with the past. In the case of crimes where complicity might extend beyond the individuals who actually fired shots to government officials, police, or other state actors, a trial rarely offers the possibility of opening up any larger discussion of responsibility or of the social and political contexts in which the violence occurred. A legal trial in these cases emphasizes narrow agency and individual punishment for crimes that could be construed much more broadly.[34] Trials, moreover, are often highly selective; at Kent State, twenty-eight guardsmen fired their guns, but only eight were ever tried. This selectivity can make the process seem unfair or arbitrary. And although trials can lead to the collection of enormous amounts of evidence, which can help make a historical record more complete, they do not have the goal of uncovering the truth of an event or resolving differences among historical accounts. As legal theorist Martha Minow argues, trials are not particularly useful if the goal is establishing consensus about "controversial, complex events."[35] The legal form itself is, another scholar notes, "ill-suited to deal with the subtleties of facing the past."[36]

Not surprisingly, then, even when the victims in Kent and Greensboro achieved some success in the courtroom, the historical record remained divided and unsettled.

In both Kent and Greensboro, victims eventually won small cash awards (the result of a civil trial in Greensboro, and of a settlement in a federal civil trial in Kent), but these payouts did little to affirm the activists' view of events or to affix responsibility for the shootings on the gunmen or on political authorities more generally. The verdict in the civil trial that held the police and the Klansmen and Nazis jointly liable for one of the five deaths did not resolve the factual issues of the case. Even though the city of Greensboro agreed to pay the cash settlement on behalf of both the police department and the Klansmen and Nazis, it refused to accept any responsibility or liability for what had happened and offered no apology.[37] Likewise, a 1979 out-of-court settlement in a federal civil case awarded wounded students and parents of the dead at Kent State $675,000, but the statement signed by the Ohio National Guard did not apologize or accept responsibility for the shootings. Indeed, the settlement statement insisted that the university had followed the law in banning the student rally and ordering protesters to disperse. It also suggested that "fearful and anxious" guardsmen may have believed that their lives were in danger, even though "hindsight suggests that another method" could have been used to resolve the confrontation.[38] This statement, a *New York Post* editorial noted, made it seem as if the deaths were an unfortunate tragedy rather than the result of actions by the Guard. As a result, despite the cash settlement, the *Post* predicted, "Kent State will remain an open and disturbing case indefinitely."[39]

But if the courtroom is not the best site for resolving these pasts, what steps can be taken to grapple with a contested past? Here, recent events in Greensboro prove instructive. More than twenty-five years after the shootings, community activists in Greensboro established an independent truth and reconciliation commission to try to uncover a more complete and accurate story of what happened on November 3, 1979, and to address the underlying causes and legacies of the violence that took place that day. While truth commissions have proven quite popular internationally since the first one was established in 1974, the Greensboro Truth and Reconciliation Commission (GTRC) represents the first full-fledged commission of this kind in the United States.[40] Commissions are typically official bodies established by a state undergoing a political transition; they investigate past human rights abuses and make recommendations to prevent future violence and to heal existing social ruptures caused by the violent past. Greensboro adapted the truth commission model to grapple with a single incident of violence and set it up as a community endeavor, rather than the act of a state.

The idea of establishing a truth and reconciliation commission in Greensboro first arose in 1999, at events marking the twentieth anniversary of the shooting, when two groups founded by survivors raised the question of whether an organization modeled on the South African Truth and Reconciliation Commission might serve as a way for Greensboro to address the continued community rifts left by the violence of November

3, 1979. With the assistance of the New York-based Institute for Transitional Justice, they worked to build support in the community for the creation of an independent truth commission to explore the event.[41] Supporters knew that only a truly independent commission could be effective. The truth commission in Greensboro, unlike most of those elsewhere in the world, would not be an official body established by a state or governing authority. The city of Greensboro did not organize the commission; in fact, the city council ultimately voted to oppose its formation. But the victims of the shootings and former CWP members could not be in charge of the commission either, if the group hoped to have any legitimacy. Thus, while former CWP activists came up with the idea for a truth and reconciliation commission, they worked hard to ensure that the commission would be autonomous and would have widespread community support; they had to be willing to cede control over the event to an independent group. By February 2004, a wide variety of community organizations, including local colleges and universities, labor groups, the mayor's office, and religious and political groups, had agreed to appoint members to a committee to select the truth commissioners. The selection committee chose seven people to serve on the commission, including a retired corporate attorney, a minister, a college professor, and several community activists. Of the seven, three were white, three were black, and one was Southeast Asian.[42] In 2005, the commission formally began its work.

From the start, the GTRC had two key goals: to help develop a more accurate record of what had happened on November 3—to find some kind of "truth" about the event—and to help Greensboro achieve some form of reconciliation or healing. As the GTRC's declaration of intent noted, the commission sought to engage with the past in order to "lead Greensboro into becoming a more just, understanding, and compassionate community."[43] In fact, these two goals of truth and reconciliation are inevitably intertwined, because a community cannot move forward and grapple with the continuing legacies of past violence without coming to at least some basic agreements about what actually happened and who was responsible. Moving forward requires engaging with, and weighing, the different versions of history that circulate about an event. Reconciliation does not mean that all memories or versions of history are necessarily granted equal legitimacy or weight. Indeed, one of the most important parts of any meaningful reckoning with violence is recognizing that myths or untruths often develop around instances of political violence, and that some histories have been silenced or marginalized. A "central task" for any truth commission, Martha Minow explains, is developing as coherent and complex a narrative of what actually happened as it can.[44]

Greensboro offers a powerful window into the potential of this kind of work to respond to wounds not healed by time more effectively than a legal trial. In order to uncover as much of the truth about the 1979 shootings as possible, the GTRC deliberately structured its work to engage a wide variety of community members and to examine both the causes and the legacies of the shootings. The commission took public statements from more than 125 community members about the causes, context, and consequences of the shootings, and the commissioners analyzed all available records, from trial transcripts to newspaper coverage.[45] They also held three public hearings in which a total of 54 people gave statements about the events in Greensboro, the history leading up to November 3, and the connections between the events of November 3 and today.[46] Speakers at the public hearings covered a broad range: Klansmen who were involved in the 1979 event, injured CWP members and family members of those who were killed, former residents of the housing project where the shootings took place, the judge and attorneys from one of the legal trials, community activists, elected officials, police officers, labor organizers, and historians. Between 300 and 500 members of the community attended each of the two-day public hearings. Other community members attended meetings or community dialogues to talk about the shootings and their legacies in Greensboro today.[47]

The final report issued by the GTRC in 2007 suggests ways in which truth commissions can help establish a more honest narrative about a contested incident, one with greater legitimacy than the stories previously told by either side in the conflict. While the commissioners admitted that they could not establish the complete truth of the event, they hoped their efforts would take the city "some distance away from the half-truths, misunderstandings, myths and hurtful interpretations that have marked the story until now."[48] Perhaps most significantly, the commission challenged the common perception that the incident was a shootout for which each side bore equal responsibility. The GTRC found that the Klansmen and Nazis came to the march deliberately to provoke violence, that they opened fire first, and that only one of the five CWP members killed was armed at the time. The commission did not absolve the CWP of all responsibility for the event; a few of the CWP members did fire back, and the incendiary rhetoric they aimed at the Klan was extremely naïve. Nevertheless, the commissioners reminded the community that the Klan also engaged in violent rhetoric, which it, unlike the CWP, had backed with violent action.[49]

The commissioners also drew very different conclusions about the role of official actors in the 1979 killings than those long put forward by political authorities. They found that the Greensboro city police had intentionally withheld adequate protection from the demonstrators and that the absence of the police was the "single most important element that contributed to the violent outcome."[50] They also concluded that the police's handling of the incident had been colored by the officers' negative perceptions of communism and of the CWP. The GTRC also criticized city officials for deliberately misleading the public about what had happened on November 3 in order to protect the police department and the city's reputation. Moreover, perhaps most fundamentally—and in direct contradiction to city officials and community members who charged that the shooting had not had any long-term negative impact on Greensboro—the GTRC found that the incident had had "devastating effects on our community" that continued to the present day. The GTRC thus concluded that "many of our elected leaders are either horribly out of touch with, willfully blind to, or simply unconcerned about the lingering pain and the stifling workings of power in this community."[51] Although it is unlikely that even this strongly worded and well-documented final report will resolve all the differences in the interpretations of the 1979 event, the GTRC has achieved what historian Michael Ignatieff has argued is one of the key benefits of truth commissions: they can narrow the range of permissible lies that can be told about the past.[52]

Will the GTRC lead Greensboro down a path toward reconciliation and healing? In truth, it is too soon to assess the long-term consequences of the GTRC's investigation and conclusions, although early indications suggest that the process has had a positive impact on Greensboro.[53] It is clear, however, that the truth commission process enabled the community of Greensboro to reckon with the historical myths and untruths that had developed around the November 3 event in a way that legal trials did not. Based on the historical record that it has put forth and helped legitimize, the GTRC called for a broad range of remedies, including recommendations that the city formally apologize and take specific steps to reduce racial and economic inequalities in Greensboro. Moreover, the process itself demonstrated that people in a community can come together, despite opposition from elected leaders, to seek truth and work toward reconciliation.[54]

Even if the GTRC succeeds only in helping to establish a more accurate historical record of what happened, it must be judged a success. Political theorist Gregory Streich argues that survivors and descendants of historical injustice must mobilize alternative memories and interpretations of the past in order to "unsettle, undermine, and alter the 'ruling memory' that a nation develops in which injustices of the past are constructed as minimally important, discrete, and non-systematic events or 'details' of history, or simply aberrations in an otherwise just society."[55] In Greensboro, the victims of violence found that the only way for them to alter a well-established ruling memory was to work for an independent commission purposefully and carefully designed to seek truth. There is no simple formula to ease the pain of a Kent State or a Greensboro, but the truth process carried out in Greensboro seems to be a first step toward putting to rest that city's past, a past that for so long has refused to lie down quietly.

Notes

1. For a good basic background on the Greensboro shootings, see Elizabeth Wheaton, *Codename GREENKIL: The 1979 Greensboro Killings* (Athens: Univ. of Georgia Press, 1987).
2. Philip Caputo, *Thirteen Seconds: A Look Back at the Kent State Shootings* (New York: Chamberlain Books, 2005), 77. In actuality, as political scientist John Logue has noted, Kent State can be viewed as an example of a long tradition of the American government using force to quell dissent. John Logue, "Official Violence," in Bills, *Kent State/May 4*, 143–49.
3. In Greensboro, it did turn out that a handful of the demonstrators were armed with handguns and that a few did shoot back once the Klan opened fire. However, none of the attackers were injured and the vast majority of the demonstrators did not have any weapons. An exact sequence of events and a detailed description of shots fired is available in Greensboro Truth and Reconciliation Commission (hereafter, GTRC), *Greensboro Truth and Reconciliation Commission Final Report*, presented to the residents of Greensboro, the City, the Greensboro Truth and Community Reconciliation Project, and other public bodies on May 25, 2006 (Greensboro, N.C.: GTRC, 2006), 178–85.
4. Bills, "Introduction," 2.
5. Thomas R. Hensley and Jerry M. Lewis note that the Kent State shootings "have certainly come to symbolize the deep political and social divisions that so sharply divided the country during the Vietnam War era." See Hensley and Lewis, "The May 4 Shootings at Kent State University: The Search for Historical Accuracy," in *Kent State and May 4th*, ed. Hensley and Lewis, 54.
6. Cited in Gordon, *Fourth of May*, 18. James Michener found countless letters to the editor in the aftermath of the shootings, some criticizing the shootings and others expressing approval for the Ohio National Guard. Michener, *Kent State: What Happened*, 434–46.
7. Gordon, *Fourth of May*, 36.
8. Only two of the four students killed and five of the nine students injured at Kent had been involved in the protests. Sandra Scheuer, who had been observing on the Commons when the rally began, was shot while on her way to her afternoon class. William Schroeder, an ROTC student, was simply observing the protests when he was killed. Ibid., 186.
9. For a summary of the local press coverage of the incident, see Scott Pryor, "A Direction of Truth and Love: Representation, Bearing Witness, and the History of November 3, 1979" (senior honors thesis, Guilford College, 2002), chap. 2; and Sandy Michele Bermanzohn, "The Media's Demonization of the Radical Left: Two Case Studies" (college honors thesis, University of Vermont, 2003).
10. Signe Waller, "A City of Two Tales: The Greensboro Massacre of November 3, 1979 in Fact, Context and Meaning," unpublished report submitted to the GTRC, Greensboro, N.C., February 2005.
11. Greensboro's mayor, Jim Melvin, insisted the day after the shooting that it had been committed "by people from outside our community" and that it had "absolutely no relationship with race problems here." Jim Melvin, quoted in *Greensboro Daily News*, Nov. 4, 1979, cited in the Greensboro, North Carolina, Human Relations Commission Report, Greensboro, N.C., Oct. 6, 1980, 9.

12. Greensboro Police Department, An Administrative Report of the Anti-Klan Rally, Greensboro, North Carolina, November 3, 1979, Greensboro, N.C., Nov. 19, 1979, Civil Rights Greensboro (website), <http://www.greensborotrc.org/1979_policewvo.pdf>, 40; Greensboro, North Carolina, Human Relations Commission Report, 2.
13. Bermanzohn, "The Media's Demonization of the Radical Left: Two Case Studies" (college honors thesis, University of Vermont, 2003), 44.
14. Greensboro, North Carolina, Human Relations Commission Report, 4.
15. Waller, "A City of Two Tales," 5. The survivors of the attack have written extensively about their perspective of the events of November 3. In addition to Waller, see Paul Bermanzohn and Sally A. Bermanzohn, *The Greensboro Massacre* (New York: Cesar Cauce Publishers and Distributors, 1980); Sally A. Bermanzohn, *Through Survivor's Eyes: From the Sixties to the Greensboro Massacre* (Nashville, Tenn.: Vanderbilt Univ. Press, 2003); Signe Waller, *Love and Revolution* (Lanham, Md.: Rowman and Littlefield, 2002).
16. For accounts of the events by guardsmen, see Edward J. Grant and Michael Hill, *I Was There: What Really Went on at Kent State* (Lima, Ohio: C.S.S. Publishing Co., 1974); and William Furlong, "The Guardsmen's View of the Tragedy at Kent State," *New York Times Magazine,* June 21, 1970, 12. Scholars and official reports have discredited the version of events recounted in the preceding sources. See, for example, I. F. Stone, *The Killings at Kent State: How Murder Went Unpunished* (New York: Vintage Books, 1970); and *The Report of the President's Commission on Campus Unrest* (Washington, D.C.: GPO, 1970).
17. Carole Barbato, Laura Davis, and Mark Seeman, "Outline of April 30–May 4, 1970" (unpublished paper, Kent State University, Kent, Ohio, March 2009), 4–5; Hensley, *Kent State Incident,* 42–48; Gordon, *Fourth of May,* 51–57.
18. Iwona Irwin-Zarecka, *Frames of Remembrance: The Dynamics of Collective Memory* (New Brunswick, N.J.: Transaction Publishers, 1994), 4–12, 17–19.
19. Michael Kammen, *Mystic Chords of Memory: The Transformation of Tradition in American Culture* (New York: Knopf, 1991), 39.
20. The term *memory work* comes from Irwin-Zarecka, *Frames of Remembrance,* 8. In Greensboro, survivors have not only written extensively about their experiences, but also worked for years to help organize a truth commission. In Kent, ongoing memory works include the oral history project conducted by the Special Collections and Archives division of the Kent State University Libraries, the May 4 Task Force work on the annual May 4 Commemorations, and the building of a May 4 Visitors Center to educate the public about the shootings.
21. Bishop Desmond Tutu, "Reconciliation in Post-Apartheid South Africa: Experiences of the Truth Commission," remarks at the Nobel Peace Laureates Conference, University of Virginia, Nov. 5, 1998, <http://www.virginia.edu/nobel/transcript/tutu.html>.
22. Michael Frisby, "Kent Case Just Won't Stay Quiet in the Grave," *Cleveland Plain Dealer,* Sept. 13, 1981, cited in Gordon, *The Fourth of May,* 89.
23. Solomon Schimmel, *Wounds Not Healed by Time: The Power of Repentance and Forgiveness* (Oxford: Oxford Univ. Press, 2004).
24. The contemporary efforts to prosecute decades-old civil rights era murders attest to the interests of families in seeing the killers of their relatives brought to justice. Since 1989, local, state, or federal authorities have reexamined evidence in nearly thirty cases of

unsolved civil rights murders. Twenty-three men have been convicted for their participation in these crimes, including James Edward Seale, who was convicted in 2007 for his role in the 1964 killing of two young black men in Mississippi. A list of cases—both those that have resulted in trials and convictions and those that are still pending or have been closed—is available at Northeastern University, "Civil Rights and Restorative Justice," <http://www.northeastern.edu/crrj/cold_cases/cold_case_watch/>.

25. GTRC, *Final Report,* 258.
26. Overviews of the Kent State trials are available in Hensley, *Kent State Incident,* 84–134; and Gordon, *Fourth of May,* 115–27; 135–57.
27. Robby Stamps, Letter to *Daily Kent Stater,* Oct. 2, 1975, qtd. in Gordon, *Fourth of May,* 141. For a full account of the 1975 federal civil trial, see Kelner and Munves, *Kent State Coverup*.
28. Hensley and Lewis, "The May 4 Shootings at Kent State University," 57.
29. GTRC, *Final Report,* 262.
30. There is some confusion about whether CWP members were even asked to testify during this first trial. Moreover, some CWP members felt that they could not testify safely because they had been indicted on riot charges and feared incriminating themselves.
31. "Jurors Say Self-Defense was Critical Factor in Klan-Nazi Trial," AP Wire Service, Nov. 18, 1980, qtd. in GTRC, *Final Report,* 276.
32. "Jury Foreman Explains Verdict," *Charlotte Observer,* Apr. 18, 1984, qtd. in GTRC, *Final Report,* 289.
33. For a discussion of the comparative benefits and limitations of legal trials, see Martha Minow, *Between Vengeance and Forgiveness: Facing History after Genocide and Mass Violence* (Boston, Mass: Beacon Press, 1998), 25–51.
34. On the inherent limitations of the form of a legal trial, see Margaret M. Russell, "Cleansing Moments and Retrospective Justice," *Mich. L. Rev.* 101 (2003): 1225; Margaret M. Russell, "Reopening the Emmett Till Case: Lessons and Challenges for Critical Race Practice," *Fordham L. Rev.* 73 (2005): 2101; and Robert Gordon, "Undoing Historical Injustice" in *Justice and Injustice in Law and Legal Theory*, ed. Austin Sarat and Thomas H. Kearns (Ann Arbor: Univ. of Michigan Press, 1999), 35–76.
35. Minow, *Between Vengeance and Forgiveness,* 47.
36. Tina Rosenberg, *The Haunted Land* 351, qtd. in Minow, *Between Vengeance and Forgiveness,* 51.
37. GTRC, *Final Report,* 307. The police and Klan were held liable for only one of the deaths, that of Dr. Mike Nathan. Although Nathan's wife was a member of the CWP, Nathan himself was not, and he was a sympathetic figure because he worked at a clinic for low-income children.
38. Settlement statement issued by the defendants in Cleveland, Ohio, Jan. 4, 1979; "Legal Chronology May 5, 1970–January 4, 1979," comp. and ed. Margaret Ann Garmon, Special Collections and Archives, Kent State University Libraries, Kent, Ohio, <http://speccoll.library.kent.edu/4may70/legalchronology.html>.
39. "The Kent State Verdict," *New York Post,* Aug. 29, 1975, cited in Gordon, *Fourth of May,* 157.
40. There is an extensive literature on truth commissions, especially on the South African Truth and Reconciliation Commission. The best overview of truth commissions available

is in Priscilla B. Hayner, *Unspeakable Truths: Confronting State Terror and Atrocity* (New York: Routledge, 2002). The GTRC's *Final Report* notes that forty truth commissions, including both official and nonofficial ones, were established between 1994 and 2005. Between 1974 and 2004, at least twenty-six different nations established official truth commissions to grapple with their histories of systematic human rights abuses, including Argentina, El Salvador, Rwanda, Yugoslavia, and, most famously, South Africa. A full list is available at <http://www.beyondintractability.org/essay/truth_commissions/>. The GTRC was not the first truth-seeking commission in the United States, but it was the first group to fully embrace the truth and reconciliation model that has been used by many other nations around the globe. There are a few important precedents for the GTRC in this country, including the official commissions set up to study and address race riots in Wilmington in 1898 and Tulsa in 1921.

41. Lisa Magarell, Senior Associate, International Center for Transitional Justice, interview by author, Jan. 21, 2005; also see "ICTJ Activity: The Greensboro Truth and Reconciliation Commission," International Center for Transitional Justice, <http://www.ictj.org/en/where/region2/517.html>.
42. On the development of the GTRC, the selection process, and the background of the commissioners, see Spoma Jovanovic, "The Greensboro Truth and Community Reconciliation Project: Communication for Community Change" (paper presented at the American Psychological Association Convention, New Orleans, La., 2006), <http://www.webster.edu/peacepsychology/Jovanovic.pdf>. See also GTRC, *Final Report,* 455–61.
43. Statement from "The Declaration" of the Greensboro Truth and Reconciliation Commission Project, reprinted in GTRC, *Final Report,* 454.
44. Minow, *Between Vengeance and Forgiveness,* 58, 60
45. GTRC, *Final Report,* 520.
46. A complete list of speakers at the public hearings and audio files and transcripts of much of the testimony are available in the Statement Archives section of the GTRC website, online at <http://www.greensborotrc.org/hear_statements.php>.
47. For more details about these community meetings and dialogues, see GTRC, *Final Report,* especially 32–36, 463–80.
48. "Executive Summary," GTRC, <http://www.greensborotrc.org/exec_summary.pdf>, 2.
49. Ibid., 15.
50. Ibid., 7.
51. Ibid., 20.
52. Quoted in Hayner, *Unspeakable Truths,* 25.
53. The truth process in Greensboro has already led to the creation of new activist groups and new efforts at community cross-racial dialogues. The local newspaper agreed to implement the GTRC's recommendation to create a citizen's advisory group, and a new grassroots effort has developed to push for the city to pay employees and contractors a living wage. Spoma Jovanovic, "The Greensboro Truth and Community Reconciliation Project: Communication for Community Change" (paper presented at the American Psychological Association Convention, New Orleans, La., 2006).
54. Lewis Pitts, the attorney who represented the survivors in their 1980 civil lawsuit against the Klan, the city, and the FBI, believes that the GTRC represents an example

of "democratic self-government." This process, Pitts argues, "paves the way towards democracy, putting into action the philosophy that government is of the people, by the people, and for the people." Lewis Pitts, "Local Vocal: Nov. 3, 1979 Reveals Police–Hate Group Complicity," *Yes! Weekly,* July 13–19, 2005, 21; Lewis Pitts, interview by author, July 14, 2005, Greensboro, N.C.

55. Gregory Streich, "Is There a Right to Forget? Historical Injustices, Race, Memory, and Identity," *New Political Science* 24, no. 4 (2002): 534.

Social Remembering and Kent State

Jerry M. Lewis

Shortly after the events of May 4, 1970, when members of the Ohio National Guard fired into a crowd of unarmed Kent State University students, killing four and wounding nine others, people began calling for ways to remember the fallen and injured students. It is generally assumed that the social remembering of an important cultural event is a good thing. This is particularly true when the remembering concerns events that have caused serious personal and public trauma. Social remembering is considered as a positive way to honor the people and institutions associated with tragic events. In the language of functional analysis, the processes of remembering are eufunctional to the equilibrium of the system and to maintaining the social health of society. The process of social remembering encourages inquiry and learning about people and events. It provides an understanding of these events and may serve as a reminder that such events could be prevented in the future. In contrast to this positive view of social remembering, however, almost every major step in the social remembering processes associated with the May 4, 1970, shootings has been characterized by controversy and debate. Social remembering at Kent State has been dysfunctional because of two major types of issues: (a) the collision of social or collective memories about the shootings and ways to commemorate them, and (b) the ethical concerns surrounding the social remembering of traumatic events.

In *Voices of Collective Remembering*, James Wertsch provides guidelines for appreciating the continuum between collective memory and analytical history. He warns that in examining these characteristics, scholars need to see them as "*tendencies* and *aspirations* of collective memory and history rather than ironclad attributes and that the opposing tendencies often operate in tension with one another."[1]

Wertsch prefers the term *social remembering* to the term *collective memory*, because the former emphasizes the process or action of remembering rather than "memories that we 'have.'"[2] He points out that even when people experience the same event (such as the shootings at Kent State) they have different interpretations or remembrances of those events. Collective remembering "comes to define eternal truth . . . and identity."[3] It is a social process of remembering by sharing stories and experiences.

Table 13.1. Social Remembering and History

Social Remembering	History
"Subjective"	*"Objective"*
Single committed perspective	Distanced from any particular perspective
Reflects a particular group's framework	Reflects no particular social framework
Unself-conscious	Critical, reflective stance
Impatient with ambiguities about motives and the interpretation of events	Recognizes ambiguities
Focus on stable, unchanging group essence	*Focus on transformation*
Denies "pastness" of events	*Focus on historicity*
Links the past with the present	Differentiates the past from the present
Ahistorical, antihistorical	Views past events as "then and not now"
Commemorative voice	*Historical voice*
Museum as a temple	Museum as a forum
Unquestionable heroic narratives	Disagreement, change, and controversy as part of ongoing historical interpretation

Source: Adapted from James Wertsch, *Voices of Collective Remembering* (Cambridge, UK: Cambridge Univ. Press, 2002), 44.[4] Used with permission.

As outlined above, Wertsch considers four major attributes or tendencies of those involved in collective/social remembering when compared with analytical history. The process of social remembering is *subjective* in nature. There is a "community of remembering" that has a clear focus on what should be remembered; it is not self-reflective and does not accept alternative explanations of the events being remembered.[5] The thrust of social remembering is resolving ambiguous interpretations of events to produce a single committed group memory that reflects a particular group's social framework. However, analytical history involves a sense of objectivity. Historians try to distance themselves from any perspective and reflect no particular social framework. They often deal with and present multiple perspectives, thus allowing themselves to live with and embrace ambiguities.

During the process of social remembering, groups tend to "focus on the stable unchanging essence of the group," whereas analytical history focuses on transformation and change over time. Although there is some transformation in social remembering, for the most part it is resistant to change. Collective remembering has no sense of the "pastness" of the events, according to Wertsch. Viewing the past within the circumstances of the present and linking the past events with the present through commemorative activities is of highest concern. Analytic history, however, has a tendency to focus on historicity—that is, the events happened "then and not now"—and, unlike collective remembering, displays little concern to connect the past events to the present. From the historical perspective, these events are part of the circumstances of the times that occurred in the past. Social remembering, in contrast, gives the past events a "commemorative voice" through the cultural tool of the heroic narrative or stories. In the social remembering process, the museum is seen as a temple that is not subject to differing interpretations and change. It places primary importance on continuing to share the stories or narratives of past actors in the events being remembered. Viewing events from an analytical historical perspective encourages people to explore the complicated motives and actions of past events, thus giving any museum the sense of a forum—an exchange of different perspectives and interpretations of events. Change and controversy are part of the ongoing historical interpretation of an event, thus giving it a historical voice.

To a great degree, Wertsch's analysis of social remembering sheds light on the difficulty that people have had over the past forty years in dealing with the Kent State shootings, or what the community associated with Kent State University and the shootings has come to call "May 4" (spoken as "May Fourth"). Because this paper is concerned with social remembering surrounding the events of May 4, 1970, the emphasis of this paper will be in discussing and analyzing the left side of Wertsch's model. The framework of social remembering will be applied to two commemorative events: the Candlelight March and Vigil and the annual May 4 Commemoration and one physical entity of remembrance, the May 4 Memorial.

There are two groups who are part of the community of remembering at Kent State. The core group is the private group of the thirteen families of the slain and wounded students, the wounded students themselves, and those who directly experienced the shootings on May 4, 1970. The members of this group are drawn together by a commonly shared tragedy. They are the May 4 family. However, a larger, public group comprising many more people has also participated in the social remembering process. This public group is represented by members of the May 4 Task Force and by all those connected to this event who carry on the traditions of remembrance and mourning. This public group links the past to the present and has become part of the extended May 4 family, or what historian Jay Winter describes as the "fictive kinship group."[6] The kinship group has bonded with the May 4 family through the commemorative activities and remembrances. The private group and the public fictive kinship group come together each year to remember and mourn the dead. The process begins on the University Commons for the Candlelight March.

The annual March and Vigil were first held on May 3 and 4, 1971, in commemoration and remembrance of the deaths of Allison Krause, Jeffrey Miller, Sandra Scheuer, and William Schroeder. Knowing the importance of social ritual, I instituted the Candlelight Vigil, with the assistance of several students, on the evening of May 3, 1971. Jeff Auld, a graduate student in sociology, recommended adding the Candlelight March in order to let more people take part in the collective remembering process. Each year, the Candlelight March begins at 11:00 P.M., on May 3. All in attendance are given a lighted candle to hold during their silent procession around the campus. The procession usually takes about forty-five minutes. The beginning point and ending points of the March are significant. The March begins at the Victory Bell on the Commons, where the noon rally on May 4, 1970, began, and ends at the Prentice

The annual Candlelight March around the Kent State campus on May 3. Photo by Gary Harwood. Reprinted with permission.

Hall parking lot, where most of the injured and students who were killed fell that same day. Generally, people having strong associations with the shootings—the wounded students, the parents of the slain or wounded students, leaders of the May 4 Task Force, and friends and family of the dead and wounded students—lead the marchers around campus, holding lighted candles in lanterns. These people are the first to stand vigil at the four places in the parking lot where the four students lay fatally wounded on May 4, 1970. This is the beginning of the actual Candlelight Vigil. Throughout the night, the silent vigils continue in half-hour segments until the beginning of the commemorative program the next day on the Commons. The Vigil concludes with the ringing of the Victory Bell at 12:24 P.M. on May 4, the moment when the Ohio National Guard fired sixty-seven rounds during thirteen seconds.

Both the Candlelight March and the Vigil illustrate the ritualistic, unchanging nature of the social remembering process and are central to it. Paul Connerton, in *How Societies Remember,* writes, "By comparison to myths, the structure of rituals has significantly less potential for *variance.* . . . It follows that if considerable precautions are to be taken to assure the identity of a culture's symbolic material, it will be advisable to direct these precautions to ensuring the identity of its ritual."[7] The Vigil, which locates the spots where the slain students fell, is commemorative through its emphasis on the sacred and through its unchanging content and ritual precision. While very little has changed since the Vigil was first created in 1971, in

Two stand vigil in the place where a slain student fell. Photo by Gary Harwood. Reprinted with permission.

recent years, senior university officials have been included in the honor of carrying the lanterns and holding them for the first half hour at each of the areas marked off in the Prentice Hall parking lot. Members of the Kent State University community and others continue to stand half-hour vigils from 11:00 P.M. on May 3 until 12:24 P.M. on May 4, when the annual commemoration begins—continuing the tradition since 1971. The only major change has been the addition of reciting the Jewish mourning prayer, the Kaddish. This began in the mid-1980s when a local rabbi asked if he could give a prayer following the march in memory of the three Jewish students who were killed. This tradition has continued since that time. In addition to the Mourners' Kaddish, the Lord's Prayer is also recited.

The ringing of the Victory Bell on the Commons is illustrative of the call to action that was used in the late 1960s and on that weekend in May 1970. Beginning the March on the Commons at the Victory Bell is symbolic as well. The Victory Bell is where the rally began on Monday, May 4, 1970. Furthermore, it represents a reclamation of the land that students claimed was theirs on that day. This was where they stood their ground when the order was given by the Ohio National Guard for them to disperse. This is where many of the students met immediately after the shootings to protest, by standing in that place, the deaths of their fellow classmates and the wounding of many others.

The Candlelight March, following the original route around campus in 1971, is likewise symbolic of the protest marches that occurred on the campus to summon students to various rallies held on the Kent State Commons throughout the 1960s and on that weekend in May 1970. In fact, immediately after the shootings, marches and vigils were held on college campuses throughout the United States in memory of the four dead students at Kent State and in protest of the United States' incursion into Cambodia.[8] At Bowling Green State University in Ohio, on May 6, 1970, seven thousand people participated in a Candlelight March in response to the shootings on the Kent State campus. President William T. Jerome III wrote, "The very silence of the Candlelight March indicates that there are times in the life of mankind when words and rhetoric are unable to convey the depth of human feeling and commitment."[9] The silence of the Candlelight March and Vigil conveys the depth of feelings of members of the private and fictive kinship groups. The events of the Candlelight March and Vigil were designed to bring the tragedy of those who were killed and wounded on May 4 to the forefront. The silent March and the silent Vigil with candles are both intended to evoke deep sadness and loss associated with the shootings. As Jay Winter suggests, silence forces people to suspend activity and remember.[10] Even breaking the tradition of the silent March and Vigil with the spoken words of the Kaddish evokes a deep emotional response within the community of remembrance.

There have been other modifications to the tradition of remembrance on May 4. In the early years of the Vigil, metal stanchions and ropes were used to cordon off the spots where the four students died or lay dying. Each spot was marked with a wooden sign with the dead student's name written on it. Also, in the early years after the shootings, many of the families did not take part in the annual Candlelight March and Vigil. Their feelings were too raw to share with anyone in public. Parents could not think of coming to the spot where their children had drawn their last breaths. With the help and support of members of the May 4 Task Force and friends of the May 4 family, however, the families of the slain students gradually became more involved. The turning point appeared to be after 1975, when Arthur Krause, father of slain student Allison Krause, stood vigil at the spot where his daughter had died. In 1999, at the insistence by the May 4 Task Force on behalf of the families, permanent bollards with lights and inscribed granite markers with the names of the four students who died were dedicated. These markers are symbols for the Vigil candles. Thus the markers, which are darkened only during the annual commemoration, are daily surrogate vigils for the annual Vigil that remembers the four slain students.

The Vigil and the markers have become sacred symbols in the social remembering process at Kent State. While there has been a strong need to keep these traditions unchanged, they have been challenged in several distinct instances by people seeking to push the collective toward a transformation of this commemorative event. In 2008, for example, two people who had been active in the remembering process got into a strong argument. One of them wanted to read aloud a list of people who had been harmed in political action throughout the United States and the world; the other wanted to keep the silent Vigil *silent,* focusing instead on the sacred honoring of the slain and wounded Kent State University students only. For the most part, the Candlelight March and Vigil remain silent.

Another challenge to the sacred rituals occurred many years ago, when Peter Davies, a writer about May 4 who led the campaign for a federal grand jury in the Kent State case, attended the Vigil and challenged particulars of the rituals. Davies became quite upset, insisting that the spot marking where Sandy Scheuer had died was in the wrong place by several feet, according to the facts. Having been involved in the federal grand jury trial, he understood the importance of being accurate about the distances separating the slain students from the guardsmen who fired at them. Davies regarded the Vigil as more than a symbolic remembrance activity. He felt so strongly about this that he moved the temporary stanchions to the correct position according to documented materials he found while researching his book.[11] Interestingly, as Wertsch points out, social remembering is more about the ritual than the actual facts involved. However, when the permanent stanchions were to be erected in the parking lot, scholars, eyewitnesses, and photographs were used to mark as accurately as possible the spots where the four students were hit by gunfire.

A second social remembering key event is the May 4 Commemoration, where a "gathering of fictive kinships" occurs each May 4.[12] The May 4 families and the fictive kinship group meet on the Commons each May 4 to remember the dead and wounded students. During the first five years after the shootings, the university sponsored a commemoration program. In 1971, there were three days of commemorative activities. On Sunday, May 2, civil rights activist Julian Bond spoke. On Monday, May 3, speakers included activist Dick Gregory and James Ahern, chief of police for New Haven, Connecticut, and a member of the President's Commission on Campus Unrest. On Tuesday, May 4, President Kingman Brewster of Yale University and civil rights activist Jesse Jackson were the key speakers. A series of similar commemoration programs followed. Then in 1975, President Glenn Olds announced that there would be no more commemorations. He believed that five years of university-sponsored commemorations were sufficient. Every year since that time, however, the May 4 Task Force has planned and conducted the May 4 commemorations on May 3 and 4.

The program for the Commemoration has remained relatively constant since 1975. At 12:24 P.M., the transition from the Candlelight Vigil in the Prentice Hall parking lot to the annual Commemoration on the Commons begins with the ringing of the Victory Bell fifteen times, in honor of the four students killed and nine students wounded at Kent State and of the two students killed at Jackson State College on May 14, 1970.[13] The time, 12:24 P.M., replicates the time when the guardsmen fired their weapons for thirteen seconds. There is a narrative reading of the events that occurred on May 1–4, 1970, to inform those present of what happened on the campus leading up to and including the shootings. After the reading, the last people standing vigil in the parking lot in memory of the four slain students march down the hill to the Commons carrying four lanterns in their honor. Pictures of the four slain students are placed in front of the stage, along with candles that are kept lit throughout the Commemoration. Then there are speeches from friends or family members on the lives of the four students. Lastly, there are invited activist speakers. In 1977, the university declared May 4 an official day of remembrance. Classes are suspended from noon until 2:00 P.M. every May 4 so that any university community member who wishes to participate in the Commemoration can do so.

Most social remembering involves resolving ambiguous interpretations of events so that there is a single committed group memory that reflects a particular group's social framework. The narrative of events leading to the shootings is an example of this. Social remembering also involves a sacred response or "voice" for remembering an event. It represents the events and mourns the deaths of the slain and the suffering of the wounded. The program of the annual Commemoration attempts to do just that. It replicates the May 4 rally protesting the presence of the National Guard on the Commons, educates those in attendance on the events of May 1–4, 1970, and attempts to keep alive the stories of the students who were killed. Witnesses of the shootings and the friends and family members of the victims become important storytellers. The traumatic events of May 4 have shaped and defined many of their lives. They bear witness to the past and tell their stories to those who have never experienced the trauma in quite the same way that they have. They become, symbolically, the voices of those who were silenced on May 4. According to Pennebaker and Gonzales, "In general, memories that are formed between the ages of 13 and 25 are the most striking events in our personal histories." Events that occur during this time period are most likely to be commemorated by this age cohort.[14] This could explain why hundreds of people make the annual pilgrimage to Kent State on May 4 to participate in this annual Commemoration on the Commons and become part of the May 4 fictive kinship.

These personal narratives provide a link to the past. According to Wertsch, collective remembering has no sense of the pastness of the events.[15] Viewing the past within the circumstances of the present and linking the past events with the present through commemorative activities is an important part of the remembering process. The commemoration process attempts to capture the events being remembered in current terms. People are less concerned about hard facts and more concerned about the symbolic meaning of the events. That is, the tragedy being remembered is not in the past, but very relevant, symbolically, to contemporary times. Therefore, social remembering has to have relevance for contemporary life. This could explain why social justice issues and speakers are part of the May 4 commemorative program each year.

The commemorative program reflects Wertsch's concept of the unquestionable heroic narratives. One of the results of the May 4 community of remembering is the portrayal of the slain students in heroic terms.[16] They are referred to as martyrs by many of the commemorative speakers. In fact, one of the wounded students, who is still active in the social remembering process, uses this term each time he refers to the four who were killed on May 4. It is an emotionally charged word that evokes the meaning of a shared sacrifice for the cause. The definition of the term *martyr,* however, suggests a peron who volunteered for suffering. At Kent State, certainly none of the slain or wounded students volunteered for their deaths or injuries.

In addition to the Candlelight March and Vigil and the May 4 Commemoration, there is a physical entity that has become part of the social remembering process for anyone who visits Kent State—the May 4 Memorial, built to preserve the memory of the slain students. Interest in constructing a major memorial dedicated to the students killed or injured during the day of May 4, 1970, arose almost immediately after the shootings occurred. The university community and the community at large were not ready for such a tribute, however. It was not until 1985 that a Kent State University committee, appointed by KSU's president, Michael Schwartz, recommended that a memorial be built. This time frame is not particularly unusual, according to collective memory scholars James W. Pennebaker and Amy L. Gonzales, who say that "monuments tend to be erected either immediately after an event or in 20–30 year cycles thereafter," regardless of whether the event being remembered was positive or negative.[17]

The May 4 Memorial. Photo by Gary Harwood. Reprinted with permission.

When people heard about plans for a May 4 Memorial, many assumed that everyone would approve of a memorial associated with recognizing the killing and wounding of unarmed students by thirteen seconds of gunfire from a military unit of the United States. In the event, the process of planning the Memorial was fraught with conflict. In the early years following the shootings, during the discussion and debate about whether to build a May 4 Memorial in memory of the four students, some argued against building any memorial to the four students slain at Kent State until Vietnam veterans were honored. The Vietnam Veterans Memorial was dedicated in Washington, D.C., on November 1984, a year before plans were begun to build a May 4 Memorial at Kent State. Once the Vietnam Veterans Memorial was dedicated, many at Kent State University seemed to feel that this issue was settled.

In 1985, President Schwartz accepted the recommendation of the memorial committee and initiated a design competition. While discussions were under way for the physical memorial, the parents of the slain students asked that the Memorial not be representational; that is, that the images and even the names of the slain students be omitted from the Memorial to avoid any chance of its components looking like gravestones. Thus, the call for submissions indicated that the theme of *four* should be part of the memorial, but not the names of the wounded and slain.[18] The competition drew almost seven hundred submissions. The winner of the competition, Chicago architect Bruno Ast, was selected in the summer of 1986. Originally, the only name on the May 4 Memorial was Ast's own. In response, some people called for putting the names of the slain students on the pylons representing them, but this was rejected by the university. This issue of whether or not the students' names should be on the May 4 Memorial became a considerable source of controversy until President Schwartz, in discussions with the students' families and others, resolved it by agreeing to place a plaque with the names of all the slain and injured students on the ground near the May 4 Memorial. The Memorial itself gives no description or explanation of the events of May 4; the only words on it are "Inquire, Learn, Reflect." However, the university does supply copies of a brochure in a box near the Memorial, which lays out the facts of the shootings and an interpretation of the May 4 Memorial.[19]

The Memorial was dedicated during the twentieth anniversary remembrances on May 4, 1990. Its description in the brochure reads:

> Constructed of carnelian granite . . . the memorial is graced by a planting of 58,175 daffodil bulbs, which symbolize the number of our country's losses in Vietnam. . . . [The memorial is entered through a plaza that has] engraved in the plaza's stone threshold the words "Inquire, Learn, Reflect." . . . A progression of four polished disks embedded in the earth leads from the plaza to four free-standing pylons aligned on the hill. The disks reflect our own image as we stand on them; the pylons stand as mute sentinels to the force of violence and the memory of the four students killed.[20]

The May 4 Memorial is abstract and ambiguous, subject to many interpretations, and reflects no particular social framework. Without the interpretation given in the brochure, visitors are left to wonder what these objects mean. To some involved in the social remembering process, this ambiguity is unacceptable. They believe that the memorial should tell a story about the shootings. Although the families requested that images of their children not be on the memorial, its abstract form was not acceptable either. The memorial did not reflect their interpretation or framework for viewing the shootings. The conflict over the May 4 Memorial is an example of the tensions between analytical history and social remembering.

Nevertheless, the debate and controversies surrounding the social remembering of the Kent State shootings serve to keep the memory of the events alive in the mind of the collective. It speaks to the contention of Avishai Margalit that societies have an ethical obligation to remember certain events—particularly those characterized by trauma.[21]

The controversy and debate that continue over the appropriateness of the Memorial is an example of the dysfunctional aspect of the social remembering process. The dysfunctional aspects of the Vigil and Commemoration activities lie primarily in the desire of some participants to move them away from the sacred and expand them to include political statements. Those involved in the social remembering process desire to keep those events as they have always been—a way to remember and honor the slain students. Yet there is a need in social remembering to link past events with the present. These tensions between honoring and remembering the dead and using the dead to advance a current cause is what is at issue in the social remembering of May 4.The dysfunctional aspects of the social remembering process pertaining to the May 4 Memorial occur when the debate slows down the processes of remembering. For example, it took fifteen years for the community even to agree to have a Memorial and twenty years before the Memorial was dedicated on May 4, 1990. Perhaps this lengthy process reflects the need of some to forget traumatic events because remembering causes such stress and suffering among its survivors.

According to Barbara A. Misztal, Freud "is commonly recognized as one of the forebears of the idea that the past continues to the present."[22] The processes of social remembering induce emotional suffering. When an individual goes through the process of remembering a past traumatic event or events, he or she often experiences deep sadness, depression, anxiety, or a sense of overwhelming loss. As discussed earlier, two categories of people experience this emotional suffering: the private group and the public group. The private group is made up of those who have a direct link to the remembered events, including the families of the slain and wounded students, the wounded students, eyewitnesses to the events, and guardsmen. The public group is made up of people who did not directly experience the remembered events but, through the collective memory processes, develop a sense of the tragedy through ritual experience and empathy—the fictive kinship.

The social remembering process, especially for a traumatic event like the shootings at Kent State, can cause emotional pain for all involved, both the private and public groups, for different reasons. Social remembering is always contextual. In the case of the May 4 tragedy, the university community becomes the backdrop or context of remembering. But added to this context is the division that occurred in our country over the Vietnam War The controversies arising from U.S. involvement in the war in Southeast Asia were amplified by people's responses to the day the war came home to the Kent State campus. Thus the war in Vietnam and the actions of the Ohio National Guard are all part of the context in which people remember the events of May 4. Given these circumstances, what are the ethical issues of social remembering? What happens when the process of social remembering causes emotional pain? What happens when the groups involved in the social remembering process collide? Do those who encourage remembering have the right to inflict emotional pain on other people in an effort to remember?

The iconic photograph most closely associated with the Kent State shootings is a powerful image evoking a variety of responses. It is the photograph of Mary Ann Vecchio (a fourteen-year-old runaway from Florida) calling out over the body of Jeffrey Miller. The photo won a Pulitzer Prize for the photographer, John Filo, who was a student at Kent State when he took the picture.

Although it serves as a symbol for the tragedy that occurred at Kent State, Filo's photograph can also cause pain among those in the private collective group. Jeff Miller's mother noted numerous times how upsetting it was seeing that image of her son lying on the ground in a pool of blood. She said that she deals with this iconic image by pretending that Jeff is asleep. John Filo for years felt guilty for trapping Mary Ann Vecchio in time and causing such pain in her life because of the photograph he took of her that day in May. They both were thrust into the international spotlight because of the photograph.

As someone who experienced May 4 directly and has written and taught about the events, I belong to a group of people who have direct experience and connection with the tragedy.[23] The emotional toll on the members of this group is tremendous each time the anniversary of the shootings approaches. It is important to keep in mind

John Filo's Pulitzer Prize–winning photograph of slain student Jeffrey Miller with Mary Vecchio calling out over his body. Photo copyright John P. Filo. Reprinted with permission.

that each of us brings our own agenda when remembering what happened at Kent State. The markers can be a reminder of what the families of the slain and wounded students have suffered. Sergeant Matthew McManus, a member of the Ohio National Guard, said, "I want people to know in their heart of hearts that the guardsmen have suffered. Not as much as some." Perhaps the markers can help us imagine it and encourage us to make the world better in honor of the four slain students. This is not an easy task. In order to remember the slain and wounded students, one has to experience what happened in May 1970, or, in the case of the private group, relive the past. We must put ourselves in the place of a student, faculty member, or staff member in the parking lot on that terrible day, or imagine being a guardsman at the top of the hill near the Pagoda, shooting his rifle. This can be quite emotionally difficult. This is the dysfunctional aspect of the social remembering of May 4.

The same is true of the May 4 rituals and site. I have taken innumerable people to the May 4 site. Every time people go to the shooting site, stand in the marker places, and look at the place where the guardsmen stood as they fired, an expression of shock or pain comes across their faces. This is particularly true of those standing at Sandy Scheuer's spot, which is more than 130 yards from the Pagoda—the site from which the National Guard fired. Each of the markers helps visitors to understand the distances that the slain students were from the National Guard when the firing commenced. Perhaps the best way to cushion this pain is simply to prepare visitors for it before they come to the May 4 site and Memorial.

Some see this outpouring of emotion as cathartic, but to others, it is simply a way of unnecessarily dredging up and dwelling on the past. "Why can't you just get on with it?" such people ask. "It happened a long time ago. Do you have to keep bringing up these events?" The literature on social remembering gives us some insight to the answer to these questions. Commemorative events, like the yearly Candlelight March, Vigil, and May 4 Commemoration, give social members a chance to share narratives, thus enabling them to link the past events to the present. Although these events can be emotional, they are viewed as a means to connect to the past in a collective way. As Jay Winter explains, "remembering the cruelties of the past is not a choice but a necessity."[24]

There is a need to explore issues around why we remember, why there is a need for a Candlelight March, Vigil, and Commemoration. Three are relevant. One, we remember to honor the fallen. Two, we remember in the hope that the events remembered, often very tragic, might never occur again. That is, as Santana said, "Those who do not remember the past are doomed to repeat it." Three, the larger society demands that we remember. The first two seem obvious, the third, less so. May 4 does not belong to Kent State University; it belongs to society. Many people were deeply affected by the events of May 4 and its aftermath. The larger community expects that Kent State will do something each year in some form to memorialize the four students. This is particularly true for major anniversaries defined by years ending in 0s and 5s. In other words, the demands for remembering are extrinsic to the university culture. When my wife and I traveled to Europe, Australia, and New Zealand and were asked about our hometown and professions, invariably the people had heard of the May 4, 1970, shooting of students at Kent State in Kent, Ohio.

There are functional dimensions of remembering. First, and most importantly, the Vigil and the May 4 Memorial honor the sacrifice of the slain and wounded students. Secondly, they encourage students and others who participate to inquire, learn, and reflect on the meaning of May 4. This charge seems to be the essence of what a university is about and hence in harmony with the basic values of objective inquiry that guide a university culture. What then is the responsibility of those who organize social remembering events to both the private and public groups to ease their suffering when reliving the experience of the trauma? Do organizers have a responsibility to warn people who are not very knowledgeable about the events that they will be remembering a situation where young, unarmed Kent State students were killed or wounded in a demonstration, many standing more than one hundred yards from the National Guard when they were shot? A core value of a college or university is the uncompromising seeking of truth, whatever the consequences. A college or university professor commits his or her perspectives—theoretical, methodological, and empirical—to this pursuit. Yet often the process of remembering creates abstractions that move the remembered event or person away from empirical reality.

Does the process of remembering, which is often based on abstraction, have the dysfunctional consequences of harming the values of truth seeking? Is Kent State University, in the processes of social remembering, harming the very thing we stand for as a university? That is, do the emotional aspects of the remembering harm or hinder truth seeking? Can we claim as scholars that we are pursuing answers to questions wherever the inquiry might take us? These questions illustrate that the processes of social remembering create a tension between ethical issues and the values of inquiry in colleges and universities. How do we resolve this tension? One obvious answer is to try not to distort, in the process of remembering, the empirical truths of the events being remembered. But, when one looks at the May 4 Memorial, such distortion may happen. The Memorial clearly is not representational. Also, it does not stand on the site of the shootings, but instead near where students were killed and wounded. It is clearly an abstraction, but one that scholars and historians can accept.

The university is now building a permanent May 4 Visitors Center exhibit in the former Kent State student newspaper office in Taylor Hall. This center will provide a central place where people can explore and better understand the events that occurred on May 4, 1970, and their impact and meaning for today.[25] In May 2010, the university dedicated a walking tour of the May 4 historical site. Seven interpretive trail markers with factual information and photographs lead the visitor through the May 4 site and relay information about what happened on that day. Scholars of public history, sociology, anthropology, communication and journalism, peace studies, and English from throughout the United States, along with many in the local campus and city community, participated in forums to discuss the content of the center and the walking tour. As Winter notes, public history attempts to create a bridge between the scholarship of history and public remembering.[26] Perhaps, with the walking tour and the completion of the May 4 Visitors Center, there will be a bridging of the social remembering and analytical history processes as described by Wertsch. It is time for such a convergence.

Notes

1. James Wertsch, *Voices of Collective Remembering,* 2.
2. Ibid., 17.
3. Ibid., 25.
4. Also see James Wertsch, "Collective Memory," in *Memory in Mind and Culture,* ed. Pascal Boyer and James Wertsch (New York: Cambridge Univ. Press, 2009), 127.
5. Avishai Margalit, *The Ethics of Memory* (Cambridge, Mass.: Harvard Univ. Press, 2002), passim.
6. The May 4 Task Force was founded in 1975 by three of the wounded students: Alan Canfora, Dean Kahler, and Robby Stamps. Maintained as a student organization at Kent State University, its purpose is to raise awareness and understanding of the shootings. Members give lectures on and off campus and hold two public forums during the academic year. They also give out an activism scholarship (investment revenue permitting) from the monies raised in a benefit concert by Peter, Paul, and Mary. Members work all year to plan the annual Candlelight March and Vigil and the Commemoration. Jay Winter's term "fictive kinship" comes from *Remembering War,* 136.
7. Paul Connerton, *How Societies Remember* (Cambridge, UK: Cambridge Univ. Press, 1989), 57.
8. *Report of the President's Commission,* 18.
9. William T. Jerome III, "Statement Concerning Candlelight March, May 7, 1970," Ohio Memory Project, Ohio Memory Collection, the Ohio Historical Society and the State Library of Ohio, Columbus, Ohio, <http://www.ohiomemory.org/cdm4/document.php?CISOROOT=%2Fp267401coll36&CISOPTR=24472&REC=16&CISOBOX=William+Jerome+III>.
10. Winter, *Remembering War,* 143.
11. Peter Davies, *Truth about Kent State.* For a detailed account of the trials related to the Kent State shootings see Hensley, "The May Fourth Trials," in Hensley and Lewis, *Kent State and May 4th,* 64–86.
12. Winter, *Remembering War,* 145.
13. Jackson State became Kent State's sister school in tragedy. At Jackson State on May 14, 1970, police killed two students, James Green and Philip Gibbs, and wounded twenty. Jackson State remembers the tragedy through a marker and the Gibbs-Green plaza. See

Christina Hange Kukuk, "The Gibbs/Green Affair," *The Burr,* special edition, May 4, 2000, <http://www.burr.kent.edu/archives/may4/jackson/cover.html>.

14. James W. Pennebaker and Amy L. Gonzales, "Making History: Social and Psychological Processes Underlying Collective Memory," in Boyer and Wertsch, *Memory in Mind and Culture,* 173.
15. Wertsch, *Voices of Collective Remembering,* 44.
16. Ibid.
17. Pennebaker and Gonzales, "Making History," 184.
18. James E. Dalton, *May 4 Memorial Design Competition* (Kent, Ohio: Kent State University, 1985).
19. Glenn W. Frank, Thomas R. Hensley, and Jerry M. Lewis, *May 4 Site and Memorial* (1990; Kent, Ohio: Kent State Univ. Communications and Marketing, 2008). The original brochure was replaced in 2010 by a new site and Memorial brochure, available from a regularly stocked stand (the box near the Memorial was not always regularly stocked) in the Prentice Hall parking lot, where the slain students fell.
20. Frank, Hensley, and Lewis, *May 4 Site and Memorial.* The 2010 brochure retains this information.
21. Margalit, *Ethics of Memory.*
22. Barbara A. Misztal, *Theories of Social Remembering* (Maidenhead, Berks., UK: Open Univ. Press, 2003), 3.
23. On Monday, May 4, 1970, shortly before noon, I went to the Commons as a faculty marshal to observe the rally that I thought might be held to protest the presence of the Ohio National Guard on campus. I moved onto the Commons and passed students who had been gathering around the Victory Bell for the past hour. I watched the crowd for about fifteen minutes, at which time the National Guard moved against the students, driving them off the Commons with a tear gas attack. Students responded very angrily to the attack, which did little more than provoke them. The Guard continued to advance on students, driving them over a hill as they moved to a practice football field. I was taking care of a student in the parking lot who had been teargassed by the Guard. I looked up and saw guardsmen retracing their steps from the practice field. As they got to the top of the hill, twenty-eight of the more than seventy guardsmen fired their rifles. Many guardsmen fired into the air or into the ground. However, a small portion fired into the crowd below, killing four Kent State students and wounding nine others. I was standing twenty yards behind the spot where Sandy Scheuer was killed. I took cover when the firing began. My experiences were typical of many that day, including those of Mary Ann Vecchio and John Filo, a Kent State student at the time who took the famous picture of Mary kneeling beside the body of Jeffrey Miller.

    When I go to the Prentice Hall parking lot markers during the annual Vigil each year, I am reminded of various conversations with parents of the slain students. The markers symbolize personal memories for me. The marker closest to the Pagoda from where members of the National Guard fired marks the spot where Jeffery Miller fell. I recall Jeffery Miller's mother, Elaine Holstein, connecting with Mary Ann Vecchio, as they walked in the Vigil March in 1995. Two women, linked in tragedy, reached out to each other. The next marker, marking the spot where Allison Krause fell, causes me to think of her father, Arthur, with his powerful frame and booming voice, saying, "Jerry, never let what happened here be forgotten." The third marker tells us where Bill Schroeder fell when the war came home from the hills of Vietnam to the plains of Ohio. At the 1990 dedication of the Ast Memorial, which at the time was engulfed in controversy, I remember his mother, Florence, moving me to tears with her simple declaration, "We think the Memorial is just fine." Lastly, I move to the place where Sandy Scheuer fell in the parking lot as she walked to class. Her parents, Martin and Sarah, often came to the annual Vigils. I remember one cold May 3 in 1979 when they learned that I was to be promoted to full professor in the fall; forgetting their pain and wishing me success, they gave me a resounding "Mazel Tov!"

24. Winter, *Remembering War,* 271.
25. Mission statement in the May 4 Visitors Center foundation document (unpublished paper), March 30, 2009, Kent State University, Kent, Ohio, 1.
26. Winter, *Remembering War,* 202.

Appendix: This We Know

Chronology of the Shootings at Kent State, May 1970

Carole A. Barbato, Laura L. Davis,
and Mark F. Seeman

> I have concluded that the actions of the enemy in the last 10 days clearly endanger the lives of Americans who are in Vietnam now and would constitute an unacceptable risk to those who will be there after withdrawal of another 150,000. To protect our men who are in Vietnam, and to guarantee the continued success of our withdrawal and Vietnamization program, I have concluded that the time has come for action. . . . We take this action not for the purpose of expanding the war into Cambodia but for the purpose of ending the war in Vietnam and winning the just peace we all desire.[1]

These words, spoken by President Richard M. Nixon on Thursday, April 30, 1970, at 9:00 P.M., represented to many an escalation of the war in Vietnam, not the de-escalation he had promised since 1968. The invasion of Cambodia was seen by many as a betrayal, "a cataclysmic move that turned the War in Vietnam into the War in Indochina."[2] As social justice advocate Peter Davies noted, "The groans on numerous campuses that night turned into impassioned and sometimes violent protests the next day." According to the analysis of political sociologist Seymour Lipset, "The reaction against the May 1970 Cambodian incursion, of course, produced the largest and most extensive student protest movement the United States has ever experienced. All the survey data document the increased extent of student participation, as well as the fact that student attitudes in general moved to the Left, not only with respect to the war, but on other issues as well."[3]

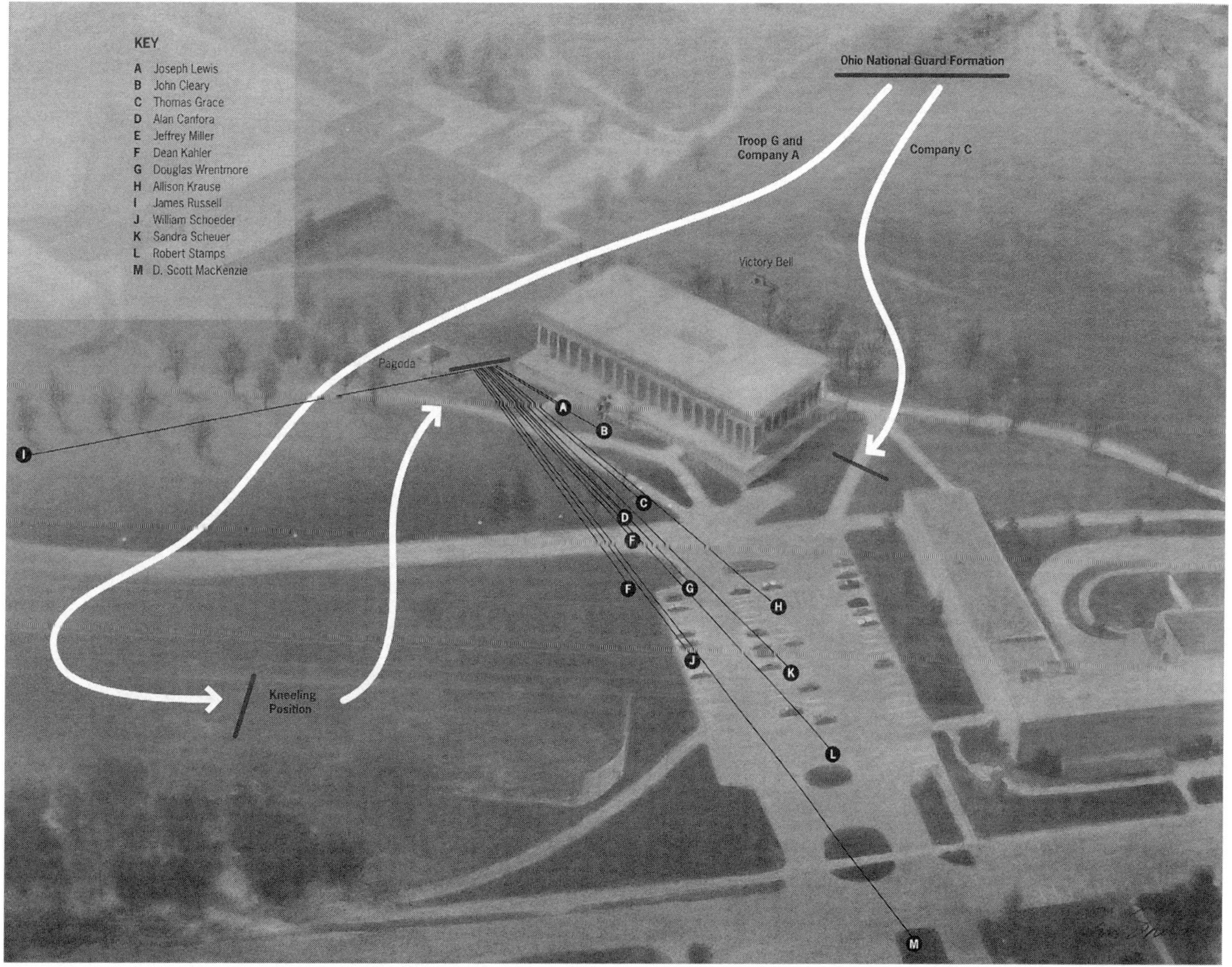

Site of the student rally and shootings on May 4, 1970. Curved lines trace the path of Ohio National Guard troops beginning at 12:05 P.M. on May 4, 1970. At 12:24, guardsmen turned 135 degrees at the Pagoda and twenty-eight fired, primarily toward students in the Prentice Hall parking lot. Map copyright Kent State University. Reprinted with permission.

On Friday, May 1, 1970, students at Kent State University, like thousands of others at hundreds of colleges and universities throughout the United States, participated in a protest against the U.S. invasion of Cambodia. While protests at some other colleges and universities were violent, this rally was impassioned but peaceful.

Kent State history graduate students Steve Sharoff and Chris Plant awoke early in the morning to plan a campus protest against Nixon's announcement of the incursion into Cambodia. By 7:00 A.M., they were distributing flyers announcing a rally at noon.[4] At noon, about five hundred students gathered at the Commons, a grassy green in the center of campus.[5] A group that called itself WHORE (World Historians Opposed to Racism and Exploitation) ceremonially buried a copy of the Constitution. According to the Justice Department Summary of the FBI Report on the shootings, "The general theme of the speeches was that the President had disregarded the limits of his office imposed by the Constitution of the United States and that, as a consequence, the Constitution had become a lifeless document, murdered by the President."[6] Someone burned his draft card, and veteran James Geary, another history graduate student who had won the Silver Star for his service in Vietnam, burned his discharge papers in protest against the invasion of Cambodia.[7] Those present agreed to meet at noon on Monday, May 4, to determine if they should join

On Friday, May 1, Kent State students protest the invasion of Cambodia by symbolically burying a copy of the U.S. Constitution at the Victory Bell on the Commons. Reprinted with permission of Kent State University Special Collections and Archives.

other universities and colleges throughout America in a national student strike. The assembly began and ended peacefully.

Later that afternoon, Kent State's Black United Students (BUS) held a rally on front campus to hear a speaker from Ohio State University talk about violence by law enforcement officials during demonstrations there. Black students advised their peers to stay away from campus activities that weekend. The short, forty-five-minute meeting disbanded peacefully. Upon hearing of the two peaceful protests, KSU's president, Robert I. White, left for Iowa, where he was to sit on the American College Testing board of trustees meeting on Sunday and take some time while there to visit with family.[8]

Friday evening was "one of the first warm Friday nights of the spring."[9] The small city of Kent had a strip of bars and clubs in the downtown area on North Water Street that attracted young people (students and nonstudents) from all over the state and the local area. Friday night was no exception. Thousands of young people were in the bars and clubs. Between 10:00 and 11:00 P.M., firecrackers were set off and a motorcycle gang called the Chosen Few was riding up and down Water Street between two bars, JB's and the Kove, performing tricks on their bikes. A police car drove past the crowd four or five times and was met with cheers as it drove by.[10] The *Report of the President's Commission on Campus Unrest* stated that ten police officers were on duty that evening, and four of these men in two patrol cars were assigned to North Water Street.[11] A trash can was dumped in the middle of Water Street, stopping the flow of traffic north and south. People danced in the street, preventing cars from passing through. Around 11:20 P.M., some members of the crowd hit the passing police car with beer bottles. According to Davies, members of the Chosen Few lit the contents of the trash can causing a small fire in the middle of Water Street.[12] It was described by some as a "bonfire," but it was a rather small trash fire.[13]

The *Akron Beacon Journal* Special Report noted that "Patrolman Robert Defluiter of the Kent Police Department said that between 11:27 and 11:41 P.M. he watched young demonstrators shouting 'Get out of town, pigs!' bombard two police cars with bottles, glasses and beer pitchers."[14] Many people who were in the bars came up to see what was going on and to escape the heat inside. "Soon the crowd blocked the street and began to stop motorists to ask their opinion about Cambodia."[15] The crowd turned revelry to an antiwar protest. According to the Justice Department Summary of the FBI Report, at 11:41 P.M. all of Kent's twenty-one police officers were summoned to duty. The nearby Stow Police Department was alerted, as well as the Portage County Sheriff Department, which sent eighty to ninety regular and special deputies to Kent. Kent police and sheriff's deputies began marching down Water Street. One squad formed at Main and Water, and the other marched down North Water Street to break up the revelry near the trash fire. The crowd, now around four hundred to five hundred in number according to the Justice Department Summary of the FBI Report, began running ahead of the police.[16] Davies noted that about twenty people started throwing bottles at buildings.[17] Within the city of Kent, forty-seven windows were broken in fifteen buildings.[18]

After consulting with Kent's police chief, Roy Thompson, Mayor Leroy Satrom declared a state of civil emergency at 12:20 A.M. and ordered all bars to be closed. He set a curfew of 11:00 P.M. for the city and 1:00 A.M. for the campus. Thompson and the Kent police enforced this order.[19] This action sent hundreds more young people into the streets and into the middle of the protesters, tear gas, and police action. Soon bystanders were being caught up in the crowd. At 12:47 A.M., Mayor Satrom called the office of Ohio's governor, James Rhodes, informing him that the SDS (Students for a Democratic Society) had taken over part of the city of Kent. In fact, the KSU chapter of the SDS had been disbanded in the spring of 1969. The governor's administrative assistant, John McElroy, called Maj. Gen. Sylvester Del Corso of the Ohio National Guard, who called the Guard liaison officer, Lieutenant Charles Barnette.[20]

Some of the crowd from downtown were forced onto campus, where they were safe from police action. When a traffic accident left an electric worker stranded—hanging on the traffic light at the corner of Lincoln and Main (the entrance to the Kent State campus)—police and members of the crowd on the campus grounds worked together to assist the worker to safety.[21] By 2:00 A.M., the streets of downtown Kent were cleared of all people; police arrested fifteen, all from Ohio—"not an unusually large number for a weekend evening in downtown Kent."[22] Although, according to the Justice Department Summary of the FBI Report, the mayor originally estimated that the disorder had caused damage to the downtown area worth $50,000 (later revising this figure to $15,000), the final figure was an estimated $10,000.[23]

Lieutenant Charles Barnette of the Ohio National Guard arrived at the city of Kent to talk with the mayor at 2:27 A.M. James Best, a Kent State political science professor, concluded, "Frustration over the Cambodian invasion, anger because they were turned out of bars, and the sting of tear gas turned what might have otherwise been a relatively harmless release of emotion into an ugly incident."[24] According to the *Report of the President's Commission,* "University Police Chief Donald L. Schwartzmiller had decided to use his men to guard campus buildings. That night, a small amount of property damage, including a broken window at the ROTC building, was done on campus." The commission concluded, "The pattern established on Friday night was to recur throughout the weekend: There were disorderly incidents; authorities could not or did not respond in time to apprehend those responsible to stop the incidents in their early stages; the disorder grew; the police action, when it came, involved bystanders as well as participants; and finally, the students drew together in the conviction that they were being arbitrarily harassed."[25]

Saturday morning began with some students assisting shop owners in cleaning up the glass from the windows broken in the stores the evening before. Sightseers examined the damage. Owners of the stores and townspeople called City Hall, demanding that something be done. The mayor and the city chief of police were convinced that the SDS Weathermen were in the area and blamed them for the destruction in downtown Kent as part of a radical plot. Conversely, KSU's police chief, Donald Schwartzmiller, later commented that the campus police did not have any information about the Weathermen being at Kent State that weekend. He noted that the city police must have seen something his own force had not.[26] According to the *Akron Beacon Journal,* "To paraphrase Voltaire's remark about God, if Weatherman did not exist, it would have to be invented. Weatherman, the most militant wing of the SDS, seems to have become a kind of policeman's shorthand for anyone who is bearded, surly and inclined toward violence."[27]

Officials met several times throughout the day. The mayor formally proclaimed a civil emergency, banning all sales of liquor, beer, firearms, and gasoline (unless it was pumped directly into a car or truck). He declared an 8:00 p.m. to 6:00 a.m. curfew for the city and the university. A meeting of the mayor, KSU officials, and Lieutenant Barnette, the Guard liaison, determined that the curfew on campus would be 1:00 a.m. At 1:00 p.m., in a meeting of Lieutenant Barnette and Vice President Matson from the university, it was agreed that if arrests were to be conducted on campus, the university would first call on its campus police, second the sheriff's department, and third the Ohio State Highway Patrol. Lieutenant Barnette warned that if the National Guard was called to assist, it would not make a distinction between the city of Kent and the university.[28] According to Lieutenant Col. Charles Fassinger, however, the role of the National Guard was to assist officials and not take over for other police enforcing agencies.[29] Lieutenant Barnette told Mayor Satrom that if he planned to request the services of the Guard, he must do so by 5:00 p.m. that day (Saturday). The Ohio National Guard already was mobilized at the time and stationed in the nearby city of Akron, because of threats and disorder associated with a Teamsters Union wildcat strike there.

For several reasons, Satrom met the Guard deadline: rumors of radical SDS involvement from outside the area, reports by shop owners of threats, a decision of the sheriff's office and campus police not to assist the city, and the availability of the Highway Patrol only for making arrests. The mayor asked for the Guard to be put on alert in the city to protect citizens and property, and Governor Rhodes authorized the troops' dispatch to Kent. The National Guard was called up and moved to Kent at 6:00 p.m.[30]

Although civil emergency and an 8:00 p.m. curfew were in effect in the city of

Kent, the curfew on Kent State's campus was set at 1:00 A.M. KSU Vice President Matson met with undergraduate student leaders to plan evening activities on campus. They sent leaflets to the dorms to announce the curfew in the city and the plans for dormitory dances and bands, and, specifically, to state that peaceful assemblies were *not banned* on campus.[31]

Rumors circulated among officials in the city and the university that the campus's Reserve Officers' Training Corps (ROTC) building would be a target.[32] By 7:00 P.M., a crowd started to form on the Commons near the Victory Bell; by 7:30 P.M., it numbered six hundred.[33] The campus police were not guarding the ROTC building, as they had the evening before when Kent State student Michael Weekly broke one of its windows. Weekly was the only one charged with doing any damage to the ROTC building that weekend.[34]

The *Report of the President's Commission* noted that KSU Police Chief Schwartzmiller called the Highway Patrol for assistance but was notified that it would come only if arrests were necessary. Since at this time the assembly was peaceful and lawful and no arrests were warranted, the Patrol was not called back. The KSU police did not go to the ROTC building at this time either.[35]

Faculty marshals wearing either blue or white armbands circulated throughout the crowd, distributing leaflets notifying participants of the 1:00 A.M. campus curfew and announcing a rumor control telephone number.[36] The crowd marched from the Commons past the dormitories, picking up more students and nonstudents as it marched around campus until its numbers had grown to between one thousand and two thousand people.[37] The *Report of the President's Commission* stated that "some were chanting, 'Ho, Ho, Ho Chi Minh,' and 'One, two, three, four, we don't want your fucking war.' As they crossed the Commons near the ROTC building, some shouted, 'Get it,' 'Burn it,' and 'ROTC has to go.'"[38] According to the Justice Department Summary of the FBI Report, "The wooden ROTC building, a target for some students because of its symbolism of U.S. involvement in Southeast Asia, was located on the western portion of the Commons. It became the focal point of the demonstration."[39] At 8:10 P.M., a few members of the crowd began throwing rocks at the ROTC building, breaking more windows. Although others threw railroad flares, they rolled off without setting it on fire. A male dipped a rag into a motorcycle gas tank and tried to set the curtains on fire, and, after thirty minutes and many failed attempts, the building started to burn. Approximately one dozen members of the crowd actively tried to set the building on fire.[40] According to the FBI report, the building was afire by 8:30 P.M., but the fire department was not notified until 8:49 P.M., when it sent trucks to the scene. Mayor Satrom, notified of the trouble on campus, called out the Ohio National Guard without conferring with university officials.[41]

At 9:00 P.M., the Kent City Fire Department arrived to put out the ROTC fire, unescorted by police. The firefighters were met with jeers and resistance from the

On the evening of Saturday, May 2, Ohio National Guard troops enter the Kent State campus when the ROTC building burns. Photo copyright Don Roese, *Akron Beacon Journal.* Reprinted with permission.

demonstrators, several of whom threw rocks, tried to cut the fire hoses, or pulled on the hoses in a tug-of-war.[42] At 9:15 P.M., just as the firefighters were leaving, the KSU police arrived at the scene. The university police used tear gas to disperse the crowd, which scattered. At this point, by all reports, the fire was out.[43] The KSU police were joined by ten officers from the Portage County Sheriff's Office.[44] Around 9:30 P.M., a small supply shed on the edge of the Commons, near the tennis courts, was set on fire, and some of the faculty marshals and students formed a makeshift bucket brigade to put out the fire and save a nearby tree.[45] The remaining students were dispersed by officers of the university police and sheriff's department. University officials called the Ohio State Highway Patrol, which was already on campus, stationed at President White's residence. Around 9:45 P.M., the fire at the ROTC building, which had been unattended by the firefighters, flared back up and burned "furiously," according to the Justice Department Summary of the FBI Report.[46] Although it is widely assumed that the building was burned by demonstrators, it also has been suggested by some researchers that the arson was the work of agents provocateurs.[47]

At 10:10 P.M., firefighters were dispatched a second time to the ROTC building, accompanied this time by the Ohio National Guard. According to the Justice Department Summary of the FBI Report, the guardsmen sent to the vicinity of the ROTC building belonged to the Ohio National Guard's Company A and Troop G. As Troop G approached campus, its vehicles were hit by rocks. Eight guardsmen reported injuries; one required medical attention.[48] Demonstrators who returned to the ROTC building found it fully engulfed in flames. By now, although the university police, sheriff's deputies, highway patrolmen, and guardsmen were helping the firefighters, the small, wooden, World War II barracks building could not be saved. From this point until midnight, the National Guard drove demonstrators into the dorms even if they were not residents of those dorms. Faculty marshals also got swept up in this action. According to the *Report of the President's Commission,* when faculty marshals tried to approach guardsmen to explain who they were, the guardsmen knelt down and raised their rifles. At this point, the faculty gave up trying to reason with the guardsmen and just ran away from them. The report further noted, "Neither Del Corso nor Canterbury requested permission of any university official before sending troops onto campus. General Canterbury said later that because the building was located on state property, the Guard needed no specific invitation to enter the campus."[49]

Sunday, May 3, 1970

On Sunday, May 3, students who lived on campus awoke to see 850 guardsmen occupying the grounds.[50] Some troops guarded the site of the ROTC building and set up camp on the football field (now the Kent Student Center parking lot). Guardsmen were posted throughout the campus with bayoneted and loaded rifles. Students were not informed, and most did not suspect, that the rifles were loaded.

At 9:00 A.M., Governor Rhodes flew into Kent by helicopter from Cleveland, Ohio, where he had been campaigning for the U.S. Senate primary election. He viewed damages in the city and on campus and met with officials at the city fire station. These officials included the Portage County prosecutor, Ronald Kane; Major General Del Corso of the Ohio National Guard; three university officials; and representatives from the State Highway Patrol and the Portage County Sheriff's Office. After a brief private discussion, the governor opened the meeting to the press and delivered a fifteen-minute law-and-order speech.[51] Thumping his fist on the table, he proclaimed that Kent State was just one of many Ohio universities being taken over by those trying to attack authority and use the universities as sanctuaries and said that officials would use any means necessary to control them. He called the disturbances at Kent State "probably the most vicious form of campus-oriented violence yet perpetuated by dissident groups and their allies in the state of Ohio." Then he added, "They're worse than the 'Brown Shirt' [*sic*] and the communist element and also the 'night riders' and the Vigilantes. They're the worst type of people that we harbor in America. And I want to say that they're not going to take over the campus. And the campus now is going to be part of the County and the State of Ohio. There is no sanctuary for these people to burn buildings down of private citizens—of businesses in a community and then run into a sanctuary. It is over with in Ohio."[52] Guardsmen stationed on campus and others in the area heard the broadcasted speech. Some agreed with Rhodes's rhetoric. Others felt the remarks were deliberately inflammatory and believed that they did in fact have a volatile effect on the situation. Many people, including university officials, interpreted the governor's statements to mean that Kent State was under martial law. However, Rhodes never did call for a state of emergency, "and indeed, Governor Rhodes's order committing the Ohio National Guard to the town of Kent, and the campus, did not become official until May 5, the day after the thirteen students were shot."[53] According to a report in *Kent* magazine, Portage County's prosecutor wanted the governor to close the university until things calmed down, but Rhodes refused to do so, saying it "would be playing into the hands of the SDS and the Weathermen."[54]

As noted earlier, Governor Rhodes was running in the Republican primary for a U.S. Senate seat, competing against a very popular candidate, Robert Taft. Since Rhodes was running on a law-and-order platform, KSU's President White, now home from his trip to Iowa, assumed that the governor was going to seek the state of emergency that would invoke martial law and believed that the National Guard was in control of the campus. With Rhodes's visit, even without the declaration of a state of emergency, the role of the National Guard changed from protecting property and assisting local law enforcement officials to one of breaking up any assembly on campus, peaceful or otherwise.[55]

Robert Matson, KSU's vice president for student affairs, and the student body president, Frank Frisina, distributed the second leaflet of that weekend. Unlike the first, this leaflet proclaimed a ban on all rallies. Few students saw the leaflets. Meanwhile, because so many people were flocking to the Kent State campus to see the burned building, all sightseers were banned from the campus by 1:00 P.M. on Sunday.[56]

By 7:00 P.M., a crowd had again gathered at the Victory Bell on the Commons, and by 8:45 P.M., it had grown so large that university officials moved up a curfew from 1:00 A.M. to 9:00 P.M. Students surveyed after the shootings reported that their motivation for attending the Sunday rally was to protest the occupation of their campus by the Ohio National Guard.[57] According to the Justice Department Summary of the FBI Report, around 9:15 P.M., a member of the university police ordered the crowd on the Commons to disperse, telling demonstrators if they did not they would be subject to arrest. The group did not disperse, but after being teargassed, it split into two directions. One group of people headed for President White's house, and the other group headed in the opposite direction, toward the gate at Lincoln and Main streets leading to town. Those who moved toward the

president's house were gassed by guardsmen and retreated back to the Commons area, when some went to join the other group at Lincoln and Main. This second group conducted a sit-in in the intersection of Lincoln and Main streets, blocking traffic in all directions.[58] "About 200 students sat down in the street there," reported the *Akron Beacon Journal,* "backed by about 500 others on the campus behind them. . . . The students sang 'Give Peace a Chance,' while a military helicopter with a searchlight circled overhead."[59] According to the Justice Department Summary of the FBI Report, "Law enforcement officers from the city and county faced the students while National Guardsmen took a position behind them. State police helicopters were overhead with searchlights being played on the crowd."[60]

At 10:10 P.M., sit-in demonstrators sought to discuss six demands with Mayor Satrom and KSU's President White: abolition of the ROTC program, removal of the National Guard from campus by Monday night, the lifting of the curfew, full amnesty for those arrested Saturday night, consideration for the demands of BUS, and a reduction in tuition. When a student used a bullhorn to read these demands aloud, the sit-in participants greeted each with cheers. One student (it is not clear whether this was the same student who read these demands) talked with police officials and then announced to the crowd that "the National Guard would be immediately leaving the front Campus . . . in response to their demands that they speak with Mayor Satrom, President White, and/or Governor Rhodes."[61]

Thinking that an agreement had been reached, sit-in participants began moving out of the intersection. Only after they had done so, the National Guard announced over a loudspeaker that the curfew had been moved up from 1:00 A.M. to 11:00 P.M. and that the crowd should disperse immediately. The demonstrators felt betrayed; some yelled obscenities and threw rocks. The guardsmen threw tear gas and advanced on the crowd, using their bayonets to break it up. About two hundred students attempted to escape into nearby Rockwell Hall, which housed the library. Two students reported being bayoneted at this time, and students were held captive in this building for about forty-five minutes.[62] Later, remaining students in the library were peacefully removed by the Ohio State Highway Patrol. The other group of three hundred students was pursued by guardsmen across campus to the Tri-Towers dormitory complex, where it was teargassed.[63] A total of sixty-eight demonstrators was arrested for curfew violation and failure to disperse.[64] According to Davies, fifty-one students were arrested for curfew violations.[65] The *Akron Beacon Journal* reported, "The first two student injuries occurred on this Sunday night—Helen Opaskar, 21, of Cleveland, and Joell Richardson, 19, of Sterling, N.Y., both pricked by Guardsmen's bayonets."[66] Anecdotal evidence

Facing page: On the evening of Sunday, May 3, students sit in at the intersection of Lincoln and Main to protest the presence of the National Guard on campus. Photo copyright *Akron Beacon Journal.* Reprinted with permission.

suggests that additional students were bayoneted but did not report their injuries. The campus was noisy and hectic during the rest of the night, as helicopters hovered overhead shining searchlights below; some students were caught unable to return to their dormitories because of the hurriedly imposed curfew.[67]

Monday, May 4, 1970

The approximately twenty thousand Kent campus students arose that sunny but brisk spring morning ready to attend their classes as usual—but there would prove to be nothing usual about the day. Morning classes began with somewhat higher than typical student absenteeism, but with a "superficial appearance of normality."[68] Several fake bomb threats (a fairly common prank) caused several classes to be canceled and one classroom building to be evacuated. Quite uncommon, Ohio National Guardsmen stood at their posts throughout campus in full gear, with bayoneted rifles, guarding the entrances to the campus, its buildings, and the remains of the ROTC building on the Commons. Their presence shocked and angered some students, especially those who, having spent the weekend at their homes or off-campus residences, were seeing the guardsmen for the first time. President White met with his cabinet at 7:00 A.M. and with the Executive Committee of the Faculty Senate at 8:00 A.M., agreeing at the latter meeting to call together the full faculty to discuss the situation on campus.[69]

At 10:00 A.M., a meeting was called by Gen. Canterbury of the Ohio National Guard. Attending it were President White and Vice President Matson representing the university; the Guard legal officer, Maj. William R. Shimp; Mayor Satrom, the police chief, Roy Thompson, and the police safety director, Paul Hershey, representing the city of Kent; and Maj. Donald E. Manly of the Ohio State Highway Patrol.[70] Because the separate curfew hours set for the city of Kent and the university were causing some confusion, those meeting decided to set a uniform curfew running from 8:00 P.M. to 6 A.M. for both. The officials raised other matters as well. General Canterbury stated his desire to withdraw his troops as soon as possible, perhaps as early as that evening. The rally scheduled for noon on the KSU campus also was discussed, although the course of the discussion was described differently in the testimony given before the President's Commission on Campus Unrest and in the courtroom trials. For example, Canterbury testified that he first learned about the rally at this morning meeting, adding that when he asked President White if it should be banned, White said it should be. President White refuted Canterbury's account, however, commenting, "From past history, all know that my response would have been affirmative to a rally." Other participants likewise disagreed over what was said at the meeting. Some did not recall President White agreeing that the rally should be banned, but in the end they did come away thinking that the rally was banned.[71]

This confusion over the planned rally extended to the campus at large. Some weren't sure if any additional rallies would be legal. Nevertheless, word spread that the rally would be held on the Commons at noon, as had been planned since May 1.

It should be noted again that although Mayor Satrom had declared a civil emergency on May 2, 1970, and troops had been called in to assist civil authority, no one had sought or obtained the injunction required for a state of emergency by noon on May 4. The extent to which the prerogatives granted the ONG within the city of Kent, as negotiated between Mayor Satrom and Major General Del Corso, would extend to the university campus likewise remained unclear; at the time, a statement by Maj. Harry Jones that the National Guard was legally empowered to forbid public gatherings on campus was accepted as truth.[72] Based on this discussion, the university prepared and distributed leaflets to students for the second time that weekend. "The leaflet listed curfew hours; said the governor through the National Guard had assumed legal control of the campus; stated that all outdoor demonstrations and rallies, peaceful or otherwise, were prohibited by the state of emergency; and said the Guard was empowered to make arrests."[73] Only the curfew hours were technically correct. In any case, many of the students were unaware of these directives either because they lived off campus and didn't receive them or because they didn't retrieve and read the leaflets from their student mailboxes until after the shootings. Other students simply disregarded them.[74]

The Victory Bell began tolling around 11:00 A.M., summoning people to the rally on the Commons. At about 11:30 A.M., General Canterbury arrived at the campus Administration Building, in which the National Guard was headquartered. Upon entering the building, he stated that the rally on the Commons was banned. "Major John Simons, chaplain of the 107th Armored Cavalry Regiment, expressed concern that the students might be unaware that the noon rally had been prohibited. He [Canterbury] said a campus official told him that the university radio station would 'spread the word.'" General Canterbury, who did not have time to change into his uniform, and Lieutenant Col. Charles Fassinger, the highest-ranked uniformed officer reporting to the Commons, arrived there between 11:30 A.M. and 11:49 A.M. They saw the crowd grow from about five hundred students to about two thousand by noon.[75] The Justice Department Summary of the FBI Report estimated that two hundred to three hundred students had gathered near the Victory Bell, with another one thousand or so behind them on the hill.[76] By 11:45 A.M., 113 ONG troops and officers took position around the site of the ROTC building at the northern edge of the Commons, 51 from Company A, 36 from Company C, and 16 from Troop G, together led by 10 officers, including General Canterbury, Lieutenant Colonel Fassinger, and Major Jones.[77] Fassinger ordered the troops to form a line near the ROTC site and to lock and load their weapons if they hadn't already done so.[78]

At the time the rally was beginning, morning classes were ending. Many students

were breaking for lunch or returning to their dorms. The student union known as the Hub, a place where students could go for lunch or to talk and relax between classes, was adjacent to the Commons and near the ROTC building. Because the Commons was the central intersection and heartbeat of the campus, the crowd there grew quickly. The lay of the land encouraged onlookers as well: "The hills made a natural amphitheater from which students could watch events on the Commons floor."[79] The motivations of those attending the rally varied: some were protesting the continuing presence of the National Guard and its treatment of students on *their* college campus; some were continuing the protest over U.S. policy begun on Friday after President Nixon announced the incursion into Cambodia; others were curious spectators or were simply passersby, crossing the Commons on their way to and from class. Faculty marshals were present at the site of this Monday rally, as they had been during the previous few days. However, as faculty marshal Ken Calkins commented, they "had been reduced essentially to the status of mere spectators . . . watch[ing] powerlessly" as the Guard took action.[80]

At 11:45 A.M., as the National Guard formed up near the ROTC building, the students were gathered around the Victory Bell, five hundred feet away. By all accounts, the assembly was peaceful.[81]

General Canterbury ordered the demonstrators to leave the Commons, but because of the noise and the distance, his order was not heard. KSU police officer Harold Rice used a bullhorn to relay the general's order for the crowd to disperse. Many students probably still did not hear the order, or if they did, they did not disperse. Next, Rice crossed the Commons in a jeep, accompanied by two guardsmen, "who rode 'shotgun' in the rear seat." Once again, Rice used the bullhorn to announce, "This assembly is unlawful. The crowd must disperse at this time. This is an order!"[82] The jeep was met with shouts and jeers by the demonstrators, some chanting, "Pigs off our campus!" "1, 2, 3, 4. We don't want your fucking war," "Power to the people," and "Strike, Strike, Strike."[83] Some demonstrators threw rocks. One bounced off a tire on the jeep. When the jeep returned to the line of guardsmen near the ROTC ruins, the students cheered, and several made unfavorable gestures at the guardsmen. While the crowd remained in place at the Victory Bell, Rice and the guardsmen approached two more times in the jeep, and each time they returned to the line their retreat was met with jeers and cheers by the students. The third time, Major Jones ran out to the jeep and ordered it to return to the skirmish line at the northwestern corner of the Commons.[84]

The dispersal announcement was ineffectual in banning the peaceful rally. General Canterbury next gave the order to shoot tear gas into the crowd to disband

Facing page: At 11:45 A.M. on Monday, May 4, guardsmen line up 500 feet away from the student rally at the Victory Bell on the Commons. Reprinted with permission of Kent State University Special Collections and Archives.

As officers issue an order to disperse to demonstrators, other students continue to pass through this hub of the campus on their way to class. Photo copyright Richard Kevern. Reprinted with permission.

it. Lieutenant Colonel Fassinger ordered eight to ten grenadiers with M-79 grenade launchers to fire two volleys of tear gas into the crowd. While this did prompt some students to scatter and retreat slightly up Blanket Hill toward Taylor Hall, most remained. Some of the tear gas canisters had fallen short because of poor aim and the fifteen-mile-per-hour winds that were blowing to the southwest. However students threw a few of the canisters back toward the line of guardsmen, raising cheers and causing some in the crowd to chant, "Pigs off campus."[85]

At this point, another announcement was made over a loudspeaker for all to disperse. The demonstrators responded with chants and jeers. According to the *Report of the President's Commission,* "Many students felt that the campus was their 'turf.' Unclear about the authority vested in the Guard by the governor, or indifferent to it, some also felt that their constitutional right to free assembly was being infringed upon. As they saw it, they had been ordered to disperse at a time when no rocks had been thrown and no other violence had been committed. Many told interviewers later, 'We weren't doing anything.'"[86]

At approximately 12:05 P.M., General Canterbury ordered the troops to advance on the demonstrators. Thirty Ohio state highway patrolmen stayed on the Commons, ready to make any necessary arrests.[87] As reported in Michener and in testimony to a federal grand jury, Canterbury said, "These students . . . are going to have to find out what law and order is all about."[88] Guardsmen—with gas masks on, bayonets

At 12:05 P.M., the Guard fires tear gas, then advances on the rally. Reprinted with permission of Kent State University Special Collections and Archives.

fixed, and rifles locked and loaded with one round of ammunition in the chamber—advanced toward the crowd. Company A was on the right flank Company C on the left flank, and Troop G in the middle. As guardsmen advanced, they launched more tear gas into the crowd. Because of the tear gas and the advancing troops, some demonstrators retreated up Blanket Hill between Taylor and Johnson Halls; others retreated toward the east between Taylor and Prentice Halls, ending in the Prentice Hall parking lot. Some of the students retreated inside the buildings to avoid the tear gas and to put water on their faces. Many in the area left. Once the guardsmen neared the Victory Bell, they split into two groups. Company C, commanded by Maj. Harry Jones, went up Blanket Hill toward the Prentice side of Taylor Hall and held the ground between Taylor and Prentice Halls. Troop G and Company A, commanded by General Canterbury and Lieutenant Colonel Fassinger, followed the majority of demonstrators up Blanket Hill between Taylor and Johnson Halls.[89]

After advancing, Company C held a line between Taylor and Prentice Halls that prevented any demonstrators from returning to the Commons through that corridor. Company A and Troop G, however, upon reaching the top of Blanket Hill near the Pagoda (the highest elevation of land), proceeded down the other side of Taylor Hall toward the Practice Field rather than simply remaining in place to block reentry to the Commons. The students in the area split to let the guardsmen pass, some moving down the hill toward Lake and Olson Halls and others going toward the Prentice Hall parking lot to the southeast of Taylor Hall. However, when some demonstrators

Students exit the Commons as guardsmen advance. Photo copyright John P. Filo Reprinted with permission.

found themselves on the Practice Field, the guardsmen who were marching toward it slowed down to give these students time to escape through the small opening in the fence. This took some demonstrators to Midway Drive and a gravel parking lot near Dunbar Hall.[90] Most students left the area entirely, however. At this point, the assembly on the Commons was disbanded and the Guard's mission accomplished.

Company A and Troop G advanced down the reverse slope of Blanket Hill past Taylor Hall, across the access road, and then onto the Practice Field. Along the field's far side was a six-foot, chain-link fence, capped with barbed wire, that formed a cul-de-sac for the advancing troops. According to the *Report of the President's Commission,* "The feeling had spread among students that they were being harassed as a group, that state and civic officials had united against them, and that the university had either cooperated or acquiesced in their suppression. They reacted to the guardsmen's march with substantial solidarity," shouting epithets at the troops. The guardsmen, for their part, "generally felt that the students, who had disobeyed numerous orders to disperse, were clearly in the wrong." Moreover, they saw the burned remains of the ROTC building as evidence of the destruction the students could cause.[91]

The *Report of the President's Commission* indicates that the crowd split at this time. Some of the more vocal demonstrators ended up in the Prentice Hall parking lot, but most students spread along the balcony of Taylor Hall or onto the hill south of Taylor Hall overlooking the Practice Field and above the access road.[92] Both the Justice Department Summary of the FBI Report and the *Report of the*

The Guard advances past Taylor Hall to the Practice Field. Members of Troop G kneel and aim at vocal demonstrators in the Prentice Hall parking lot. Photo copyright John P. Filo. Reprinted with permission.

President's Commission concluded that while the guardsmen were on the Practice Field, demonstrators threw rocks at them; both reports also speculated that a nearby construction site near Dunbar Hall provided rocks and stones to throw. Guardsmen then threw tear gas canisters at the demonstrators in the parking lot and toward those standing on the hill below Taylor Hall; some threw rocks as well. Students retaliated by lobbing some canisters back at the Guard, prompting cheers from the onlookers on the hill near Taylor Hall. One account described this exchange of projectiles by students and guardsmen as a "tennis match."[93] The distance between the guardsmen and the students made many of the rocks ineffective, although four guardsmen claimed they were hit with rocks at this time.[94] "The distances between the mass of the students and the Guards were later stepped off by expert judges, who concluded that students would have required good right arms like Mickey Mantle's to have reached the guardsmen with even small stones."[95]

During a ten-minute stay on the Practice Field, some members of Troop G were ordered to kneel and point their rifles toward the demonstrators as a gesture of force.[96] The demonstrators in the Prentice Hall parking lot, directly in the line of fire of the kneeling guardsmen, were between 150 and 200 feet away.[97] Student Alan Canfora, who would later be shot, went inside the practice fence and waved a black flag to protest the Guard's actions. Although both the Justice Department Summary of the FBI Report and the *Report of the President's Commission* concluded that this was the time that the Guard was receiving the most verbal and physical insults, guardsmen aimed their rifles but did not shoot in self-defense. Later they would claim self-defense as the reason for shooting from Blanket Hill. Major Jones, who had accompanied Captain Snyder and the members of Company C to the Prentice side of Taylor Hall to block access to the Commons, "walked through the crowd to find out if General Canterbury wanted assistance."[98] Based on the ease with which Jones passed through the crowd, Davies concluded: "If the demonstrators were as dangerous as Canterbury claimed after the killings, could a solitary officer have elbowed his way through them without some kind of incident? Yet that is exactly what happened."[99]

At the time that Major Jones was on the Practice Field, there was a huddle of the Guard leadership, prompting some to speculate that it was at this time that tactics were developed that included firing directly on the demonstrators. While Michener concluded that there was not an order to fire shared at this time, he added, "It seems likely, however, that on the football field, when the students were being obnoxious and stones were drifting in, that some of the troops agreed among themselves, 'We've taken about enough of this crap. If they don't stop pretty soon we're going to let them have it.'" He further concluded, "It seems likely that some kind of rough verbal agreement had been reached among the troops when they clustered on the practice field."[100]

According to the *Report of the President's Commission*, General Canterbury realized that there was nothing more his troops could do on the Practice Field, so he ordered them to retrace their steps up Blanket Hill and then back down to the remains of the ROTC building on the far side of the Commons. "My purpose," Canterbury explained, "was to make it clear beyond any doubt to the mob that our posture was now defensive and that we were clearly returning to the Commons, thus reducing the possibility of injury to either soldiers or students."[101] There was some speculation that the troops spent all of their tear gas while on the Practice Field and had left none for the return march to the ROTC building. This was not the case. "Both Captain Srp and Lieutenant Stevenson of Troop G were aware that a limited supply of tear gas remained and Srp ordered one canister loaded for use at the crest of Blanket Hill."[102] General Canterbury and Major Jones both claimed under oath that the guardsmen spent all of their tear gas canisters while on the Practice Field. As they marched back up Blanket Hill, they assumed a common V-shaped formation, perhaps to accommodate the terrain of the land. According to Davies, a sequence of photographs used in the trials illustrated that members of Troop G appeared to lag behind the others and seemed to be more concerned with the demonstrators in the parking lot, rather than those who appear in the photographs to be closer to them and to the other troops. Photographs show guardsmen other than members of Troop G looking forward as they advance up the hill.[103]

On seeing what they perceived as a retreat of the Guard, some students felt that everything was over. Several followed behind the Guard at a distance of sixty feet or greater. An eight-millimeter film by student Christopher Abell shows that

As guardsmen march from the Practice Field to the top of Blanket Hill at the Pagoda, students think that the troops are returning to their station on the Commons. Photo copyright John P. Filo. Reprinted with permission.

> A member of Troop G, looking over his shoulder and down toward the parking lot, would have seen five students at a distance of 60 to 85 feet, 25 students between 85 and 175 feet, and 30 students between 175 and 325 feet. . . .
>
> The evidence of the film is that at no time before Troop G opened fire were they being approached by more than 17 students, that none of the approaching students was closer than 85 feet, and that 10 of them were more than 175 feet away. . . .
>
> The film provides conclusive evidence that the guardsmen had not been rushed.[104]

As the Guard marched up the hill, the crowd ahead parted to let them by. Some demonstrators threw rocks at them as they marched up the hill toward the Pagoda. However, rocks were not thrown at the time of the shooting.[105]

As the Guard approached the Pagoda around 12:24 P.M., apparently en route to the ROTC building straight ahead down the slope, some guardsmen on the trailing edge of the right flank, mostly from Troop G, wheeled 135 degrees to the right to face the direction of the Prentice Hall parking lot. By all eyewitness accounts and photographic evidence, these guardsmen turned in unison, lifted their rifles in unison, pointed their weapons, and began shooting for thirteen seconds, spending sixty-seven rounds.[106]

At 12:24 P.M., the line of Guard unexpectedly wheels 135 degrees. During thirteen seconds, twenty-eight of the seventy-six guardsmen on the hill fire sixty-seven shots toward the Prentice Hall parking lot. Photo copyright John A. Darnell. Reprinted with permission.

After the firing had begun, Lieutenant Colonel Fassinger, Major Jones, and General Canterbury yelled, "Cease Fire!" Major Jones hit several men on the helmet to stop their firing.[107] Students dove for cover during the thirteen seconds of gunfire—some unsuccessfully.

Four Kent State students were killed. William Schroeder, a nineteen-year-old psychology major and member of the ROTC, was shot in the back at the seventh rib while lying prone 390 feet from the firing position. Sandra Scheuer, a twenty-year-old speech pathology and audiology major, was shot in the front side of her neck on her way to a speech therapy class. She also was 390 feet away from the line of fire. Jeffrey Miller, a twenty-year-old psychology major, was shot in the mouth while facing the Guard 265 feet away. Allison Krause, a nineteen-year-old Honors College art major, was diving for cover in the Prentice Hall parking lot when she was shot. She was 343 feet away from the line of guardsmen as a bullet passed through her left upper arm.

Nine Kent State students were wounded. Joseph Lewis (60 feet away) was shot twice, in the right abdomen and the left lower leg. He was closest to the Guard among the wounded students, on a sidewalk near Taylor Hall. John Cleary (110 feet away), who fell near the Solar Totem sculpture in front of Taylor Hall, was shot in the left upper chest. Thomas Grace (200 feet away) was shot in the left ankle. Alan Canfora

(225 feet away) was shot in the right wrist as he dove for cover behind a tree. Dean Kahler (300 feet away) was shot in the left side of the small of his back while lying prone on the ground near the access road. He was permanently paralyzed by the bullet. Douglas Wrentmore (329 feet away) was wounded in the right knee. James Russell (375 feet away) was the only person wounded who was outside the angle of the gunfire leading to the parking lot. He was standing near the Memorial Gymnasium, around 90 degrees from the other students, when he was wounded in the head and right thigh by birdshot. Robert Stamps (495 feet away) was shot in the right buttock. The wounded student farthest from the Guard, D. Scott Mackenzie (730 feet away) was shot in the left rear of the neck.[108] All of those shot on KSU's campus on May 4, 1970, were students of the university. They were not outside agitators or SDS Weathermen. Michener, Mayer, and syndicated columnist Victor Riesel (reported in Davies) have suggested or stated that outside agitators were to blame for much of what happened on May 4, 1970.[109] However, other sources reject the validity of this conclusion.[110] No disruptive outsiders have been identified as participating in the demonstration on May 4.

While sources vary slightly in their accounting, Kelner and Munves place "72 armed guardsmen on the top of the hill" at the time of the shooting. According to the *Report of the President's Commission,* "Twenty-eight guardsmen have acknowledged firing from Blanket Hill. Of these, 25 fired 55 shots from rifles, two fired five shots from .45 caliber pistols, and one fired a single blast from a shotgun."[111] General Canterbury, Lieutenant Colonel Fassinger, and Major Jones all claimed to hear a nonmilitary shot which triggered the rest of the volley The Justice Department Summary of the FBI Report concluded, "The FBI has conducted an extensive search and has found nothing to indicate that any person other than a Guardsman fired a weapon."[112]

Terry Strubbe, a student at Kent State, set his tape recorder on his dorm window on the first floor of Johnson Hall and left for the rally at noon on the Commons nearby. In 1974, the U.S. Department of Justice paid for an analysis of that tape recording by engineering firm Bolt, Beranek, and Newman of Cambridge, Massachusetts. The report indicated that the first three shots came from M-1 rifles that were located between the Pagoda and the corner of Taylor Hall. It also established that sixty-seven shots were fired, not sixty-one as previously reported.[113] Reexamination of a copy of the Strubbe tape by audio analysts Stuart Allen and Tom Owen in 2010 suggested a verbal order to fire was given before the volley of shots.[114] This agrees with the claims of some students and guardsmen who say they heard an order to fire.[115]

The shooting was done primarily by members of Troop G and Company A, along with two members of Company C who got separated from their company and went with the main body of troops to the Practice Field and back up Blanket Hill.[116] The shooting began with no announcement or warning to the students and no immediate provocation. Some guardsmen claimed they fired because their lives were in danger. However, the Justice Department Summary of the FBI Report noted first that "six Guardsmen, including two sergeants and Captain Srp of Troop G stated pointedly that the lives of the members of the Guard were not in danger and that it was not a shooting situation" and second that "the claim by the National Guard that their lives were endangered by the students was fabricated subsequent to the event."[117] Furthermore, the FBI concluded that students had neither surrounded the guardsmen nor were throwing rocks at the time of the shootings, as some guardsmen alleged. The *Report of the President's Commission* concluded that the "indiscriminate firing of rifles into a crowd of students and the deaths that followed were unnecessary, unwarranted, and inexcusable."[118]

After the thirteen seconds of gunfire, an eerie silence fell. As students lay wounded and dying on the ground, members from Troop G and Company A turned and marched back to the site of the ROTC building, unimpeded by either the hundreds of students on Blanket Hill on the north side of Taylor Hall or observers on the Student Activities Center roof between Stopher and Johnson Halls to the west of the Commons.

Company C, which held its position on the other side of Taylor Hall near Prentice Hall to the east, did not fire during those thirteen seconds. Following the shootings, Capt. James Ronald Snyder took seven of his men to assess the conditions of the students wounded in the parking lot. He reportedly looked at two young men and concluded they were dead. Jeffrey Miller had died instantly, but William Schroeder lived for some time after reaching the hospital. Several of Snyder's men were near the

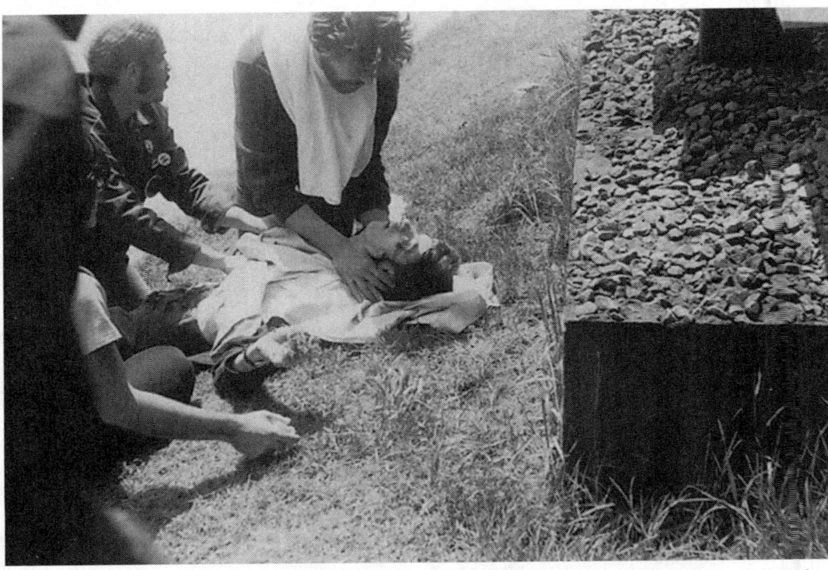

Students are left on their own to care for their wounded classmates. Photo copyright John A. Darnell. Reprinted with permission.

body of Jeff Miller when some angry students, having just witnessed the slaughter of their fellow classmates by the other guardsmen, yelled obscenities at them. One of the guardsmen threw a tear gas pellet at the student group in response.[119] The members of Company C returned to their skirmish line and eventually back to the Commons. Captain Snyder later would tell a federal grand jury that he found a pistol and brass knuckles on Jeff Miller's body, although he finally admitted that he concocted this account as a self-defense story for the group of guardsmen in case of legal action.[120]

The students who had witnessed the horrors of the shootings were now left on their own to care for their fellow classmates, who lay dead, dying, and wounded in the Prentice Hall parking lot and on the ground surrounding Taylor Hall. Some ran into the nearby dorms of Prentice and Dunbar Halls to call for ambulances and to find help; some went into Taylor Hall to seek out telephones and to find assistance from those inside. Others linked arms around the dead and wounded or administered first aid to those who could still be helped. Still others were frozen in place, unable to respond to what they had just witnessed, or running to the Commons, screaming for ambulances that had not yet arrived. Faculty marshal Glenn W. Frank, a popular geology faculty member, rode with an ambulance from the Commons and assisted in getting the dead and wounded into the ambulances.

As some students helped with the dead and wounded, others began to gather on the hill above the Commons. After ambulances took many of the dead and wounded to hospitals, shocked students began milling around in a daze, eventually joining the other students at the Victory Bell on the Commons. Although the students did not realize it, the potential for another slaughter was extremely high at this time. The *Report of the President's Commission* estimated the crowd that reconvened on the Commons was between two hundred and three hundred. The National Guard stood at one end of the Commons while the students clustered near the Victory Bell. In response to orders from the Guard, students moved away from the Victory Bell to a grassy slope along the edge of the Commons, near Stopher and Johnson Halls, where they staged a sit-in. Some expressed anger; others were quiet with shock. General Canterbury and Major Jones were still determined to disperse the crowd. According to the *Report of the President's Commission,* Glenn Frank persuaded General Canterbury to give the faculty marshals some time to try to disperse the students, to avoid any further military action by the Guard. Frank, along with psychology professor Seymour Baron, political science professor Mike Lunine, and history graduate student Steve Sharoff, tried to get the students to leave the site.[121]

James Michener provides the most detailed account of this standoff between the Guard and the students following the shootings.[122] He focuses particularly on the efforts of Professors Frank, Lunine, and Baron to avert more bloodshed. Michener reports that a tape recorder captured a voice from the crowd asking: "Are we going to have any kind of retaliation?" Baron argued that there should be no retaliation, asserting that the Guard who shot and killed the students were "going to sweat blood." At this point, Baron went to the line of guardsmen and asked who was in charge. When an officer pointed to General Canterbury, Baron approached him and pleaded with him to prevent further action by the Guard. Canterbury reportedly brushed him aside, growling, "Take this man away." A captain took Baron by his arm, escorting him away, but when Baron asked the captain to release him so he could return to the student group to help, the captain replied, "Good Luck."[123]

When Baron returned to talk with the crowd of students, he had little luck in getting them to disperse and go to their dorms or homes; the students were as steadfast as the Guard. Michener reports the students saying: "If they kill us all, let them do it now." Baron ran back to General Canterbury with the hope of averting additional violence, pleading with Canterbury, "'You've got to give those kids some kind of sign.' Canterbury asked, 'Sign of what?' and Baron said, 'That you're not going to shoot. That we can quieten [*sic*] this thing down. Isn't there some kind of order, like 'parade rest'?" The Guard, hearing the words "parade rest," reportedly dropped their guns from their shoulders, but Canterbury ordered them to shoulder them again, and they responded to his orders. Again Baron pleaded, "'General, can't you make them stop pointing those guns as if they were going to fire?' General Canterbury reflected, looked at the massed students, and said, 'Parade rest.'"[124]

Baron went back to the students and pleaded with them to realize that they were dealing with a general and troops with guns they were willing to use again. "Now if you walk down toward them," he warned, "I promise you they'll kill you. Now the reason they'll kill you is because they're scared to death. . . . There is only one way you're going to stay alive, and that is to stay here. I don't want you going down there."[125] Someone from the crowd asked, "Who ordered them to shoot?" and Baron replied that he didn't know.

The faculty members again sent a representative to the Guard. This time Mike Lunine ran down toward the Guard in search of General Canterbury. Lunine pleaded that there must be no more shooting. Canterbury did not reply. According to Michener, two university personnel standing with the Guard stated, "'Those students shouldn't be on that hill. There has to be a line drawn somewhere. We've got to have law and order.'" Upon hearing this, Lunine ran back to those on the hill and warned them of what might happen if they didn't move. Lunine returned to the Guard and once again begged the Guard not to shoot, and again one of the university personnel said, "'Professor Lunine, the National Guard does not negotiate under siege.'" Lunine asked whom they were talking about, and the official pointed to the students on the hill. This frightened him deeply and he went back to the students again and pleaded, "'Students, the imminence of slaughter is great.'"[126] A taped exchange makes clear the severity of the situation:

Baron: I'm scared to death that somebody else is going to get shot and killed.
Voice: Man, you take Martin Luther King. He wouldn't be scared.
Baron: Martin Luther King would not have stayed. Martin Luther King was a man who understood that to win you must live. If you die, you cannot win anything. You must live to win. I don't want you kids to die. That won't win you kids peanuts.
Voice: Let them splatter us right now.
Baron: There are too many of you who are too damned good to die in this stinking field here.[127]

After this exchange, graduate student Steve Sharoff approached the Guard. He pointed to his faculty marshal armband and stated that he wanted to speak with General Canterbury. When the Guard led him to Canterbury, Sharoff told the general that the students on the hill would not be moved. The general told him to get them out of there. Sharoff replied that they had just seen four of their friends killed. "'I have my orders,'" Canterbury replied. "'They have got to go.'" When Sharoff tried to argue, Canterbury repeated the same phrase again. It was at this point that Sharoff realized that both groups were determined to hold their ground, and a horrific outcome was imminent.[128]

Glenn Frank was the next faculty member to try to talk with General Canterbury. On his way to the Guard position, he was met by a group of guardsmen led by Major Jones. Frank thought that Major Jones was moving his men out to confront the students. According to Michener, Frank pleaded, "'For God's sake, don't come any closer.' Jones replied, 'My orders are to move ahead,' and Frank said quietly, 'Over my dead body.'" Jones did not move forward. Approaching Canterbury, who was talking with Capt. Ron Snyder, Frank pleaded with the general to give him and the others more time to move the students off the hill. Michener was told that the general said, "They're going to have to find out what law and order is all about." The general told Frank he had five minutes to move the students out; however, Major Manly, who commanded the 181 members of the Ohio State Highway Patrol now on the Commons, effectively told Frank to take all the time he needed.[129] Additional troops were now massing on Blanket Hill above the Commons, effectively surrounding the student sit-in on the hill. Frank approached the students fully convinced of the severity of the situation. A tape from a radio station recorded yelling, threats, cursing, and general noise, followed by Frank's desperate plea:

Voice (over the mob): Here's Glenn Frank.
Voice (over the mob): Hold on, hold on. Wait a minute. Hold it.
Frank (with deep, choking emotion): I don't care whether you've never

> listened to anyone before in your lives. I am begging you right now. If you don't disperse right now, they're going to move in, and it can only be a slaughter. Would you please listen to me? Jesus Christ, I don't want to be a part of this.[130]

Frank's final plea succeeded. By 1:30 P.M., the Commons and the surrounding area were cleared.[131]

The university president, Dr. White, having returned from his lunch at the Brown Derby restaurant, ordered the university closed for the rest of the week as of 1:20 P.M. In addition, Judge Albert L. Caris of the Common Pleas Court of Portage County signed an order granting the injunction request of Portage County's prosecutor, Ronald J. Kane, to close the university until "conditions merit the reopening."[132] Because they were forced to evacuate immediately and could not make arrangements for their departure, students in the dorms left without many of their belongings. At 1:00 P.M., Kent Bell Telephone had shut down phone service to the dormitories, so that students could neither make nor receive calls. "Most of them [were] without access to transportation," as well. "David Ambler, dean for student residence life, had the . . . idea of wheeling out the thirty-six university buses, loading them with students, and starting them off to Cleveland or Columbus, from which spots frantic students could catch what airplanes were available" or otherwise make their way home as best they could.[133] All traffic in and out of the city of Kent was stopped by roadblocks, obstructing parents' efforts to retrieve their children from campus and others from entering or leaving the city. Military personnel patrolled the city and campus and enforced a dusk to dawn curfew.[134]

Aftermath

On May 13, the court order closing the university was modified, permitting some personnel access to the university. Because the spring quarter was not over, many faculty corresponded with students by U.S. mail or held courses in their homes or at off-campus sites so that Kent State students could complete the quarter. On June 13, 1970, 1,250 seniors and graduate students returned to Kent State to take part in commencement ceremonies. On June 15, 1970, the court injunction was lifted.[135]

Facing page: Students stage a sit-in near Stopher-Johnson Dormitories to protest the shootings. Faculty marshal Glenn Frank convinces students to leave to avoid further tragedy. Photo copyright Don Roese, *Akron Beacon Journal*. Reprinted with permission.

Notes

1. Richard M. Nixon, "Cambodia: A Difficult Decision," *Vital Speeches of the Day* 36, no. 15 (1970): 450–52.
2. Eszterhas and Roberts, *Thirteen Seconds,* 25
3. Davies, *Truth About Kent State,* 12; Seymour M. Lipset, "Polls and Protests," *Foreign Affairs* 49, no. 3 (1971): 549.
4. See the special report on the Kent State shootings in the *Akron Beacon Journal*, "Tragedy in Our Midst."
5. Davies, *Truth About Kent State,* 12.
6. For the Justice Department's Summary of FBI Reports on the Kent State Shootings, see I. F. Stone, *Killings at Kent State,* 62.
7. "Tragedy in Our Midst."
8. James Best, "The Tragic Weekend of May 1 to 4, 1970," in Hensley and Lewis, *Kent State and May 4th,* 9; "Tragedy in Our Midst."
9. Davies, *Truth About Kent State,* 13; *Report of the President's Commission,* 241.
10. *Report of the President's Commission,* 241; Stone, *Killings at Kent State,* 63; Best, "Tragic Weekend," 10.
11. *Report of the President's Commission,* 241.
12. Davies, *Truth About Kent State,* 13.
13. See, for example, Michener, *Kent State: What Happened,* 125.
14. "Tragedy in Our Midst."
15. *Report of the President's Commission,* 241.
16. Stone, *Killings at Kent State,* 63.
17. Davies, *Truth About Kent State,* 13.
18. *Report of the President's Commission,* 241; Stone, *Killings at Kent State,* 64.
19. Davies, *Truth About Kent State,* 14.
20. *Report of the President's Commission,* 242.
21. Best, "Tragic Weekend," 11; Michener, *Kent State: What Happened,* 131–35.
22. "Struggle to Recovery," 4.
23. Stone, *Killings at Kent State,* 64; Best, "Tragic Weekend," 10; *Report of the President's Commission,* 242.
24. Best, "Tragic Weekend," 11.
25. *Report of the President's Commission,* 242–43.
26. Eszterhas and Roberts, *Thirteen Seconds,* 46.
27. "Tragedy in Our Midst."
28. Best, "Tragic Weekend," 12; *Report of the President's Commission,* 245.
29. Charles Fassinger, interview by Carole A. Barbato and Laura L. Davis, Apr. 1, 2007.
30. *Report of the President's Commission,* 246–47; Stone, *Killings at Kent State,* 65.
31. Davies, *Truth About Kent State,* 17; *Report of the President's Commission,* 245.
32. *Report of the President's Commission,* 244; Davies, *Truth About Kent State,* 16.
33. Best, "Tragic Weekend," 13.
34. Stone, *Killings at Kent State,* 66; Best, "Tragic Weekend," 14.

35. *Report of the President's Commission,* 247.
36. "Struggle to Recovery," 5.
37. Best, "Tragic Weekend," 13; Davies, *Truth About Kent State,* 16–17; *Report of the President's Commission,* 248.
38. *Report of the President's Commission,* 243.
39. Stone, *Killings at Kent State,* 66.
40. *Report of the President's Commission,* 249; Stone, *Killings at Kent State,* 66–67.
41. Stone, *Killings at Kent State,* 67; Best, "Tragic Weekend," 14; *Report of the President's Commission,* 250.
42. "Struggle to Recovery," 5; *Report of the President's Commission,* 249.
43. Best, "Tragic Weekend," 14; Stone, *Killings at Kent State,* 67; *Report of the President's Commission,* 249; Davies, *Truth About Kent State,* 18.
44. Stone, *Killings at Kent State,* 67.
45. Jerry M. Lewis, personal communication with the authors, Feb. 5, 2008; *Report of the President's Commission,* 250; Stone, *Killings at Kent State,* 68.
46. Best, "Tragic Weekend," 15; Stone, *Killings at Kent State,* 68.
47. Bills, "Introduction," 13; Davies, *Truth About Kent State,* 17; Peter Davies, "The Burning Question: A Government Cover-up?" in Bills, *Kent State/May 4,* 151; Charles A. Thomas, "Chapter 4: The Burning Question," in *Blood of Isaac,* Charles Thomas Papers, 1970–2003, box 64s, series 10, May 4 Collection, Special Collections and Archives, Kent State University Libraries, Kent, Ohio, <http://speccoll.library.kent.edu/4may70/IsaacFour.htm>.
48. Stone, *Killings at Kent State,* 68; Davies, *Truth About Kent State,* 18–19.
49. *Report of the President's Commission,* 250.
50. Stone, *Killings at Kent State,* 73.
51. Best, "Tragic Weekend," 16; Stone, *Killings at Kent State,* 69.
52. James A. Rhodes, Rhodes Speech on Campus Disorders in Kent, May 3, 1970—Fire House Speech, Political Science Department, Records, 1970, box 70, folder 27, May 4 Collection.
53. Bills, "Introduction," 13; Kelner and Munves, *Kent State Coverup,* 71; "Struggle to Recovery," 5; *Report of the President's Commission,* 254; Davies, *Truth About Kent State,* 22–23, 25.
54. "Struggle to Recovery," 5.
55. "Tragedy in Our Midst"; Davies, *Truth About Kent State,* 22.
56. Best, "Tragic Weekend," 18.
57. Taylor et al., *Violence at Kent State,* 48.
58. Stone, *Killings at Kent State,* 70–71; Best, "Tragic Weekend," 17.
59. "Tragedy in Our Midst."
60. Stone, *Killings at Kent State,* 71.
61. Stone, *Killings at Kent State,* 71–72; Best, "Tragic Weekend," 17–18; *Report of the President's Commission,* 257–58.
62. Best, "Tragic Weekend," 18; Davies, *Truth About Kent State,* 26–28.
63. Stone, *Killings at Kent State,* 72.
64. "Struggle to Recovery," 6.
65. Davies, *Truth About Kent State,* 28.
66. "Tragedy in Our Midst."
67. Harold M. Mayer, *Commission on KSU Violence,* Vols. 1–4, unpublished report (Kent,

Ohio: KSU Printing Service, 1972), 22.

68. Mayer, *Commission on KSU Violence,* 22.
69. *Report of the President's Commission,* 259.
70. *Report of the President's Commission,* 260–61; Davies, *Truth About Kent State,* 31.
71. Best, "Tragic Weekend," 19; *Report of the President's Commission,* 260–61.
72. Michener, *Kent State: What Happened,* 324–25.
73. *Report of the President's Commission,* 255.
74. Michener, *Kent State: What Happened,* 325.
75. *Report of the President's Commission,* 261, 263–65.
76. Stone, *Killings at Kent State,* 75.
77. Davies, *Truth About Kent State,* 34; Michener, *Kent State: What Happened,* 32[illegible]–30.
78. *Report of the President's Commission,* 263.
79. Ibid., 265.
80. Kenneth R. Calkins, "The Frustrations of a Former Activist," in Bills, *Kent State/May 4,* 104.
81. Stone, *Killings at Kent State,* 75; *Report of the President's Commission,* 288.
82. "Struggle to Recovery," 6.
83. "Struggle to Recovery," 6; *Report of the President's Commission,* 263; Stone, *Killings at Kent State,* 76.
84. *Report of the President's Commission,* 264; Stone, *Killings at Kent State,* 77.
85. *Report of the President's Commission,* 265–66; "Tragedy in Our Midst"; Stone, *Killings at Kent State,* 77.
86. Stone, *Killings at Kent State,* 77; *Report of the President's Commission,* 267.
87. Stone, *Killings at Kent State,* 78.
88. Michener, *Kent State: What Happened,* 331; and James Ronald Snyder, whose testimony provided the same account, transcript of *Arthur Krause et al. v. James A. Rhodes et al.,* District Court of the United States for the Northern District of Ohio Eastern Division, 1975, vol. 20, p. 4751, May 4 Collection.
89. Stone, *Killings at Kent State,* 78–79.
90. Ibid., 79–80; Davies, *Truth About Kent State,* 34; *Report of the President's Commission,* 266–67.
91. Michener, *Kent State: What Happened,* 337; *Report of the President's Commission,* 266–67.
92. *Report of the President's Commission,* 267.
93. Stone, *Killings at Kent State,* 81; *Report of the President's Commission,* 267.
94. Stone, *Killings at Kent State,* 81.
95. Michener, *Kent State: What Happened,* 336.
96. *Report of the President's Commission,* 268; Stone, *Killings at Kent State,* 81–82; Kelner and Munves, *Kent State Coverup,* 139.
97. Davies, *Truth About Kent State,* 41.
98. Stone, *Killings at Kent State,* 82; *Report of the President's Commission,* 267.
99. Davies, *Truth About Kent State,* 38–39.
100. Davies, *Truth About Kent State,* 41–42; Michener, *Kent State: What Happened,* 361, 409–10.
101. *Report of the President's Commission,* 268.
102. Stone, *Killings at Kent State,* 82.
103. Davies, *Truth About Kent State,* 42.

104. Kelner and Munves, *Kent State Coverup,* 174–75; *Report of the President's Commission,* 270.
105. *Report of the President's Commission,* 270–71; Stone, *Killings at Kent State,* 87.
106. Davies, *Truth About Kent State,* 45; Kelner and Munves, *Kent State Coverup,* 177; Michener, *Kent State: What Happened,* 340.
107. Best, "Tragic Weekend," 25; *Report of the President's Commission,* 272.
108. Davies, *Truth About Kent State,* 52–55; *Report of the President's Commission,* 273–76.
109. Michener, *Kent State: What Happened,* 352, 409, 411; Mayer, *Commission on KSU Violence,* 4, 2–23; Davies, *Truth About Kent State,* 142.
110. Robert M. O'Neil, John P. Morris, and Raymond Mack, *No Heroes, No Villains: New Perspectives on Kent State and Jackson State* (San Francisco, Calif.: Jossey-Bass, 1972), 7; *Report of the President's Commission,* 239; Stone, *Killings at Kent State,* 61; "Tragedy in Our Midst."
111. Kelner and Munves, *Kent State Coverup,* 192; *Report of the President's Commission,* 273.
112. Stone, *Killings at Kent State,* 89.
113. Kelner and Munves, *Kent State Coverup,* 177.
114. John Mangels, "New Analysis of 40-Year-Old Recording of Kent State Shootings Reveals that Ohio Guard Was Given an Order to Prepare to Fire," Cleveland.com, May 9, 2010, <http://blog.cleveland.com/metro/2010/05/new_analysis_of_40-year-old_re.html>.
115. *Report of the President's Commission,* 275.
116. Ibid., 277.
117. Stone, *Killings at Kent State,* 84; Captain Snyder testified that he fabricated the self-defense story for the Guard to use, transcript, vol. 20, 4850–56.
118. Stone, *Killings at Kent State,* 87; *Report of the President's Commission,* 289.
119. Best, "Tragic Weekend," 25; *Report of the President's Commission,* 277.
120. Kelner and Munves, *Kent State Coverup,* 124–25; Snyder testimony, transcript, vol. 20, 4850–56.
121. *Report of the President's Commission,* 278.
122. The dialogue in this passage is taken from the interpretive account in Michener, *Kent State: What Happened,* 400–408. Michener wrote the dialogue after listening to a tape recording.
123. Michener, *Kent State: What Happened,* 401–2.
124. Ibid., 402.
125. Ibid., 404.
126. Ibid., 404, 405.
127. Ibid., 405.
128. Ibid., 405, 406.
129. Ibid., 406.
130. Michener, *Kent State: What Happened,* 407; *Report of the President's Commission,* 278.
131. Best, "Tragic Weekend," 24.
132. *Report of the President's Commission,* 285–86; "Struggle to Recovery," 11.
133. Michener, *Kent State: What Happened,* 419–20.
134. "Struggle to Recovery," 11.
135. Ibid., 19.

Bibliography

Abrahamson, David. *Magazine-Made America: The Cultural Transformation of the Postwar Periodical.* Cresskill, N.J.: Hampton Press, 1996.

Alexander, Jeffery C. "Toward a Theory of Cultural Trauma." In *Cultural Trauma and Collective Identity,* edited by Jeffrey C. Alexander et al., 85–108. Berkeley: Univ. of California Press, 2004.

Anderson, Benedict. *Imagined Communities.* London: Verso, 1983.

Ashmore, Harry S. *Hearts and Minds: The Anatomy of Racism from Roosevelt to Reagan.* New York: McGraw-Hill, 1982.

Assmann, Aleida. *Erinnerungsräume: Formen und Wandlungen des kulturellen Gedächtnisses.* Munich: C. H. Beck, 1999.

Augé, Marc. *Les forms de l'oubli.* Paris: Payot and Rivages, 1998.

Badger, Tony. "The Forerunner of Our Opposition: Arkansas and the Southern Manifesto of 1956." *Arkansas Historical Quarterly* 56, no. 3 (1997): 353–60.

Barbato, Carole, Laura Davis, and Mark Seeman, "Outline of April 30–May 4, 1970, Kent State University." Unpublished paper, Kent State University, Kent, Ohio, Mar. 2009.

Barker, Pat. *Another World.* New York: Viking, 1998.

Barringer, Mark. "The Antiwar Movement in the United States." In *Encyclopedia of the Vietnam War: A Political, Social, and Military History,* edited by S. C. Tucker, 34–36. <http://www.english.illinois.edu/maps/vietnam/antiwar.html>.

Barthel, Diane. *Historic Preservation: Collective Memory and Historical Identity.* New Brunswick, N.J.: Rutgers Univ. Press, 1996.

Bartley, Numan V. "Looking Back at Little Rock." *Arkansas Historical Quarterly* 25, no. 2 (1966): 101–16.

———. *The Rise of Massive Resistance: Race and Politics in the South During the 1950's.* 1969. Baton Rouge: Louisiana State Univ. Press, 1997.

Bates, Daisy. *The Long Shadow of Little Rock: A Memoir by Daisy Bates.* Fayetteville: Univ. of Arkansas Press, 1986.

Baughman, James L. *Henry R. Luce and the Rise of the American News Media.* Boston, Mass.: Twayne Publishers, 1987.

Baumeister, Roy F., and Stephen Hastings. "Distortions of Collective Memory: How Groups Flatter and Deceive Themselves," In Pennebaker, Paez, and Rimé, *Collective Memory of Political Events,* 277–94.

Beals, Melba Pattillo. *Warriors Don't Cry: A Searing Memoir of the Battle to Integrate Little Rock's Central High.* New York: Washington Square Press, 1994.

Bennett, W. Lance. *News: The Politics of Illusion.* 7th ed. New York: Longman, 2006.

Ben-Ze'ev, Efrat. "Imposed Silences and Self-censorship: *Palmach* Soldiers Remember 1948." In Ben-Ze'ev, Ruth Ginio, and Jay Winter, *Shadows of War,* 181–96. New York: Cambridge Univ. Press, 2010.

———, Ruth Ginio, and Jay Winter, eds. *Shadows of War: A Social History of Silence in the Twentieth Century.* New York: Cambridge Univ. Press, 2010.

Bermanzohn, Paul, and Sally A. Bermanzohn. *The Greensboro Massacre.* New York: Cesar Cauce Publishers, 1980.

Bermanzohn, Sally A. *Through Survivors' Eyes: From the Sixties to the Greensboro Massacre.* Nashville, Tenn.: Vanderbilt Univ. Press, 2003.

Bermanzohn, Sandy Michele. "The Media's Demonization of the Radical Left: Two Case Studies." College honors thesis, University of Vermont, 2003.

Best, James. "The Tragic Weekend of May 1 to 4, 1970." In Hensley and Lewis, *Kent State and May 4th,* 4–31.

Bethlehem, Louise. "Now That All Is Said and Done: Reflections on the Truth and Reconciliation Commission in South Africa." In Ben-Ze'ev, Ginio, and Winter, *Shadows of War,* 153–70.

The Big Chill. Directed by Lawrence Kasdan. Beverly Hills, Calif.: Carson Productions, 1983.

Bills, Scott L. "Introduction: The Past in the Present." In Bills, *Kent State/May 4,* 1–61.

———, ed. *Kent State/May 4: Echoes Through a Decade.* 1982. Kent, Ohio: Kent State Univ. Press, 1988.

Bissonette, Devan L. "Between Silence and Self-Interest: *Time, Life,* and the Unsilent Generation's Coming-of-Age." *Journalism History* 35, no. 2 (Summer 2009): 62–71.

Blake, Mariah. "Tim Golden on Digging Deep, Timing, and Sourcing." The Water Cooler. *Columbia Journalism Review.* May 27, 2005. <http://cjr.org/the_water_cooler/tim_golden_on_digging_deep_tim.php>.

Blanchot, Maurice. *The Writing of the Disaster.* Translated by Ann Smock. Lincoln: Univ. of Nebraska Press, 1995.

Blight, David W., ed. *Beyond the Battlefield: Race, Memory, and the American Civil War.* Amherst: Univ. of Massachusetts Press, 2002.

Blossom, Virgil T. *It Has Happened Here.* New York: Harper, 1959.

Boyer, Pascal, and James V. Wertsch, eds. *Memory in Mind and Culture.* New York: Cambridge Univ. Press, 2009.

Boyle, Michael, Michael R. McCluskey, Douglas M. McLeod, and Sue E. Stein. "Newspapers and Protest: An Examination of Protest Coverage from 1960 to 1999." *Journalism & Mass Communication Quarterly* 82 (2005): 638–53.

Branch, Taylor. *Pillar of Fire: America in the King Years, 1963–65.* New York: Simon and Schuster, 1998.

Brewer, Vivian L. *The Embattled Ladies of Little Rock: The Struggle to Save Public Education at Central High.* Fort Bragg, Calif.: Lost Coast Press, 1999.

Bryant, Jennings, and Mary Beth Oliver, eds. *Media Effects: Advances in Theory and Research.* New York: Routledge, 2009.

Calkins, Kenneth R. "The Frustrations of a Former Activist." In Bills, *Kent State/May 4*, 100–104.

Calloway, Paul. *Soviet and Western Psychiatry.* London: Moor Press, 1992.

Campbell, E. Q., and Thomas Pettigrew. *Christians in Racial Crisis: A Study of Little Rock's Ministry.* Washington, D.C.: Public Affairs Press, 1959.

Campbell, James T. "Settling Accounts? An Americanist Perspective on Historical Reconciliation." *American Historical Review* 114 (Oct. 2009): 963–77.

Caputo, Philip. *Thirteen Seconds: A Look Back at the Kent State Shootings.* New York: Chamberlain Books, 2005.

Carmichael, Stokely, with Ekwueme Michael Thelwell. *Ready for Revolution: The Life and Struggles of Stokely Carmichael (Kwame Ture).* New York: Scribner, 2003.

Carter, David. E. "The Changing Face of *Life*'s Advertisements, 1950–1966." *Journalism Quarterly* 46, no. 11 (1969): 87–93.

Cayrol, Jean. "Nuit et brouillard, comme un dispositive d'alerte." Extrait des *Lettres françaises*, n. 606, février 1956. <http://www.arte-boutique.com/detailProduct.action?product.id=2706&productDetail.id=2724>.

Chafe, William H., et al., eds. *Remembering Jim Crow: African Americans Tell about Life in the Segregated South.* New York: New Press, 2001.

Chandler, Michael, writer. *Freedom on My Mind* (documentary film). Directed by Connie Field and Marilyn Mulford. San Francisco: California Newsreel, 1994. DVD, 1995.

Coakley, R. W. *Operation Arkansas.* OCMH Monograph 158M. Washington, D.C.: Histories Division, Office of the Chief of Military History, Department of the Army, 1967.

Cobb, Orso. *Orso Cobb of Arkansas: Memoirs of Historical Significance.* Little Rock, Ark.: Rose Publishing Co., 1989.

Cohen, Bernard C. *The Press and Foreign Policy.* Princeton, N.J.: Princeton Univ. Press, 1963.

Cohen, Lizabeth. *A Consumers' Republic: The Politics of Mass Consumption in Postwar America.* New York: Vintage Books, 2003.

Collins, Cathy. "Forgetting and Remembering the Desegregation of Central High School in Little Rock, Arkansas: Race, Community Struggle, and Collective Memory." Ph.D. diss., Fielding Graduate University, 2004. Dissertation Abstracts International, AAT 3140183; DAI-A 65/07 (Jan 2005): 2779.

Combined Universities Campaign for Nuclear Disarmament: Student Union for Peace Action : New Left Committee Fonds. 1960–68. McMaster University Archives and Special Collections, Hamilton, Ontario, Canada.

Communist Party of Canada Fonds, 1905–82. Library and Archives of Canada, Ottawa, Ontario, Canada.

Connerton, Paul. *How Societies Remember.* Cambridge, UK: Cambridge Univ. Press, 1989.

Conrad, Margaret, and Alvin Findel. *Canada: A National History.* 4th ed. Toronto: Peason-Longman, 2007.

Cope, Graeme. "A Thorn in the Side? The Mother's League of Central High School and the Little Rock Desegregation Crisis of 1957." *Arkansas Historical Quarterly* 57 (Summer 1998): 160–90.

Counts, Will. *Life Is More than a Moment: The Desegregation of Little Rock's Central High.* Bloomington: Indiana Univ. Press, 1999.

Crozier, Michel, Samuel P. Huntington, and Joji Watanuki. *The Crisis of Democracy: Report on the Governability of Democracies to the Trilateral Commission.* New York: New York Univ. Press, 1975.

Dalton, James E. *May 4 Memorial Design Competition.* Kent, Ohio: Kent State University, 1985.

Daniel, Pete. *Lost Revolutions: The South in the 1950s.* Chapel Hill: Univ. of North Carolina Press, 2000.

Dardis, Frank E. "Marginalization Devices in U.S. Press Coverage of Iraq War Protest: A Content Analysis." *Mass Communication and Society* 9 (2006): 117–35.

Davies, Peter. "The Burning Question: A Government Cover-up?" In Bills, *Kent State/May 4*, 150–59.

———. *The Truth About Kent State: A Challenge to the American Conscience.* New York: Farrar, Straus, and Giroux, 1973.

Davis, Peter. "Commentary." *Hearts and Minds* (documentary film). Directed by Peter Davis. 1974. DVD, Criterion Collection, 2002.

DeBenedetti, Charles, with Charles Chatfield. *An American Ordeal: The Antiwar Movement of the Vietnam Era.* Syracuse, N.Y.: Syracuse Univ. Press, 1990.

Desai, Kiran. *The Inheritance of Loss.* New York: Atlantic Monthly Press, 2005.

Donovan, Hedley. *Right Places, Right Times: Forty Years in Journalism, Not Counting My Paper Route.* New York: Henry Holt and Co., 1989.

Doss, Erika, ed. *Looking at* Life *Magazine.* Washington, D.C.: Smithsonian Institution Press, 2001.

Dudziak, Mary L. *Cold War Civil Rights: Race and the Image of American Democracy.* Princeton, N.J.: Princeton Univ. Press, 2000.

Edey, Maitland. *Great Photographic Essays from* Life. Boston, Mass.: New York Graphic Society, 1978.

Edy, Jill. "Journalistic Uses of Collective Memory." *Journal of Communication* 49, no. 2 (Spring 1999): 71–85.

Elson, Robert T. *Time Inc.: The Intimate History of a Publishing Enterprise, 1923–1941.* Vol. 1. Edited by Duncan Norton-Taylor. New York: Atheneum, 1968.

———. *The World of Time Inc.: The Intimate History of a Publishing Enterprise, 1941–1960.* Vol. 2. Edited by Duncan Norton-Taylor. New York: Atheneum, 1973.

Eszterhas, Joe. "Ohio Honors Its Dead." *Rolling Stone,* June 10, 1971, 14–18.

———, and Michael D. Roberts *Thirteen Seconds: Confrontation at Kent State.* New York: Dodd, Mead, and Co., 1970.

Evans, Richard J. *In Hitler's Shadow: West German Historians and the Attempt to Escape from the Nazi Past.* New York: Pantheon Books, 1989.

Felman, Shoshana. "Paul de Man's Silence." *Critical Inquiry* 15, no. 4 (Summer 1989): 704–44.

Ferrándiz, Francisco. "The Return of Civil War Ghosts: The Ethnography of Exhumations in Contemporary Spain." *Anthropology Today* 22, no. 3 (2006): 7–12.

Foley, Michael. *Confronting the War Machine: Draft Resistance during the Vietnam War.* Chapel Hill: Univ. of North Carolina Press, 2003.

Frank, Glenn W., Thomas R. Hensley, and Jerry M. Lewis. *May 4 Site and Memorial.* 1990. Kent, Ohio: Kent State University Communications and Marketing, 2008.

Frank, Thomas. *The Conquest of Cool: Business Culture, Counterculture, and the Rise of Hip Consumerism.* Chicago, Ill.: Univ. of Chicago Press, 1997.

Freed, James Ingo. Quoted in "Inside the Museum: The Architecture." United States Holocaust Memorial Museum. <www.ushmm.org/museum/a_and_a/>.

Freeman, Jo. *At Berkeley in the Sixties: The Education of an Activist, 1961–1965.* Indianapolis: Indiana Univ. Press, 2004.

Freyer, Tony A. *The Little Rock Crisis: A Constitutional Interpretation.* Westport, Conn.: Greenwood Press, 1984.

———. "The Little Rock Crisis Reconsidered." *Arkansas Historical Quarterly* 56, no. 3 (1997): 361–70.

———. "The Past as Future: The Little Rock Crisis and the Constitution." In Jacoway and Williams, *Understanding the Little Rock Crisis,* 141–51.

———. "Politics and Law in the Little Rock Crisis, 1954–1957." *Arkansas Historical Quarterly* 40, no. 3 (1981): 195–219.

Frisch, Michael. "American History and the Structures of Collective Memory: A Modest Exercise in Empirical Iconography." *Journal of American History* 75, no. 4 (Mar. 1989): 1130–55.

Furlong, William. "The Guardsmen's View of the Tragedy at Kent State." *New York Times Magazine,* June 21, 1970.

Fussell, Paul. *The Great War and Modern Memory.* 25th anniversary ed. New York: Oxford Univ. Press, 2000.

Garrow, David. *Bearing the Cross: Martin Luther King Jr. and the Southern Christian Leadership Conference.* New York: Vintage, 1988.

Gates, Lorraine. "Power from the Pedestal: The Women's Emergency Committee and the Little Rock School Crisis." *Arkansas Historical Quarterly* 55, no. 1 (1996): 26–57.

Gibney, Alex. "Commentary." *Taxi to the Dark Side* (documentary film). DVD. Directed by Alex Gibney. New York: THINKFilm, 2007.

Giffels, David, Chuck Klosterman, and Michael Weinreb. "Of Loss and Learning." *Akron Beacon Journal,* Apr. 30, 2000.

Gitlin, Todd. *The Sixties: Years of Hope, Days of Rage.* New York: Bantam Books, 1987.

———. *The Whole World Is Watching: Mass Media in the Making and Unmaking of the New Left.* Berkeley: Univ. of California Press, 1980.

Godfrey, P. C. "'Sweet little girls'? Miscegenation, Desegregation, and the Defense of Whiteness at Little Rock's Central High, 1957–1959." Ph.D. diss., State Univ. of New York at Binghamton, 2001. *Dissertation Abstracts International* 62 (07), 2585A, UMI No. 3019499.

Golden, Tim, et al. "In U.S. Report, Brutal Details of 2 Afghan Inmates' Deaths." *New York Times,* May 20, 2005. <http://www.nytimes.com/2005/05/20/international/asia/20abuse.html?pagewanted=1&_r=2>.

Goltermann, Svenja. "On Silence, Madness, and Lassitude: Negotiating the Past in Post-war West Germany." In Ben-Ze'ev, Ginio, and Winter, *Shadows of War,* 91–112.

Gordon, Robert. "Undoing Historical Injustice." In *Justice and Injustice in Law and Legal Theory,* edited by Austin Sarat and Thomas H. Kearns, 35–76. Ann Arbor: Univ. of Michigan Press, 1999.

Gordon, William A. *The Fourth of May: Killings and Coverups at Kent State.* Buffalo, N.Y.: Prometheus Books, 1990.

Grace, Thomas M. *Kent State: Death and Dissent during the Long Sixties, 1958–1973.* Amherst: Univ. of Massachusetts Press, forthcoming.

———. "Kent State: The Struggle for Memory and Meaning." *The Sixties: A Journal of History, Politics and Culture* 2, no. 2 (Dec. 2009), 245–49.

Graham, Mark W. "Memorializing May 4, 1970, at Kent State University: Reflections on Collective Memory, Public Art and Religious Criticism." *Literature and Theology* 20 (Dec. 2006): 424–37.

Grant, Edward J., and Michael Hill. *I Was There: What Really Went on at Kent State.* Lima, Ohio: C.S.S. Publishing Co., 1974.

Greensboro, North Carolina. "Human Relations Commission Report." Oct. 6, 1980.

Greensboro Police Department. "An Administrative Report of the Anti-Klan Rally, Greensboro, North Carolina, November 3, 1979.' Greensboro, N.C. Nov. 19, 1979. Civil Rights Greensboro (website). <http://www.greensborotrc.org/1979_policewvo.pdf>.

Greensboro Truth and Reconciliation Commission. *Greensboro Truth and Reconciliation Commission Final Report.* Presented to the residents of Greensboro, the city, the Greensboro Truth and Community Reconciliation Project and other public bodies, May 25, 2006. Greensboro, N.C.: Greensboro Truth and Reconciliation Commission, 2006.

Gregory, Sanford W., and Jerry M. Lewis. "Symbols of Collective Memory: The Social Process of Memorializing May 4, 1970 at Kent State University." *Symbolic Interaction* 11 (1988): 213–33.

Griffin, Larry J. "'Generations and Collective Memory' Revisited: Race, Region, and the Memory of Civil Rights." *American Sociological Review* 69, no. 4 (Aug. 2004): 544–57.

Grossberg, Lawrence. *Dancing in Spite of Myself.* Durham, N.C.: Duke Univ. Press, 1997.

Halberstam, David. *The Fifties.* New York: Villard Books, 1993.

Halbwachs, Maurice. *On Collective Memory,* edited and translated by Lewis A. Coser. Chicago, Ill.: Univ. of Chicago Press, 1992.

Haldeman, H. R. *The Haldeman Diaries: Inside the Nixon White House.* New York: G. P. Putnam's Sons, 1994.

———, with Joseph DiMona. *The Ends of Power.* New York: Time Books, 1978.

Hall, K. L. "The Constitutional Lessons of the Little Rock Crisis." In Jacoway and Williams, *Understanding the Little Rock Crisis,* 123–40.

Hall, Mitchell. *Because of Their Faith: CALCAV and Religious Opposition to the Vietnam War.* New York: Columbia Univ. Press, 1990.

Hallin, Daniel. *The "Uncensored War": The Media and Vietnam.* Berkeley: Univ. of California Press, 1989.

Halstead, Fred. *Out Now! A Participant's Account of the Movement in the U.S. against the Vietnam War.* New York: Pathfinder Press, 1978.

Hare, A. Paul. "The Nonviolent Alternative: Research Strategy and Preliminary Findings." In *Collective Violence.* Edited by James F. Short Jr. and Marvin E. Wolfgang. New Brunswick, N.J.: AldineTransaction, 2009.

Haridakis, Paul, and Amber Ferris, "The Use of 'Speech Zones' to Control Public Discourse in Twenty-First-Century America." In *The Impact of 9/11 and the New Legal Landscape: The Day that Changed Everything?* edited by Mathew J. Morgan, 39–56. New York: Palgrave Macmillan, 2009.

Harkness, Sarah, and Jerry M. Lewis. "Student Interest in May 4, 1970, at Kent State University." Unpublished manuscript. Sociology Department, Kent State University, Kent, Ohio, 2003.

Hawken, Paul. *Blessed Unrest: How the Largest Movement in the World Came into Being and Why No One Saw It Coming.* New York: Viking Press, 2007.

Hayner, Priscilla B. *Unspeakable Truths: Confronting State Terror and Atrocity.* New York: Routledge, 2002.

Hearts and Minds (documentary film). Directed by Peter Davis. BBS Productions, 1974; DVD, Criterion Collection, 2002.

Heineman, Kenneth J. *Campus Wars: The Peace Movement at American Universities in the Vietnam Era.* 1993. New York: New York Univ. Press, 1994.

Heiskell, Andrew, with Ralph Graves. *Outsider, Insider: An Unlikely Success Story.* New York: Marian-Darien Press, 1998.

Hensley, Thomas R. *The Kent State Incident: Impact of Judicial Process on Public Attitudes.* Westport, Conn.: Greenwood Press, 1981.

———. "The May Fourth Trials." In Hensley and Lewis, *Kent State and May 4th*, 64–86.

———, and Jerry M. Lewis. *Kent State and May 4th: A Social Science Perspective.* 3rd ed. Kent Ohio: Kent State Univ. Press, 2010.

Herman, Edward, and Noam Chomsky. *Manufacturing Consent: The Political Economy of Mass Media.* 2nd ed. New York: Pantheon, 2002.

Herring, George C. *America's Longest War: The United States and Vietnam, 1950–1975.* 4th ed. Boston, Mass.: McGraw-Hill, 2002.

Hoffman, Paul. *Moratorium: An American Protest.* New York: Tower Publications, 1970.

Holstein, Elaine. "Anniversary: May 4, 1988." *Vietnam Generation* 2, no. 2 (1990): 46–49.

Huard, Victor. "The Canadian Peace Congress and the Challenge to Postwar Consensus, 1948–1953." *Peace and Change* 19, no. 1 (1994): 25–49.

Huckaby, Elizabeth. *Crisis at Central High: Little Rock 1957–58.* Baton Rouge: Louisiana State Univ. Press, 1980.

Hunt, Andrew. *The Turning: A History of Vietnam Veterans against the War.* New York: New York Univ. Press, 1999.

Huyssen, Andreas. *Present Pasts: Urban Palimpsests and the Politics of Memory.* Stanford, Calif.: Stanford Univ. Press, 2003.

———. *Twilight Memories: Marking Time in a Culture of Amnesia.* New York: Routledge, 1995.

Hynes, Samuel. *The Soldiers' Tale.* New York: Penguin, 2000.

"ICTJ Activity: The Greensboro Truth and Reconciliation Commission." International Center for Transitional Justice. <http://www.ictj.org/en/where/region2/517.html>.

IMDb.com, Inc. Internet Movie Data Base. Copyright 1990–2011. <http://www.imdb.com/title/tt0854678/fullcredits#cast>.

Irwin-Zarecka, Iwona. *Frames of Remembrance: The Dynamics of Collective Memory.* New Brunswick, N.J.: Transaction Publishers, 1994.

———. *Neutralizing Memory: The Jew in Contemporary Poland.* New Brunswick, N.J.: Transaction Publishers, 1990.

Isserman, Maurice, and Michael Kazin. *America Divided: The Civil War of the 1960s.* New York: Oxford Univ. Press, 2000.

Jackson, Miriam R. "Vietnam War Refought: Kent State, 1977." *Vietnam Generation* 4, nos. 3–4 (Summer–Fall 1992): 110–18.

Jacoway, Elizabeth. "Down from the Pedestal: Gender and Regional Culture in a Ladylike Assault on the Southern Way of Life." *Arkansas Historical Quarterly* 56, no. 3 (1997): 345–52.

———, and C. Fred Williams, eds. *Understanding the Little Rock Crisis: An Exercise in Remembrance and Reconciliation.* Fayetteville: Univ. of Arkansas Press, 1999.

Jeffrey, Jaclyn, and Glenace Edwall, eds. *Memory and History: Essays on Recalling and Interpreting Experience.* Lanham, Md.: Univ. Press of America, 1994.

Jerome, William T., III. "Statement Concerning Candlelight March, May 7, 1970." Ohio Memory Project. Ohio Memory Collection. The Ohio Historical Society and the State Library of Ohio, Columbus, Ohio. <http://www.ohiomemory.org/cdm4/document.php?CISOROOT=%2Fp267401coll36&CISOPTR=24472&REC=16&CISOBOX=William+Jerome+III>.

Joseph, Branden W. "John Cage and the Architecture of Silence." *October* 81 (Summer 1997): 80–104.

Jovanovic, Spoma. "The Greensboro Truth and Community Reconciliation Project: Communication for Community Change." Paper presented at the American Psychological Association Convention, New Orleans, Louisiana, 2006.

Kammen, Michael. *Mystic Chords of Memory: The Transformation of Tradition in American Culture.* New York: Knopf, 1991.

Kaplan, John. "The *Life* Magazine Civil Rights Photography of Charles Moore, 1958–1965." *Journalism History* 25, no. 4 (Winter 1999): 126–39.

Kasinsky, Renée G. *Refugees from Militarism: Draft-Age Americans in Canada.* New Brunswick, N.J.: Transaction Books, 1976.

Kastiaficas, George. *The Imagination of the New Left: A Global Analysis of 1968.* Boston, Mass.: South End Press, 1987.

Kellner, Douglas. *Television and the Crisis of Democracy.* Boulder, Colo.: Westview Press, 1990.

Kelner, Joseph, and James Munves. *The Kent State Coverup.* New York: Harper and Row, 1980.

Kimball, Roger. *The Long March: How the Cultural Revolution of the 1960s Changed America.* San Francisco, Calif.: Encounter Books, 2000.

Kirk, John A. *Redefining the Color Line: Black Activism in Little Rock, Arkansas, 1940–1970.* Gainesville: Univ. Press of Florida, 2002.

Kitch, Carolyn. "Anniversary Journalism, Collective Memory, and the Cultural Authority to Tell the Story of the American Past." *Journal of Popular Culture* 36, no. 1 (2002): 44–67.

Klapper, Joseph T. *The Effects of Mass Communication.* New York: Free Press, 1960.

Kosnac, Erin, and Melissa Hostetler. "Then I Was Shot. Tom Grace: Discovered the Irony." *The Burr.* Special edition, May 4, 2000. <http://www.burr.kent.edu/archives/may4/shot/shot4.html>.

Kostash, Myrna. *Long Way from Home: The Story of the Sixties Generation in Canada.* Toronto: James Lorimer and Co., 1980.

Kozol, Wendy. Life*'s America: Family and Nation in Postwar Photojournalism.* Philadelphia, Pa.: Temple Univ. Press, 1994.

Kukuk, Christina Hange. "The Gibbs/Green Affair." *The Burr.* Special edition. May 4, 2000. <http://www.burr.kent.edu/archives/may4/jackson/cover.html>.

Lamis, Alexander P., and Mary Anne Sharkey, eds. *Ohio Politics.* Kent, Ohio: Kent State Univ. Press, 1994.

Lang, Kurt, and Gladys Engel Lang. "Collective Memory and the News." *Communication* 11 (1989): 123–39.

Langer, Lawrence. *Holocaust and the Literary Imagination.* New Haven, Conn.: Yale Univ. Press, 1975.

Langguth, A. J. *Our Vietnam: The War, 1954–1975.* New York: Simon and Schuster, 2000.

Lentz, Richard. *Symbols: The News Magazines and Martin Luther King.* Baton Rouge: Louisiana State Univ. Press, 1990.

Leuchtenburg, William E. *A Troubled Feast: American Society since 1945.* Boston, Mass.: Little, Brown, 1979; reprint, Glenview, Ill.: Scott, Foresman and Co., 1983.

Levant, Victor. *Quiet Complicity: Canadian Involvement in the Vietnam War.* Toronto: Between the Lines, 1986.

Levi, Primo. *Survival in Auschwitz.* New York: Basic Books, 2002.

Levinas, Emmanuel. *Basic Philosophical Writings.* Edited by Adriaan Peperzak, Simon Critchley, and Robert Bernasconi. Bloomington: Indiana Univ. Press, 1996.

———. *Entre Nous: Thinking-of-the-Other.* European Perspectives. Translated by Michael B. Smith and Barbara Harshav. New York: Columbia Univ. Press, 1998.

Lewis, Jerry M., and Thomas R. Hensley. "The May 4 Shootings at Kent State University:

The Search for Historical Accuracy." *Ohio Council for the Social Studies Review* 34, no. 1 (Summer 1998). <http://dept.kent.edu/sociology/lewis/lewihen.htm>.

Lewis, John. Interview by Brian Williams. "Decision 2008: Election Night, 11:00 P.M.," NBC. Nov. 4, 2008. <http://www.lexisnexis.com/lnacui2api/delivery/PreviewFrameDisplay.do?jobHandle=2826%3A304585627&fromCart=false&dnldFilePath=%2Fl-n%2Fshared%2Fprod%2Fdiscus%2Fqds%2Frepository%2Fdocs%2F7%2F62%2F2826%3A304585627%2Fformatted_doc&fileSize=5000>.

Lexier, Roberta. "Student Activism at the University of Saskatchewan, Regina Campus, 1961–1972." Master's thesis, University of Regina, Regina, SK, Canada, 2003.

Lippmann, Walter. *Public Opinion.* New York: Macmillan, 1922.

Lipset, Seymour M. "Polls and Protests." *Foreign Affairs* 49, no. 3 (1971): 548–55.

Lipsky, Michael. "Protest as a Political Resource." *American Political Science Review* 62 (Dec. 1968): 1144–58.

"Live Election Coverage." CNN. Meridien, ET: Nov. 4, 2009.

Loengard, John. *Life Photographers: What They Saw.* New York: Little, Brown, and Co., 1998.

Loftus, Elizabeth. *Eyewitness Testimony.* Cambridge, Mass.: Harvard Univ. Press, 1979

Logue, John. "Official Violence." In Bills, *Kent State/May 4,* 143–49.

Lowrey, Wilson. "Media Dependency during a Large-Scale Social Disruption. The Case of September 11." *Mass Communication and Society* 7 (2004): 339–57.

Luce, Henry R. *The Ideas of Henry Luce.* Edited by John Jessup. New York: Atheneum, 1969.

Lytle, Mark H. *America's Uncivil Wars: The Sixties Era from Elvis to the Fall of Richard Nixon.* New York: Oxford Univ. Press, 2006.

Macpherson, Kay, with Christine Donald. *When in Doubt, Do Both: The Times of My Life.* Toronto: Univ. of Toronto Press, 1994.

Maier, Charles. "Consigning the Twentieth Century to History: Alternative Narratives for the Modern Era." *American Historical Review* 105, no. 3 (2000): 807–31.

Marcus, Daniel. *Happy Days and Wonder Years: The Fifties and the Sixties in Contemporary Cultural Politics.* New Brunswick, N.J.: Rutgers Univ. Press, 2004.

Margalit, Avishai. *The Ethics of Memory.* Cambridge, Mass.: Harvard Univ. Press, 2002.

Martin, Ralph G. *Henry and Clare: An Intimate Portrait of the Luces.* New York: G. P. Putnam's Sons, 1991.

May 4 Collection. Special Collections and Archives. Kent State University Libraries, Kent, Ohio.

May 1970: Birth of the Antiwar University. New York: Pathfinder Press, 1971.

May 4 Visitors Center foundation document mission statement. Unpublished paper. Mar. 30, 2009. Kent State University, Kent, Ohio.

Mayer, Harold M. "Commission on KSU Violence." Vols. 1–4. Unpublished report. Kent State University, KSU Printing Service, Kent, Ohio, 1972.

McCarthy, Cormac. *The Road.* New York: Knopf, 2006.

McCombs, Maxwell, and Amy Reynolds. "How News Shapes Our Civic Agenda." In Bryant and Oliver, *Media Effects,* 1–16.

McMillen, Neil R. "White Citizen's Council and Resistance to School Desegregation in Arkansas." *Arkansas Historical Quarterly* 30, no. 2 (Spring 1971): 95–122.

McMillian, John, and Paul Buhle, eds. *The New Left Revisited.* Philadelphia, Pa.: Temple Univ. Press, 2003.

Michener, James A. *Kent State: What Happened and Why.* New York: Random House, 1971.

Miller, Judith. *One by One by One: Facing the Holocaust.* New York: Simon and Schuster, 1990.

Minow, Martha. *Between Vengeance and Forgiveness: Facing History after Genocide and Mass Violence.* Boston, Mass.: Beacon Press, 1998.

Miroff, Bruce, Raymond Seidelman, and Todd Swanson, eds. *Debating Democracy: A Reader in American Politics,* 6th ed. Boston Mass.: Houghton Mifflin, 2009.

Misztal, Barbara A. *Theories of Social Remembering.* Maidenhead, Berks., UK: Open Univ. Press, 2003.

Moffatt, Gary. *History of the Canadian Peace Movement until 1969.* St. Catharines, Canada: Grape Vine Press, 1969.

Morgan, Edward P. "The Good, the Bad, and the Forgotten: Media Culture and Public Memory of the Civil Rights Movement." In Romano and Raiford, *The Civil Rights Movement in American Memory,* 137–66.

———. *The Sixties Experience: Hard Lessons about Modern America.* Philadelphia, Pa.: Temple Univ. Press, 1991.

———. *What Really Happened to the 1960s: How Mass Media Culture Failed American Democracy.* Lawrence: Univ. Press of Kansas, 2010.

Murphy, Sara A. *Breaking the Silence: Little Rock's Women's Emergency Committee to Open Our Schools, 1958–1963.* Fayetteville: Univ. of Arkansas Press, 1997.

Nadel, Alan. *Containment Culture: American Narratives, Postmodernism, and the Atomic Age.* Durham, N.C.: Duke Univ. Press, 1995.

Nasstrom, Kathryn L. "Beginnings and Endings: Life Stories and the Periodization of the Civil Rights Movement." *Journal of American History* 86, no. 2 (Sept. 1999): 700–711.

Night and Fog [Nuit et brouillard] (documentary film). Directed by Alain Resnais. Narration written by Jean Cayrol. Translated by Alexander Alan. Neuilly-sur-Seine, France: Argos Films, 1955; DVD, Criterion Collection, 2003. This edition of the film restores the original version, before censorship.

The 1983 Pix 38 (yearbook). Central High School. Little Rock, Ark: 1983.

Nixon, Richard M. "Cambodia: A Difficult Decision." *Vital Speeches of the Day* 36, no. 15 (1970): 450–52.

Nourkova, Veronica, Daniel M. Bernstein, and Elizabeth Loftus. "Biography Becomes Autobiography: Distorting the Subjective Past." *American Journal of Psychology* 117, no. 1 (2004): 65–80.

O'Neil, Robert M., John P. Morris, and Raymond Mack. *No Heroes, No Villains: New Perspectives on Kent State and Jackson State.* San Francisco, Calif.: Jossey-Bass, 1972.

On Strike . . . Shut It Down! A Report on the First National Student Strike in U.S. History, May 1970. Chicago, Ill.: Urban Research Corporation, 1970.

Oropeza, Lorena. *¡Raza Si! ¡Guerra No! Chicano Protest and Patriotism during the Viet Nam War Era.* Berkeley: Univ. of California Press, 2005.

Paez, Dario, Nekane Basabe, and Jose Luis Gonzalez. "Social Processes and Collective Memory: A Cross-Cultural Approach to Remembering Political Events." In Pennebaker, Paez, and Rimé, *Collective Memory of Political Events,* 147–74.

Parks, Gordon. *Voices in the Mirror: An Autobiography.* New York: Doubleday, 1990.

Pennebaker, James W., and Amy L. Gonzales. "Making History: Social and Psychological Processes Underlying Collective Memory." In Boyer and Wertsch, *Memory in Mind and Culture,* 171–93.

Pennebaker, James W., Dario Paez, and Bernard Rimé, eds. *Collective Memory of Political Events: Social Psychological Perspectives.* New York: Sage, 2006.

Peterson, Theodore. *Magazines in the Twentieth Century.* Urbana, Ill.: Univ. of Illinois Press, 1964.

Powers, Murray. Pulitzer Prize nomination letter, Jan. 24, 1971. Pulitzer Collection, Columbia University Libraries, New York.

Powledge, Fred. *Free at Last? The Civil Rights Movement and the People Who Made It.* New York: HarperPerennial, 1991.

Prendergast, Curtis, with Geoffery Colvin. *The World of Time Inc. The Intimate History of a Changing Enterprise, 1961–1980.* Edited by Robert Lubar. New York: Atheneum, 1986.

Pryor, Scott. "A Direction of Truth and Love: Representation, Bearing Witness, and the History of November 3, 1979." Senior honors thesis, Guilford College, 2002.

Rabiger, Michael. *Directing the Documentary.* 4th ed. Burlington, Mass.: Focal Press, 2004.

Raiford, Leigh, and Renee C. Romano. "Introduction: The Struggle over Memory." In Romano and Raiford, The *Civil Rights Movement in American Memory,* xvi–xx.

Reed, Roy. "The Contest for the Soul of Orval Faubus." In Jacoway and Williams, *Understanding the Little Rock Crisis,* 98–105.

———. *Faubus: The Life and Times of an American Prodigal.* Fayetteville: Univ. of Arkansas Press, 1997.

Reeves, Richard. *President Nixon: Alone in the White House.* New York: Simon & Schuster, 2001.

Renan, Ernest. *Qu'est-ce qu'une nation?* edited by Philippe Forest. Paris: Pierre Bordas et fils éditeur, 1991.

The Report of the President's Commission on Campus Unrest. Washington, D.C.: GPO, 1970.

Ricoeur, Paul. *La mémoire, l'histoire, l'oubli.* Paris: Seuil, 2000.

Rimé, Bernard, and Véronique Christophe. "How Individual Emotional Episodes Feed Collective Memory." In Pennebaker, Paez, and Rimé, *Collective Memory of Political Events,* 13–46.

Rittenhouse, Jennifer. *Growing Up Jim Crow: How Black and White Children Learned Race.* Chapel Hill: Univ. of North Carolina Press, 2006.

Robert S. Kenny Collection, University of Toronto Thomas Fisher Rare Book Library, Toronto, Ontario, Canada.

Romano, Renee C. "Narrative of Redemption: The Birmingham Church Bombing Trials and the Construction of Civil Rights Memory." In Romano and Raiford, *The Civil Rights Movement in American Memory,* 96–134.

———, and Leigh Raiford, eds., *The Civil Rights Movement in American Memory.* Athens: Univ. of Georgia Press, 2006.

Ross, Doug. *In the Interests of Peace: Canada and Vietnam, 1954–1973.* Toronto: Univ. of Toronto Press, 1984.

Roy, Beth. *Bitters in the Honey: Tales of Hope and Disappointment across Divides of Race and Time.* Fayetteville: Univ. of Arkansas Press, 1999.

Royal Canadian Mounted Police (RCMP) Records, RG 146. Canadian Security Intelligence Service. Library and Archives of Canada, Ottawa, Ontario, Canada.

Rukeyser, Muriel. *The Book of the Dead.* In *The Muriel Rukeyser Reader,* edited by Jan Heller Levi, 29–48. New York: W. W. Norton and Co., 1995.

Russell, Margaret M. "Cleansing Moments and Retrospective Justice." *Michigan Law Review* 101 (2003): 1225.

———. "Reopening the Emmett Till Case: Lessons and Challenges for Critical Race Practice." *Fordham Law Review* 73 (2005): 2101.

Sale, Kirkpatrick. *SDS.* New York: Random House, 1973; New York: Vintage Books, 1974.

Sanbonmatsu, John. *The Postmodern Prince: Critical Theory, Left Strategy, and the Making of a New Political Subject.* New York: Monthly Review Press, 2004.

Sandage, Scott A. "A Marble House Divided: The Lincoln Memorial, the Civil Rights Movement, and the Politics of Memory, 1939–1963." In *Time Longer than Rope: A Century of African American Activism, 1850–1950,* edited by Charles M. Payne and Adam Green, 492–535. New York: New York Univ. Press, 2003.

Schacter, Daniel. *The Seven Sins of Memory.* Cambridge, Mass.: Harvard Univ. Press, 1999.

Schimmel, Solomon. *Wounds Not Healed by Time: The Power of Repentance and Forgiveness.* Oxford: Oxford Univ. Press, 2004.

Schudson, Michael. *Watergate in American Memory: How We Remember, Forget, and Reconstruct the Past.* New York: Basic Books, 1992.

Schuzter, Paul. "Untitled" (photograph). From "Asking for Trouble and Getting It," *Life,* June 2, 1961, 46–47.

Scott, Joan W. "The Evidence of Experience." *Critical Inquiry* 17, no 4 (1991): 773–97.

Serbyn, Roman. "Photographic Evidence of the Ukrainian Genocidal Famine, 1932–1933." Address, 2009 Symposium on Democracy, Kent State University, Kent, Ohio, May 1, 4–5, 2009.

Shakespeare, William. *King Lear,* edited by Alfred Harbage. Baltimore, Md.: Penguin Books, 1973.

Sitkoff, Harvard. *The Struggle for Black Equality.* Rev. ed. New York: Hill and Wang, 1993.

Skowronek, Stephen. "The Changing Political Structures of Presidential Leadership." In *Debating Democracy: A Reader in American Politics,* edited by Bruce Miroff, Raymond Seidelman, and Todd Swanson, 295–309. 6th ed. Boston, Mass.: Houghton Mifflin, 2009.

Small, Melvin. *Covering Dissent: The Media and the Anti–Vietnam War Movement.* New Brunswick, N.J.: Rutgers Univ. Press, 1994.

Society of Professional Journalists. "SPJ Code of Ethics." Copyright 1990–2011. <http://www.spj.org/ethicscode.asp>.

Sontag, Susan. *On Photography.* New York: Farrar Straus, and Giroux, 1977.

———. *Regarding the Pain of Others.* New York: Farrar, Straus, and Giroux, 2003.

Special Collections. University of Arkansas, Fayetteville, Ark.

Special Collections. University of Arkansas, Little Rock, Ark.

Spencer, Otha B. "Twenty Years of *Life:* A Study of Time, Inc.'s Picture Magazine and Its Contributions to Photojournalism." Ph.D. diss., University of Missouri, 1958.

Spofford, Tim. *Lynch Street: The May 1970 Slayings at Jackson State College.* Kent, Ohio: Kent State Univ. Press, 1988.

Stein, J. G. "Image, Identity, and Conflict Resolution." In *Peace, Conflict and Violence: Peace Psychology for the 21st Century,* edited by Daniel J. Christie, Richard V. Wagner, and Deborah DuNann Winter, 189–208. Englewood Cliffs, N.J.: Prentice-Hall, 2001.

Steinbeck, John. *Cannery Row.* 1945. New York: Penguin Books, 1994.

Stone, I. F. *The Killings at Kent State: How Murder Went Unpunished.* New York: Vintage Books, 1970.

Streich, Gregory. "Is There a Right to Forget? Historical Injustices, Race, Memory, and Identity." *New Political Science* 24, no. 4 (2002): 525–42.

"Struggle to Recovery," *Kent* 3, no. 6 (1970): 4–22.

Swanberg, W. A. *Luce and His Empire.* New York: Charles Scribner's Sons, 1972.

Swerdlow, Amy. *Women Strike for Peace: Traditional Motherhood and Radical Politics in the 1960s.* Chicago: Univ. of Chicago Press, 1993.

Taxi to the Dark Side (documentary film). Directed by Alex Gibney. THINKFilm, 2008. DVD.

Taylor, Stuart, et al. *Violence at Kent State, May 1 to 4, 1970: The Students' Perspective.* New York: College Notes and Texts, 1971.

Tewksbury, David, and Dietram A. Scheufele. "News Framing Theory and Research." In Bryant and Oliver, *Media Effects,* 17–33.

"35 Years Later: Black and White Student Reunions." *Oprah Winfrey Show.* Jan. 15, 1996. Transcript, Chicago, Ill.: Burrelle's Information Services.

Thompson, Edward K. *A Love Affair with* Life *and* Smithsonian. Columbia: Univ. of Missouri Press, 1995.

Thompson, E. P. *The Making of the English Working Class.* London: Victor Gollancz, 1963.

Thompson, Paul. "Believe It or Not: Rethinking the Historical Interpretation of Memory." In Jeffrey and Edwall, *Memory and History,* 1–16.

———. *The Voice of the Past: Oral History.* 2nd ed. New York: Oxford Univ. Press, 1988.

Todorov, Tzvetan. *Hope and Memory: Lessons from the Twentieth Century.* Princeton, N.J.: Princeton Univ. Press, 2003.

"Tragedy in Our Midst—A Special Report." *Akron Beacon Journal,* May 24, 1970.

Tutu, Desmond. "Reconciliation in Post-Apartheid South Africa: Experiences of the Truth Commission." Remarks at the Nobel Peace Laureates Conference, University of Virginia, Nov. 5, 1998. <http://www.virginia.edu/nobel/transcript/tutu.html>.

United States Holocaust Memorial Museum. "Inside the Museum: The Architecture." <www.ushmm.org/museum/a_and_a/>.

Vincent, Mary. "Breaking the Silence? Memory and Oblivion since the Spanish Civil War." In Ben-Ze'ev, Ginio, and Winter, *Shadows of War,* 47–67.

Wainwright, Loudon. *The Great American Magazine: An Inside History of* Life. New York: Alfred A. Knopf, 1986.

Wallace, David. "Orval Faubus: The Central Figure at Little Rock Central High School." *Arkansas Historical Quarterly* 39, no. 4 (1980): 314–29.

Waller, Signe. "A City of Two Tales: The Greensboro Massacre of November 3, 1979 in Fact, Context and Meaning." Unpublished report submitted to the Greensboro Truth and Reconciliation Commission, Feb. 2005.

———. *Love and Revolution.* Lanham, Md.: Rowman and Littlefield, 2002.

Ware, Vron, and Les Back. *Out of Whiteness: Color, Politics, and Culture.* Chicago, Ill.: Univ. of Chicago Press, 2002.

Weldes, Jutta, and Mark Laffey. "Learning to Live with U.S. Foreign Policy and Its Discontents: The Politics of Public Memory at Kent State, 1970–2001." Prepared for presentation to the Annual Meeting of the International Studies Association, New Orleans, Mar. 2002.

Wells, Tom. *The War Within: America's Battle over Vietnam.* Berkeley: Univ. of California Press, 1994; New York: Henry Holt and Co., 1996.

Wertsch, James. "Collective Memory." In Boyer and Wertsch, *Memory in Mind and Culture,* 117–37.

———. *Voices of Collective Remembering.* Cambridge, UK: Cambridge Univ. Press, 2002.

Wheaton, Elizabeth. *Codename GREENKIL: The 1979 Greensboro Killings.* Athens: Univ. of Georgia Press, 1987.

Whitaker, Reg, and Gary Marcuse. *Cold War Canada: The Making of a National Insecurity State.* Toronto: Univ. of Toronto Press, 1994.

Whited, Charles. *Knight: A Publisher in the Tumultuous Century.* New York: E. P. Dutton, 1988.
Wilder, Carol. "The War that Won't Die." <http://www.carolwilder.net/index.html>.
Will, George. Foreword to *Reassessing the Sixties: Debating the Political and Cultural Legacy,* edited by Stephen Macedo, 3–8. New York: Norton, 1997.
Williams, C. Fred. "Class: The Central Issue in the 1957 Little Rock School Crisis." *Arkansas Historical Quarterly* 56, no. 3 (1997): 341–44.
Williams, Juan. *Eyes on the Prize: America's Civil Rights Years, 1954–1965.* New York: Penguin Books, 1988.
Winter, Jay. "Céline and the Cultivation of Hatred." In *Enlightenment, Passion, Modernity: Historical Essays in European Thought and Culture,* edited by Mark S. Micale and Robert L. Dietle, 230–48. Stanford, Calif.: Stanford Univ. Press, 2000.
———. "Remembering Injustice and the Social Construction of Silence." Keynote address, 2009 Symposium on Democracy, Kent State University, Kent, Ohio, May 1, 4–5, 2009.
———. *Remembering War: The Great War between Memory and History in the Twentieth Century.* New Haven, Conn.: Yale Univ. Press, 2006.
———. "Thinking about Silence." In Ben-Ze'ev, Ginio, and Winter, *Shadows of War,* 3–31.
———, and Emmanuel Sivan. "Setting the Framework." In *War and Remembrance in the Twentieth Century,* edited by Jay Winter and Emmanuel Sivan, 6–39. Cambridge, UK: Cambridge Univ. Press, 1999.
Women's Emergency Committee to Open Our Schools (documentary film). Produced and directed by Sandra Hubbard. Little Rock, Ark.: Morning Star Studio, 1993.
Wood, Nancy. *Vectors of Memory: Legacies of Trauma in Postwar Europe.* Oxford: Berg, 1999.
Young, James E. *At Memory's Edge: After-images of the Holocaust in Contemporary Art and Architecture.* New Haven, Conn.: Yale Univ. Press, 2000.
Zelizer, Barbie. "Reading the Past against the Grain: The Shape of Memory Stories." *Critical Studies in Mass Communication* 12, no. 2 (June 1995): 214–39.
Zimmerman, Richard G. *Plain Dealing: Ohio Politics and Journalism Viewed from the Press Gallery.* Kent, Ohio: Kent State Univ. Press, 2006.

Contributors

Carole A. Barbato is professor of communication studies at Kent State University and author of a book, several chapters, and journal articles, including essays reflecting her research on the Kent State tragedy. With Laura L. Davis, she cocreated Kent State's May 4 walking tour and with Davis, Mark F. Seeman, and Jerry M. Lewis coauthored the nomination to place the site on the National Register of Historic Places. She and Davis led the design of the May 4 Visitors Center exhibit, for which they received a $300,000 grant from the National Endowment for the Humanities in 2011.

Kenneth J. Bindas is professor and chair of the Department of History at Kent State University. His work in the area of memory and culture includes authoring *Remembering the Great Depression in the Rural South* (2007) and *Swing, That Modern Sound: The Cultural Context of Swing Music in America, 1935–1947* (2001) and producing/assistant directing the documentary *Invisible Struggles: Stories of Northern Segregation* (2007).

Devan Bissonette earned his Ph.D. in history from Binghamton University, where his dissertation, "The *Time* of Our *Life:* Packaging the News for America's Busy Readers, From Little Rock (1957) to the End of Life as We Knew It (1972)," was awarded a distinguished dissertation award in 2009. His research interests include media history and visual culture. He is currently a contributing faculty member at Walden University.

Suzanne Clark is professor of English at the University of Oregon, where her teaching focuses on modernist culture and theory. In addition to publishing books and articles on the effects of gender on cultural history, she has written on the areas of literature and film, notably the books *Sentimental Modernism: Women Writers and the Revolution of the Word* (1991) and *Cold Warriors: Manliness on Trial in the Rhetoric of the West* (2000). She also has copresented with Daniel L. Miller on the subjects of film and argument and the filmmaking of Ernest Hemingway and Joris Ivens.

Cathy J. Collins, Ph.D., is a nonprofit leader and social science scholar committed to bridging theory, research, and action to achieve social justice and transformative social change. Collins was the first executive director of the Racial and Cultural Diversity Commission for the City of Little Rock, Arkansas. She currently serves as executive director of Habitat for Humanity of Greater Newburgh, New York.

CLAIRE A. CULLETON is professor of modern British and Irish literature at Kent State University. Her books focus on twentieth-century culture and include *Names and Naming in Joyce* (1994); *Working-Class Culture, Women, and Britain, 1914–1921* (2000); and *Joyce and the G-Men: J. Edgar Hoover's Manipulation of Modernism* (2004). She is also coeditor of two collections, *Modernism on File: Writers, Artists, and the FBI, 1920–1950* (2008) and *Irish Modernism and the Global Primitive* (2009), and serves as general editor of Palgrave Macmillan's Irish Studies series.

LAURA L. DAVIS is professor of English and faculty coordinator for May 4 initiatives at Kent State University. Her published work includes editing "Freya of the Seven Isles" in the *'Twixt Land and Sea* volume of the Joseph Conrad edition by Cambridge University Press (2008) and editing and coediting three volumes of essays. With Carole A. Barbato, she is cocreator of Kent State's May 4 walking tour and, with Barbato, Mark F. Seeman, and Jerry M. Lewis, she coauthored the nomination to place the site on the National Register of Historic Places. She also led the design of the May 4 Visitors Center exhibit with Barbato, for which they received a $300,000 grant from the National Endowment for the Humanities in 2011.

THOMAS M. GRACE, Ph.D., is the author of *Kent State: Death and Dissent during the Long Sixties*, forthcoming from University of Massachusetts Press, Amherst. He teaches as an adjunct professor of history at Erie Community College and is a consultant for Kent State University's May 4 Visitor Center. He was among the casualties of National Guard gunfire in May 1970.

PAUL HARIDAKIS is professor and director of the School of Communication Studies at Kent State University. He conducts research on freedom of speech, media use and effects, law, public policy, political communication, and sports communication. His recent research has focused on restrictions on public discourse and access to information in the United States and on social media use in political contexts.

JANET LEACH is assistant professor in the School of Journalism and Mass Communication at Kent State University. She is director of Kent State's Media Law Center for Ethics and Access and an Ethics Fellow at the Poynter Institute. She is past editor of the *Akron Beacon Journal* and held reporting or editing positions at the *Cincinnati Enquirer*, the *Phoenix Gazette*, and the *Arizona Republic*.

JERRY M. LEWIS is professor emeritus of sociology at Kent State University. He has been an active researcher and teacher on issues related to the shootings at Kent State on May 4, 1970, and is the cofounder of the annual Candlelight March and Vigil discussed in his essay in this volume. His published work on May 4 includes coediting, with Thomas R. Hensley, *Kent State and May 4th: A Social Science Perspective*, now in its third edition from Kent State University Press. His teaching also has focused on courses in introductory sociology, collective behavior, and sociology of religion. He received several of Kent State's teaching awards, including the Alumni Association's Distinguished Teaching Award.

MITCH MCKENNEY is assistant professor in the School of Journalism and Mass Communication at Kent State University at Stark. He spent eighteen years in newsrooms, including a decade as an editor at the *Akron Beacon Journal* and Ohio.com, where he supervised coverage of politics, crime, features, and other topics. Earlier in his career, he was a reporter and editor at the *Palm Beach Post* in Florida and the *Times-Union* in Rochester, New York.

DANIEL L. MILLER is an associate professor in the University of Oregon's School of Journalism and Communication, where he teaches classes on documentary production and documentary history. In particular, his class titled "Documenting War," as well as his research, raises questions about war, peace, and reconciliation in the films that have tried to record, remember, and question the history of war and conflict. He is director and producer of a number of documentary films, including *Fire in the Heartland,* which examines student activism at Kent State through the sixties and the demonstrations there in May 1970.

EDWARD P. MORGAN is University Distinguished Professor of Political Science at Lehigh University, where he teaches the courses "Social Movements and Legacies of the 1960s," "Propaganda, Media, and American Politics," and "Organizing for Democracy." He is the author of *What Really Happened to the 1960s: How Mass Media Culture Failed American Democracy* (2010), as well as *The Sixties Experience: Hard Lessons about Modern America* (1992).

CHRISTOPHER POWELL has taught Canadian and U.S. history at the University of New Brunswick and the University of Alberta. His forthcoming book, from the University of British Columbia Press, is a study of the transnational relationship between the anti–Vietnam War movements in Canada and the United States. He also pursues research on the 1960s, peace, labor, and the cold war.

RENEE ROMANO, associate professor of history at Oberlin College, is the author of *Race Mixing: Black-White Marriage in Postwar America* (2003), and coeditor of *The Civil Rights Movement in American Memory* (2006). She currently is writing a book about the many civil rights era murder cases that have been reopened and prosecuted since the mid-1990s.

MARK F. SEEMAN is an archaeologist and professor of anthropology at Kent State University. He has a long-term interest in the preservation of cultural resources and actively has promoted this agenda in a variety of leadership and professional capacities, including his membership on the Ohio Historic Site Preservation Advisory Board. He recently led the successful nominatation to place the site of the Kent State shootings of May 1970 on the National Register of Historic Places.

JAY WINTER is the Charles J. Stille Professor of History at Yale University. He is the author of numerous books, including *Sites of Memory, Sites of Mourning: The Great War in European Cultural History* (1995), *Remembering War: The Great War Between Memory and History in the Twentieth Century* (2006), and *Dreams of Peace and Freedom: Utopian Moments in the Twentieth Century* (2006). He received an Emmy award for best documentary series in 1997 as coproducer and co-writer of *The Great War and the Shaping of the 20th Century,* an eight-hour series broadcast on PBS and the BBC, and shown subsequently in twenty-eight countries.

Index